Routledge Revivals

Industrial Relations in the British Printing Industry

First published in 1967, *Industrial Relations in the British Printing Industry* was written to provide a comprehensive picture of the development of organisations of both employers and those employed in the British printing industry.

The book traces the story from the seventeenth century Craft Guilds and the Stationers Company, through the development of trade unions and union rule in the nineteenth century and up to the technical revolution of the early 1900s. Later chapters cover in detail problems such as restrictive practices and productivity bargaining in the thirty years prior to the original publication of the book. It also explores how their aims and strategies are related to changing technological and economic conditions.

Industrial Relations in the British Printing Industry will appeal to those with an interest in social history and the history of industrial relations, particularly with regards to the printing industry.

Industrial Relations in the British Printing Industry

The Quest for Security

By John Child

First published in 1967
by George Allen & Unwin Ltd.

This edition first published in 2021 by Routledge
2 Park Square, Milton Park, Abingdon, Oxon, OX14 4RN
and by Routledge
605 Third Avenue, New York, NY 10017

Routledge is an imprint of the Taylor & Francis Group, an informa business

© George Allen & Unwin Ltd., 1967

All rights reserved. No part of this book may be reprinted or reproduced or utilised in any form or by any electronic, mechanical, or other means, now known or hereafter invented, including photocopying and recording, or in any information storage or retrieval system, without permission in writing from the publishers.

Publisher's Note
The publisher has gone to great lengths to ensure the quality of this reprint but points out that some imperfections in the original copies may be apparent.

Disclaimer
The publisher has made every effort to trace copyright holders and welcomes correspondence from those they have been unable to contact.

A Library of Congress record exists under LCCN: 67079390

ISBN 13: 978-0-367-74675-9 (hbk)
ISBN 13: 978-1-003-15903-2 (ebk)

Book DOI: 10.4324/9781003159032

INDUSTRIAL RELATIONS IN THE BRITISH PRINTING INDUSTRY

THE QUEST FOR SECURITY

JOHN CHILD

London

GEORGE ALLEN & UNWIN LTD

RUSKIN HOUSE MUSEUM STREET

FIRST PUBLISHED IN 1967

*This book is copyright under the Berne Convention.
Apart from any fair dealing for the purposes of private
study, research, criticism or review, as permitted under
the Copyright Act, 1956, no portion may be reproduced
by any process without written permission. Inquiries
should be made to the publishers.*

© *George Allen & Unwin Ltd.*, 1967

PRINTED IN GREAT BRITAIN
in 10 on 11 point Plantin type
BY UNWIN BROTHERS LTD
WOKING AND LONDON

PREFACE

The study of Industrial Relations is gradually becoming accepted in British Universities as suitable for inclusion in undergraduate courses of study. It has long been accepted in the U.S.A. There have been many studies of trade unions, as a glimpse at the bibliography will confirm; there have been remarkably few studies of employers' associations, and fewer still of industrial relations in particular industries.

The teaching of the subject has been, inevitably, handicapped by the lack of suitable textbooks, and indeed the lack of a commonly recognized body of concepts. I have come to the view that the theoretical outline put forward by Professor John T. Dunlop, of Harvard University, in his book *Industrial Relations Systems*, provides a useful framework in which to study industrial relations at the level of either the firm, the industry, or the nation. This book is a study at the industrial level. While I have not, in general, used Dunlop's vocabulary, I am very conscious of my intellectual debt to his writings.

I wish, also, to express my grateful thanks to Mr Allan Flanders, of Nuffield College, Oxford, who guided my original researches in this field. I owe much, too, to the insight which I gained during attendance at the Nuffield Seminar in Industrial Relations, conducted by Mr Flanders, Mr Hugh Clegg, and Mr Kenneth Knowles. Without the direct and indirect help of these men, and of the students who participated in the seminar, this book would have had less merit. They must not, of course, be held responsible for any of its imperfections of fact or interpretation. I wish also to thank the many officers of the British Federation of Master Printers, and of the trade unions in the industry, who gave me access to their documents and libraries. In particular, I wish to thank Mr L. E. Kenyon, and Mr C. W. D. Alister, of the B.F.M.P., and Mr G. Eastwood and Mr S. Carter, of the Printing and Kindred Trades Federation, for their willing co-operation. Mr Alister and Mr Carter read the final draft, and made many valuable suggestions.

Every research worker realizes his debt to the numerous library officers without whose co-operation his studies could not have proceeded. Finally, I should like to thank Miss Wheeler, of Oxford University Press, for typing the manuscript with such speed and accuracy.

CONTENTS

PREFACE   *page* 7

PART I   CONTROL BY CIVIL AUTHORITY
 I. Craft Gilds and Stationers' Company (–1660)   15
 II. Decline of Stationers' Company (1660–1780)   32

PART II   TRADE SOCIETIES AND TRADE UNIONS (1780–1848)
 III. Unlawful and Dictatorial Combinations   47
 IV. The Birth of Collective Bargaining   61
 V. Regional and National Unions   74
 VI. The Problem of Unemployment   93

PART III   REGULATION BY UNION RULE (1848–90)
 VII. Consolidation of the Craft Unions   107
 VIII. Control of Labour Supply   124
 IX. Regulation by Union Rule   137

PART IV   BILATERAL BARGAINING (1890–1920)
 X. The Technical Revolution   156
 XI. Composing Machines   165
 XII. Flood Tide of Trade Unionism   184
 XIII. Bilateral Collective Bargaining   203
 XIV. War and Boom 1914–20   219

PART V   PERIOD OF COMPROMISE (1920–45)
 XV. Uneasy Truce   232
 XVI. The Joint Industrial Council   254
 XVII. Terms of Employment   267
 XVIII. The Second World War (1939–46)   284

PART VI   THE NEW WORLD—FULL EMPLOYMENT
 XIX. Search for a Wages Structure (1947–51)   309
 XX. Bargaining on Labour Supply (1952–56)   326
 XXI. Productivity Bargaining (1959–64)   343
 XXII. Epilogue   361

GLOSSARY   372

BIBLIOGRAPHY   373

INDEX   376
A*

ABBREVIATIONS

A.S.L.P.   Amalgamated Society of Lithographic Printers.

A.M.P.   Association of Master Printers (London).

B.M.R.C.U.   Bookbinders' and Machine Rulers'
Consolidated Union.

F.M.P.   (British) Federation of Master Printers.

F.S.E.S.   Federated Society of Electrotypers and
Stereotypers.

G.T.A.   General Typographical Association (Scotland).

· I.T.U.   Irish Typographical Union.

J.I.C.   Joint Industrial Council.

L.S.C.   London Society of Compositors.

L.C.S.J.B.   London Consolidated Society of Journeymen
Bookbinders

L.T.S.   London Typographical Society.

L.U.C.   London Union of Compositors.

M.P.A.   Master Printers' Association

N.A.T.   National Arbitration Tribunal.

N.P.A.   Newspaper Proprietors Association
(London dailies).

N.T.A.   National Typographical Association.

N.T.U.   Northern Typographical Union.

N.U.B.M.R.   National Union of Bookbinders and
Machine Rulers.

N.U.P.B. & P.W.   National Union of Printing,
Bookbinding and Paper Workers.

P. & K.T.F.   Printing and Kindred Trades Federation.

P.M.M.T.S.   Printing Machine Managers' Trade
Society (London).

P.T.A.   Provincial Typographical Association.

S.L.A.D.E.   Society of Lithographic Artists, Designers
and Engravers.

S.T.A.   Scottish Typographical Association.

PART ONE

CONTROL BY
CIVIL AUTHORITY

CHAPTER I

CRAFT GILDS AND STATIONERS' COMPANY

*It is ordeyned, that all Occupations of the Citie of London
shall be lawfullie ruled and governed every one in his
Nature, in due Manner, so that no Falsehoode or Deceipt
be founde in any Manner of Occupations aforesaid,
for the Honour of the good Company of the said
Occupations, and for the common Profit of the People. . . .*
Ordinance of the Council of London,
R. R. SHARPE, *Calendar of Letter Books* . . G, p. 135

MANUSCRIPT BOOK PRODUCTION

The high artistic quality of the medieval manuscript book was the result of centuries of development of fine manual skills. Each craftsman concentrated his energies on a narrow field of work, developing greater dexterity with his tools and a nice knowledge of the characteristics of his materials. Thus the finest manuscript books are of great beauty and almost incredibly painstaking craftmanship.

Most books were written on parchment made from the skins of sheep or goats, or vellum made from calfskin. Sometimes the skins were prepared by leather workers and sold to the bookmen; sometimes the book producers employed their own men to prepare the skins and cut them to the required size.[1] The major task, that of copying out the text of the book, was done by men called Textwriters, Scribes or Scriveners. Later, however, the term 'Scrivener' was restricted to those scribes who wrote out formal legal documents such as charters, deeds, wills, and conveyances of property. In earlier times presumably some scribes did both kinds of work.[2]

When the page of plain text was completed it was passed to the Limners or Illuminators who added the ornately decorated capital letters, the marginal illustrations, and the gilt border. When these were finished

[1] MSS. Harl. 5910. I. (British Museum.)
[2] *The Case of the Free Scriveners of London*, 1749, pp. 20-26.

16 CONTROL BY CIVIL AUTHORITY

the leaves were collated and sent to the binders. A joiner cut wooden boards to fit the book, a binder covered the boards with leather and embossed it in gold leaf; perhaps a claspmaker added a metal clasp to prevent the book from springing open. The completed manuscript book was an object of great beauty. It was also, inevitably, very expensive.

Much of the work was done by monks whose efforts were naturally concentrated on the production of religious books for use in churches and their own libraries, but they sometimes produced books for sale to the public. This branch of the industry was obviously beyond the control of the secular authorities.

Outside the monasteries the production of books for the market was carried on in small establishments. Contemporary accounts suggest that at one stage the entrepreneur in a book establishment was a Textwriter by trade. As a master he was, however, concerned not only with the production, but also with the sale of his product. The separation of the commercial from the manufacturing function developed much later. In fact, in the era of manuscript books, much of the work was bespoke, done to the order of a particular customer, and not simply for sale to the general public. The term 'workshop', which now means a place where manufacture is carried on, reveals how, in earlier times, the 'working' and 'shopping' functions were combined. George Unwin and other scholars have emphasized that the typical 'master craftsman' of the late Middle Ages was primarily a shopkeeper or tradesman (with emphasis on the *trade*) rather than a producer.[1]

THE CRAFT GILDS

The most important secular institutions of the medieval city were the Craft Gilds. In the days when the State authority was weak or uncertain, when feudalism was crumbling, when the town was gradually assuming important economic and political functions, the tightly organized Craft Gild gave cohesion and stability to the social structure. Inevitably, over the centuries, in different industries or under different economic or political conditions, the influence and function of the gilds showed great variation. Even their origin is masked in obscurity, and authorities differ as to how they arose. Were they free, voluntary associations of craftsmen, later given formal recognition by the City Council and the State? Or were they created by the latter as agents of local authority? The whole truth may never be known. Nevertheless, by the end of the fifteenth century the Craft Gilds had an established part in the social, religious, economic and political life of their times.

[1] G. Unwin, *The Gilds and Companies of London*, 1938, p. 62.

CRAFT GILDS AND STATIONERS' COMPANY

The typical gild was, according to its charter, a semi-official organization owing its authority and privileges to the fiat of the City Council. In return for jurisdiction over its members in certain matters the gild was supposed to protect the interests of the public. Thus the Mayor and Aldermen granted the petition of the Textwriters to set up a gild expressly 'for the reason that it concerneth the common weal and profit'. By ensuring that standards of craftsmanship were maintained, that apprentices were properly indentured, that foreigners and interlopers were not allowed to practise, and that those who produced shoddy work were punished, the gild was an important part of the civil administration.

This was its official function, the one which concerned the authorities. But to the ordinary member the gild's main function was quite different. To him it was a fraternity of men united by the bond of common participation in a certain trade, and therefore with a number of common interests and enemies. By providing opportunities for friendly social intercourse the gild lessened to some extent the animosities inseparable from commercial competition. Many gilds assumed responsibility for the welfare of their members by providing relief for the sick or poor, by looking after their widows or dependants, and by other charitable activities.

Thirdly the gild performed several economic functions, mainly by its regulation of working conditions and enforcement of customs to ensure that all legitimate craftsmen received a reasonably fair share of the available work. It was on constant watch to prevent interlopers or foreigners from usurping the privileges of freemen, claiming, with some justification, that it could not be held responsible for standards of work if people other than its own members were allowed to practise the trade. In 1373 the Scriveners expressly mentioned the 'many mischiefs' which had arisen because of the incompetence of foreigners who had recently set up shop in the city. At the same time they claimed frankly that as they had spent time and money in learning their craft, they should be given preference in the exercise of it.[1]

Details of the structure of the different gilds varied in response to the needs of the trade, and the changing policy of the civic authorities. The general rules for the constitution and government were usually contained in a Charter granted by the City Council, or in a set of ordinances by which the Council granted a petition for self government of the craft. Although the gild was apparently given a *carte blanche* to compose its own regulation it was always subject to any State or City decrees on such matters as the employment of 'strangers', the taking of apprentices, or the fixing of prices. Furthermore it was always subject to the vague

[1] Riley, *Memorials*, pp. 372–3.

CONTROL BY CIVIL AUTHORITY

condition that it should act for the general good of the public, and breach of this fundamental condition could be punished by revocation of the Charter.

The most important officers were the Masters—in a small gild usually two in number—who were elected annually. After election they attended a ceremony at the Guildhall where they swore an oath of obedience to the Charter and loyalty to the City. In the joint gild of Textwriters and Limners one master was elected from each craft.[1] Annual elections and limitations on re-election gave experience of office to most members, and prevented the abuses which might follow if the same officers held power for long periods. Alterations in the rules could be made only by a general meeting of the gild. The Masters of the Textwriters and Limners had authority 'to call together all the men of the said trades honourably and peaceably when need shall be, as well for the good rule and governance of the said City as of the Trades aforesaid'.[2]

Discipline within the gild was obtained largely by that popular device of medieval government, the oath. Thus the Masters were under oath to observe the Charter and Ordinances, and the men were under oath to obey the officers. After 1403 obedience to the Masters and Wardens was enforced by a State decree, on pain of punishment for rebellion.[3] Although the larger gilds were allowed to set up their own courts for the settlement of disputes and the punishment of miscreants, the smaller ones such as the Textwriters had to report serious breaches of their rules to the Guildhall.[4]

There is no direct evidence of the number of masters and workmen connected with the production of manuscript books in London. There were, however, sufficient for the establishment of several craft gilds. As early as 1357 it was ordered and agreed by Henry Pykard, Mayor, and the Aldermen, that the Writers of Court Letter and Text Letter, and the Limners and Barbers should be given certain privileges.[5] This ordinance does not show clearly whether the trades mentioned were in separate gilds, or a joint one, but it is probable that at this time most of the bookworkers were in the one gild. Bookbinders may well have been more closely associated with leather workers.

The stationers, or booksellers, standing between the producer and consumer, were obviously in the best position for gauging the demands of the market, and controlling the supply of the product. By virtue of their strategic economic position they came to dominate the industry, gradually squeezing out the Textwriter masters. By the time of the

---

[1] Riley, *op. cit.*, p. 557.   [2] *Ibid.*, p. 558.
[3] *Liber Albus*, p. 424.   [4] Riley, *op. cit.*, p. 558.
[5] R. R. Sharpe, *Calendar of the Letter Books of the Corporation of London*, Letter Book G, f.61. (Henceforth cited as: Sharpe, *Letter Book*, etc.)

CRAFT GILDS AND STATIONERS' COMPANY 19

introduction of printing it was the Stationer, and not the Textwriter, who was the master of the typical 'bookshop'.

In 1403 the Textwriters, together with the 'Limners and other folks of London who are wont (also) to bind and sell books' petitioned the Mayor for permission to set up a Joint Gild, basing their case on an ancient ordinance of the time of Richard III which had required that all occupations of the City should be 'lawfully ruled and governed'.

The petitioners for the Joint Gild of 1403 also emphasized the need for stricter supervision, and laid stress on that favourite method of gild control, restriction of the right to practise a trade to the legitimate craftsmen. The Wardens took the oath to govern the trade 'to the praise and good fame of the loyal good men of the said trades, and to the shame and blame of the bad and disloyal men of the same'.[1]

Little is known of the history of this Joint Gild during the fifteenth century, but it was certainly functioning between 1420 and 1440 when its masters were sworn in at the Guildhall. A clue to its evolution is given by an entry for 1417 when the Masters of the Scriveners, Limners and Stationers were sworn in. As the stationers came to dominate the industry, they gave their name to the gild to which they belonged. Mention of a Stationers' organization is found almost continuously from this date until 1557 when the Stationers' Company was granted its Charter of Incorporation.[2]

To sum up, about 1350 the book crafts were probably in a Joint Gild which split up into the separate crafts about 1370. Early in the fifteenth century they came together again, and gradually became known as the Stationers. There is little reason to doubt the claim made by the officers of the Stationers' Company in 1645:

'That your petitioners' predecessours were made a brotherhood in the 4th year of the reigne of King Henry 4th, and had then ordinances for the good government of their fellowship . . . by which . . . the said Corporation had byn governed for the space of 240 years without interruption.'[3]

INTRODUCTION OF PRINTING

In the autumn of 1476 a wealthy merchant, member of the Mercers' Company, rented the almonry at Westminster Abbey, and some weeks later the room resounded to the blows of workmen labouring to erect a

---

[1] Riley, *op. cit.*, p. 558.
[2] G. Pollard, 'The Company of Stationers before 1557', *The Library*, 1938.
[3] E. Arber, *Transcript of the Registers of the Stationers' Company*, Vol. I, p. 593.

20 CONTROL BY CIVIL AUTHORITY

gaunt wooden structure of a kind never before seen in England. The merchant was William Caxton, and the crude frame the first printing press set up in the country. Before his death (c. 1491) Caxton printed more than one hundred books and documents and firmly established the art and mystery of printing from movable type.

Briefly the new invention consisted of two basic processes which remained practically unchanged in the following four centuries. First there was the arrangement of the separate letters to form the words and lines of the text; this operation was called *composition*, and was done by *compositors*. The second process consisted in applying ink to the printed surface, and pressing it against the paper on which it was to be printed; this process was called *presswork*, and was done by *pressmen*. To save time, and for ease of binding, several pages of a book were printed on the one sheet of paper; the sheet was then folded so that the printed pages all appeared in correct order. This was called a signature. The various signatures were then placed in order and sewn on to the spine of the book. This folding of the sheets and collating of the signatures were simple, unskilled operations and were later performed by women and girls.

Bookbinding operations were divided into two groups. The first steps—cutting the boards, cutting of leaves, sewing on the boards and glueing on the leather—were called *forwarding*. The final operations—working the design, embossing the lettering, gilding the edges, etc.—were called *finishing*.

As a substantial amount of capital was required to purchase a press and a quantity of type, and to pay wages to the workmen, the early master printers were often men of considerable means. According to Christopher Barker's report, written when he was the Queen's Printer (c. 1582):

'In the tyme of King Henry the Eighte [1509–1547] there were fewe Printers, and those were of good credit and compotent wealth; at which tyme and before there was another sort of men that were writers, lymners of bookes and dyverse thinges for the Churche and other uses, called stacioners; which have and partly to this daye do use to buy theire bookes in grosse of the saide Printers, to bynde them up, and sell them in their shops, whereby they well mayntayned theire families.'[1]

The master printer was properly concerned only with the production of printed sheets, but if he was also a stationer he would organize the assembly of sheets into a book, and when he sold a copy would perhaps undertake to complete the binding to the design of the customer. Very

[1] Arber, *op. cit.*, Vol. I, p. 114. Christopher Barker's Report.

CRAFT GILDS AND STATIONERS' COMPANY 21

often, however, the bookbinding was done in a separate establishment. Much of the work of the smaller master printers was of ephemera such as broadsides and pamphlets which were not bound or stitched at all.

Printing had been established on the continent for some decades before it reached England. It was inevitable therefore that the first English printers should rely on alien craftsmen; indeed many of the best known masters themselves came from the Netherlands. With the increase in the number of printing presses, and the gradual training of English apprentices to learn the mysteries of composition and press-work, the native printers began to show the hostility towards the alien craftsmen which developed in London during the early sixteenth century. In 1484 an Act restricting the entry of alien workmen into England had specifically exempted those connected with the printing trades,[1] but in 1534 this protective clause was cancelled, and severe restrictions were imposed on the buying and selling of books printed on the continent.[2] It is difficult to decide whether this was intended primarily to protect the 'infant industry', or to control a growing source of seditious literature. Probably the Government hoped to kill two birds with one stone.

THE STATIONERS' COMPANY CHARTER, 1557

The authority of the old Stationers' Gild was severely shaken by the rapid growth of printing in the early sixteenth century. The alien workmen were difficult to control, as they were not strictly eligible for membership; furthermore the new skills did not fit any of the old categories, and it seemed doubtful, for a while, whether the gild could continue to function effectively. Many of the old manuscript stationers had, naturally, invested in printing presses, and learned how to operate them. The printing press completed the extinction of the craft of Text-writers.

The gild was saved, in a radically modified form, by two considera-tions: first, the desire of the authoritarian State to control sources of seditious literature, and second, the aspirations of the wealthy stationers for a higher social and civic status. About this time many of the wealthy gilds had been transformed into City Companies with all the parapher-nalia of an elaborate livery, important economic privileges, and enhanced political power. The ambitious stationers therefore petitioned for incorporation—not of course on these grounds—but as a means of controlling the 'disorders' of the industry for the common welfare. They were fortunate in the times. The Government was desperately anxious

[1] I Richard III. c. 9.
[2] 25 Henry VIII. c. 15. An Act for Prynters and Bynders of Bookes.

CONTROL BY CIVIL AUTHORITY

to combat the flood of blasphemous, heretical and seditious propaganda that had been released by the new invention. The Charter of Incorporation was granted in 1557.

For the following century the Stationers' Company played a dual role. It regulated the internal or domestic matters of the industry, settling disputes among members, making rules relating to apprenticeship and other customs, and to some extent fixed the terms of employment of the journeymen. It also acted as an agent of the State for the control of printing, the registration of printing presses and publications, and the detection and destruction of illegal presses.

All Freemen, masters and journeymen, in the printing industry and associated trades, belonged to the Company, and in theory enjoyed equal rights and status, as in the ancient gilds. But in fact the position was very different.

The Executive body of the Company was the Court of Assistants, which had very wide powers, and actively intervened to settle disputes between masters, or between employers and employed. Originally it was elected by the whole membership, which would obviously have given the journeymen a dominant voice in the Company's affairs. This did not suit the stationers. The custom soon developed, and was later made constitutional, of filling vacancies in the Court by the Court itself. The body of the members were thus excluded from the franchise.

The titular head was the Master, but in fact the Wardens were the most powerful officers. They had extensive powers of search and entry, to detect irregular printing, and to intervene in all matters affecting the good conduct of the industry. Originally these officers too, were elected by the whole membership; later however the Court took over their appointment. Thus with a self-perpetuating Executive controlling the appointment of the most powerful officials, the original democratic constitution was subverted in the interest of the wealthy members.

The journeymen and small master printers were deprived of any real voice in the conduct of the company. Most of the wealthy and influential members were stationers, publishers and booksellers, with commercial rather than industrial interests. Subsequently there were several violent and prolonged disputes between these two factions, and sometimes the journeymen printers sided with the small masters against the commercial oligarchy.

In 1560 the cleavage of economic and social status was made more evident by the division of the members into Yeomen and Liverymen. Election to the Livery was supposed to be an honour given in recognition of honourable service to the Company. It carried certain civic privileges and enhanced social status, as well as the perquisite of an extra appren-

CRAFT GILDS AND STATIONERS' COMPANY 23

tice. Election was made by the Court of Assistants. It required payment of high entry fees, and the purchase of the regalia; it was therefore effectively beyond the means of the poorer masters, no matter how well they might, in theory, be entitled to the honour. It was, in fact, another way of buttressing the power of the wealthy members against the poorer.

Thus by their control of election to the Livery, to the Court, and to the main offices, the wealthy stationers obtained an unshakable hold on the control of the Company, and thus of the industry. By their monopoly of the licences and patents for the printing of standard, highly profitable works, and the use of their influence to obtain government patronage for themselves, and by the repression of potential competitors, they maintained this dominance for the best part of a century.

The old gild principles of equality and fraternity, which had been its main source of strength, were completely lost; so too was the democratic system of election and rotation of office. Nor did the Company show much intention of exercising the other gild function of protecting the public, though this was one of the grounds for its incorporation. On the other hand it did, on a few occasions, concern itself with the welfare of its poorer members. Several times, when journeymen or small masters applied for relief, for employment, the Court ordered the richer masters to forego, at least temporarily, some of their privileges, in order to provide sustenance for the others.[1] This was perhaps due less to unalloyed charity than to the realization that unemployed journeymen, or deperate small masters, would be sorely tempted to take work on some of the 'illegal presses' which, for all the vigilance of the Wardens and the agents of the Star Chamber, continued to flourish in well hidden cellars of the Government's many enemies. Every time another seditious pamphlet appeared in the streets, or an anti-Government broadside or ballad sheet began to circulate in the inns and coffee houses, the unfortunate Wardens of the day incurred the lively wrath of the Government. Indeed the office of Warden, though giving great power to the incumbent, with considerable opportunity for nepotism, bribery and the persecution of private enemies, was not altogether a sinecure.

MASTER PRINTERS

The number of printing houses in London in 1557 is not known, but in 1582 when Christopher Barker presented his *Note of the State of the Company of Printers*, he complained that there were then twenty-two printing houses in London, whereas eight or ten would, he thought,

[1] Greg and Boswell, *Records of the Court of the Stationers' Company*, 1557–1602, p. 4.

24 CONTROL BY CIVIL AUTHORITY

have sufficed for all of England and Scotland.[1] He proposed that there should be even stricter supervision to suppress illegal printing and raise the technical standards. After a bitter dispute within the Company, the Star Chamber issued the famous Decrees of 1586 under which it was ordered that no new printing offices were to be opened until the existing 'excessive' number was abated. All master printers were to be licensed, and the number of apprentices limited. For the next fifty years, despite periods of laxity in enforcing the Decrees, the number of masters did not rise above twenty-two, while the number of presses could not have exceeded sixty. During the turbulent years of the early Commonwealth there was a great burst of new master printers, and by 1660 their numbers had risen to sixty, though many of them were in a small way, and probably had only one press each.

Although the Stationers continued to dominate the industry the restriction of the number of masters tended to establish virtual monopolies for those who were fortunate enough to secure a licence, and many of the masters rose in wealth and social eminence. Although the rank of 'Master Printer' was not formally recognized by the Company's constitution, it was one of considerable importance, and elevation to it was attended with due ceremony. In 1588 when Thomas Orwin was elected to be a Master Printer, he was presented to the Lieutenant of the Tower, the Recorder, the Dean of Westminster, and other dignitaries.[2]

While the number of masters was limited, the succession to the place of a deceased or retired master was an affair of general interest. Often the place was handed down from father to son, or bequeathed to a successor. The rank of Master Printer was not strictly tied to any particular establishment, and it was possible to transfer the rank to an outsider.

JOURNEYMEN

In the Middle Ages it was customary for the journeymen, as well as the apprentices, to live in the master's home. This custom persisted into the sixteenth century, but was then dying out. In 1577 a master was ordered by the Court of Assistants to provide 'meate, drinke, lodginge and wasshinge of his lynen' for his journeymen.[3] But by this time it was more usual for a journeyman to set up his own household, certainly if he were married. The distinction between householders and other journeymen is indicated in a writ issued in 1549 to the King's officers, ordering them to help Edward Whitchurche, the King's Printer, to take

[1] Arber, *op. cit.*, Vol. I, p. 114.
[2] Greg and Boswell, *Records*, p. 28. [3] *Ibid.*, p. 3.

CRAFT GILDS AND STATIONERS' COMPANY 25

up 'as manye prynters, composytours, and founders, as well house-holders as prentyces and jornymen and others', as he needed for his work.[1]

The records of the Court of Assistants show that there was hardly an aspect of industrial organization with which it was not called upon to deal. As its jurisdiction was limited to members of the Stationers' Company, a large part of its work was concerned with internal quarrels, —disputes between masters over their respective patents and monopolies, and disputes between masters and journeymen over the terms of employment.

As there was little change in technique or the size of industry, custom was an important determinant of the code of industrial rules. Thus when the Court of Assistants was required to decide a disputed point, it considered first the Law, and second the custom—either of the City or of the Trade. The Court did not, except on a few occasions, make new rules itself; it attempted to interpret and enforce rules which it derived from custom and law.

From the earliest records there are fragmentary scraps of evidence regarding wage disputes. In 1577 a claspmaker was ordered to serve out with his master 'so muche tyme as he hath before covenanted to serve him ffor 2s a weeke to be payde at every weeke ende'.[2] This journeyman obviously lived in the master's house and received board and lodging. Although he was on time wages, he was required to execute a certain minimum amount of work, namely, five dozen clasps a day.

Several other pieces of evidence hint at the existence of the method of payment by the piece, but they are all ambiguous. In the seventeenth century, with the increase in printing of news sheets and topical pamphlets, piece payment for composition and presswork may have been introduced. The regulations framed by the Master, Wardens and Assistants in 1635 for the compositors were not specific on this point, but clause 8 suggests that compositors were paid by piecework:

'That where a journeyman and an Apprentice worke together, they shall take theire Worke as it falles out, and not otherwise, the one the ffirst part and the other the last, as at ffirst they agree.'[3]

The wage bargain was settled between the individual employer and

[1] Calendar of Patent Rolls, Edw. VI, Vol. II, p. 98.

[2] Greg and Boswell, *op. cit.*, p. 1.

[3] Arber, *op. cit.*, Vol. IV, pp. 21–23. More than two centuries later the London compositors' trade union had to fight to achieve recognition of the same rule, to prevent the piece-worker from being given the difficult composition which would take a long time, while the apprentices took the 'fat', or straightforward matter.

26 CONTROL BY CIVIL AUTHORITY

workman. Nevertheless there was, at least in the larger offices, a very strong 'custom' that certain minimum rates should be paid. Any employer who infringed the custom would find himself subjected, not to the threat of a strike, but to a series of petty embarrassments which would convince him of the error of his ways. After all, the journeymen's workshop organization—the Chapel—described in the following chapter was very firmly established by 1682 when Joseph Moxon wrote of its customs, although many of the practices he describes could have occurred only in the larger offices.

If however the master remained adamant and the men wished to persevere in their dispute, they could appeal to the Court of Assistants. Thus in 1577 when the journeymen printers petitioned, 'That they maie be well and truelie paide for their worke', the Court admitted the justice of the plea but asked that the men should be more specific. Journeymen were certainly discouraged from attempting to enforce wage increases by direct methods. In 1587 when the orders were made restricting the right of the masters to keep standing forms (i.e., type set up ready to be used in a later printing) it was added that:

'If any workman shall over hardly behave himself, either in his work or in Demaunding of Wages, then the controversie (is) to be decided by the Master, Wardens and Assistants.'[1]

Similarly in the regulations of 1635 it was provided:

'That no workman shall rayse his wages above the now usuall Rates. Nor noe Master Printers abate the prices they now give. But in case of difference, the Master and Wardens to decide it.'[2]

Throughout this period the officers of the Company assumed at least a nominal responsibility for seeing that the workmen were provided either with employment or with some form of relief. In 1577 in answer to the simple prayer of the printers 'that they maie have work' it was ordered that the rich booksellers should give up some of their contracts to their poorer brethren. It is not clear whether they were supposed to give out work directly to the journeymen—though this was sometimes the custom—or were to give orders to the small masters who would then find work for the men. Again in 1587 the Court made six highly 'restrictive' orders with the object of providing more work. In these it was conceded that the journeyman's right to employment took priority over the commercial interest of the master. Firstly it was ordered that

[1] Arber, *op. cit.*, Vol. II, p. 883.   [2] *Ibid.*, Vol. IV, p. 21.

CRAFT GILDS AND STATIONERS' COMPANY 27

'no forms of letters be kept standinge to the prejudice of Workemen at any tyme'; secondly, strict limitations were placed upon the number of copies printed in each impression, and of the number of impressions; thirdly it was ordered:

'That no apprentice nowe beinge be employed either in composinge or workinge at the presse while any workman prynter able to discharge suche worke and reasonably requiring the same (beinge of honest and good behaviour) shall want work'.[1]

Some years later when the journeymen again applied for 'reformation' of working conditions, the code of proposed regulations explicitly recognized their right to maintenance during sickness:

'Seeing journeymen having wife and children, some more and some less . . . and their daily wages will but find them in the week, if that sickness comes upon a man as he is in work (or by age falls sick and lame) I could desire some course might be taken for their relief—I mean not such as be mis-spenders of their time in drinking and idleness, but I mean such as I know have been faithful in their callings.'[2]

APPRENTICESHIP

Apprenticeship was a vital institution in the organization of the medieval city. Legally the apprenticeship contract was often a formal deed, registered at the Guildhall, containing the covenants of the three parties —the parent or guardian, the master, and the youth. The apprentice lived in the home of his master, and in return for food and lodging, and instruction in the craft, was required to lead a moral life and apply himself diligently to his work.

The system served three main functions. Firstly it provided for the technical education of the future craftsmen. A master was legally bound to teach the apprentice all the arts and mysteries of the trade. In return the apprentice was required to make satisfactory progress, and in some trades was required to produce an elaborate 'masterpiece' as evidence of his competence before he could claim to be set free. Usually the term of the apprenticeship lasted for seven years or more, and it was often so timed that the youth came out in his twenty-first year.

Secondly it was an important method of qualifying for citizenship. Only Freemen were allowed certain privileges in the City, such as the right to work at certain trades, and to vote for the municipal offices.

---

[1] A Copie of Certain Orders Concerning Printing, 1587.
[2] MSS. Tanner (Bodleian) Vol. 33, p. 33. (n.d.).

28 CONTROL BY CIVIL AUTHORITY

Serving an apprenticeship was the commonest method of earning the freedom of the city. The municipal authorities were therefore concerned that the system should be preserved and regulated according to custom. In this they were often at odds with the masters in various trades who found the old regulations irksome and restrictive. At times the Council of London took active steps to see that the regulations were observed; in the reign of Edward the First it ordained:

'That no person shall henceforth receive an apprentice if he be not himself free of the City, and cause their covenant to be enrolled, of whatever condition such apprentice may be. And that no apprentice after his term fully served, shall follow his trade in the City before he shall have been sworn of his freedom, and thereupon enrolled. And that no apprenticeship shall be received for a term of less than seven years, according to the ancient and established usage.'[1]

Thirdly the apprenticeship system ensured that there was some rough equality between the demand for, and the supply of labour in the trade. Limitation of numbers was sometimes effected directly by decree of the City Council, or an ordinance of the controlling gild, but indirectly it was effected by the rule that the apprentice should live in the master's house. Sometimes the existing masters were keen to take on more apprentices, in order to obtain the cheap labour, for the apprentice received no wages. At such times the authorities intervened to prevent masters from taking on too many apprentices, for they wisely feared the social consequences—unemployment, distress, and unrest— which would follow from the training of too many men in any branch of trade.

In practice the well-being of the apprentice varied enormously according to the status and temper of the master. Thus one who served with a wealthy stationer, after paying a high premium, would live *en famille*, be accorded care and attention, and might reasonably aspire to the hand of his master's daughter. But many of the smaller masters engaged apprentices for the sake of the premium or the cheap labour, and took pains to exact from the unfortunate youths more in the value of service than the cost of board, lodging and instruction. The apprentice was committed for seven years or more to a kind of bond slavery from which he could hardly escape, except to the prisons or the gallows. Contemporary records are full of stories of runaway apprentices, and of the riotous behaviour of apprentices revolting against their restrictions. Their hours of work, mealtimes, holidays and so forth were completely at the discretion of the master, who was also allowed a fair degree of

[1] *Liber Albus*, Book III, Part II, p. 237.

CRAFT GILDS AND STATIONERS' COMPANY 29

latitude in the infliction of corporal punishment for alleged misdemeanours.

For two centuries after the introduction of printing the Government tried to restrict the industry to a definite size and location to facilitate the detection of seditious printing. But any attempt to reduce the number of presses inevitably threatened a number of journeymen with unemployment. Furthermore, if the number of masters and presses were fixed, as the Government desired, there would be a definite proportion of apprentices to journeymen which would ensure an adequate supply of future craftsmen. If this ratio were exceeded, some journeymen would be faced with unemployment and distress, and would be tempted to take work wherever it was offered. This danger was recognized by the inclusion of an apprentice quota in the celebrated Star Chamber Decree of 1586, 'for the avoyding of the excessive number of Prynters within this Realm'. The permitted quota was as follows:

A Master or Upper Warden of the Company: 3 apprentices.
A Liveryman of the Company: 2 apprentices.
A Master who was a yeoman of the Company: 1 apprentice.[1]

Had this rule been strictly enforced it might have provided a workable formula for regulation of entrance to the industry, but by relating the quota to the master's status in the Company, and not to his economic importance (i.e. to the number of presses he operated, or the number of journeymen he employed) it permitted some sharp practices by the hierarchy. A rapid turnover of Masters or Wardens, or a large number of elections to the Livery, would have defeated the purpose of the scheme. Apparently the authorities hoped that the 'haves' and 'have-nots' would strike a balance of power which would coincide with the future needs of the industry. However, by the early seventeenth century the Decree was a dead letter. In 1635 the workmen complained of 'the excessive numbers of persons brought up to the art of printing, some of which learn the trade and are not bound at all by Indenture to any, others bound to men free of this Company and other Companies, and turned over to Prynters to serve out their tyme . . .'.[2]

This custom of 'turning over' an apprentice, from one master to another, originally sanctioned to permit some flexibility, or to alleviate distress or hardship (for example on the death or insolvency of the master) was one of the commonest ways of avoiding the regulations. These 'turnovers' were for centuries a fruitful source of journeymen's complaints.

But with the abolition of the Star Chamber a few years later, and a

[1] Arber, *op. cit.*, Vol. II, pp. 807–12.
[2] S. P. Dom. Charles I, Vol. 301, No. 105. Arber, *op. cit.*, Vol. IV, p. 21.

CONTROL BY CIVIL AUTHORITY

great expansion of the industry during the Commonwealth, most of the 'restrictive' customs were abandoned. This period was one of full employment and prosperity for the journeymen, and it was not until the State attempted to re-impose restrictions on the size of the industry in 1662 that the latter were moved to call for complementary restrictions on the intake of apprentices.

Apprenticeship remained by far the commonest way of obtaining a right to a Freedom. As a Freeman could, in law, follow any profession, the civic authorities kept a wary eye on the apprentice policy of every company, for laxity on the part of one would nullify the restrictions of the others. On taking an apprentice the master registered him at the Stationers' Hall and paid a small fee:

'Receved of John Daye for presentinge of Edwarde Robynson to be his apprentis for VII yeres from the feaste of saynte John babteste . . . VI d.'[1]

The apprentice was entitled to provision of full board and adequate clothing. As he received no wages he was often forced to borrow to provide himself with any of the needs not specified in the indentures. Hence he often finished his servitude in debt to his master who, if unscrupulous, was able to dictate terms of future employment on the threat of imprisonment for debt. The provision of clothing was a custom so well established that often it was not expressly mentioned in the indentures, but on several occasions masters were ordered by the Court to provide suitable attire. One apprentice was to be given:

'Beside his ordenarie Workedaie apparell, one suite of newe apparell with a faire newe Cloke, fytt and mete for him in the Judgment of the Master and Wardens.'[2]

The master was required to give the youth full instruction in the trade, 'without concealing his Cunning or Workmanship from him, and without any outrage or other misusing to be done him'.[3]

Standing *in loco parentis* the master was held responsible for the youth's misdemeanours, and in the case where a printing apprentice assaulted a freeman, the master was required to pay damages, enter into a bond against repetition of the offence, and continue to take charge of the apprentice.[4]

The master was however entitled to use reasonable corporal punishment to enforce discipline, and in some unhappy households the wretched apprentice, as well as being the drudge, was cuffed and

---

[1] Arber, *op. cit.*, Vol. 1, p. 167. [2] Greg and Boswell, *op. cit.*, p. 14.
[3] *Ibid.*, pp. 8, 14. [4] *Ibid.*, pp. 62, 71.

CRAFT GILDS AND STATIONERS' COMPANY 31

whipped by every ill tempered adult. When the term was expired, the master presented the apprentice to the Wardens of the Company for the granting of his Freedom. Again a small fee was paid, and a donation given towards the cost of the celebration of the event.

Later the masters of the Company presented the apprentices at the Guildhall to receive the Freedom of the City.

Under the ancient custom of patrimony a master printer was permitted to bring his eldest son up to the trade, and present him for his Freedom when he had served the customary time, but he was not allowed to train other kinsmen without a proper deed of apprenticeship.

CHAPTER II

DECLINE OF THE
STATIONERS' COMPANY
1660–1780

GENERAL CONDITIONS

With the restoration of the monarchy in 1660, 'indiscriminate' printing was again subject to state control. Under the Licensing Act of 1662 the number of master printers was reduced to twenty in order to secure effective control of all printed matter and the prompt discovery and punishment of offenders.

For the next three decades the industry laboured under the watchful eye of officers of the Government. After the Revolution, however, control was relaxed considerably, and in 1695 the Licensing Act was allowed to lapse. 'From that date', wrote Timperley, with commendable caution, 'the press in England has been commonly considered to be free.'[1]

The number of master printers fell from sixty or seventy in 1660 to thirty-five in 1668, partly from the Plague, and partly by the Great Fire in which many printers' and booksellers' establishments were destroyed. Even those who survived were hard hit by the ensuing paralysis of the literary and commercial life of the capital. This period of contraction and stagnation was followed by one of slow expansion, especially after 1700. Between 1696 and 1709 the number of London weekly papers rose from nine to sixteen, and in the latter year there was also the first daily, the *Daily Courant*.[2] The early eighteenth century is famous for such periodicals as Defoe's *Review*, Steele's *Tatler*, and Addison's *Spectator*. This expansion was impeded by the duties on paper, pamphlets and advertisements which were imposed in the early eighteenth century with the primary object of discouraging political pamphleteering. These duties were bitterly opposed by the paper manufacturers and printers. The growing importance of periodical printing is shown, after

[1] C. H. Timperley, *Encyclopedia*, p. 531.
[2] Charles Knight, *The Old Printer and the Modern Press*, 1838, p. 218.

DECLINE OF STATIONERS' COMPANY

allowance has been made for the exaggeration natural in such an exigency, by the gloomy comment of the printers:

'That of many Master Printers and Journeymen in this City, two Thirds do entirely depend upon the printing of small Papers and Pamphlets, especially the latter . . . and therefore two Thirds of the said Printers, with their Families, must be entirely Ruin'd.'[1]

Despite these pessimistic forecasts of its demise, the newspaper continued to flourish. By 1785 there were nine morning and ten evening dailies in London, as well as nine others, while in the provinces there were about fifty regular newspapers most of which appeared once weekly.[2] Overall expansion was coupled with some degree of specialization. Pendred's list includes six type-founders, three ink-makers, forty-four engravers and thirteen copper-plate printers. The commercial side was equally diversified with entries for stationers, booksellers, print sellers and paper merchants.

DECLINE OF THE STATIONERS' COMPANY

When the monarchy was restored in 1660, an attempt was made to re-impose limitations on the printing industry. Roger L'Estrange recognized the connection between the poverty of the printers and the incentive to seditious printing:

'One great evil is the multiplicity of private presses, and consequently of printers, who for want of public and warrantable employment, are forced to play the knaves in corners, or want bread.'[3]

To reduce the danger it was necessary to keep the number of printers to a minimum, and ensure reasonably full employment for them all. No branch of the industry should remain unregulated; even the carpenters and joiners who built the presses, the typefounders and smiths, the authors and the readers—all were to be kept under watch, and encouraged to act as spies and informers. Journeymen were to be strictly controlled:

'Let no journeyman be employed, without a certificate from the master where he wrought last; Let no master discharge a journeyman nor he leave his master, under fourteen dayes notice, unless by consent.'[4]

---

[1] *The Case of the Manufacturers of Paper* (Bodleian MM Jur. 29). V. also *The Case of the Poor Printers and Papermakers Farther Stated*, 1712 (Goldsmiths).

[2] J. Pendred, *The London and Country Printers' and Stationers' Vade Mecum.* London, 1785.

[3] Roger L'Estrange, *Considerations and Proposals in Order to the Regulation of the Press*, 1663, p. 2.   [4] *Ibid.*, p. 4.

B

34 CONTROL BY CIVIL AUTHORITY

Who was to be entrusted with this strict supervision? At this time the master printers were in dispute with the merchant oligarchy in the Company, and indeed had in 1660 petitioned for incorporation as a separate company, complaining of the wrongs they suffered at the hands of the stationers, and suggesting that they should be given the requisite authority to regulate the industry.[1] But the sceptical L'Estrange brusquely dismissed their claim:

'It were a hard matter to pick out twenty master printers who are both free of the trade, of ability to manage it, and of integrity to be trusted with it: most of the honester sort being impoverished by the late times, and the great business of the Press being engrossed by Oliver's creatures.'[2]

In regard to the Stationers' Company claims he was even more forth-right:

'It seems a little too much to reward the abusers of the Press with the credit of superintending it; upon a confidence that they who destroyed the last King for their benefit will now make it their business to pre-serve this to their loss.'[3]

L'Estrange considered that the only way to control the industry securely was to employ officers who were not financially connected with it. Thus the police powers of the Company were, though not abolished, severely limited.

The new set of Ordinances approved in 1678 confirm that the Company was also ceasing to exercise much authority in the other field—the determination of terms of employment—where it had once been supreme. Most of the new clauses were concerned with the mode of election of officers, and with settling disputes among the more exalted members. Discipline within the company was tightened by specifying, more precisely than before, the responsibilities and duties of the different ranks and officers. The Court of Assistants was given nominal power of search for illegal presses, and authority to punish offenders, but these were seldom used.[4]

The only aspect of industrial relations mentioned in the new Ordinances was apprenticeship. The practice which had developed of transferring an apprentice from one master to another, sometimes

---

[1] *A Brief Discourse Concerning Printing and Printers.* S. P. Dom. Charles II, Vol. 88, No. 133.

[2] Roger L'Estrange, *op. cit.*, p. 26.　　　　　　　　　　　　　[3] *Ibid.*, p. 25.

[4] *Orders, Rules and Ordinances . . . of the Mystery or Art of Stationers,* 1678.

DECLINE OF STATIONERS' COMPANY

outside the Stationers' Company, was incompatible with the object of maintaining a strict check on all printing. Masters were therefore prohibited from instructing any youths—except their own sons—in the art of printing, unless such youths were actually bound as apprentices to a lawful printer.

This attempt to re-impose something of the old restrictive code ended in failure, for with the spread of printing to the provinces in the eighteenth century neither the Court of Assistants nor the Government could exercise effective control. This breakdown of regulation was not welcomed by the masters, many of whom feared the competition of enterprising journeymen willing and able to set up small establishments with very little capital. The master printers therefore revived the idea that control of the industry should be given to an organization in which they should dominate, thus eliminating the remnants of authority of the merchant clique in the Stationers' Company.[1] This idea was not adopted. Throughout the eighteenth century effective control by the Stationers' Company continued to decline.

JOURNEYMEN'S ORGANIZATION—THE CHAPEL

In the interval between the control of the industry by the Stationers' Company and the rise of autonomous organization of journeymen the latter were not completely at the mercy of their masters in regard to the determination of working conditions. Almost from the very introduction of printing, the men in each office had exercised a certain degree of self-government through the venerable institution of the *Chapel*. According to Joseph Moxon's *Mechanick Exercises*, published in 1683:

'Every *Printing House* is by the Custom of Time out of Mind, called a *Chappel;* and all the Workmen that belong to it are *Members of the Chappel*; and the Oldest Freeman is *Father of the Chappel* . . . There have formerly been customs and Bye Laws made and intended for the well and good Government of the *Chappel*, and for the more Civil and Orderly Deportment of all its Members while in the *Chappel*; and the penalty for the breach of any of these Laws and Customs is in Printers' Language called a *Solace*. And the Judges of these *Solaces* and the Controversies relating to the *Chappel*, or any of its Members, was plurality of Votes in the *Chappel*. It being asserted as a Maxim, *That the Chappel cannot Err*. But when Controversie is thus decided, it always ends in the Good of the Chappel.'[2]

[1] *A Certain and Necessary Method of Regulating the Press*. (Goldsmiths. Broadsides, 232 (II).)
[2] Reprinted in Ellic Howe, *The London Compositor*, Introduction.

36 CONTROL BY CIVIL AUTHORITY

The printers' Chapel is undoubtedly one of the most fascinating forms of workers' organization ever evolved. Even in Moxon's time the tradition was so firmly established that its origin was lost to contemporaries, and he could use only such vague phrases as 'formerly' or 'time out of mind' in attempting to show its beginnings.

Membership was compulsory; journeymen joined when they were engaged by the master on a more or less permanent basis, apprentices when they came out of servitude. In the early eighteenth century an elaborate initiation ceremony was generally performed. It began with a procession of the journeymen around the office, to the chant of a non-sensical alphabetical anthem. This was followed by a mock conferment of knighthood—Thomas Gent was made Lord High Admiral over all the bogs in Ireland,[1] and a mock baptism in which beer or ale replaced the customary water. Masters often insisted that new journeymen should submit to the rigours of initiation, presumably because they knew there would be trouble from the 'Chapellonians' if a non-member was allowed to work beside them. Benjamin Franklin discovered this when he worked as compositor and pressman in a London office in 1725.[2]

A newly bound apprentice was often required to go through a corresponding ordeal in order to be made a Cuz or Deacon, a kind of novitiate order of the Chapellonians.[3] Although the actual ceremony seems at this time to have become something of a farce, the authority of the Chapel within the office was very real. A workman who refused to join or to obey the Rules soon found himself the object of the tiresome attentions of the *Chapel Ghost* who made life uncomfortable for the 'excommunicate' by mixing up the letters in his case, hiding his inkballs, and playing other annoying tricks. After a few weeks of such treatment most journeymen were only too willing to conform. By the end of the century the Chapel Ghost was commonly known as Ralph or Ralpho. The Chapel's income was made up of entry fees, fines for infringement of rules, and general contributions. According to Moxon:

'Every new workman to pay half-a-Crown; which is called his *Benvenue*: this *Benvenue* being so constant as Custome is still lookt upon by all Workmen as the undoubted Right of the *Chappel*, and therefore never disputed; yet he who has not paid his *Benvenue* is no Member of the *Chappel*, nor enjoys any benefit of *Chappel-Money*. If a Journeyman Wrought formerly upon the same Printing House and comes again to Work on it, he pays but half a Benvenue.'[4]

[1] Thomas Gent, *Life*, 1832, p. 16.
[2] Benjamin Franklin, *Memoirs*, 1818, Vol. I, p. 69.
[3] *The Country Journal*, 24 May, 1740.
[4] J. Moxon, *op. cit.*, p. 360.

DECLINE OF STATIONERS' COMPANY

The method of formulating Chapel Rules varied considerably. Moxon did not state precisely how they were made at this time, but he certainly implied that the journeymen exercised a good deal of authority in workshop matters. Although there were only nine Rules 'usually and generally accepted', there were many others made by general consent for each office. The following were the nine misdemeanours generally punished:

'1. Fighting in the Chapel.

2. Swearing in the Chapel.

3. Abusive Language, or giving the Ly in the Chappel.

4. To be Drunk in the Chappel.

5. For any Workman to leave his Candle burning at Night.

6. If the Compositor let fall his composing stick, and another take it up.

7. Three Letters and a Space to lye under the Compositors Case.

8. If a Pressman let fall his Ball or Balls, and another take it up.

9. If the Pressman leave his Blankets in the Tympan at Noon or Night.'[1]

Moxon also listed a number of others which prohibited sending out for drink, gambling for money, or playing practical jokes. Strangers who perpetrated hoary puns about galleys at sea, or made references to horses or pigs (nicknames given to the pressman on account of their strength and the grunting they made when pulling) were liable to contribute to the funds. These general rules were concerned almost equally with two aspects of workshop life: firstly, the regulation of personal relationships, and secondly, the promotion of workshop efficiency.

The Chapel was thus a democratic workplace institution with authority to legislate on a wide variety of matters connected with the organization of production and the personal conduct of its members. This authority was enforced by a number of sanctions. In the first place the Chapel could inflict a fine varying with the severity of the offence, usually according to a predetermined scale. If an offender would not pay up, the members of the Chapel might use physical force, laying the recalcitrant on the imposing stone and beating him on the buttocks.[2] More probably they would proceed in a less spectacular but no less effective fashion by invoking the assistance of the ethereal Ralpho.

The Chapel had another ingenious method of resolving disputes among members, known as the 'purchasing of a solace'. According to Moxon:

[1] v. *Rules and Orders to be Observed by the Members of this Chapel.* 1734.

[2] J. Moxon, *op. cit.,* p. 357.

38 CONTROL BY CIVIL AUTHORITY

'Any of the Workmen may purchase a *Solace* for any trivial Matter, if the rest of the *Chappel* consent to it. As if any of the Workmen sing in the *Chappel*, he that is offended at it may, with the *Chappel's* consent purchase a penny or twopenny *Solace* for any Workman singing after the *Solace* is made; Or if a Workman or Stranger salute a Woman in the Chappel after the making of the *Solace*, it is a *Solace* as of such Value as is agreed on.'[1]

The workman who wished to introduce the new rule 'purchased the solace' by laying a penny on the imposing stone and asking the Father of the Chapel to call a Meeting. He then outlined the reasons for the suggested rule, and suggested a fine for its infringement. The Chapel then decided whether or not to make the rule, and the amount of the fine. This procedure persisted well into the nineteenth century as the description given by the writer of 'The Composing Room' shows:

> 'But now the Father damps the angry flame,
> And the full Chapel empties every frame.
> Sam Brown, the plaintiff, duly has paid down
> With solemn phiz the customary brown;
> For here, as in King William's courts of law,
> There must be current coin as well as jaw.
> The clerk cries Silence! and the Father spreads
> His hand, in view of the assembled heads.
> And thus commences, "Gentlemen, in your
> Collective wisdom we must find a cure".'[2]

That rules for the smooth conduct of the work should have been enforced in the larger offices of the eighteenth century was to be expected; but it is amazing that such an elaborate code, buttressed by such an ingenious system of penalties, should have been common in the seemingly chaotic workshops of the sixteenth and seventeenth centuries. The older the Chapel rules, the more apparent is the essentially democratic nature of its organization: its most persistent tradition was that each issue should be dealt with by the *whole* of the members. As fines went into Chapel funds which were used to provide benefits for members in distress, or for the purchase of drink, each member had an interest in seeing that the rules were enforced. The interest was not, however, so direct as to encourage malicious spying, and the procedure of general discussion and an open vote probably ensured that in the majority of cases justice

[1] J. Moxon, *op. cit.*, p. 359.
[2] G. Brimmer, 'The Composing Room'. Reprinted in C. H. Timperley, *Encyclopaedia*, p. 516.

DECLINE OF STATIONERS' COMPANY 39

was done,—and was seen to be done. As an added safeguard some Chapels had a specific rule against abuse of the system:

'As nothing is proposed by these Orders but Good Rule, and what shall be equally for the Advantage of Everyone, all Cavilling, Stratagems, or Snares to promote Forfeitures, otherwise called Polling, is agreed to be avoided.'[1]

Comparison of Moxon's rules of 1682 with those of a century later shows that the status of the Chapel had changed significantly. In the latter period it was more under the direct control of the employer, and there was in consequence a greater emphasis on rules relating to workshop efficiency. For example, the master could intervene to enforce Chapel fines by deducting them from wages. Sometimes the master was called in to arbitrate if the Chapel could not come to a decision.[2]

In the eighteenth century there was also a decline in the sense of professional etiquette and dignity; in a period notorious for excessive alcoholism of the working classes the printers were certainly no exception. Nor is this surprising considering the long hours, the erratic employment, the emphasis on speed, the deterioration in craftsmanship and the waning of the old conception of industrial unity. But in an age when *laissez-faire* was coming to be regarded as the almost divinely inspired doctrine of social organization, the Chapel sustained in the ranks of the journeymen printers the spirit of industrial comradeship and endured to form the basis of the new organizations in which they would recover their sense of common purpose and unite to resist a depression of their traditional standard of life in the bleak age of industrialization.

APPRENTICESHIP

In October 1666, a few weeks after the Great Fire of London, the journeymen printers issued a broadsheet containing a plea for stricter control of entry into the trade. The one hundred and forty legal workmen, they said, 'were reduced to great necessity and temptations from want of lawful employment, occasioned partly by the encroachment of foreigners and partly by supernumary apprentices and turnovers'. The temptations discreetly referred to were undoubtedly high wages offered by opponents of the Government to those who would print their seditious pamphlets. The men then put forward the following proposals as a basis for reform, but were prepared to submit themselves

[1] Rules and Orders . . ., 1734. *The London Compositor*, p. 32.
[2] MSS. Harl. 5915, f. 112 (Brit. Mus.).

CONTROL BY CIVIL AUTHORITY

'to what other course or provision soever authority shall judge more expedient for their redress':

'1. That no foreigner (that is to say) such a one as hath not served seven years to the art of printing, under a lawful master printer as an apprentice, may be entertained or imployed by any master printer for the time to come.

2. That a provision may be made to hinder the increase of apprentices, and a limitation appointed as to the number . . .

3. That no turnovers be received by any master printer, but from a master printer; and that no master printer turning over an apprentice may be permitted to take any other apprentice in his place, till the full term of said apprentice so turned over be expired; for otherwise the restraint and limitation of apprentices will be evaded, and the number supplied by turnovers; under which name is understood, such persons as being bound to one master, are turned over to serve the residue of their time with another.'[1]

These proposals were not adopted by the authorities. However, with the subsequent expansion of the industry, and the opening of opportunities for enterprising men in the provinces, London journeymen probably grew less concerned with limitation of entry to the trade. Later in the eighteenth century, when the country offices began to discharge large numbers of apprentices who drifted to the capital to seek their fortune, London journeymen clamoured again for restriction of entry. But by then the Stationers' Company, even had it wished to meet their demands, was incapable of exercising authority over the provincial firms.

One important effect of the engagement of large numbers of apprentices by comparatively small masters was the breakdown of the system of 'indoor' apprenticeship, for a small master could not give board and lodging in his home to half-a-dozen lusty youths. At the end of the century this change in custom was deeply deplored by the journeymen, primarily because it encouraged the taking of an excessive number of apprentices. Furthermore it symbolized the separation of the social classes and economic interests of masters and men.

At its best the old 'indoor' system had much to commend it. John Dunton told how his father advised him (c. 1675):

---

[1] *The Case and Proposals of the Free Journeymen-Printers in and about London,* 1666. Reprinted in J. Toulmin Smith, *English Gilds,* 1870, p. clxi n.

Note the definition of the term 'foreigner'. This term was still in use in the early nineteenth century.

DECLINE OF STATIONERS' COMPANY 41

'Serve your full time with cheerfulness and delight endeavouring to acquaint yourself with all the Mysteries and Improvements of your Trade; and, if you find not convincing reasons to the contrary, serve as a Journeyman for one year.'[1]

The almost continuous record of trouble with London apprentices is, however, eloquent evidence that the system placed too great a strain on either the forbearance of the Masters or the capacity of the average youth to labour for seven long years without regular payment. Even John Dunton, in composing somewhat Utopian resolutions to be made by a new apprentice, unwittingly revealed the burden of the system:

'I'd reckon my Master and Mistress as another Father and Mother. . . . There's no way but this to make the Chains of a Seven Years Bondage sit easily, without galling. . . .'[2]

The following extract from an apprentice's petition to the Court of the Company to grant him his freedom, despite the refusal of his master to present him, shows some of the worst aspects of the system:

'Finding myself very much injured by the many specious charges of Mr Heath with whom I served my Apprenticeship, all of which he has already laid before the Chamberlain, for which I suffered ten days imprisonment since which confinement I have done nothing to offend him.—

'Having suffered many hardships during my Apprenticeship, such as my Father dying when I had served but two years and left me friendless, in so much that I had no one to find me in Cloaths but my Master, which he refused, in consequence of which I had not any to appear decent in, and for the last three years of my time was actually obliged to remain at home for want of them.

'For trifling faults I may have committed I have been frequently knocked down, knelt on and beat in a most unmerciful manner.

'The hours of my labour were from six o'clock in the morning till nine, ten, sometimes eleven and twelve at night, for which I received not the least gratuity or encouragement.

'I am led to believe that the reason of Mr Heath's present cruel behaviour is on account of my refusing to work for him after I was out of my time, but as I was desirous of improving myself in the business . . . and Mr Heath having kept the best part of the work to himself rendered it impossible for me to gain any further knowledge of it had I staid with him.

[1] John Dunton, *Life and Errors*, 1705, p. 45.   [2] *Ibid.*, p. 55.

B*

CONTROL BY CIVIL AUTHORITY

'It has been recommended to me to wait on Mr Heath, my wife has already been and not withstanding her condition, her tears and entreaties could not prevail. I have already made every concession in my power, have asked pardon in open Court, which I hope, Gentlemen, you will take into Consideration, and not deprive me of my Freedom (as I have suffered the Law for any faults I have committed). The loss of it would be punishing an Innocent yet unborn, whom I wish should be born free.'[1]

As it became apparent to the journeymen that the change in practice was leading to a greater *number* of apprentices, with the inevitable consequence that future employment was uncertain, they became alarmed. In 1775 the London pressmen asked the Court of the Stationers' Company to enforce more rigid control, but although the Court made a gesture of acquiescence, it was in reality powerless in the matter.[2] It was partly to deal with this problem that the early journeymen's trade societies came into existence.

ORGANIZATION OF WORK—THE COMPANIONSHIP

The compositors in the typical printing office of the eighteenth century were usually organized in a *companionship*, especially if they were engaged on newspaper work where speed of production was more important than craftsmanship. Usually a 'ship consisted of from three to six compositors who elected a leader called the *Clicker*. The Master then gave out the copy to the Clicker, who apportioned it among the members of the 'ship. The Master paid the group according to the size of the job at the standard piece rates, and the 'ship decided how to divide the lump payment. Usually the basis of decision was the number of letters each had set, for the clicker had kept a record of lines given out and composition given in by each worker. In his spare time the clicker set up headings, numbers, etc., and did the impositions. He needed to be a good workman who could turn his hand to any job and command respect and obedience from the companionship. Furthermore he needed no mean capacity for organization in order to preserve a smooth flow of work to all members, and minimize stoppages and disputes over the distribution of the 'fat' work on which high wages could be made. The clicker's wage, which came from the lump pay-

---

[1] Petition of Francis Allchin . . . (Jaffray MSS.). In a letter to the Court of Assistants the master did not deny the apprentice's statements regarding his treatment, but made counter charges of insolence, spoiling of material, etc.

[2] E. Atkinson, *An Account of the Rise and Progress of the Dispute between the Masters and Journeymen Printers*, 1799. (Goldsmiths), p. 11.

DECLINE OF STATIONERS' COMPANY

ment, was usually made equal to that of the most highly paid compositor.

From the point of view of the employer the purpose of the companionship was to speed up the production and release him from detailed management of the work; from the compositors' viewpoint its function was to increase piecework earnings by ensuring that those who were directly interested in high output took over the organization. Stower recommended it as 'the best means of expediting pamphlets and other works of a temporary and urgent nature' for it excited a spirit of emulation and induced the men 'to pursue their work with vigour'.[1] In his *Printers' Grammar* he included a set of 'Rules to be Observed in Companionships' which had been in operation since at least 1760.

'Each sheet should be divided into as many parts as the companionship may consist of and the choice of each part, if it materially varies, should be thrown for.

If parts of the copy be particularly advantageous or otherwise, each of the companionship should throw for the chance of it. . . . It frequently happens that a litigious man will otherwise argue half an hour on a point that would not have made five minutes' difference to him in the course of his day's work.'

These illustrate the general method of approach: first, an attempt was made to frame reasonably equitable rules; second, provision was made for the rapid settlement of disputes by a quick gamble. Towards the end of the century, as piecework became the general rule in composing rooms, there was increasing variety in the practice of different companionships, and the term came eventually to apply to *any* composing room staff, whether or not they were working under a clicker.

WAGES AND HOURS OF WORK

Fragmentary evidence on wages and hours of work before 1785, when the first Compositors' Scale of Prices was printed, gives only a rough guide to the prevailing terms of employment. In 1683 Moxon stated that men's earnings varied from half-a-crown to four shillings per day. Unfortunately it is not clear whether these were time rates or piece rates. Probably piece rates for composition and presswork did not become general until the eighteenth century, when newspaper offices put greater emphasis on speed. Caleb Stower suggested that piecework was introduced about 1700.[2]

---

[1] Caleb Stower, *The Printers' Grammar*, 1808, p. 468. These were the very characteristics which made the early unions hostile to the system.

[2] *Ibid.*, p. 418.

44   CONTROL BY CIVIL AUTHORITY

Throughout the eighteenth century the wages of a craftsman varied considerably according to his individual skill. In 1713, for example, James Watson stated that he would rather pay five shillings a day to a good pressman than one and sixpence to a careless one.[1] In 1747 a contemporary writer gave the following estimate of earnings in the various printing trades.

TRADE	AVERAGE WEEKLY EARNINGS (*shillings*)
Compositor	16–21
Pressman	16–21
Copper Plate Printer	15–18
Paper Maker (Moulder)	15–18
Bookbinder	12

Source: *A General Description of All Trades*, Lond. 1747

The figure for bookbinders is probably too low, for the finishers generally received as much as the compositors.

These earnings-agree broadly with Gilboy's detailed survey of wages in eighteenth-century England, which showed that the average weekly wages of London craftsmen rose from 15s in 1700 to 18s in 1780.[2]

Hours of work varied a great deal according to the amount of work in hand, the urgency of the contract, and the season of the year. Men on time wages naturally tended to work more regular hours than piece-workers. An important change in this century was the tightening of industrial discipline, and the attempt by the employers to promote greater regularity. Pressure of commercial competition which followed the decline of the old monopolies worked in the same direction. In 1747 the hours of work in most printing trades were from six in the morning to eight or nine at night. Usually an hour was allowed for breakfast, and an hour for lunch, but there was no break for tea, and the men had their supper at the end of the day at home. As late as 1786 bookbinders worked fourteen hours a day, with two hours off for meals, but by this time a large number of compositors and pressmen were on piecework, and their hours were consequently irregular.

[1] J. Watson, *History of Printing*, 1713, p. 21.
[2] E. W. Gilboy, *Wages in Eighteenth Century England*, 1934, Appendix.

PART TWO

***

TRADE SOCIETIES AND TRADE UNIONS
1780–1848

CHAPTER III

UNLAWFUL AND
DICTATORIAL COMBINATIONS
1780–1825

> *It appears from the unlawful and dictatorial combinations*
> *of the compositors, that not only the Bookselling Trade,*
> *and Authors and Literature in General, but the Master*
> *Printers in Particular, have suffered great inconvenience,*
> *and considerable loss and detriment; and that the*
> *prosperity of the Printing Business is thereby in*
> *imminent danger.*
>
> Resolution of Master Printers, May 1, 1807.

GENERAL CONDITIONS

In the late eighteenth and early nineteenth centuries—the classical period of the 'industrial revolution'—there were no dramatic changes in technology or industrial organization. Iron machinery and steam power were the main elements in the development of the factory system. In printing, however, they played a very minor part. The work of the hand compositor remained unchanged. True, the iron press, introduced about 1810, swiftly replaced the wooden one, but the work of the pressman was scarcely changed. Only in the office of *The Times*, which for so long used revolutionary techniques to propagate conservative views, was there a symbol of the new industrial era—a steam-driven printing press.

Bookbinding, considered either as a craft or an industry, had changed even less than letterpress printing. The typical binder's shop employed only a few workmen, capital equipment was negligible, and skilled journeymen could, with comparative ease, set up as masters. The small master bookbinders were not industrial capitalists but rather independent master craftsmen, executing orders for customers in their own houses. Hence many of them regarded the booksellers, rather than the journeymen, as the main enemy.

48 TRADE SOCIETIES AND TRADE UNIONS

The number of master printers in London rose from 124 in 1785 to 233 in 1818 and to more than 300 in 1825.[1] There are no accurate figures for the numbers of journeymen or apprentices. The following estimates are based on information contained in various petitions for wage increases.

	1785	1818*	1825
Compositors, Men	500	1300	1600
Compositors, Apprentices	180	600	700
Pressmen, Men	200	500	600
Pressmen, Apprentices	80	200	250
Bookbinders, Men	180	500	650

*v. Article in *The Gorgon*, 1818.

These figures show that the average establishment was still small— five compositors, two pressmen and three apprentices. But as the larger offices were easier for the trade societies to organize, the majority of the 'non-society' men were to be found in the smaller ones, the 'cock robin' shops which throughout the nineteenth century, and even later in the provinces, were to prove the bane of union organizers.

MASTERS' ORGANIZATIONS

The evidence relating to masters' associations in the letterpress printing industry is scanty and ambiguous. Whenever the workmen agitate for a rise in wages, or some limitation on apprentices, the masters appear as a semi-organized body, but this is only to be expected. The great strategic difference between masters and men, in the nineteenth century was that the men's organization had to be formal, and enduring, if resources were to be built up. The masters, on the other hand, needed only to come together intermittently, when a crisis threatened; at other times the state of the labour market was sufficiently in their favour to make further organization unnecessary.

For example, when the journeymen compositors presented a petition for an increase in piecework prices, in 1785, the masters held a general meeting and appointed an *ad hoc* committee to meet a deputation from the men, and inform them of the masters' decisions.[2] The committee was more of a go-between than a representative body. At this period there was no attempt at negotiation, for the masters denied that the men had a right to address them collectively.

The master bookbinders, however, seem to have had a more formal

[1] John Johnson (*Typographia*, 1824) gave 306; The London Trade Society of Compositors (*Rules*, 1826) gave 323.
[2] E. Howe, *The London Compositor*, Doc. I.

UNLAWFUL AND DICTATORIAL COMBINATIONS   49

and enduring organization. Probably its main function was to formulate and enforce the elaborate price-lists which governed the trade about this time. In 1781 the bookbinders had united to present a petition to the booksellers for permission to raise the standard prices.[1] Twelve years later when Faulkner, the astute leader of the journeymen, learned that the master bookbinders were compiling a new scale of prices to submit to the booksellers, he decided that the time was opportune for another reduction in journeymen's hours of work.

Action by the men led to a short dispute. When it was over the masters formed an Association, not to oppose the journeymen, but to co-operate with them to prevent 'under-cutting' of prices by 'unfair' employers. This venture in co-operation was short-lived, and the Association was dissolved at the end of the century. In 1806 the masters united temporarily to resist the strike of the men over the Tea Half-hour.[2]

Maintenance of prices was an honoured medieval tradition; price-cutting was inevitably associated with 'foreigners' and shoddy workmanship. As nearly all of the master bookbinders had served their apprenticeships to the trade, and were in business in a small way, they were immune to the new doctrines of mass production, specialization, and lowered prices.

According to Francis Place, the master type-founders had had a very close organization which exercised strict control over both the price of type and the wages of workmen.[3] This combination of employers was sufficiently strong to crush the strike of 1818. By the use of 'character notes' and the dismissal of militant employees the masters prevented the formation of any journeymen's society in their section of the industry.[4]

In general, in this period formal Associations of masters were ephemeral, *ad hoc* bodies which seldom survived for long. Those which did carry on continuously were more concerned with regulation of prices than with collective bargaining.

JOURNEYMEN'S TRADE SOCIETIES—ORIGINS

Throughout the eighteenth century journeymen in many trades formed organizations to protect their standard of life from the depressing effects of industrialization, and the breakdown of the old methods of industrial regulation. Such 'combinations', as long as they aimed at the enforce-

[1] E. Howe, *The London Bookbinder*, Appendix I.
[2] E. Howe and J. Child, *The Society of London Bookbinders*, ch. VII.
[3] Select Committee on Artizans and Machinery, 1824, *First Report*, p. 45.
[4] *The Gorgon*, 1818, p. 169.

50 TRADE SOCIETIES AND TRADE UNIONS

ment of existing laws, were tolerated by the authorities.[1] On the other hand combinations to raise wages or shorten hours were illegal under several old statutes against restraint of trade, or the raising of prices, as well as the common law of conspiracy. Thus the journeymen who organized the first trade societies before 1800 ran a risk of being indicted for conspiracy, and several printers, pressmen and bookbinders were imprisoned on this charge.

In 1799 and 1800 the Government, alarmed at the spread of revolutionary ideas from the Continent, passed the notorious Combination Acts, which, in effect, made all journeymen's trade societies illegal. But more important, from a practical point of view, was that the Acts provided for summary conviction of offenders.[2] Instead of the lengthy process of indictment and trial by jury, offenders could be dealt with by magistrates. In practice, however, many of the employers were reluctant to resort to the law, and in the printing trades the masters frequently met representatives of the men's societies in order to negotiate about terms of employment. Nevertheless the Combination Acts hung like the sword of Damocles over the trade society leaders, and intimidated the less militant of the journeymen. In 1825, largely through the efforts of Francis Place, the Combination Acts were repealed.[3]

Surviving records of the first autonomous organizations of journeymen printers leaves it uncertain whether they were 'trade societies' or 'benefit societies'. The former term was used for those which aimed directly at securing some control over the conditions of employment of their members. Some trade societies, however, developed from benefit clubs, and during the transitional stage a superficial examination of a society's rules might give a misleading impression of its main function. The bookbinders, for example, continued to call their organization a 'Friendly Society' for some decades after it had definitely taken an active part in the regulation of working conditions.[4] As friendly societies were generally approved by the authorities, while trade societies were anathematized, the journeymen continued to emphasize the friendly benefit side of the activities and to maintain discreetly philanthropic titles for their trade organizations.

In 1799 the pressmen who attempted to negotiate with the masters on the limitation of apprentices, were prosecuted for conspiracy. At the trial it was shown that the men were members of the Pressmen's Friendly Society whose headquarters was the Crown, near St Dunstan's

[1] S. and B. Webb, *The History of Trade Unionism*, ch. II.
[2] M. D. George, 'The Combination Laws Reconsidered', *Ec. Hist.*, 1927.
[3] Graham Wallas, *The Life of Francis Place*, ch. VIII.
[4] E. Howe and J. Child, *op. cit.* ch. I.

UNLAWFUL AND DICTATORIAL COMBINATIONS 51

Church in Fleet Street. The prosecutor, however, contended that this was only a cloak:

'It was called a Friendly Society; but, Gentlemen, by means of some wicked men amoung them the society degenerated into a most abominable meeting for the purpose of a conspiracy: those of the trade who did not join their society were summoned, and even the apprentices, and were told unless they conformed to the practices of these journeymen, when they came out of their time they would not be employed.'[1]

COMPOSITORS

The original stimulus to the formation of a society of compositors was the need for a set of rules to regulate payment to piece workers. Little is known of the manner of settlement of the first Scale of Prices in 1785. By 1793 the men had a permanent committee, which collected regular 'contributions', organized meetings of delegates from different offices, and attempted to limit the number of apprentices.[2] Its headquarters were at the Hole-in-the-Wall, Fleet Street. In 1801 the compositors formed the Union Society (whose title suggests that it was the result of an amalgamation) 'with the design of correcting irregularities, and endeavouring to promote harmony between the employers and the employed, by bringing the modes of charge from custom and precedent into one point of view, in order to their being better understood by all concerned'.[3]

This Society conducted negotiations on revision of the Scale of Prices in 1805 and 1810, but after the vicious prosecution of *The Times* compositors in the latter year it appears to have lapsed. In the 1820's two societies of compositors and one of news compositors were founded. Similarly the pressmen's society, which flourished from about 1790 to 1810, lapsed for a decade or more, and was eventually re-established in 1834.

PAPERMAKERS

The first trade societies of papermakers probably developed from the informal benefit clubs based on each mill. When supplies of French paper were cut off during the Napoleonic Wars, the industry enjoyed a

---

[1] E. Atkinson, *An Account of the Rise and Progress of the Dispute . . .*, 1799, p. 12 (Goldsmiths).

[2] Circular *To Compositors*, 24 November 1794; *The London Compositor*, Doc. XXVII.

[3] *The London Scale of Prices*, 1836, p. 17.

52 TRADE SOCIETIES AND TRADE UNIONS

period of expansion in which skilled journeymen enjoyed comparatively high wages. By 1794 the men had an extensive link-up of the different areas into a national organization. According to an Act of 1795:

'Great numbers of journeymen papermakers in various parts of this kingdom, have lately entered into unlawful meetings and combination to obtain an unreasonable advance of their wages, and for other illegal purposes. . . .'[1]

The passing of the Act to prohibit such combination had little effect, for in 1797 the men of Kent struck effectively, and in 1801 the organization was remodelled on even more ambitious lines. The following letter from society headquarters, intercepted by an employer, illustrates the intrepidity and vision of the enthusiasts for unionism:

'This is to acquaint you that we have now made our fifth subscription of 2/6d each, which makes 12/6d per man. . . . I have been to Maidstone by appointment, where I was met by a very respectable body of our trade, 44 in number where I produced the sick and secret articles of our trade which were generally and universally approved and signed, and are to be printed; also the cards of freedom. Everything bears a favourable aspect, and I hope will have a favourable issue. It would be a pity, after spending so many hundreds, to lose the cause at last for want of support. Manchester and Wells approve our plan, and they say that they will establish it in every mill from Benwick to Lands End.'[2]

The papermakers' society was undoubtedly one of the largest and best organized in the kingdom, and indeed the Webbs suggested that it formed the model for many later national unions, including the Owenite ones.[3] Certainly the Rules printed in 1823 revealed considerable experience in the art of organizing over a wide territory, a task which in the days of mail coaches, police spies and hostile government was fraught with difficulties and dangers much greater than those facing a local society.

The Rule Book of the Papermakers ended with these delightful verses:

[1] 36 Geo. III. c.3. Preamble.
[2] H.O. 42/62. Reprinted in A. Aspinall, *The Early English Trade Unions*, 1949, (Doc. 39). Note the distinction between the 'sick' Articles for public display, and the 'secret' Articles, relating to trade matters.
[3] S. and B. Webb, *Industrial Democracy*, 1898, p. 12 n.

Unlawful and Dictatorial Combinations 53

> May masters with their men unite,
> Each other ne'er oppress,
> And their assistance freely give,
> When men are in distress.
>
> We covet not our masters' wealth,
> Nor crave for nothing more,
> But to support our families,
> As our fathers have before.
>
> Then may the God that rules above,
> Look on our mean endeavour,
> And masters with their men unite,
> In hand and hand forever.[1]

This was another item in the campaign to persuade the authorities that the Society meant no harm. The 'hand in hand' in the last line refers to the emblem of two clasped hands, which was a favourite device on the early trade society membership cards. It symbolized the comradeship and unity of the journeymen. In these verses the papermakers are suggesting, tongue in cheek, that it symbolizes the unity of journeymen and masters!

BOOKBINDERS

The development of a trade society is shown most clearly by the history of the London bookbinders, for many of their earliest records have been preserved. In 1785 the journeymen formed three Lodges, as they were called, with the pleasant titles of 'The United Friends', 'The Society of Brothers', and 'The City Brothers'. These Lodges developed from coteries of journeymen who used to meet regularly at the One Tun in the Strand, the Green Man in Bow Street, and the Three Jolly Butchers in Warwick Lane. The object of the Lodges was to raise a fund to support a claim for a reduction in hours from fourteen to thirteen daily (including meals). In other words, it was a Strike Fund. Ironically the journeyman who first suggested the reduction had become a master by the time of the actual dispute. The men won the hour, and the Lodges flourished; a fourth was set up in 1793 and a fifth in 1795. Four of the originals survived the dangerous years of the Combination Acts, and formed the nucleus of later trade unions. For some years after the end of the first major dispute a small clique of members agitated for more centralized control of funds, a working ticket common to all

[1] Rules and Articles of Journeymen Papermakers, 1823. Select Committee on Artizans and Machinery, *Second Report* 1824

54 TRADE SOCIETIES AND TRADE UNIONS

Lodges, and stricter rules regarding admission. Following the successful strike for a reduction of hours, these reforms were incorporated in the Articles of 1784. By this time the so-called Friendly Society of Journeymen Bookbinders was in reality a full-fledged trade society. Its Articles made no mention of friendly benefits but contained quite elaborate rules relating to working conditions, and it had negotiated an important agreement with the Master Bookbinders' Association.

SOCIAL PHILOSOPHY

The most striking feature of the early printers' societies' pronouncements and activities was their fundamental conservatism. There was hardly a breath of radical social reform, and not a hint of unorthodoxy in political economy or social ethics. Whatever novel views may have been held privately by a few individuals, the majority of the members were in general interested only in maintaining their previous position in the social system. They looked back nostalgically to a (largely mythical) golden age of full employment, reasonable wages, and a fairly regulated intake of apprentices.

They had a profound dislike for the new doctrine of *laissez-faire* which the masters were invoking to justify practices which they had long been pursuing. Thus the men's first reaction to the brute facts of persistent unemployment and lower real wages was to look for some authority which could enforce corrective regulation. They turned first to the Stationers' Company. When this failed, the men turned to a greater authority—the State—and appealed for the enforcement of the Elizabethan Statute of Apprentices. But the current of *laissez-faire* was flowing too strongly and the last shreds of legislative protection were removed in 1813 by the repeal of the Statute.

The Societies then turned, almost reluctantly, to the task of enforcing reforms by collective action of the men. What were these reforms? Broadly they were reasonably continuous employment and a fair rate of pay. The concept of a 'fair price' for labour was largely based on tradition. It suggested that the worker should be paid enough to maintain his family at their accustomed standard; sometimes it implied that he should keep his position in the social scale relative to other craftsmen. Seldom was it suggested that the men should enjoy a gradually *rising* standard of living. The relentless move to make his labour a mere market commodity shocked the skilled artizan very deeply. While he could witness with philosophical detachment the servile status of the domestic servants, the ill-paid toil of the manual labourer, or the monotonous drudgery of the factory operatives, the attempt to lower his own status—to substitute the impersonal cash nexus for the social-economic

UNLAWFUL AND DICTATORIAL COMBINATIONS 55

relationship of the old order—seemed to him an offence against justice and decency. Hence the predominance of the more highly paid workers —the skilled artizans—in the earliest trade societies; they expressed the protest of an intelligent, educated, and relatively well-paid aristocracy of labour against this transformation of the relation between master and man. Thus they frequently demanded a return to an *ethical* basis of behaviour. Witness the bookbinders in 1786:

'It is their desire at all times to conduct themselves with submission to their superiors, considering themselves in a subordinate state. Nevertheless they cannot help reflecting that they are men, and as such, sensible of the oppression they labour under. They hope none will believe them actuated with motives adverse to the interest of their employers, or linked in combination to obstruct their business; they reprobate every idea repugnant to justice, and ground no claim but on principles of equity.'[1]

This is not the language of social revolution. The appeal to justice fell frequently on stony ground, for competition among master printers was becoming sharper and the booksellers were continuing their old conspiracy to dominate the printers and binders. And even if the principle was accepted, the application of it to particular instances was fraught with difficulty. When the journeymen realized that this line of attack was fruitless, they relied on a less ambiguous principle—the maintenance of their traditional standard of life.

CONSTITUTION OF TRADE SOCIETIES

When the organization of journeymen extended beyond the confines of a single work place, or beyond the number of men who had found a common interest in their habit of meeting together for drinking and talking, it was necessary to consider how the members of the wider group could be brought to obey the discipline of the constituted authority. Within the bookbinders' Lodge or the printers' Chapel this problem was not so acute, for close personal contact between all members tended to promote solidarity in the face of outsiders, whether masters or other workmen. In the large societies this personal acquaintance with other members was attenuated and sometimes a divergence of interest between sub-divisions of the Trade became a serious threat to the unity of each society.

Thus the news compositors, with different conditions of work, eventually broke away from the society of book compositors; in the

[1] Address to the Public, *Morning Herald*, May 9, 1786.

56   TRADE SOCIETIES AND TRADE UNIONS

bookbinders' society there was friction between the highly-skilled finishers who were paid by the week, and the less skilled forwarders who were often paid by the piece; later the Vellum Binders broke away from the parent society to form their own; in papermaking the 'wet' workers were often at loggerheads with the 'dry' workers. Faced with the task of reconciling these varying interests the early leaders developed some basic techniques of solidarity which changed but little in the following half century. The problems with which they were confronted and the solutions which were devised can be shown most clearly by a study of two highly successful organizations, those of the bookbinders and the papermakers.

The earliest surviving set of bookbinders' *Articles*, those of 1794, reveal the detailed structure of their society.[1] It consisted of four Lodges, each of which had its own officers.[2] The Friendly Sir (President) and Friendly Assistant (Secretary) were elected quarterly, but the Secretary was chosen annually, possibly because the number of literate members was fairly small. The Secretary collected subscriptions and fines which he paid over to the Friendly Sir for safekeeping in the Society Chest. The early unionists had a strict sense of democratic responsibility; substantial fines were inflicted for refusal to take office, or for lateness or non-attendance at meetings. Absence on Quarterly Night sometimes met with expulsion. The Secretary kept a record of the proceedings at each meeting and forwarded any important resolutions to the Trade Committee.

The latter consisted of three representatives from each Lodge, one of whom retired every quarter. Its function was to co-ordinate the work of the Lodges and to frame byelaws for the maintenance of the just 'rights of the Trade'. It met every second Tuesday night (the Lodges met on Mondays) received money and reports from the Lodges, and considered cases of breach of Society customs or trade rules. Its authority to frame new rules or alter the old ones was subject to the approval of a majority of the members assembled in special meetings.

However cumbrous this constitution might appear, it had indisputable advantages for a small Society. As each member was expected, indeed compelled, to take a full share in both the ordinary and the official business, and as rotation of officers took place quarterly, every member obtained a fairly clear notion of how the Society worked. There was no chance of a self perpetuating bureaucracy maintaining power by its monopoly of the principal offices.

But the reason for the success and stability of the Bookbinders'

---

[1] *Articles of the United Friendly Society of Journeymen Bookbinders*, 1794 (Jaffray Coll.).

[2] E. Howe and J. Child, *op. cit.*, ch. VIII.

Unlawful and Dictatorial Combinations 57

Society did not lie only in the democratic safeguards of their constitution. Hundreds of similar societies were formed in the early nineteenth century in the face of an immediate threat, or in the excitement of a trade dispute, only to fade away when the danger or excitement had subsided. Men needed something more than the dim awareness of a future contingency to induce them to devote time and money to maintaining a trade society during long intermissions of comparative calm. The bookbinders' leaders therefore adopted many of the devices used with success by contemporary friendly societies. In the first place admission was made into much more than an economic obligation; it was treated as the conferment of a high honour, and an elaborate ritual, borrowed partly from that of the Freemasons, impressed upon the neophyte the gravity of the occasion. The three knocks on the door, the purple sash with flaming gilt heart, the robes, the incantations, the formal solemnity of the exhortation, and finally the greeting, 'Sir, I hail you by the sacred name of Friend'; these were no idle trappings perfunctorily employed. The high seriousness of the proceedings was considered appropriate to an organization dedicated to maintaining the welfare and dignity of 'the trade'. Secondly the binders showed their political acumen by making their society meetings occasions for the enjoyment of informal conviviality. Stewards were appointed to superintend the distribution of beer and tobacco and after the conclusion of the business the rest of the evening was spent in drinking and singing. Puritanical members might object to this diversion of the Society's time and money, but these regular jollifications had incalculable importance in sustaining the 'spirit of unionism' during periods of industrial armistice.

But perhaps nothing united the men so strongly as a sense of their common oppression, or danger of oppression, and to sharpen this the binders had a very apposite example—the 'Martyrdom' of the five men who in 1786 had been imprisoned for conspiracy, and the death of one of their members in Newgate. On the anniversary of the day of the liberation of the survivors, June 28th, a great annual celebration was held and stories were retailed (losing nothing in richness of detail as the years rolled on) of the fortitude of the Victims, the loyalty and ingenuity of their Friends, the solidarity of the Trade and the brutality and inhumanity of the Persecuting Masters.

While other printing trades had their heroes and martyrs, in no other society was there comparable official recognition and perpetuation of the incident. Yet this can hardly explain the failure of other trades to maintain organizations as stable as that of the binders. Perhaps in the letterpress trade the numbers may have been too great for the primitive type of society, for in 1818 there were about 1300 journeymen com-

58 TRADE SOCIETIES AND TRADE UNIONS

positors and 500 pressmen in London. What they needed, possibly, was some unit intermediate between the Chapel and the Union, with about one hundred members, small enough to excite a spirit of personal responsibility and loyalty, and large enough to widen their horizons beyond the Chapel. After 1825 both the compositors and the pressmen formed those peculiar infra-union organizations, the Gifts, which played something of the same role, and presumably served the same psychological needs, as the bookbinders' lodges.[1]

Member in distress were given help through the Petition, according to the following procedure. Two friends of the distressed person would apply to the Trade Committee for permission to take around a subscription list. If this was granted the Petition was officially circulated around the shops, and a grant of two pounds made to provide immediate sustenance. When the list was complete the Committee paid over the total subscribed (less the two pounds). The merit of the system lay in the fact that the sum subscribed became a debt to the Society if not paid on the date due, and was therefore almost certain to be collected. On the other hand the total was related less to the real needs of the petitioner than to his popularity and the energy of his 'vouchers'. Crude though it was, for over a century the Petition was retained by the London societies as a means of relieving special cases of distress, even when more regular methods had been devised for the common misfortunes. The right to ask for a petition was thus an important factor in obtaining loyalty and discipline from society members.

The binders' was the most stable society, but the palm for the most complex organization must be awarded to the papermakers. Theirs was one of the first successful attempts to build a nationwide 'union'. England was divided into five Grand Divisions of which the oldest and largest, Maidstone, was made the Senior Division. Each area was then further divided into sub-divisions, and within each mill the journeymen were formed into a Mill Company.[2] This method of basing the unit of organization on the workplace, adopted from purely practical and geographical considerations, was an important factor in promoting essential solidarity. The Mill Company was rather similar in function to the printers' Chapel, but did not have so ancient a tradition. The Clerk, or Constable as he was sometimes called, checked the cards of applicants for work, kept a wary eye on apprentices, collected subscriptions and sent a monthly report and financial statement to the Clerk of the Sub-Division.

The affairs of each Sub-Division were managed by a Clerk and a com-

[1] *Typographical Protection Circular*, 1849, p. 43. Copies of later Gift Rules are in the Webb Coll.
[2] Select Committee on Combination Laws, 1825, *Report*, App. 18.

UNLAWFUL AND DICTATORIAL COMBINATIONS 59

mittee of eight members of the Mill Companies. This committee kept a check on the mills in its area and every quarter sent a financial statement to its Grand Division. The latter was again under the control of a Clerk and committee of eight members, four of whom retired each quarter. Each Grand Division was almost a supreme authority in its own area of jurisdiction, but in cases of special interest it was expected to consult the committee of the Maidstone Grand Division. There was at first no form of national delegate meeting or national executive.

The early trade society invariably had its headquarters in some conveniently situated public house. The Call Book was kept there, with the names of journeymen wanting work; there the members held meetings and festivals, or congregated for informal entertainment; there would journeymen on tramp repair for sustenance and hospitality. The landlord of the public house was a trusted friend of the Society; the Box or Chest containing the hard-won funds was often left in his care, and surplus monies were sometimes given to him for safe keeping. In times of slack trade or prolonged dispute, when the society approached insolvency the landlord often came to the rescue with a grant or loan. During the operation of the Combination Act he carried no mean responsibility for he could have been forced by the authorities to divulge whatever information he possessed regarding the leaders, the funds and the purposes of the societies which met on his premises.

CONCLUSION

This survey supports the Webbs' generalization that trade societies sprang from every kind of opportunity for the journeymen to meet together—at work, during leisure, for 'friendly society' business, for 'trade discussions', for drinking and making merry.

But far more striking than the diversity of the immediate origins is the astonishing way in which several societies burst upon the scene almost simultaneously. Was this sheer coincidence? If not, what general causes or conditions brought them into being in the decade 1780–90?

The explanation does not lie in any special development within the industry at this time. But throughout the eighteenth century the evident decline of the Stationers' Company control of the industry led to a breakdown of customary rules and practices. The journeymen resented this change. The sharp deterioration in their standard of life caused by the rapid rise in the cost of living during the French Wars sparked the movement for collective adjustment of wages. Early successes, due to a favourable labour market, gave encouragement to continue the experiment. Other trades were infected with the 'mania for combination' which the authorities deplored.

60 TRADE SOCIETIES AND TRADE UNIONS

The roots of the beliefs and traditions of the early craft societies lie deep in history, in the ideal of the stable social framework, where each man had a right to his trade, where prices and wages were fixed by law, where the supply of labour was regulated to suit the demand. All of these traditions survived the impact of *laissez-faire* and the industrial upheaval of the nineteenth century. A knowledge of them is essential to the understanding of modern craft unionism.

CHAPTER IV

THE BIRTH OF
COLLECTIVE BARGAINING

*We have all, both Journeymen and Masters talked too
long at a Distance; it is Time, without we mean to ruin
the Trade in general, to come to the Point, and to
consider and ascertain more clearly the Rights of every
Individual in the Trade.*
*James Fraser's First Memorandum to the Masters and
Journeymen, 1787.*

COLLECTIVE BARGAINING

The distinctive feature of the new Trade Societies which distinguished
them from the sick or benefit societies was that they were formed to
conduct collective bargaining on behalf of their members. In other words,
terms of employment were no longer to be settled between each master
and each man separately. The men in each trade would bargain as a
group to determine certain basic terms of employment. The advantages
of this are obvious. In the case of individual bargaining the employer,
having usually more capital at his command, could afford to stand out
longer than the individual workman. The latter was thus forced, eventually, to accept the employer's terms. As long as there was some
unemployment in the industry the workmen, individually, were at a
grave disadvantage. But when the workers joined together, and built
up a fund to support members out of work, their collective bargaining
power was greatly increased.

In sixteenth and seventeenth centuries when they petitioned various
authorities for redress of grievances, they had thrown themselves on
their mercy. Doubtless, if there was no improvement in their condition
they would show resentment by spontaneous stop-work meetings, or by
slowing down production, or by spoiling material, but naturally there
was no mention of such techniques of persuasion in old petitions. Once
they had funds and organization, however, they were able to plan the

62 TRADE SOCIETIES AND TRADE UNIONS

strategy of industrial conflict with greater prospect of success. The bookbinders' disputes vividly illustrate the evolution of tactics during this period.

About 1782 John Lovejoy, an enterprising journeyman bookbinder, suggested that men in the trade should put aside regular contributions to build up a fund to support a movement for a shorter week. For three years the Lodges collected their subscriptions, and in 1786 their committee decided to take the initiative. The plan was for men in the four largest shops to ask simultaneously for a reduction of one hour, and if this was refused, to hand in one week's notice.

The masters' response was unequivocal: immediate discharge of *all* their workmen in the hope that the Lodge funds would be rapidly exhausted. The booksellers supported the masters by agreeing to take inferior bindings during the dispute, and the masters attempted to train women and boys to do the semi-skilled work involved in the cheaper bookbinding. The Lodges sent delegates to the shops to promise the women that they would be paid the equivalent of their wages if they came out in support of the men. When many of the women left, the masters attempted to recruit labour from the country towns, promising high wages and good conditions.[1]

The men's leaders were indicted for conspiracy and six were committed to Newgate. The dispute appeared to end in a confused stalemate, but one by one the employers gave way and by the time the Martyrs were released the first Hour had been generally conceded. The journeymen won because they had the advantage of careful preparation and solid organization. The masters, united in the face of the emergency, had not been able to stick together and many had later defaulted in order to retain valued workmen or to gain new contracts.

In 1794, however, when the journeymen asked for the second Hour, the masters formed an Association, and were rumoured to be taking out surety bonds of fifty pounds against capitulation to the men. This time victory of the masters appeared certain until Faulkner, one of the journeymen's leaders, hit on the idea of threatening to establish a co-operative bindery run by the journeymen. The masters immediately convened a meeting at which they agreed to give way to the men's demand.

The bookbinders' third dispute was also over a reduction in hours. Until 1806 there was no generally established custom in regard to an afternoon break for tea, and men on overtime were required to work right through from lunch time until eight or nine o'clock. The men formed a committee to conduct an organized agitation for the introduction of a standard half hour for tea. Within a few weeks of the start of

[1] E. Howe and J. Child, *op. cit.*, ch. I.

THE BIRTH OF COLLECTIVE BARGAINING 63

the campaign most of the West End firms had given way, but others were holding out. The Trade Society decided to attack these by a series of 'bumper' strikes, taking on one shop at a time and paying full wages to the men withdrawn. But after these tactics had been applied to a few shops the recalcitrant masters rallied their forces and gave simultaneous notice to *all* of their men. This time although the men had no fund, a high proportion of them were still at work; these paid 4s weekly to a pool from which those locked-out drew 15s weekly. When the masters again attempted to glean labour from the country the men issued circulars asking country workers to keep out of London. These appeals were not wholly successful; after fifteen weeks the men's finances were exhausted and they returned to work individually on the best terms they could obtain. The effort seemed to have been in vain, but in the flourishing state of trade the masters were not disposed to vengeance, and within a few weeks of the end of the dispute the Tea Half Hour had been granted in almost every shop.

That the journeymen were thus eventually successful in three major conflicts within two decades was a good omen for the future of the strike weapon. Within twenty years hours of work had been reduced by two and a half per day: it was one hundred and fifty years before an equivalent reduction was achieved. Undoubtedly their early success was due less to the efficiency of their organization than to the precarious economic position of the master bookbinders. Yet *without* the organization of their Society their advance would have been much slower. Knowing that the Fund could support them for a reasonable time most of the journeymen showed no hesitation in obeying the order to hand in a week's notice.

In letterpress printing, too, the men's first attempts at collective bargaining were highly successful. In 1785 the London compositors presented a Memorial to their masters, asking for eight rules to govern piecework. Five of their requests were granted. In 1793 the men obtained more concessions, and in 1805, despite the Combination Acts, representatives of the Compositors' Trade Society conducted lengthy negotiations with the masters to settle the detailed clauses of the new Scale of Prices which was to remain the basis of piecework prices for the rest of the century. Again in 1816 when the masters wished to reduce the rates, the Trade Society conducted the negotiations on behalf of the journeymen and was successful in moderating the masters' demands.[1] In none of these prolonged negotiations did the journeymen explicitly use the threat of a strike, but the employers were well aware that the Trade Society could withdraw labour from shops which did not observe 'fair' conditions.

[1] E. Howe and H. Waite, *The London Society of Compositors*, passim.

64 TRADE SOCIETIES AND TRADE UNIONS

The compositors developed the technique of concentrating on one firm at a time, a method particularly effective against newspaper firms owing to the fierceness of commercial competition in that branch of the industry. The pressmen, on the other hand, favoured the 'general' strike, but owing to the looseness of their organization they were not very successful. The relative merits of the two methods were discussed by a writer in *The Gorgon*:

'It has been suggested that when Workmen find it necessary to strike for an advance of Wages, that they should not do it *en masse*, all the Workmen striking at the one time, but that they should attack their employers in detail, selecting a few of the masters for which they will not work, reduce them to submission, and then attack the remainder. There appears to be good generalship in this suggestion of our correspondent and we doubt not but it would be found very efficient in practice. The men who continue at their work would be able to support those who had "turned out". . . .'[1]

In the transition period, when combinations to raise wages, reduce hours, or otherwise alter terms of employment, were illegal, either under the common law of conspiracy, or the Combination Act of 1800, the men relied on the old *form* of approach, namely the 'humble petition'. But their respectful, even obsequious, demeanour, was more of a public guise, and the masters soon learned that behind it was the determination to employ effective sanctions.

APPRENTICESHIP

Almost from their inception the early trade societies were confronted with the need for regulation of entry into each trade. This was no new problem; the novel feature was the determination of the journeymen themselves to exercise some control over the matter. From their point of view there were really two problems. Firstly they wished to restrict the 'right to the trade' to those who had served a full seven-year apprenticeship. On this point they had the legal backing of the ancient Statute of Apprentices, passed in 1563, although it had not been strictly enforced for many years. Secondly however the trade societies wished to limit the number of apprentices. Again this was in itself no new departure, for in the seventeenth century the number had been strictly related to the master's rank in the Stationers' Company. But with the decline of the Company as a regulative institution in the industry, some new basis, more appropriate to the altered conditions, was required.[2]

[1] *The Gorgon*, 1818, p. 192.
[2] E. Howe and H. E. Waite, *op. cit.* 1948, ch. III.

THE BIRTH OF COLLECTIVE BARGAINING 65

As long as the system of indoor apprenticeship had been retained, the need for a numerical quota of apprentices had not been so urgent, for there was a 'natural' limit set by the accommodation available in the master's house. When the indoor system broke down this limitation was removed. Even so, conditions might have been tolerable, from the men's point of view, had the other rule been strictly enforced. But with the growth of larger establishments the masters were able to apply a division of labour which permitted the employment of an increasing proportion of unskilled labour. The master bookbinders, for example, engaged non-apprenticed men to do the simple operation of beating the sections flat, and took on women to do much of the preliminary work hitherto reserved to craftsmen.

By 1750 the two older forms of control—of numbers, by the Stationers' Company, and of the right to the trade, by the State—had almost completely broken down. By the end of the century the journeymen's trade societies were campaigning vigorously for their restoration, or for the imposition of some new restrictions. They began with an attack on the system of Outdoor Apprenticeship:

'Outdoor apprentices are those who do not board and reside in the houses of their masters, but only resort to their offices for the purposes of business. They receive a regular weekly stipend, or a certain proportion of their earnings, to board themselves. This mode of apprenticeship has long had the reprobation of every person who has had an opportunity of observing its effects. It is peculiarly dangerous in an extensive city like this, teeming with incentives to vice and profligacy. Numerous have been its victims to the violated laws of the country; and by it vice and dissipation have been diffused to a lamentable extent.

'Every person must likewise be struck with the illegality of it, for it is a direct violation of the indenture. There it is said that the youth is to serve from the day of the date of his indenture "after the manner of an apprentice", but this novel practice has nothing of the manner of an apprentice in it. It might as well be said "after the manner of a journeyman". . . . The youth are neither found in drink, apparel, lodging or any other necessaries, but are converted into a kind of indentured journeyman. Every idea of apprenticeship is violated.'[1]

The objections of the journeymen went deeper than mere indignation at the corruption of youths by the temptations of city life; in the break-up of the indoor system they sensed that another blow was being struck, however unconsciously, for the objective of reducing labour to a

[1] *Address to the Booksellers* . . . (B.M. MSS. Add. 27799, f. 97).

C

66 TRADE SOCIETIES AND TRADE UNIONS

market commodity. However bad the old system might have been in practice, and at its worst it reduced the apprentice to little better than a bond slave, at least the employer accepted nominal responsibility for the welfare of his apprentices, and in the last resort could be brought to Court to answer for any breach of the deed. But under the new system the employer was under much less obligation, moral or legal, to take any personal interest in his employees; the cash nexus was to form the only enduring bond between master and man. Small wonder that the journeymen expressed profound moral indignation at the change.[1]

The craftsmen believed, with religious intensity and unquestioning faith, that only the servitude of a formal apprenticeship conferred on a man the precious 'right to the trade'. For two centuries and a half this belief was supported with the legal sanctions of the Statute of Apprentices. But in 1813 the Statute was repealed. The restrictive and regulative provisions of the old code were at variance with the temper and doctrine of the new generation of free enterprise industrial capitalists.

Indeed, for some time past the Courts had seldom offered recognition of the men's rights. As early as 1786 the compositors failed to obtain an injunction against John Walter, proprietor of *The Times*, forbidding him from setting up as a master printer, on the grounds that he had not served an apprenticeship to the trade.[2] In the next two decades consensus of opinion among the master printers swung strongly in favour of repeal of the Statute. They issued a broadsheet containing many expressions of disapproval of it by eminent legal and judicial authorities, and concluded:

'It is to be observed that this Check upon Trade viz., not being able to employ any hands that are able to do the work without such hands having served an Apprenticeship in Compliance with the Directions of the said Act of Queen Elizabeth, greatly enhances the Price of all Articles especially at a time when the population is daily increasing, and the Demand proportionately increasing. And this Statute is not only a restraining Statute as to the Masters, but also an enabling Statute as to the Men, as it empowers the Workmen to enter into Combinations against their Masters, and to dictate their own terms. . . .'[3]

In 1806 the master printers tried to procure the introduction of a Bill into the House of Commons to exempt the printers from the apprentice laws. When this failed they petitioned Parliament for a special exemption, claiming that only thus could they execute urgent orders for

[1] See the lively letters of Miles's Boy, *The London Compositor*, pp. 118-22.
[2] J. Walter, *Address to the Public*, 1789.
[3] *Master Printers' Circular*, 1805 (C.U.P. Doc. 7).

THE BIRTH OF COLLECTIVE BARGAINING

printing work. In particular they wished to have the term of apprenticeship reduced in order to be able to train journeymen more quickly.

The journeymen remained obdurately opposed to any reduction in the term. In 1805 the compositors reaffirmed their policy:

'It is a known fact that some gentlemen of the profession (even in the City) have taken apprentices for the term of four, five, and six years, according to the extent of the premium—against established usage and to the detriment of the lads themselves, who will not be allowed their privilege to the trade without serving the full term of seven years.'[1]

The masters were particularly annoyed by the fact that the Statute gave the men a pretext for forming combinations, ostensibly to see that the Statute was enforced. Even in the repressive atmosphere of the times, it was difficult to prosecute men for combining to ensure that the laws of the country were observed! The most prominent in this campaign were the bookbinders. In 1811 they formed a Secret Committee to make a survey of existing conditions and prepare evidence for the prosecution of the offending masters. After compiling a 'very considerable list of persons who clandestinely follow our profession' the Secret Committee consulted a lawyer. He advised them that an action could be taken against employers contravening the Statute, but stressed that the Trade Society should not be in any way associated with it. A leading journeyman then acted as plaintiff, and brought charges against a firm employing 'illegal' men.[2] The firm was found guilty, but the fine of four pounds which the judge imposed had no effect, and the firm continued to employ the illegal men.

Some of the masters agreed with the journeymen that the old laws should be enforced; those who employed only 'legal' men, and who executed high-class work were often threatened with undercutting by firms which took on unskilled labour at low wages and turned out shoddy work. At one point these 'fair' masters were disposed to co-operate with the journeymen to enforce the regulations, but negotiations broke down when the men recklessly made some other extravagant demands. At the conclusion of a desultory correspondence with the masters, the men's delegate reported to the Society:

'We were apprized of having many friends, but they were too divided among themselves to come to a determination. Had we succeeded we are satisfied an appeal to the law would have been seldom, if ever,

---

[1] To Master Printers, 1805. (*The London Compositor*, Doc. X.)
[2] *Pratt v. Fraser . . .*, 6 June, 1811 (Jaffray Coll.).

68 TRADE SOCIETIES AND TRADE UNIONS

necessary. As it is we must rely on our own resources and firmness for the accomplishment of any measures that may ultimately be deemed necessary.'[1]

Shortly afterwards another action was brought against an employer who had taken on unskilled men. The action failed miserably, and a few months later the Statute of Apprentices was repealed.[2] The journeymen's appeal to the law had failed; henceforth they would have to rely on their own methods and sanctions to bring employers to recognize the doctrine of the Right to the Trade.

Running almost parallel with the effort to prevent the incursion of illegal men was the campaign to limit the number of apprentices. In this the compositors were the most active. In 1787 they simply resolved to exclude from the trade all who had not served their full time, but in 1794 they supplemented this with an *Appeal to Parents and Guardians*. This first effort met with little success. In the first place a parent was unlikely to be convinced by the men's arguments if he had previously heard from a master a glowing account of the prospects of the trade. An unscrupulous master, eager to obtain the premium, could easily find some parent eager to apprentice his son to the genteel trade of a printer. In the next few years the compositors launched an intensive, but quite ineffective, propaganda campaign against those offices which had 'excessive' apprentices.[3]

The majority of members gradually became convinced that more direct action was needed. After prolonged debates they adopted the principle that the number of apprentices should be related to the number of journeymen, as a reasonably fair way of distributing the quota among the offices. A general meeting agreed that the ratio should be one apprentice to five men, and that members working in offices where this ratio was exceeded should be punished.[4] But in 1807 the masters, learning that the society was planning a campaign of direct action, stole the initiative by resolving to make a substantial *increase* in the numbers of apprentices, allegedly in order to compensate for the drift of trained men to newspaper and periodical houses which, from a time-honoured tradition, did not train any apprentices. The masters quickly received the support of the booksellers, who were naturally anxious to ensure an adequate labour supply, not only to facilitate the prompt execution of orders, but also to forestall any attempt by the society to raise wages,

[1] Reports of the Secret Committee, MSS. (Jaffray Coll.).
[2] *Pratt v. Annereau . . .*, 1812 (Jaffray Coll.).
[3] *v.* Selection in *The London Compositor*, Doc. XXIX.
[4] *Agenda for a General Meeting of the Union Society* (*The London Compositor*, Doc. XXX).

THE BIRTH OF COLLECTIVE BARGAINING 69

and consequently costs. Thus encouraged the master printers decided to press on with their scheme for taking more apprentices:

'. . . this danger of ruin to the masters arises from the aforesaid artful, pertinacious, and unlawful combinations of the Compositors; who by attempting to limit the number of Apprentices would, if not frustrated, have completely within their power the means of enhancing the price of labour, and would render the Trade unable to enter into competition with other markets where such causes do not operate; and thus obstructing the increase of workmen, the employment and extent of our Capital would be materially cramped, and the spirit of enterprise and the liberty of trade, so congenial to British literature, would be in danger of being extinguished.'[1]

The compositors replied with a lengthy address *To the Book-Sellers of London and Westminster* in which they related in detail the grievances which they suffered from the change in the nature of apprenticeship, and the lack of regulation of numbers. They continued to withdraw members from offices with excessive apprentices, but they were eventually defeated by the masters' determined intake of new lads, for the Society could not afford to support the large numbers of journeymen who should have been withdrawn. The Society was undoubtedly hampered by the need to tread warily, and keep its operations reasonably covert, for the masters might have lost patience and invoked the Combination Laws had the men been too overbearing. The Society did attempt a 'bumper' strike, attacking the worst offices one by one, and withdrawing men. The masters retaliated, however, by circulating a blacklist of such men, and the Society had to admit defeat. The final blow to the journeymen's campaign was a large influx of unemployed from the provinces. Many of them, with no experience of trade society 'principles', came eagerly to the capital when they heard that there was a dispute in progress, hoping to obtain the jobs made vacant. Nor was this problem confined to the compositors. In 1824 the London Bookbinders received a letter from Edinburgh, saying:

'The shoals of Apprentices who are bred in Edinburgh and who annually inundate London are well known to you, and will require our joint efforts to stop. In the meantime we are sorry to say they are increasing. . . .'[2]

Thus the first determined effort of the men to apply a numerical ratio

[1] *General Meeting of Master Printers*, 1807 (*The London Compositor*, Doc. XXXIII).
[2] London Bookbinders' Society, Minute Book (Jaffray Coll.).

70   TRADE SOCIETIES AND TRADE UNIONS

of apprentices to journeymen ended in failure. In 1818 there were approximately three journeymen to every apprentice, both at case and at press, but owing to the slackness of trade the employers were taking on fewer lads. Nevertheless the masters regarded their freedom to take more apprentices as the fundamental basis of their bargaining power vis-à-vis the Society. A strike, or a threatened strike could always be broken with a nucleus of 'rats' and a new batch of apprentices. The mere threat to take on more lads was often enough to quell the militant spirits among the men. On the other hand many masters realized the necessity of general rules to regulate prices and conditions of work, and were prepared to permit the men to combine to obtain such uniform rules, as long as the masters were left free to regulate the intake of apprentices.[1]

WAGES AND HOURS

The earliest document containing details of a systematic scale of payment for printing workers is the Compositors' Scale of Prices of 1785 which listed piece rates for many kinds of work. The basic rate was raised from 4d to 4½d per 1000 letters. Thenceforth piece rates tended to prevail in this branch of the industry, and the original scale was enlarged and modified until it assumed a bewildering complexity.[2]

The basis of payment remained the number of letters which the compositor had set. Obviously if all type of a given size had a body of the same width, an approximate estimate of the number of letters on a page could be obtained by dividing the area of the page by the area of the type body. Masters and men did indeed carry Ready Reckoners which showed at a glance how many letters of each sort would be contained in a page of given dimensions.

One of the first problems to arise, even on straightforward book work, or common matter, was how to measure the size of the page. Was the heading, or the page number, or the direction line, to be included in the length? Were side notes, or numbers, or em quadrats placed at the beginning and end of each line to count in the width? Another set of problems arose from attempts to estimate the relative ease or difficulty of setting different sorts of type. Small type, for example, was more difficult to handle than large, and deserved a higher basic rate. Italic type presented its own problems to the compositor. A third complication arose from the variations in the complexity of the material; for example, dictionaries in two languages obviously required more care and attention from the compositor, and reduced his rate of working.

Although the 1785 Scale recognized some of these complexities, it

[1] Select Committee on Artizans and Machinery, 1824. *Second Report.*
[2] For this and other piecework scales, *v. The London Compositor*, passim.

THE BIRTH OF COLLECTIVE BARGAINING 71

was not until 1805 that they were set out in a systematic and unequivocal way. Small types *were* paid for at a higher basic rate; ems or ens at the ends of lines *were* included in the width of the page. Because of the difficulty of framing a general rule to cover side notes and footnotes, these were left to be settled between each employer and his journeymen. The basic rate for medium types, raised to $5\frac{1}{4}$d per 1000 in 1800 remained unchanged.

During the Napoleonic War the cost of living in Britain rose fairly consistently, and in 1809 the compositors used this to press for an increase in piece rates. They quoted from the *Wealth of Nations* the five principal circumstances which Adam Smith had maintained should justify an equalization of the net advantages of each occupation; on every score the compositors claimed that a rise was overdue. For good measure they added that 'the proximity of the art of composing to the high professions and the liberal arts and sciences would seem to entitle it to rank above mechanical and manufacturing employments'. After prolonged negotiations, the masters agreed to raise the basic rate to 6d per 1000.

For the next eighty years this scale regulated the payment of piece rates for hand composition. Although numerous additions were made, often by joint agreement, and the original clauses were supplemented by many paragraphs of explanations, exceptions, and examples, the basic clauses were not altered, except for the slight changes in the rates. This is all the more remarkable when it is remembered that for long intervals there was no effective organization of masters or men, and hence no authority (other than custom and convenience) to enforce its observance. The London Scale came to enjoy something of the force of a hallowed tradition more enduring than the organizations which had brought it forth.

Although the masters were most reluctant to admit that wages should rise with the cost of living, they were not laggardly in pressing for a reduction when the cost of living fell, after the Napoleonic War. In 1816 a meeting of influential masters agreed to reduce the scales for composition and presswork, and despite some sporadic opposition (for the trade societies were defunct) they carried through a small decrease.

In contrast to the compositors the bookbinders were hostile to the system of payment by piecework, and fought strenuously to prevent its extension, though many masters were keen to adopt it to facilitate accurate costing. The journeymen's opposition stemmed mainly from the Finishers, the highly skilled men who executed the embossing and gilding of the leather bindings, and who were paid by weekly wages. They tended to dominate in the councils of the Trade Society at this time. As long as the typical binder's shop was a small establishment

72 TRADE SOCIETIES AND TRADE UNIONS

executing orders to the requirements of individual customers, there was no scope for division of labour, the simplification of operations, and the assignment of workmen to long 'runs' of similar work for which piece rates were suitable. But with the expansion of the binding business in the early nineteenth century, and with the growth in size of publishers' editions—itself a consequence of the cheapening of printing—some binders' shops grew into small factories. By 1824 the threat of the extension of piecework was so immediate that a daring member of the Trade Society suggested that the Anniversary dinner should be cancelled, and the funds used for an all-out campaign against the system. Admitting the danger, the majority considered the proposed remedy to be far too drastic.[1]

In every trade there were some journeymen on time rates who were paid by the day instead of the week. Indeed throughout the nineteenth century the trade unions had to fight continuously against the tendency of the employers to reduce their permanent hands to a minimum, and rely on engaging casual labour by the day to help out with urgent work. As long as there was a pool of unemployed, this was possible. But as the Trade Societies gained greater control of the labour supply, and helped to regulate the filling of vacancies, by the system of the Call Book, the evils which usually attend the casualization of labour were substantially reduced.

Each Trade Society had to decide whether to fix a minimum rate, and admit only men who were receiving at least this rate, or to enrol all 'legal' journeymen, build up its funds, and try to fix standard rates later. In this respect there was a significant contrast between the policy of the bookbinders, who were mainly on time rates and the compositors who were mostly on piece rates. According to the compositors' code the cardinal sin was to accept work 'below scale'; for this a society member could be expelled. But to the bookbinders, the major crime was to work with non-society men without reporting them to the officers. The bookbinders were not so strict about the actual wage rate; although they had a minimum, they frequently allowed society members to accept less, for example if they were engaged on the semi-skilled work such as beating.

The table on page 73 shows the changes in the time rates of weekly wages for the main trades during this period.

According to these figures the standard weekly time rates rose about 50 per cent in this period. But for most of the period the cost of living rose more rapidly than the wage rates. After 1814 however the cost of living fell, and from 1820 until 1830 it was seldom more than 10 per cent above the level for 1790. Therefore those journeymen who could obtain full-time employment at the standard rates enjoyed a fairly

[1] E. Howe and J. Child, *op. cit.*, ch. X.

THE BIRTH OF COLLECTIVE BARGAINING 73

high level of real wages. But the general trade depressions which accompanied the fall in the cost of living were reflected in the high rates of unemployment in printing and bookbinding trades after 1815.

TRADE	STANDARD WEEKLY WAGE RATE					
	(*Shillings*)					
	1785	1795	1805	1810	1815	1825
Bookbinders (finishers)	21	23	25	27	30	30
Daily News Compositors						
Evening	31	34	37	43	43	43
Morning	31	36	40	48	48	48
Book Compositors	24	30	33	36	36	33
Pressmen	21	24	27	33	32	32

Sources: Bookbinders Documents (Jaffray Coll.)
New Compositors' Report, 1820.
London Scale of Prices, 1836.
The Gorgon, 1818, p. 220.

Actual hours of work varied from trade to trade and from season to season, but throughout this period there was a perceptible tendency for hours to become more standardized, at least in the organized trades where time rates prevailed. By 1806 the bookbinders had reduced their normal working day from fourteen to twelve hours (including one and a half hours for meal times), in line with the accepted hours for compositors and pressmen. But in those trades where piece work was dominant, and especially in the newspaper offices where earnings were comparatively high, the societies were not concerned with the standardization of hours of work. The ten and a half hour working day, and a six day week, remained the norm in the printing trades for more than fifty years.

C*

CHAPTER V

REGIONAL AND NATIONAL UNIONS
1825–48

> *Let the compositors of London, then, decide this night for*
> *Union, and forty united Societies in the country are*
> *prepared to take you by the hand, and call you brothers—*
> *nearly one thousand individuals are willing to aid your*
> *cause and second your efforts—but, if fearful, timorous*
> *and lukewarm, you longer hesitate, then farewell to every*
> *hope of independence!*
> Report of General Trade Committee, March 4 and 11,
> 1834

LONDON LETTERPRESS SOCIETIES

In 1825, the year of the repeal of the Combination Acts, there were two societies of compositors in London, one established in 1820 for journeymen on daily newspapers,[1] and one purporting to serve the needs of the whole trade. In fact the latter, the London Trade Society of Compositors established in 1816, seems to have functioned for the first ten years mainly as a benefit society providing out-of-work pay and accident compensation. After the repeal of the Combination Acts it devoted more attention to the defence of the London Scale and in 1828 altered its objects to include 'the protection of the rights of the trade'.[2] Its somewhat timid policy had, in 1826, provoked the secession of a militant faction which set up a rival society.[3]

With three bodies claiming overlapping jurisdiction it was inevitable that disputes should arise which would weaken their bargaining power vis-à-vis the employers. After a prolonged controversy on the relative merits of a benefit society or a 'pure trade society', the leaders of the two 'General' societies, chastened by a progressive deterioration in working conditions, agreed to put aside their differences of philosophy and to

---

[1] The Society of London Daily Newspaper Compositors.
[2] London Trade Society of Compositors, *Rules*, 1828.
[3] London General Trade Society of Compositors, *Rules*, 1826.

REGIONAL AND NATIONAL UNIONS

co-operate on a practical programme of enforcement of the London Scale. This rapprochement resulted in 1833 in the formation of a Union Committee charged with the co-ordination of their trade policies and the settlement of intersociety disputes.[1] The Union Committee took the bold step of recommending an amalgamation of the three compositors' societies, and the creation of a fund 'from which men might be immediately remunerated when compelled to quit their situations'.[2]

This idea was enthusiastically supported and in 1834 over 1500 compositors joined the new body, the London Union of Compositors. Its first *Rules and Regulations* indicate clearly that the protagonists of the trade protection school of thought had been influential in drafting its constitution:

'1. That for the better protection of the rights of the Journeymen, the Compositors of London and its Vicinity shall be formed into one Society.

2. That the said Union shall have for its object the protection and regulation of the wages of labour, agreeably to the Scale and acknowledged practice of the Trade.

3. That every Compositor of fair character, while working in London . . . shall belong to the Union and shall pay Fourpence per month, *to form a fund which shall be applied entirely to Trade Purposes.* . . .'[3]

The daily news compositors refused to join the L.U.C. unless they were given complete autonomy on newspaper matters. This provoked the indignation of the book compositors who had been ready to make substantial concessions to win over the newsmen. There were no apprentices in newspaper offices (except 'unfair' ones such as *The Times*), and newspaper compositors were trained in book houses. As newspaper work was very exhausting, older men, unable to stand the strain, were often forced to return to the more leisurely book houses. The L.U.C. therefore claimed that the interests of the newsmen were inseparably linked with those of the bookmen:

'It therefore becomes necessary for the Committee to declare that the News Compositors have no right to a separate jurisdiction. And the

[1] Note that the term 'Trade Union' was at first restricted to an organization formed by the *union* of two or more trade societies.

[2] L.U.C., *Report of Union Committee*, 1833. (*Lond. Comp.*, Doc. LVIII). Cf. S. & B. Webb, *The History of Trade Unionism*, 1920, p. 198. By inadvertently mixing two quotations taken out of context the Webbs completely missed the point. The 'opponents' referred to in their quotation were not the employers but non-Society men! The L.U.C. was a militant Trade Society.

[3] L.U.C., *Rules and Regulations*, 1834 (*italics supplied*).

76 TRADE SOCIETIES AND TRADE UNIONS

first argument which they use to support this opinion is—that newsmen have no separate interest, for their prices depend upon what is paid in book offices.'[1]

The L.U.C. then established its own News Section in direct rivalry with the older society, and although several efforts were made to effect an amalgamation, the newsmen remained divided until 1852. At first the L.U.C. made spectacular progress. In 1836, with over 2,000 members, and a network of officials in all main offices, it seemed to be entering an era of unprecedented power. Sounding a new note of militant class consciousness, it gave generous assistance to the Owenite Builders Federation, and to other unions on strike:

'The Council mentions this to point out the impolicy of standing aloof in the struggles which are continually going on between the employers and employed, and to suggest to you how essential it is that we should stand well with the various trade societies in the metropolis. . . . And, indeed, we do not judge wisely if we do not regard these disputes as so many skirmishes and trials of strength, preparatory to that grand action which must eventually be fought between the labourers and capitalists of England.'[2]

The L.U.C., though sympathetic to Owenite ideals, did not join the Grand National Consolidated Trade Union.[3]

In the late 1830's, however, the L.U.C. began to crumble. A prolonged spell of bad trade exhausted its funds, and a series of costly disputes revived the old controversy of the relative merits of 'trade' and 'benefit' society. The London men therefore took a keen interest in the schemes being discussed in the columns of the *Compositors' Chronicle* for a National Association of unions in the printing trades.[4]

REGIONAL TYPOGRAPHICAL UNIONS

About a dozen local typographical societies were established before the repeal of the Combination Acts in 1825. In the following five years their number was trebled, and many organizations which had hitherto appeared to be benefit clubs began to try to regulate working conditions.[5]

---

[1] L.U.C., *Report of General Trade Committee*, 1835.
[2] L.U.C., *Annual Report of Trade Council*, 1837, p. 24.
[3] L.U.C., *First Annual Report*, 1835.
[4] L.U.C., *Final Report of Trade Council*, 1845.
[5] See P. H. J. H. Gosden, *The Friendly Societies in England*, 1815–1875, Manch. Univ. Press, 1961, p. 71.

REGIONAL AND NATIONAL UNIONS

Like the London societies of the previous period they were generally conservative in outlook, aiming to protect or to regain the privileges and rights established in a previous era. Owing to the small number of journeymen printers in each town there was usually no separation of compositors, readers and pressmen. In the provinces a youth served his time as a 'printer' and on coming out of his servitude drifted into that branch of the trade for which he felt best suited, or in which there was a convenient vacancy. All legal 'printers' were therefore eligible for membership of the local typographical society. Sometimes even bookbinders were included. Thus in 1840 the Delegate Meeting of the Northern Typographical Union resolved:

'That persons who have served a legal seven years' apprenticeship to printing and bookbinding, or the printing and stationery business, shall be eligible to become members of the N.T.U. provided they adopt the printing business alone when out of their time.'[1]

The objects of the Oxford Compositors' Trade Society were:

'1. To protect and maintain the wages agreeable to the London piece scale; and on the establishment according to the acknowledged practice of the trade in Oxford.

2. To promote the due performance of all engagements entered into, as well by journeymen as employers.

3. For the relief of compositors passing through the town in search of employment.'[2]

In the thirties the majority of the local *societies* joined up with the three regional *unions*. The main impetus to this movement came from the need for more effective administration of the system of tramp relief.[3] A second impulse came from the need for more effective control of the number of apprentices, for it was patently futile for one society to impose restrictions if in the neighbouring towns there were flourishing 'nurseries'.[4] A third reason lay in the popular belief that a pooling of funds would give greater strength, for in case of a dispute with an employer, all of the resources could be concentrated on one point and the workers would be invincible.

---

[1] Northern Typographical Union, *Report of Delegate Meeting*, 1840.
[2] Oxford Compositors' Trade Society, *Rules*, 1840.
[3] See R. E. Musson, *The Typographical Association*, Oxford, 1954, pp. 27, 52.
[4] *Ibid.*, p. 42.

78 TRADE SOCIETIES AND TRADE UNIONS

'If union be good for anything, the more extended it is, the more power-ful it will be.'[1]

The common error in the optimistic calculations of the advantage of more extensive unionism was to stress the increased income without making a proper estimate of the probable commitments in which the union would be involved. Although the arguments for uniting appeared irrefutable, and the weakness of the isolated societies was only too obvious, most of the members showed no great enthusiasm to join up in regional organizations. Parochial isolationism, national rivalry and jealous zeal for local autonomy all contributed towards the delay.[2] Gradually however the opposition was broken down and most of the typographical *societies* in the provinces joined up with one of the three regional *unions*.

The first of these was the Northern Typographical Union established in 1830 as a loose federation of local societies in Yorkshire and Lanca-shire. The following were its main 'principles of action':

'1. That each town in the Union shall have a stated sum as its standard wages, and any individual working under that standard shall not be regarded as an honourable member of the profession.

2. That each society shall have a fund from which to relieve all honourable members in search of employment.

3. That no employer shall have more than two apprentices, unless he regularly employs more than four men—that then he shall have three; but in no case shall he have more.

4. That each society shall subscribe a small sum towards the general Union Fund, formed to enable us to support every trade movement, to remunerate persons sacrificing their situations in support of our principles, and to defray the incidental expenses of the Association.'[3]

As a matter of convenience and economy, in days when travel and communications were slow and expensive, the Executive of the local Society in the town selected as the Seat of Government acted as the executive of the union. The annual or biennial meeting of delegates from the member societies controlled the general policy of the union, altered the constitution, and selected the Seat of Government for the following period. Inevitably, in a federal type of organization, there was

[1] General Typographical Association (Scotland), *Eighth Annual Report*, 1844. Note that the term 'Union' referred to a Union of *Societies*, not *men*.
[2] See Correspondence in *Compositors' Chronicle*, 1840–41.
[3] Address from the Committee of Management, N.T.U., 1841.

REGIONAL AND NATIONAL UNIONS 79

continual friction between the central authority and powerful local blocs unwilling to cede their autonomy in certain matters. Thus when the Central Executive wished to standardize conditions throughout the area it often ran up against the opposition of powerful local societies who believed that they had nothing to gain, and perhaps something to lose from the proposed change.[1] It was only after some decades of experiment that the provincial unions evolved a constitution which achieved a reasonable balance between these conflicting interests.

The subscription was at first only 3d per member monthly, but in 1837 another 1d per month became payable on account of the tramp relief Reimbursement Fund. From the central funds strike allowance was paid to members withdrawn from unfair offices on the order of the Committee. In 1840 the Strike Allowance was raised to £4 payable in weekly instalments of 15s–20s according to the decision of the local committee. All members were of course also required to subscribe to the funds of their local society.[2] Local subscriptions varied according to the local standard wage, and to the number of benefits provided.

In 1840 the Northern Typographical Union consisted of forty-four member societies and almost 1,000 journeymen. Its area of influence extended steadily southwards, but it failed to gain much support in Wales where unionism had always been very weak.[3] In towns where there was no society the Northern Union sometimes established a tramp relief station in the hope that in future years this would develop into a full trade society. Its leaders were keenly aware of the need for more complete membership and conducted many organizing campaigns in 'weak' towns and districts.

The main 'trade' object of the Northern Typographical Union was the limitation of apprentices. Although the importance of this policy was explained to the members with almost monotonous regularity by the Secretary, John Backhouse, many branches were extremely reluctant to incur any financial loss through too rigid an adherence to the prescribed quota. In 1842–43 many local societies were so impoverished that they were quite impotent to enforce the Union rules. The Central Funds, too, had been drained by a number of small strikes.[4]

Under these circumstances it was not surprising that the Northern Union—then the most vigorous of the printing trade unions—should have been the most energetic canvasser of the project of a great National Association of all printing trade unions. This project was the main item

---

[1] See Musson, *op. cit.*, pp. 36 et seq. N.T.U. *Rules*, 1836.
[2] N.T.U. Report of Delegate Meeting, *Compositors' Chronicle*, 1840.
[3] N.T.U. Eleventh Annual Report, *Compositors' Chronicle*, 1841.
[4] N.T.U. Report of Delegate Meeting, 1844. *The Printer*, pp. 161–4.

80 TRADE SOCIETIES AND TRADE UNIONS

on the agenda at a large Delegate Meeting of the N.T.U. held in Derby in 1844. Representatives of all other typographical unions and societies were invited to attend.

The second regional union of letterpress societies was the General Typographical Association of Scotland, a loose federation set up in 1836. Government was in the hands of a Central Board made up of members of the Committee of the Society in the town selected as the Seat of Government. Delegate meetings were held annually to revise the rules and frame general policy.[1] The Central Fund was at first intended only for the payment of strike allowance to members withdrawn in defence of rules, but it was not long before several branches were agitating for a general tramp fund.

While the G.T.A. did not ignore the control of apprentices, it did not attempt to enforce as rigid or restrictive a quota as that of the N.T.U. In some towns apprentices were so numerous that it was considered an improvement if their numbers could be reduced to parity with the journeymen. In 1841 the Central Board claimed that the 'conciliatory and moderate measures' which it had consistently taken had resulted in an appreciable drop in the proportion of apprentices.[2] The masters were, however, beginning to rebel against this steady pressure, and in 1841 the Association was involved in five disputes on this question. In the next few years there was a depression of trade, and with great numbers of tramps on the road the Union was unable to enforce its policy. The Report of 1844 stated that strikes had been numerous, vexatious and expensive, and a prolonged dispute at Stirling had resulted in the dissolution of the local society. The Central Board therefore recommended members to vote for the formation of the National Typographical Association.[3]

The third of the regional unions was the Irish Typographical Union formed in 1837. Its objects and structure were basically the same as the others, but it suffered more than they from a fatal lack of control by the Central Committee. The result was that branches entered upon 'forward movements' without consulting the Committee, and often in ignorance of what was happening in other branches.

In consequence a number of simultaneous disputes in 1841 brought the union to the verge of insolvency. As delegate meetings were held only once in three years members frequently complained that the Central Committee was out of touch with the rank and file.[4] The tradition of aggressive local independence popularly ascribed to the Irish

[1] G.T.A., *Rules*, 1836.
[2] G.T.A., Fifth Annual Report, *Compositors' Chronicle*, 1841.
[3] G.T.A., Eighth Annual Report, 1844.
[4] Correspondence in *Compositors' Chronicle*, passim.

REGIONAL AND NATIONAL UNIONS

national character certainly seems to have been in evidence in the chequered history of the I.T.U.

Although the Committee was opposed to the linking up of the I.T.U. with the proposed National Association, the Irish delegates to the Derby conference returned convinced that in this lay the only hope of salvaging their union.

THE NATIONAL TYPOGRAPHICAL ASSOCIATION, 1845–48

During the widespread depression of 1842–43 various plans for the rehabilitation of the printing profession were put forward in the columns of the *Compositors' Chronicle*. Some sought stricter control of apprentices, some the reform of the tramping system, others the formation of a national strike fund. The Editor of the paper was sceptical of the success of such schemes.

'The great difficulty to be overcome is the indisposition which the majority feel to devote a sufficient portion of their earnings to the maintenance of trade principles. This indisposition has been injurious, and will be destructive. . . .'[1]

In 1844 as the time for the N.T.U. Delegate Meeting approached there was a marked renewal of interest in plans for re-organization. A detailed constitution for a United Typographical Association was published in *The Printer* and a keen debate followed in the correspondence columns.[2] After the Delegate Meeting at Derby in August 1844, attended by representatives of almost all the larger societies and guest delegates from other unions, a set of rules for a National Association was drafted and submitted to the trade throughout the country. By the end of the year most of the main unions and independent societies had agreed to join. A special delegate meeting at Manchester in 1844 decided to bring the National Typographical Association into being in January 1845.[3] The changeover was effected by making all members of the founding unions free members of the National Typographical Association. All of the old regional unions, the London Union of Compositors, and many independent societies joined the new Association.

The principle object was the centralization of authority in regard to the conduct of strikes and disputes, in order to conserve resources and deploy forces to the best advantage. One of the major weaknesses of the old system was that each Society had the right to open or close offices within its area of jurisdiction, without consulting the others. This

[1] *Compositors' Chronicle*, 1843, p. 269.
[2] *The Printer*, 1844, p. 97.   [3] *Ibid.*, p. 161.

82   TRADE SOCIETIES AND TRADE UNIONS

frequently led to friction and misunderstanding, allegations of treachery, and waste of effort through lack of co-ordination.[1]

Secondly it aimed at providing 'an equitable remuneration to the unemployed and those who make sacrifices for the interests of the trade'. Hitherto a man on strike had been given a special tramp card which entitled him to double the normal relief. But this was generally felt to be inadequate compensation for the deliberate giving up of one's job. This inadequacy had resulted in a weakening of union control, for non-members in 'unfair' offices were reluctant to join the union, in case they should be asked to withdraw from their jobs, and even staunch members were reluctant to report breaches of trade customs, for the same reason. Under the rules of the N.T.A. a member called on to withdraw was to receive an allowance at the rate of three quarters of his average earnings, for a maximum of six months.

The third reform was the abolition of the tramp relief for unemployed and the introduction of an out-of-work allowance of 7s weekly. The London compositors frankly expected that this feature would improve their position immensely by removing the threat of an influx of tramps from the country.[2]

The first year of operation was highly successful; membership exceeded 4,000, and despite the settlement of fifty-one small disputes and the payment of £700 to strikers, funds in hand were almost £1,000.[3]

But in the following year, 1846, the high hopes began to wane. Heavy unemployment, especially in the London area, made severe inroads on the resources. Despite months of double subscriptions, funds and membership were falling by the end of the year. At this critical time, when the union was trying to avoid a large-scale dispute, the master printers of Edinburgh forced a show-down by introducing a system of 'certification' under which they agreed to give preference to non-unionists, and to blacklist all strikers. When the local journeymen resolved to expel any member who applied for a 'certificate' and to withdraw members from shops which used the certificate system, a large-scale stoppage followed.[4] Over 200 journeymen were discharged and the book trade brought almost to a standstill. Strike pay cost the N.T.A. over £2,000, and the burden of double subscriptions was too heavy for many societies. The final blow to the N.T.A. was the decision of the London compositors, in February 1848, to withdraw.[5]

[1] *Compositors' Chronicle*, 1841, p. 35.
[2] L.U.C., *Report of the Trade Council to the Compositors of London on the proposed National Typographical Association*, n.d.
[3] N.T.A. Second Half-Yearly Report, December 1845.
[4] *Typographical Gazette*, 1847, p. 197.
[5] L.S.C. (N.T.A.), Report of Third Annual General Meeting. *The London Compositor*, Doc. LXXIV.

REGIONAL AND NATIONAL UNIONS

Thus ended in disaster the first attempt of the printing journeymen to form a national union.

BOOKBINDERS

The history of the bookbinders' union in this period is remarkably similar to that of the letterpress printers. First there was the amalgamation of the London lodges, and the linking up of the provincial societies to control the tramping system. This was followed by the formation, growth, and swift collapse of a National Union.

The reorganization in London began with the formation of a Trade Committee, elected by the whole of the members of all Lodges, to supervise matters of general interest, such as the credentials of applicants for admission, the numbers of apprentices, the payment of out-of-work relief, and to report on the state of the trade throughout the country. The Committee kept up a correspondence with provincial societies.[1]

On the other hand the collection of subscriptions remained the responsibility of the Lodges. It was obviously unwise to have one organization raising the money and another one spending it, and this frequently resulted in the Society getting into financial difficulty. Furthermore there were always factions in the Lodges who resented the over-riding authority of the Trade Committee, and wished to regain their old autonomy.[2]

The society was racked by a bitter dispute between piece-workers and time-workers. Many of the piece-workers were in the large Bible binding shops, where large scale methods of production facilitated the standardization of productive processes, and the use of piece rates to speed up production. In 1826 the Society for Promoting Christian Knowledge, a body of clerics and wealthy philanthropists, oblivious to the welfare of British workers, induced the Bible binders to reduce their prices by twenty per cent. When the masters tried to reduce piece rates by the same proportion, the Bible hands went on strike, without the prior approval of the Trade Committee, which was then hard pressed for funds. The strike was soon broken, but the piece-workers harboured a grievance against the Society. In 1832 a number of them formed a break-away organization, known as the Equitable Society. Another large scale dispute occurred in 1833 when the masters, perhaps taking advantage of the schism in the trade society, tried to enforce another reduction in piece rates.

In 1837 the masters formed an Association and in the next two years challenged the authority of the Society's rules regarding limitation of

[1] E. Howe and J. Child, *op. cit.*, ch. X.
[2] *Ibid.*, pp. 139–40 and ch. XVII.

84 TRADE SOCIETIES AND TRADE UNIONS

apprentices. The long dispute of 1839, 'The Struggle', ended in the financial exhaustion of the Society. The severe reduction in members, owing to the high contributions necessary to repay loans, gave added strength to the movement for 'consolidation' of the Lodges, as the only way of improving administrative efficiency, and preventing waste and misappropriation of the funds. In 1840 the London Consolidated Society was duly constituted, and the Lodges abolished. The first full-time secretary was Thomas Joseph Dunning, who played a prominent part in trade union affairs in the next thirty years.[1]

In 1839 when the Committee was set up to consider the consolidation of the Lodges, a more grandiose scheme for a national union was being canvassed by a few energetic members, and the Committee was eventually instructed to prepare a 'Plan of Union for the Whole Trade in Great Britain and Ireland'. There were then some twenty or thirty bookbinders' societies in provincial towns, but the only liaison between them was through the Bookbinders' Consolidated Relief Fund (established in 1836) which financed the system of paying mileage relief to tramps.[2] Encouraged by information that many provincial societies were keen to join a national union, the London committee set to work, basing the constitution on the following objectives:

'To afford the means of relief to its members out of work, by providing them with the means of travelling from one place to another in search of employment; to afford the means of immediate communication and relief to each and every point of the Union where its rights and privileges are threatened with invasion.'[3]

In short the plan was to link London up with the provincial tramp relief fund and transform the whole organization into a trade union. It was proposed to separate the societies into several geographical divisions each of which would send delegates to the annual meeting of the legislative council, while the executive would be elected by the largest member, London. Each local society was left free to provide out-of-work benefit from its own funds if it so desired, but the national union retained the tramp relief system. Each local secretary was required to send regular reports of the state of trade to the Chief Secretary so that he could issue advice on the most promising tramping routes.

---

[1] T. J. Dunning is cited in S. & B. Webb, *History of Trade Unionism*, 1920; Karl Marx, *Capital*, Everyman, ch. 19, and J. S. Mill, *Principles of Political Economy*, 1920, p. 939 n. His essay *Trades Unions and Strikes, their Philosophy and Intention*, London, 1860 is his most important publication.

[2] Bookbinders' Consolidated Relief Fund, *Rules*, 1836.

[3] *Report of Committee appointed to prepare a Plan of Union*, 1839.

REGIONAL AND NATIONAL UNIONS

A meeting of delegates at Manchester in April 1840, resolved that the plan should come into operation in the following month. By the end of the year the Bookbinders' Consolidated Union had a membership of 1,300, of which 700 were in the London Lodge. In the meantime the latter had become involved in the great 'struggle' with the masters over the limitation of apprentices. During this dispute it incurred a heavy legacy of debt, and was unable to maintain its contributions to the Consolidated Union. It therefore decided to withdraw 'temporarily'. Thus ended the first attempt at a national union of bookbinders.

In the provinces, after the withdrawal of the London Lodge in 1840, the Consolidated Union continued to function, though its activities were little more than those of the old Relief Fund. The seat of government was moved to Dublin. Although the local society was strong in support of unionism, difficulties of administration were enhanced by the extra delay in communication. Rumours of impending insolvency and accusations of inefficiency and neglect were frequent. In vain did the Committee issue a series of circulars designed to restore confidence and unity.[1]

In 1847 the larger English societies took matters into their own hands, convened a delegate meeting, and resolved to transfer the seat of government to Liverpool. When this was effected the Consolidated Union had thirty-eight branches but only £56 in general funds.[2] The constitution was revised to improve the system of communication between the Central Committee and the branches, to provide for publication of the results of all ballots, and for the establishment of a regular *Circular* by which members could be kept fully informed of the Executive's actions. Admittance fees were temporarily reduced as part of a campaign to enrol new members. These reforms injected a new lease of life into the moribund Consolidated Union and in the second half of the century it flourished as a fairly successful 'New Model' union.

PAPERMAKERS

In 1826 the Original Society of Papermakers was torn by an internal dispute over the rates of pay for a new method of making light-weight paper for ledgers. The issue was hotly debated for nearly two years, and ended in the formation of a break-away society. The two factions, known as the 'Star' and the 'Deckle' vied to gain control of the mills throughout England, and relaxed their qualifications for admission.[3] When the two

[1] For an account of internal dissension, see Bundock, *The National Union of Printing, Bookbinding and Paper Workers*, 1959, pp. 19–23.

[2] Bookbinders' Consolidated Union, *Circular*, No. 2, 1848.

[3] *World Paper Trade Review*, 1901–1902. Series of articles on 'History of Papermakers'.

86 TRADE SOCIETIES AND TRADE UNIONS

unions were reunited, in 1837, the foolishness of this rivalry was apparent: the market was over-supplied with labour, and unemployment was heavy.[1]

In 1847 the members were organized into three classes for regulating payment of subscriptions:

	WAGES	NUMBER OF MEMBERS
I	22s +	320
II	17s — 22s	671
III	— 17s	54

The Society was prepared to support strikes which occurred in the effort to prevent a reduction in wages, and strike allowance included provision for wife and children on a more generous scale than was usual at this time, but no allowance was paid to the man.[2] On some occasions strikes had been supported by the Society when the masters refused an increase in rates, especially if the increase was necessary because wages were depressed in that locality. All strikes were authorized by the Central Committee in Kent but a complete strike was an unusual occurrence.[3] At the zenith of its power in the decade 1840–50, the Society claimed over 1,000 members, in almost every mill in the United Kingdom, but with the predominance of the machine process, its influence suffered a steady decline. Many workers in machine factories did not join the Society, and their own union was not founded until 1853.

INTERNAL REFORMS

Grand schemes for 'reform' on a national scale seemed doomed to failure, but there were two internal reforms of the societies of this period which were of great importance for the future success of the unions. The first was the removal of the House-of-Call from a public house, to either a coffee house or an office, with an accompanying campaign against alcoholism. The second was the formation of a responsible unit of the organization in each work place, in order to provide stricter supervision of the manner in which trade customs were observed or 'innovations' attempted.

After 1825 there was a general reaction against the use of public houses. It is impossible to read trade union documents in the thirties without being impressed by the enthusiasm of the workers' leaders for

[1] Bundock, *op. cit.*, ch. 39.
[2] A. D. Spicer, *The Paper Trade*, 1907, 'Social Conditions'.
[3] National Association for the Promotion of Social Science, *Report on Trades' Societies . . .*, 1860, p. 376.

REGIONAL AND NATIONAL UNIONS

improvement of social conditions by means of thrift, sobriety and education. The L.U.C. Council in 1836 painted a depressing picture of the contemporary scene:

'The working classes have therefore by their sloth and ignorance become the inhabitants of a region redolent of pauperism and crime. Poverty is the parent of every vice, but more especially of dissipation; and those who make the mass of mankind poor are amongst the first to upbraid them with the consequence of their avarice, and loudly denounce the working class as an improvident and dissipated race.'[1]

Trade societies first attempted to break the vicious circle of poverty and vice by a direct attack on the former—raising wage rates, protecting earnings, and guarding the skilled jobs. But towards the middle of the century they also made a deliberate effort to tackle the other part of the problem. Responsible union leaders, believing that the ultimate mission of their organization was the moral rehabilitation of the workers, fought against the practice of alcoholic intemperance, which was reputed to be a prominent factor in the depression of health and efficiency of the printers.[2]

The holding of society meeting in public houses did not conduce to the efficient transaction of business. An L.U.C. Special Committee reported:

'. . . the liquors drunk during the discussion, and the noise created by the publicans' servants, joined to the jingle of pots and glasses, must be alike injurious to the proper discharge of the duties to which they (the members) are entrusted, as they are known to be repugnant to the taste of a large number of our members.'[3]

Shortly afterwards the L.U.C. removed its offices from the Red Lion public house to unlicensed premises in Bouverie Street, and Robert Thompson was appointed full-time Office Keeper at a salary of £90 per annum. Two years later the bookbinders' committee also gave its opinion 'that it is absolutely necessary to withdraw, as soon as possible, all meetings and business of the Society, Houses of Call, as well as every other, from Public Houses'. It recognised that the old convivial Lodge meetings had played an important part in promoting the solidarity of the members, and suggested that this function could in future be

[1] L.U.C., *Annual Report of Trade Council*, 1836.
[2] C. T. Thackrah, *The Effect of Arts, Trades and Professions . . . on Health and Longevity*, 1832.
[3] L.U.C., *Report of Committee*, 1837.

88   TRADE SOCIETIES AND TRADE UNIONS

performed by purely social gatherings. Within the Society a bitter conflict raged between the traditionalists and the reformers. With Puritan zeal the latter were determined to put an end to the worst feature of the old system:

'The desire to meet in Lodges is simply the desire to meet for the transaction of business, accompanied by the means of intoxication. Progressing as the human mind undoubtedly is, and exploded as the habit of drinking on every occasion has become in all classes of society, it is not a little singular that retrograde movement should find advocates. It is simply a contradiction in terms to meet for business when you provide the means of excitement which shall render you incapable of deliberation in the transaction of it.'[1]

The bookbinders therefore moved their office to the Magnet Coffee House in Drury Lane. The supporters of the Lodge meetings expressed their disgust in a song, 'On the Coffee Shop Dodge'.

> Oh, what are poor bookbinders come to ?
> Stop a bit, and we shall see.
> Consolidated and undone too,
> With nought to drink but vile coffee.
>
> There was a time, I well do know,
> When Gin and Beer were to be got,
> And round the table they would flow
> With pipes and drink from glass or pot.
>
> But mark how different now the case is!
> No pipes, nor Gin or Squirt abounds,
> For want of which they make wry faces,
> And Squirts they get from coffee grounds.[2]

This was no trivial issue; it kept the London Society divided for no less than ten years, and seriously impaired the effectiveness of its control of working conditions. In the finish the reformers won but a large number of the others seceded from the Society and set up a rival, The Dayworking Bookbinders Society, which led a separate existence for sixty years.

Many influential leaders of the compositors and binders were influenced by the Moral Force wing of the Chartist movement. T. J.

[1] *Bookbinders' Trade Circular*, 1857, p. 69.
[2] E. Howe and J. Child, *op. cit.*, p. 174.

REGIONAL AND NATIONAL UNIONS

Dunning, secretary of the binders, had been in touch with Francis Place, and had contributed articles on political economy to *The Charter*.[1] Jaffray, another leader of the bookbinders, was acquainted with William Lovett, and a member of his National Association for Promoting the Social and Political Improvement of the People. Thompson, the architect of the L.U.C. and a keen advocate of a national printers' union, was tireless in his exhortations to the workers to better their lot by education and the use of reason.

None of them had much sympathy for the visionary ideas of Robert Owen. In the *Compositors' Chronicle* and *The Printer* which Thompson edited there were long philosophical articles attacking 'atheistic socialism', and only once did a correspondent plead for a consideration of Owen's Utopian plans. Industry, sobriety and self-education—these were to be the means of liberating the workers from poverty and vice. The reaction against meeting in public houses must be seen therefore as a symptom of a much wider change in objectives and social philosophy.[2]

The most important internal reform in organization in this period was the incorporation of the Chapel in the Union structure. The prime need of the Compositors, if they wished to continue to enforce the Scale of Prices, was close supervision of working conditions, in order that 'encroachments' should be promptly reported, for if employers were allowed to whittle away at the extras, or interpret ambiguous clauses to their own advantage, the men's earnings would be seriously reduced. The Union Committee advised that a system of supervision by responsible shop delegates should be instituted:

'By the arrangements proposed under this plan, no man could in future plead ignorance of the customs and laws in the trade—for, if the whole trade were united in one society, and the business managed by a council of delegates, delegated meetings—if there were but one journeyman in a house, that individual would be constrained occasionally to attend, to take a part in the proceedings of the trade. Thus no malpractices could be hidden nor would innovations any longer creep in by degrees, until it became difficult to ascertain what is really the custom of the trade upon certain points. . . .'[3]

In offices where chapels were already in existence these took over the

---

[1] *The Charter*, January 27, 1839.
[2] See M. Hovell, *The Chartist Movement*, p. 217. A. Briggs (ed.) *Chartist Studies*, 1959, ch. 9.
[3] *Report from the Union Committee* (*The London Compositor*, Doc. LVII).

90 TRADE SOCIETIES AND TRADE UNIONS

function of electing the Trade Delegates. ('Shop Steward' is the term used in other trades.) Where there was no old-style chapel, it was but natural that the meetings to elect Trade Delegates should be called chapel meetings, and that the Delegate should be called the Father-of-the-Chapel. At first the two offices were distinguished, but as union organization improved and the Trade Delegate became an important official, the chapel became more and more a unit in the structure of union organization. By 1840 the transition was generally complete, for then the Trade Council report expressly mentioned the chapel:

'Now it often happens that the monies received in Chapels from the members of the Union are not paid in regularly, and it is therefore now particularly necessary for the Delegates, Clerks and Members of Chapels to see that the monies collected are paid in as soon as possible.'[1]

This reform in the mode of government was of great value to the Executive. Firstly it made it easier for the Union to collect subscriptions, and for the journeymen to pay; thus there was less likelihood of members being erased for arrears. Secondly it provided an efficient means of checking the observance of trade rules and customs in each office, and provided a channel of communication between executive and membership.

By 1840 the tradition of disciplining offending Chapel members by the use of Ralph, the Chapel Ghost, had lapsed. In 1841 Ralph wrote to the *Compositors' Chronicle*, bemoaning the fact that he had 'fallen so much into disrepute of late as not to have had a single job for some months, although (he) . . . might have been of some assistance in one or two refractory cases'. Thompson, the Editor, replied:

'We are really glad to find that Master Ralph's occupation is gone, and that the days of violence are succeeded by the age of reason. We are no friend to coercion in any shape, and at all times prefer moral to physical force. It would be well however, as Master Ralph is about to quit England, if compositors would more actively employ those moral means which seldom prove ineffectual.'[2]

Later generations of printing union leaders were unanimous in ascribing the stability of their organizations to the fact that the unit of government was based firmly on the place of work. It was fortunate that at this critical juncture they had at hand the ancient and venerable institution

[1] L.U.C., *Report of Trade Council*, 1840.
[2] *Compositors' Chronicle*, 1841, p. 60.

REGIONAL AND NATIONAL UNIONS 91

of the Chapel which with a little ingenuity could be adapted to serve a vital function in the Union.

These two internal reforms at the local level were important in providing a sound basic unit on which more extensive organization could be built in future.

REGULATION OF TERMS OF EMPLOYMENT

In the provinces regulation of wages, hours and working conditions was in the hands of the local societies and unions. Though masters' associations enjoyed brief life in larger centres, such as Dublin, Edinburgh or Glasgow, in the smaller towns there was no formal organization. It may be presumed, however, that Adam Smith's observation about the prevalence of informal 'conspiracies', to keep wages down and prices up, was still valid.

Why did the masters not combine? The main reason seems to be that in the prevailing conditions of surplus labour, they had little to fear from the unions. In fact, in so far as the unions standardized rates and hours, they were welcomed by many employers, for this eliminated the possibility of price-cutting by low-wage firms. On the other hand, when the unions attempted to enforce apprentice restrictions, the masters often reacted swiftly and effectively, as in the London book-binders' struggle of 1839, and the Edinburgh printers' lock-out of 1847. Furthermore most of the local societies, and even the first unions, were basically conservative in their ambitions, aiming at maintaining wage rates and preserving privileges. In this they often enjoyed the sympathy of some employers. It was when the unions attempted to *raise* wages and *shorten* hours that they came up against fiercer and often concerted, opposition.

Each local society had an established rate of weekly wages, which varied considerably throughout the country. Hours varied too, and were less frequently mentioned in the Rule Books. As work was seasonal, and irregular, men were expected to balance their slack days by working overtime without pay in rush periods.

There were no standard rates for Sunday work, night work, or over-time; these were at the discretion of the employer. In half-a-dozen large provincial towns piecework lists, largely modelled on the London scale, were in operation.

When the regional unions were formed in the thirties, the main reform which they attempted was the standardization of an apprentice quota. Even so, the formula which they adopted had, perforce, to remain an ideal to aim at, rather than the rule to be strictly enforced. This was why the important power to open or close offices was taken

92 TRADE SOCIETIES AND TRADE UNIONS

from the local society and vested in the central committee. Only the latter was in a position to take an overall view of the situation, and plan the union's strategy with full knowledge of the resources at its command. Lists of closed offices were circulated to all branches, and sometimes to other unions, so that tramps might be forewarned against accepting employment there.

CHAPTER VI

THE PROBLEM OF UNEMPLOYMENT

*But alas! a change has come over the scene. No longer
are the services of compositors in requisition; no longer is
their worth appreciated; the commodity which before they
sold on demand, and on which was set fair value, has
now become stale and unprofitable.*
Typographical Gazette, 1845, p. 49.

DIAGNOSIS OF THE PROBLEM

Full employment ended with the Napoleonic Wars; the enforcement of wage reductions by the master printers in 1816 was possible only because of a pool of unemployed journeymen.

Throughout the second quarter of the nineteenth century the printing trade societies were almost continuously occupied with the problem of unemployment. Perhaps the worst year was 1826 when conditions were so bad that the men appealed to public charity. This experience gave a temporary set-back to the advocates of a militant trade policy, for it was impossible to raise sufficient funds to give regular relief to the unemployed and prevent them from taking work on 'unfair' terms.

The journeymen were not content, however, with an attempt to alleviate the distress caused by persistent unemployment. They wanted to get to the root of the trouble, to diagnose the causes of this phenomenon in order that they could effect a cure. One school of thought laid the blame on the introduction of machinery:

'Machinery must be regarded as a monster that devours the bread of thousands. It is an insatiable Moloch. It is callous to all feeling; it is insensible at the sight of the emaciated form, the hollow cheek, and the sunken eye; it turns like the deaf adder from the appeal of misery.'[1]

[1] *The Advocate,* February 16, 1833.

94 TRADE SOCIETIES AND TRADE UNIONS

In point of fact, however, the introduction of power-driven machinery into printing was such a gradual process that little unemployment was directly due to this cause. A few particular inventions did threaten the livelihood of small groups of men. In the bookbinding trade, for example, the rolling machine which flattened out the book signatures prior to binding eliminated the monotonous and arduous work of the hand beaters. The latter raised an agitation and their Society sent out an urgent circular to the Lodges:

'The pressure of extreme distress that is now so generally felt amongst us, calls for our serious and immediate attention. Machinery—the principle cause of our complaint—is making rapid strides towards reducing a considerable number of our body to a state of pauperism, and to bring those who have for years supported their families in credit to exist for a time on our funds, and finally become dependent on casual bounty.'[1]

The men sent a memorial to the employers asking them to refrain from using the rolling machines. As they were chiefly used in the Bible binding shops, the Society also issued an appeal to the great Bible distributing agencies. The arguments that machines improved the lot of working classes were refuted in a pamphlet, *The Reply of the Journeymen Bookbinders*, probably written by T. J. Dunning.[2] This claimed that as the machine was not *technically* superior to the hand beater, its only advantage lay in its cheapness. As this was being obtained at the expense of the beaters who were being deprived of their livelihood, it was unjust to put the small advantage to the public above the grave distress caused to the men. These arguments were of no avail. The masters in large establishments continued to use the machines, and as the Society could not take effective action against them, the matter was quietly dropped when trade improved.

The hand pressmen whose trade was threatened by the use of steam driven printing machinery seem to have put up little concerted opposition, although there were numerous cases of isolated, and therefore ineffective, protests against the way in which the new machines were operated. In Dublin, for example, the journeymen stood firmly by the principle that such machines should be manned by pressmen, not by apprentices.[3]

[1] E. Howe and J. Child, *op. cit.*, p. 105.
[2] See *Results of Machinery, &c.* Published by The Society for the Diffusion of Useful Knowledge, 1831. *The Reply of the Journeymen Bookbinders. . . .* Published for the Society by William Smith, London, 1831.
[3] Select Committee on Combination of Workmen, 1838. *Second Report.*

THE PROBLEM OF UNEMPLOYMENT

In the early forties the compositors were seriously perturbed by the invention of the Young-Delcambre composing machine. The editor of the *Compositors' Chronicle* tried to prove that the machine could not possibly be used to reduce the cost of printing, but there was evidently widespread uneasiness:

'We are constantly receiving letters containing anxious enquiries respecting the "progress" of the composing machine and requesting our opinion as to its probable effect on the interests of the trade . . . we think now, as we did at first, that composition by the machine can never be done *cheaper* or *quicker* than it is done by hand.'[1]

A more general diagnosis of the cause of unemployment ascribed it to the severity of competition among employers. Competition, it was said, worked in two ways to reduce the number of jobs. Firstly, some employers, eager to gain contracts, cut their prices so low that they were unable to make a profit and were driven into bankruptcy. Secondly, some were forced to make continuous efforts to reduce costs and to dispense with the highly paid labour of the skilled journeymen. Hence the societies' struggle against the 'evils' of boy labour, female labour, 'porter' labour, and excessive apprentices.

Often it was the small masters who were the worst offenders in regard to excessive apprentices, for it was in the small jobbing sector of the industry that competition was most acute. As the capital required to set up as a jobbing master was negligible, many an unemployed journeyman attempted to eke out a living by using some obsolete plant and the cheap labour of apprentices. Thus, it was claimed, a vicious circle was set up:

'Little masters, without journeymen, execute work with apprentices at unremunerative prices; while journeymen without work are forced to tramp. Thus the weight of the evil falls upon the journeymen in two ways; first it deprives them of employment; and then it drives others into the market already overstocked, to compete with them. . . .'[2]

REMEDIES

If machinery was the cause of the evil of unemployment, then machinery should be abolished. This was the argument used by the journeymen bookbinders. The craftsmen did not usually, at this stage, claim the right to man the machines, especially where this would have entailed the use of new skills. But the temper of the age of the industrial revolution was against them, and the machines were kept running.

[1] *The Printer*, 1844, p. 31. [2] *Compositors' Chronicle*, 1843, p. 247.

96   TRADE SOCIETIES AND TRADE UNIONS

If, however, the root of the trouble was the severity of competition between private firms, one solution was the setting up of co-operative workshops run by the journeymen for the benefit of the unemployed. Although many plans for 'self-employment schemes' were canvassed in trade journals, few were ever put into operation. Such schemes were frequently put forward during a strike or lock-out as a way of convincing the master that he was more dependent on the men than they were on him. In 1839 during the Bookbinders' struggle there were several suggestions of a co-operative bindery; in 1843 the type-founders on strike quoted Byron:

> Ye have the letters Cadmus gave,
> Think ye he meant them for a slave?

and urged support for a journeymen's foundry;[1] in 1846 the printers were almost converted to the idea of a printing office run by the National Association:

'If we are producers, why not set to and produce for ourselves? Why always be dependent upon the whims of the capitalist, or upon the taste of those who profess to walk in a higher sphere? . . . By the possession of a co-operative printing office much employment would fall our way, from the general production of the 'hive of nations', from matters connected with the economy of our Association, and from the creation of literature not at present dreamed of.'[2]

In the previous period most of the London societies made intermittent attempts to secure some form of limitation of apprentices, and came to realize that the most sensible and practicable method was to fix a ratio of apprentices to journeymen. The employers, infected with the expansionist fever of the era of *laissez-faire*, would not agree to such a scheme. In the quarter century after the repeal of the Combination Acts the unions continued with their fumbling search for a policy which would even up the supply and demand for labour.

As limitation of apprentices had long been discussed it seems strange that it was not adopted much earlier. Partly the delay was due to the weakness of the unions owing to division of their ranks and the large proportion of unemployed. Partly it was due to the fact that the rank and file required a long experience of the effects of non-restriction before they would agree to embark on a full scale campaign to enforce

[1] *The Printer*, 1844, p. 153.
[2] *The Typographical Gazette*, 1846, p. 69.

The Problem of Unemployment 97

a definite quota. By 1840, however, the men clearly had no other alternative:

'If the trade are by their fears deterred from adopting the restrictive system—have they no fears of what may result from rejecting them? In our opinion they ought much more to fear that state of things, now hourly approaching, when our streets shall be thronged with unemployed workmen, whose necessities will compel them to take work under any circumstances.'[1]

A practical difficulty lay in the fact that the problem was a national one, and until all unions could agree to co-ordinate their efforts, there was little point in any one society making an attempt to reform conditions in its area. One difficulty was the high social esteem in which the printing trades were held; many parents, unaware of the poor prospects of full-time employment, were keen to apprentice their sons to the trade. The reputation for respectability—even gentility—which had accrued in the eighteenth century persisted for some generations after conditions had changed radically for the worse.[2] Although the unions occasionally attempted to educate the public on the true conditions, their accounts were naturally regarded as unduly distorted and pessimistic.

In 1836 The London Society of Bookbinders resolved to limit apprentices, according to the following scale:

JOURNEYMEN	APPRENTICES	(PLUS)		
6	2			
10	2	1 Bookbinder's son		
15	3	1	,,	,,
20	4	1	,,	,,
30	5	1	,,	,,
40	6	1	,,	,,
50	6	2	,,	,,

Some master bookbinders agreed to observe this rule, though they had not been consulted in the making of it, but others ignored it. The Society gradually became embroiled in the great 'Struggle' which exhausted its funds and practically forced its withdrawal from the Consolidated Union.[3]

In 1840 the provincial unions which had been trying to enforce apprentice restriction for some years realized that their efforts were being nullified by the lack of control in London, and issued an appeal

[1] *Compositors' Chronicle*, 1841, p. 61. [2] *Ibid.*, p. 43.
[3] E. Howe and J. Child, *op. cit.*, ch. XIV.

D

98 TRADE SOCIETIES AND TRADE UNIONS

to Societies in the capital to join in a national campaign.[1] In 1841 the L.U.C. resolved to enforce a quota of one apprentice to four journeymen but it lacked the funds or organization to carry out its resolution.[2] In 1845 the major letterpress unions amalgamated in the National Typographical Association with a policy based on strict limitation of apprentices. Indeed it was the payment of strike pay to the large number of Edinburgh men, who were locked out because they stood by the restrictive rule, which finally broke the finances of the N.T.A. and caused its dissolution.

Thus the two great National unions of bookbinders and letterpress printers foundered because they could not cope with the apprentice problem.

RELIEF OF UNEMPLOYED—THE TRAMPING SYSTEM

The strategy of the printing unions of the nineteenth century cannot be understood without a knowledge of the tramping system. The custom was much older than the trade societies, and in the printing industry it probably developed about the middle of the eighteenth century when the industry expanded from London to the provinces. At that time there was a growing demand for the services of skilled London journeymen; and enterprising apprentices on coming out of their servitude were tempted by the prospect of travel, a carefree life, and the chance of a good job.[3]

In the earliest documents of the London bookbinders (1797–99) are entries recording the applications of members for Honourable Leave to 'go into the Country'. Before such leave was granted the member had to 'clear the books', i.e. pay all arrears of subscriptions. He was then issued with a society tramping card and a small sum of money to start him off.

He then set out for the nearest town on the approved route. If there was a local Society he called on the secretary and on presenting his credentials was informed of possible vacancies; if there was no society he walked from shop to shop. If he could not obtain work he applied to the local secretary for relief or took the hat round the shops. The form and amount of society relief varied from place to place but usually consisted of a small sum of money and a bed of clean straw in the attic of the House-of-Call.[4]

[1] *Address of the Northern Union . . . to the Compositors and Pressmen of London,* 1840.

[2] *Address from the Compositors to the Master Printers of London,* 1841.

[3] *v.* 'Life of Wimble Flash', serial in *Compositors' Chronicle,* 1843.

[4] A detailed account of the tramping system is given by E. J. Hobsbawn, 'The Tramping Artizan', *Ec. Hist. Rev.,* 1951.

The Problem of Unemployment

Originally relief was paid to a tramp by virtue of his membership of the trade. Even if he was not a member of a Society the presentation of his indentures to show that he was a 'legal' journeyman sufficed to win him some subsistence.[1] With the development of trade societies a number of rules and customs respecting the conduct of tramping were evolved. The men in each local society realized that the removal of the local unemployed from the town when trade was slack was necessary if they wished to preserve the standard rate, especially if there were some 'closed' offices in the locality. The tramping system, therefore, changed from a method of reducing unemployment and providing relief to a method of supporting the standard rate of each society.[2]

Before the establishment of the regional unions in the thirties, each society simply decided for itself how much tramp relief it would pay. How adequate this amount was depended mainly on the distance to the next relief station. Furthermore the provision of tramp relief sometimes placed an intolerable burden on the members of a small society on a popular tramping route. In the thirties many societies came to favour some means of linking up the local societies and paying Mileage Relief. Under this system a tramp was paid from a central fund in proportion to the distance travelled (usually at the rate of 1d per mile). In 1836 the bookbinders, after rejecting a scheme for a national union, agreed to a more limited form of co-operation in the Bookbinders' Consolidated Relief Fund.[3]

The B.C.R.F. took great pains to overcome one of the main objections to Mileage Relief, namely the possibility of fraud. Tramping documents were issued on parchment to minimize the risk of forgery, and the tramp's movements were carefully circumscribed in order that any misdemeanour could be promptly punished. The Document contained a map which showed the approved tramping routes; in 1840 they ranged from Truro to Wick and included deck passages to Ireland. A common circuit included a crossing from Glasgow to Belfast, a tramp through Ireland and a return from Cork to Bristol.[4] A selection of 'Rules to be Particularly Observed by Members Travelling' was printed on the back.

Generally a tramp was required by rule to call at the office of the local secretary before trying to get work in the town. This enabled the secretary to check his credentials and advise him of the whereabouts of 'closed' or 'unfair' offices, and of any vacancies. Most Societies required the tramp to lodge his Document with the secretary in return for a

[1] London Society of Journeymen Bookbinders, *Rules*, 1820 (Goldsmiths).
[2] Musson, *op. cit.*, pp. 50–52.
[3] Bookbinders' Consolidated Relief Fund, *Rules*, 1836.
[4] B.C.R.F. Tramping Document (Jaffray Coll.).

TRADE SOCIETIES AND TRADE UNIONS

temporary 'working ticket' which would gain him admittance to any fair office. As local secretaries were invariably working men it was often stipulated that tramps should not call upon them in working hours.[1] The interruptions to their work not only brought them into disfavour with their employers, but also served to indicate to the latter the state of trade in neighbouring towns and the availability of replacements in case of a trade dispute. Discreetly worded notices such as the following were often inserted in the journals:

'Persons visiting Chester, Lancaster and Worcester are required to call upon the secretaries before applying. The non-observance of this precaution will be of some inconvenience to them if discovered.'[2]

In the provinces the tramping Document also served in lieu of strike pay to men who had been withdrawn from unfair offices. As it had been recognized from an early date that the positive act of 'sacrifice of a situation' deserved a more generous recompense than the allowance to the involuntarily unemployed, the Strike Card entitled the bearer to double relief at the tramping stations. As such cards were especially valuable they offered a strong inducement to forgery and local secretaries were instructed to examine them with particular care. Some of the unions printed their Strike Cards on coloured parchment.

This then was the tramping system as it had developed under the regional unions of the eighteen thirties. In times of reasonably good trade it achieved something of its objects. In-so-far as it reduced the reserve army of unemployed in any one town it strengthened the hand of the local society; in-so-far as it reduced overall unemployment by promoting labour mobility it strengthened the unions by reducing the number of potential 'rats'.

At every successive stage in its development, however, the tramping system raised more problems than it solved. First, the proliferation of local societies resulted in such a variety of tramp cards and documents that local secretaries could not distinguish true from false, and it was common knowledge that many fraudulent characters were receiving regular relief from several cards simultaneously. Second, the burden of tramp relief was not shared equally among the journeymen, for a small society on a busy route would have to pay out more, in proportion to its membership, than a large society in an isolated town. Thirdly relief bore no relation to a tramp's needs, for a society might be able to pay only a shilling although the next station was fifty miles away.

Each of these problems had two aspects, the strategic and the humanitarian, which were not always clearly distinguished. Every act

[1] *Compositors' Chronicle*, 1841, p. 124.　　　　　　　[2] *Ibid.*, p. 149.

The Problem of Unemployment 101

of real or fancied injustice which turned a genuine tramp bitter against the unions made another enemy and weakened their control of working conditions. In explaining to members why his union could not work more actively to raise wage rates, the secretary of the Northern Union wrote:

'Some plan must first be brought into operation by which we can, more effectively than at present, secure ourselves against the inroads of rats and an influx of tramps to defeat our objects. . . .'[1]

Union leaders had great difficulty in convincing local secretaries and members that funds should not be expended on purely charitable grounds unless the latter coincided with the strategic interest of the union:

'The chief ground of relief upon a card is not the poverty or distress of the applicant; the design is that every individual possessed of a recognized card who had occasion to travel in search of employment shall receive such support as to be under no necessity to enter an unfair office.'[2]

This point was made very clearly by a correspondent to the *Compositors' Chronicle* who tried to awaken the members of the London trade to the danger of refusing to provide relief for the unemployed:

'I have been accustomed to work in a small country town where I have often shared my evening meal with a forlorn tramp, and this I considered not merely charitable, but politic, for had I not done so, what security had I that the traveller would not, on the following morning, by underworking me, have turned me out of house and home?'[3]

In the second quarter of the century much of the time and energy of union leaders was occupied in attempts to provide solutions to these administrative and strategic problems. Some offered remedies in the form of improvements in the issuing, checking and control of tramp Documents, or in the linking up of local societies into regional unions which could standardize procedure. By issuing all Documents in a standard form a regional union could reduce opportunities for fraud; by pooling funds it could equalize contributions and standardize benefits. Thus the Northern Typographical Union which covered the north of England, The Irish Typographical Union and the General

---

[1] N.T.U., *Sixth Annual Report*, 1836.
[2] N.T.U., *Tenth Annual Report*, 1840.
[3] *Compositors' Chronicle*, 1841, p. 66.

102   Trade Societies and Trade Unions

Typographical Association (Scotland) were largely concerned with improving the administration of tramp relief in their respective areas.[1] The Northern Union had a Reimbursement Fund from which local societies were paid for expenditure on tramp relief in excess of 9d per member per month.

In times of brisk trade a small number of tramps on the road did not constitute much of a threat to union control, but in a depression the situation was very different, for then employers were keener to break customary working rules in order to reduce costs and gain contracts. The number of tramps served to indicate to employers the state of trade in neighbouring towns, and to suggest that union funds would probably be at a low level. The local society was of course vitally concerned to prevent the tramps from entering any unfair offices. As many of the tramps came from far afield, and were not members of any society, they felt little obligation to observe the rules of the local society, and especially if they were refused relief, preferred to work at low pay rather than continue to face the hazards of the road, particularly in winter.[2]

The system lost favour firstly because it had become a positive threat to union control of working conditions. 'Tramping Makes Rats', argued a writer to the *Compositors' Chronicle*. In 1842 the Northern Typographical Union tried to establish a *cordon sanitaire* around each town in which a trade dispute was in progress, and to warn all tramps to make a detour.[3] Secondly it was common knowledge that a long bout of tramping, associating with vagabonds and other ruffians of the road often reduced a respectable journeyman to a shiftless, irresponsible rogue. Thirdly there was a reaction against the futile physical suffering which the tramp had often to endure.

'We have now before our eyes the case of an individual who, after travelling several hundred miles in the vain hope of employment, arrived in London bare-foot, ragged and spirit-broken. . . . Destitute of means to procure a lodging he slept in the streets, caught a cold attended with fever, took refuge in a Union workhouse, where in a few days he perished. And this man, thus left to endure horrors at which even the most callous must shudder, had sacrificed situations for the interest of a profession which calls itself intelligent. . . .'[4]

Finally, tramping became discredited because it failed in its function of reducing unemployment.

[1] I.T.U., *Sixth Annual Report*, 1843.
[2] *Compositors' Chronicle*, 1841, p. 110.
[3] N.T.U., *Report of Delegate Meeting*, 1842.   [4] *The Printer*, 1844, p. 132.

The Problem of Unemployment

'Tramping cannot now, however, be properly denominated a searching for employment; and many men know, by sad experience, that in a few months they have travelled from one end of the kingdom to the other, often without obtaining more than a few days' work.'[1]

The alternative to tramping was the provision of out-of-work pay for the unemployed in their home towns. Leaders of the printers struggled continually to bring home the point that care of the unemployed was not only a charitable duty, but also the essential condition of success of trade union activity. The London societies of bookbinders and compositors had provided out-of-work pay as early as 1820, but their subsequent neglect of other methods of trade regulation had brought the provision of such benefits into undeserved disrepute. Naturally enough, some members of these societies came to regard the Society funds rather as an insurance against unemployment than as the 'sinews of war' in the struggle with employers.

By 1840, however, the tramping system had failed so lamentably that opinion swung again in favour of the provision of weekly unemployed benefit. No fewer than nine advantages were claimed for the latter! It would furnish data regarding the state of trade, enable secretaries to supply men promptly to fill vacancies, permit more accurate computation of the number of apprentices needed, enable the union to punish 'dishonourables', promote the principles of unionism, prevent trivial strikes, help to maintain the price of labour, reserve knowledge of the state of trade to union secretaries, and generally raise the character of the profession![2]

Throughout the country the local societies keenly debated the merits of the proposal; for several years union journals and reports were concerned with little else. The unions were handicapped by the lack of data on unemployment which would have permitted accurate estimate of the cost of different benefit rates, and in consequence there was a wide variation of opinion on the financial basis of the scheme. As it was apparent that many of the societies could not afford to pay an adequate benefit out of their own funds, it followed that they would have to link up in a wider organization. Thus there occurred the paradox that whereas the *growth* of the tramping system had been instrumental in promoting the development of regional unions from local societies, it was the *failure* of the system which largely prompted the first attempt to form a national union.

In 1845 the National Typographical Association was formed, comprising all of the older unions and most of the 'independent' local

[1] N.T.U., *Thirteenth Annual Report*, 1843.
[2] *Compositors' Chronicle*, 1841, p. 114.

104 TRADE SOCIETIES AND TRADE UNIONS

societies. Tramping relief was discontinued and arrangements made for the payment of an out-of-work benefit of 7s per week. The change was hailed with enthusiasm:

'The tramping system is to be abolished—this monster evil has destroyed itself; and we rejoice that we have lived to see the day in which better feelings prevail, and when it is at length admitted that the unfortunate unemployed, and those men who quit their situations to uphold the principles of the trade, are no longer to be exposed to the demoralizing and debasing tramping system, but are henceforth to be provided for as they ought to be.'[1]

[1] *The Printer*, 1844, p. 116.

PART THREE

REGULATION BY UNION RULE
1848–90

CHAPTER VII

CONSOLIDATION OF THE CRAFT UNIONS. 1848–90

The instinctive impulses of working men to intrench around the field of labour the associative means of defence, have their origin in a consciousness of the inability of labour to cope single-handed with capital in those struggles for a fair adjustment of wages which . . . threaten, at times, almost perfect ruin to the comforts and hopes of working men.

A. WAINHOUSE, *Trades Unions Justified*, 1861, p. 5.

CHANGES IN THE INDUSTRY

Throughout the second half of the nineteenth century the printing industry continued its steady expansion. The growth of commerce, the extension of education and the development of advertising were important external factors contributing to a heightened demand for printing products. Within the industry itself the cheapening of paper and the increasing use of power machinery led to substantial reductions in costs. The repeal of the 'taxes on knowledge'—advertisement duty (1853), newspaper stamp (1855), and paper duty (1861)—gave a great fillip to the production of newspapers, especially in the provinces where daily papers were established in the larger cities.

NO. OF MEN ENGAGED IN ENGLAND AND WALES
(000)

	1851	1871	1891	Percentage Increase
Bookbinding	5·5	7·9	11·5	110
Printing	23·6	44·1	82·0	250
Lithography	2·0	3·8	8·6	330
Papermaking	6·1	10·1	12·0	100

Source: Censuses of Population

The relative growth of newspaper and jobbing printing is shown by

REGULATION BY UNION RULE

the relative decline in bookbinding. The smaller growth in employment of papermakers was due to the substitution of machine-made paper for hand-made.

In almost all branches of the trade there was an increase in the size of the average establishment, for the expanding market encouraged entrepreneurs to adopt mass production methods and attempt to reduce costs by mechanization and the division of labour. Increase in size of firm was accompanied, perhaps inevitably, by a sharper distinction between employer and employee. The typical printing office of the early nineteenth century with the master, himself a 'practical printer', taking an active part in the supervision and execution of the work, gave place gradually to the joint stock firm in which supervision was in the hands of managers and foreman.[1] There was a consequent sharpening of the division of economic interests. Although in the sixties trade union leaders were prone to stress the 'identity' of interests of masters and men, by the end of the century statements of their fundamental divergence were increasingly common.

Southward, the great authority on the industry of the nineteenth century, expressed his concern at the change and pleaded for a return to the old sentiment of 'fellowship and brotherly regard' which had animated the ancient gilds, and exhorted employers to be sympathetic to such traditional organizations as the chapel and the companionship 'Nowadays', he wrote 'the employer is often merely a capitalist'.[2] But he pleaded in vain.

Competition was, indeed, so keen that master printers could rarely be induced to present a united front to the unions. In the competitive struggle for survival in the heyday of British capitalism personal relationships were of necessity subordinated to commercial ruthlessness. Most of the businessmen who controlled the larger printing firms believed, rightly or wrongly, they could not afford the luxury of taking an altruistic interest in their employees. Some, however, took an active part in promoting printers charities, such as the London Pension Corporation.

Although there was no dramatic technical change in this period there was steady if unspectacular improvement in the mechanics of the art.[3] By the end of the century the flat-bed cylinder presses had almost reached the limit of their possible speed and exactness of adjustment. They were, however, unsuitable for the jobbing work which was the bread and butter of the small printing shops. Cards, circulars and small

---

[1] See J. Southward, *Practical Printing*, 1882, p. 609, for a nostalgic comment.

[2] J. Southward, *op. cit.*, pp. 609–10.

[3] J. Southward, *Progress in Printing and the Graphic Arts during the Victorian Era*, 1897, passim.

CONSOLIDATION OF THE CRAFT UNIONS 109

bills were produced on hand presses such as the Albion and the Columbian until 1866 when the treadle platen was introduced from the United States. Feeding this high-speed machine by hand was a notoriously dangerous occupation.[1]

The most important technical development was the evolution of the rotary press in which a curved stereo plate was fitted to a cylinder rotating against another cylinder. As high speed operation of the rotary made it impossible to feed in separate sheets by hand the continuous reel of paper was invented. With varying qualities and strengths of paper it required a high degree of skill in the manipulation of tension devices to prevent frequent breakages. A second necessary accessory to the high speed press was a quick drying ink which would reduce the amount of 'set-off'. Inventors produced devices for cutting, counting, folding and clearing away the printed sheets as they came off the presses.[2]

There was continuous search for some method of speeding up the typesetting process to eliminate the laborious, unhealthy and expensive work of the hand compositor. Several inventors applied the idea of using racks filled with different letters which could be released by an operator from a keyboard like a piano's. Several such machines were in actual use in the eighties. Although the most efficient models, the Thorne, Hattersley and Kastenbein, increased the speed of actual composition, they achieved no reduction of cost, for the distribution of used type and the filling of the racks had to be done by hand. The machines were seldom used except in newspaper offices where speed of composing was of prime importance.[3]

Technical and economic changes were reflected in the composition of the work force in the industry. The most important of these were the growing proportion of women workers, of 'semi-skilled' operatives and of juvenile 'learners'.

In bookbinding most of the women were engaged in folding the printed sheets, collating the signatures and doing the preparatory stitching. These operations had long been tacitly recognized by the journeymen as women's work. After 1840, however, the development of cloth binding and the mass production of such standard works as Bibles and Prayer Books led to a complete change in the organization of large establishments. Aiming at cheap mass production for an assured market, the proprietors attempted to break down all binding operations to simple routine tasks which could be performed by women. As the latter had no trade protective society, conditions in the workshops,

[1] J. Southward, *Practical Printing*, p. 463.
[2] G. Isaacs, *The Story of the Newspaper Printing Press*, 1931, p. 55.
[3] E. Howe and H. Waite, *op. cit.*, ch. XIII.

REGULATION BY UNION RULE

especially of some large Bible contractors, were shocking. Arbitrary discipline, inadequate ventilation, lack of sanitation and miserable wages frequently prevailed where the unfortunate women toiled to produce the Word of God.[1]

NO. OF WOMEN ENGAGED IN ENGLAND AND WALES
(ooo)

	1851	1871	1891	Percentage Increase
Bookbinding	3·5	7·6	14·2	300
Printing	0·3	0·7	4·5	1400
Envelope making	—	1·5	2·5	—
Papermaking	3·5	6·6	8·0	130

Source: Censuses of Population

The journeymen were not indifferent to the lot of the women. In 1848 they supported them during a struggle to improve conditions in Watkins' Bible Shop, and in 1874 they lent support and encouragement to the founding of the Society of Women Employed in Bookbinding.[2] They became increasingly concerned, too, with the encroachment of female labour on to work traditionally regarded as journeymen's, and were fairly successful in persuading employers to abide by the customary demarcation. In 1891, a Joint Trade Committee of the London bookbinders' societies reported, 'Female labour does not exist to any great extent amongst us. . . .'[3] By this they meant that women were not seriously encroaching on craft work.

In the same period the number of women employed in Printing rose from almost nil to 4,500. Some of these were engaged as feeders on printing machines, but the majority probably were counting, folding, collating and stitching in printing shops which did their own binding. The employment of women on type setting was not a very grave threat to the hand compositors, for long training was necessary for all-round competence as a compositor. On straight matter such as bookwork, however, women could learn the elements of the craft in a few months, and as they worked at wages about half of the men's, were economical to employ.[4] After the great dispute of 1872 a large number of women compositors were engaged in Edinburgh book printing houses, but despite the efforts of Emily Faithfull to establish co-operative printing societies employing female compositors, they were not important

[1] E. Howe and J. Child, *op. cit.*, p. 161.
[2] B. Drake, *Women in Trade Unions*, n.d., p. 12.
[3] Bookbinders' Joint Trade Committee, *Report*, 1891.
[4] J. R. MacDonald (ed.) *Women in the Printing Trades*, passim.

CONSOLIDATION OF THE CRAFT UNIONS

elsewhere.[1] In 1895 a Special Committee of the London Society of Compositors listed 'female labour' eighth as a cause of unemployment among male compositors.[2] Envelope and Stationery manufacture was the only branch of the industry in which the number of women greatly exceeded the number of men. The men operated the guillotines which cut out the paper, but the remaining operations were performed by women and girls.

After 1870 the skilled journeymen bookbinders became alarmed at reports that 'porter labour', i.e. untrained men, was being used to work cutters, and in London at least they succeeded in forcing the majority of employers to restrict such work to legal journeymen. In the cloth-binding branch of the trade the societies had much less control and in 1888, perturbed at reports of numerous encroachments, appointed a Joint Trade Committee to investigate the position. It found that in twelve large firms employing 781 workers, fifteen per cent were un-skilled men or unapprenticed boys.[3]

But the most important branch of the industry in regard to the employment of non-apprenticed labour was newspaper printing where the introduction of rotary presses gave employment to thousands of 'semi-skilled' men. The mechanics of the rotary press with continuous reel of paper were so different from those of the old flat-bed presses that men trained on the latter were of little use. Frequently the man in charge, the machine-minder, was a trained engineer, rather than a printer, and not eligible for membership of a typographical union. The other workers on a large machine such as the Hoe Double Supplement were a 'brake hand' who controlled the tension of the paper, an oiler, a 'sup hand' who looked after the part where the supplement was printed, two 'fly hands' who carried in the stereo plates from the foundry and cleared the printed papers from the delivery end, a 'reel hand' who mounted the great reels of paper, and numerous carriers-away who washed down the rollers and helped the fly hands.[4] Thus, one large rotary might have from ten to twenty men, not one of whom was a skilled printer according to the tenets of the old craft unions. As rotaries became firmly established a system of promotion by merit through the various grades became customary. Starting as a carrier-away, an able man worked his way up through fly hand, reel hand, sup hand, oiler, brake hand and finally became a machine-minder. Although such men carried more responsibility and had more technical skill than

[1] The Report of the National Association for Social Science on Trades Societies in 1860 was printed by women.

[2] L.S.C., *Report of a Special Committee on Unemployment*, 1895.

[3] E. Howe and J. Child, *op. cit.*, p. 208.

[4] G. Isaacs, *op. cit.*, p. 59.

112 REGULATION BY UNION RULE

many of the apprenticed printers they remained ineligible for membership of the craft unions.[1]

In their continuous struggle to reduce wage costs employers were frequently tempted to engage more and more juvenile labour on the unskilled, routine, 'dead-end' jobs such as feeding paper into machines or carrying away the printed sheets. Girls as well as boys were engaged, often in flagrant contravention of the Factory Act. The unions of course kept a sharp watch for any such malpractice in shops where their members were employed. In regard to the legitimate employment of boys and girls they often preferred the latter for they were not so likely to 'pick up the trade' and later try to encroach on the skilled jobs.

ORGANIZATION OF EMPLOYERS

Until 1880 there was almost no attempt on the part of the printing employers to organize, even at local level. Indeed with the dissolution of the former associations of London master printers and bookbinders, there was hardly a masters' organization of any consequence throughout the country. In the last decade of the period, however, there was a revival of interest in the formation of local associations, almost invariably provoked by the desire to resist some 'forward movement' by a local society. Frequently they were successful, as in the case of the Edinburgh masters in 1872, but once the crisis had passed the organization tended to disintegrate for it had no reason for continuous existence.[2] That there were so few attempts to form associations was mainly due to moderation on the part of the unions. To some extent this was due to the legal disabilities under which unions laboured until 1875; but it was also due to the deliberate policy of cautious consolidation pursued by the main unions until about 1880.

London was an exception, for there the dissolution of the masters' association was precipitated by the intransigence of the L.S.C. In 1866 the A.M.P. received separate memorials from the three letterpress societies of compositors, pressmen and machine managers, all requesting a reduction of hours of work and a rise in wage rates. In particular the unions wished to obtain some agreement on standard rates for overtime, in order to discourage employers from working systematic overtime.

Although the A.M.P. attempted to resist the increases, chiefly on the grounds that any increase in costs would drive trade from London to the provinces, in November 1866, a joint committee of Master Printers and compositors, 'empowered to settle finally all matters relating to the

[1] G. Isaacs, *op. cit.*, p. 60.

[2] M. Sessions, *The Federation of Master Printers: How it Began*, 1952.

CONSOLIDATION OF THE CRAFT UNIONS

subjects comprised in the Memorial' reached agreement on the main points. The minimum stab wage was raised from 33s to 36s, hours were reduced from 63 to 60, basic piecework rates were raised ½d per 1,000 letters and a schedule of extras for overtime and Sunday work was compiled.[1] It should be noted that these clauses, eight in all, only supplemented the twenty-five clauses and numerous explanatory paragraphs of the old London Scale as settled in 1847.

Shortly afterwards agreements were signed with representatives of the unions of pressmen and machine managers. The pressmen were granted a stab wage of 36s for a 60 hour week, and the extras for overtime and Sunday work similar to those given to the compositors. Pressmen employed on time were to receive 7½d per hour. There was no alteration in the piecework scale which was apparently falling into disuse.[2] The machine managers' agreement included provision for a 60 hour week but made no mention of a minimum wage. The 'apportionment' of the 60 hours was 'to be mutually agreed upon between the Employers and the Journeymen in each office'. Overtime and Sunday work was to carry the same extras as in the other agreements.[3]

Immediately after being signed these agreements were circulated 'to every Printer known to employ journeymen'. Each was signed by the four negotiating officers of the A.M.P. and by representatives of the appropriate union. In the following year the Committee of the A.M.P. congratulated the members upon the 'more settled state of feeling throughout the London printing business, after the anxious and protracted negotiations'.

The repite was only brief.[4] During the next two years there was a succession of small disputes over interpretations of the Scale and the customs of the trade. The Committee complained that:

'The compositors evince a spirit of aggression in preferring claims and attempting to introduce innovations on the grounds of customs of the existence of which most employers have never heard, and they exhibit a determination to enforce those claims by appealing to legal process.'[5]

Relations between the L.S.C. and the A.M.P. became increasingly embittered; in 1870 the latter declared, 'The Society have not shown any disposition to assist the Masters to meet the views of their cus-

---

[1] *Agreement with the Compositors*, November 21, 1866 (*London Compositor*, Doc. LXXXI).

[2] *Agreement with the Pressmen*, November 27, 1866.

[3] This agreement, together with the others, was reprinted by the A.M.P. in pamphlet form. (St. Brides.)

[4] A.M.P., *Report of the Committee*, June 1868.

[5] A.M.P., *Report of the Committee*, June 1869.

114   REGULATION BY UNION RULE

tomers', and again mentioned that the union had been successful in
several cases in which claims against employers had been taken to
Court. It was suggested, rather forlornly, that these legal defeats showed
'the desirability of having a trade tribunal to decide trade questions,
instead of the present Law Courts'. At the Annual General Meeting in
October 1870, the masters decided to dissolve the Association.[1]

UNION ORGANIZATION

The Typographical Association, 1849–1890[2]

With the collapse of the National Typographical Association in 1848,
following on the disintegration of the national bookbinders' union
some years earlier, pessimists concluded that only a reversion to local
societies held any prospect of success. On the other hand the apostles of
amalgamation, undaunted by previous failures, promptly arranged
another delegate meeting to consider reorganizing the unions on a
national basis. Delegates from the L.S.C. attended, but in an advisory
capacity only, for their society had decided to retain its autonomy. The
Address approved by the meeting and later circulated to other societies
contained a clear statement of the need for wider union:

'. . . no locality is or can be safe under a system of isolation. . . . The
small towns of England, unless strengthened by the co-operation of
larger communities will become the nurseries of apprentices and thus an
evil will be created which no subsequent legislation can remedy.'[3]

As the Sheffield Society had been the most active in promoting the
delegate meeting, the headquarters of the new Provincial Typographical
Association were established there, and the Committee of the local
society acted as the first executive. The objects of the P.T.A. were:

'The limitation of the number of apprentices, restriction of the hours
of labour, regulation of the standard of wages, and a general supervision
of all matters affecting the interests of the printing profession.'[4]

Admission was limited to those who had served a seven year apprenticeship to the trade. Although both compositors and pressmen (or machine-
minders) were eligible to join, in practice the membership was for
several decades recruited mainly from composing rooms. The first

[1] A.M.P., *Report of the Committee* . . ., 1870.
[2] For a detailed account, see Musson, *op. cit.*, ch. VII.
[3] Quoted in T.A. *Fifty Years' Record.*
[4] Provincial Typographical Association, *Rules*, 1849.

CONSOLIDATION OF THE CRAFT UNIONS 115

subscription was 2d per week, in return for which the only benefit was strike pay (at three quarters of local standard rate) for three months. This payment was made only for strikes which had been authorized by the Central Executive.

In the first four years, before the delegate meeting of 1853, there was a high turnover of member branches, partly because of failure to pay subscriptions, partly because the Executive used its authority to expel local societies which did not show reasonable concern for enforcing the rules. The Executive refused to accept affiliation of local societies where there was an excessive number of apprentices in the local offices.[1] Some, indeed, were expelled for having given false information on this head when they applied for membership.[2] In other cases branches were struck off when they refused to obey instructions to oppose increases in the number of local apprentices. Clearly in these early formative years the Executive pursued a wise policy of establishing a sound foundation rather than attempting too rapid an expansion.

In several large towns—for example, Liverpool and Birmingham— there were two local societies operating, often at loggerheads over some comparatively minor issue. The result was inevitably a weakening of the bargaining position of the workmen. In consequence conditions in these towns were usually so 'unfair', especially in regard to the number of apprentices, that neither society could be admitted to the P.T.A. As these centres constituted a serious threat to the effectiveness of union control of the area, the P.T.A. made several attempts to unify the local societies as a pre-condition to removing local 'abuses' and qualifying the Society for membership. In most cases, however, the local quarrel had become so bitter, with each society regarding the members of the other as a 'nest of rats', that unification took a long time.

At every delegate meeting the pros and cons of the tramping system provided lively debates. In 1861 the delegates decided to institute a system of Mileage Relief, paying the usual 1d per mile to travellers. In order to keep the finances of this department separate from those of the union, they set up the Mileage Relief Association. Societies which were not members of the union were permitted to join the Relief Association on payment of a subscription of 1d per member weekly, but administration of the scheme was vested entirely in the executive of the P.T.A.[3]

It was the 1872 Delegate Meeting which inaugurated an era of

[1] P.T.A., *Report of Delegate Meeting*, 1853.
[2] P.T.A., *Sixth Half-Yearly Report*, 1852.
[3] P.T.A., *Report of Delegate Meeting*, 1861.
    Rules of the Association for the Relief of Journeymen Printers, 1862.

116   REGULATION BY UNION RULE

expansion in the history of the union. First, it decided to increase the attractiveness of membership by providing additional benefits. Believing that the unemployment benefits would tend to lighten the burden of tramp relief the Executive decided to pay them from the Mileage Relief Association funds, thus avoiding the necessity of increasing the subscription. Second, the Executive was instructed to embark on a comprehensive campaign to enrol new members and 'to extend the principles of unionism throughout the country'. In the next five years the membership grew from 2,812 to 5,309. The period of consolidation was over; the period of expansion had begun.[1]

By 1890 the Typographical Association (the 'Provincial' was dropped in 1877) had a membership of almost 10,000, a General Fund of £17,000 and a Superannuation Fund of £7,000.[2] It was then the largest, though not the wealthiest union in the industry, and in the following quarter century it played a dominant role in trade union affairs.

Scottish Typographical Association, 1853–1890[3]

Of the fifteen typographical societies in Scotland, only two—Edinburgh and Glasgow—survived the collapse of the National Typographical Association in 1848, and five years elapsed before the establishment of the Scottish Typographical Association which linked up these survivors with smaller societies in Dumfries, Kilmarnock and Paisley. The S.T.A. was a loose federation of trade societies, governed by a Central Board which had authority to direct the opening and closing of offices, and the payment of strike allowance to members withdrawn in the process of 'resisting encroachments'.[4]

Its activities for the first seven years were on a modest scale. Like those of the Provincial Typographical Association, its leaders emphasized the virtues of caution and financial prudence. Hence by 1860 it had grown to twenty-three branches with a membership of over 1,000, and funds of 10s per head. Official strikes had been few and far between, and only £28 10s had been spent in the defence of working conditions.[5]

Another decade of financial consolidation and steady growth brought membership to 1,540 and funds to £1 per head, but in 1872 the union was almost broken by two large-scale disputes in Edinburgh. The first was a strike against the proprietors of *The Scotsman* for an infraction of the news scale; the second was a more general strike of book and jobbing

[1] P.T.A., *Report of Delegate Meeting*, 1872. See Musson, p. 95.
[2] T.A., *Half-Yearly Report*, December 1890.
[3] For a detailed account, see S. Gillespie, *A Centenary of Progress*. See also, S.T.A., *A Fifty Years Record*.
[4] S.T.A., *Regulations*, 1852.   [5] S.T.A., *Report of Delegate Meeting*, 1860.

CONSOLIDATION OF THE CRAFT UNIONS

hands for an increase in basic wages and a reduction of hours. The latter, involving some 750 journeymen, lasted three months and ended in the defeat of the unionists by an influx of 'rats' gathered by the employers from non-union areas in England. The most important outcome was the employment of women compositors in many firms, a practice which persisted for almost half a century.[1]

In 1877 the Delegate Meeting, following the lead given by the P.T.A., decided to introduce a number of benefits. Opposition from some of the larger branches which operated benefit schemes of their own delayed their introduction, but a Special Delegate Meeting in 1878 decided to push ahead with schemes for funeral benefits, removal grant and tramp relief.[2] In 1881 these were augmented by the institution of out-of-work pay and sick benefit. This meeting was described by a contemporary as 'marking an epoch in the history of the Association, on account of its being the last of our proceedings as a purely trade protective organization'.[3]

In 1887 another effort was made to settle the dispute between the S.T.A. and the Edinburgh Press and Machinemen's Society which had broken away from the local typographical society in 1872 and had subsequently applied for admission to the S.T.A. as a separate branch. The union, however, stood by the principle that there should be only one branch in each town. An arbitration award by a panel of prominent printing trade unionists was rejected by the machinemen and for another twenty years they retained a separate organization. As in England the problem of the admittance of rotary machine-minders who had not served a full apprenticeship proved difficult to solve. Although it was debated at several delegate meetings, and although members recognized the absurdity of not admitting the machinemen, they would not waive the formal apprenticeship qualification which was so important in the tradition of their craft.[4]

In 1889 there was a further extension of benefits; Superannuation and Emigration Grants were introduced. Membership in 1890 stood at 2,622, funds at the healthy figure of £3,500.

The London Society of Compositors, 1848–1900.[5]

The London Society of Compositors was reconstituted after its withdrawal from the ill-fated National Typographical Association in 1848:

[1] S.T.A., *Annual Report,* 1872.

[2] S.T.A., *Report of Special Delegate Meeting,* 1878.

[3] S.T.A., *Fifty Years' Record,* p. 74. See also S.T.A., *Report of Delegate Meeting,* 1881.

[4] S.T.A., *Report of Delegate Meeting,* 1889.

[5] For a detailed account see E. Howe and H. E. Waite, *The London Society of Compositors,* 1948.

118   REGULATION BY UNION RULE

'for the purpose of protecting and regulating the wages of labour agreeably to the London Scale of Prices . . . as also the Scale of Prices regulating News and Parliamentary work; together with such customs and usages as belong to the profession'.[1]

In 1853, after a joint campaign against the introduction of non-union labour, on the *Morning Post* and the *Sun*, the Society of London Daily News Compositors amalgamated with the L.S.C.

As a majority of the compositors were on piecework, subscriptions varied in proportion to earnings.[2] The main benefit, apart from Strike Pay, was Unemployment Relief, but later the institution of Removal Grants helped to reduce slightly the cost of unemployment. Emigration grants totalling £800 were made during a burst of enthusiasm in the early fifties, but they were discontinued when it became apparent that the union could not eliminate the surplus labour by this method. They were revived in 1871 when the steady increase in Unemployment Relief—from 1s 6d per member in 1860 to 23s 4d in 1870 led to a desperate search for measures which would ease the burden on union finances.[3]

With the introduction of Funeral Benefit in 1868 and Superannuation in 1877 the L.S.C. joined the other unions in the effort to attract new members and to tighten internal discipline. It was soon made acutely aware of the difficulties attending this policy. In 1879 unemployment relief totalled more than £5,000 (21s 7d per head), caused a substantial drop in the General Fund, and provoked concern for the future solvency of the society. In the following year a special committee appointed to review the structure of the L.S.C. finances reported that, with the introduction of numerous benefits,

'. . . the character and objects of your Society have greatly altered. So great have been the metamorphoses, that at the present time it exists more in the nature of a benefit society than, as formerly, a society solely for the purpose of protecting trade interests.'[4]

According to another writer the L.S.C. was far from holding its own in the control of working conditions:

'If we glance from end to end of our so-called 'fair' houses, what do we find to be the state in many of them ? Is it not a fact that they contain abuses of all kinds,—abuses that are as a rule all in favour of the

[1] L.S.C., *Report of Delegate Meeting*, February 1, 1848.
[2] London Society of Compositors, *Rules*, 1848.
[3] Financial statistics are taken from *Annual Reports* of L.S.C.
[4] L.S.C., *Report of the Special Committee on the financial conditions* . . . 1881.

CONSOLIDATION OF THE CRAFT UNIONS 119

employers and antagonistic to the interests of the workmen employed therein? . . . Our employers well know that we have no consistent mode of working in the London Trade, and that what one house is allowed to do, another one, possibly next door, is called to account for.'[1]

In the next decade there was a reaction against this state of affairs. C. J. Drummond who succeeded to the secretaryship on the retirement of Henry Self was by no means a militant, but he was an energetic organizer and a believer in union co-operation. Under his leadership the L.S.C. membership rose to 9,000 in 1890. The union emerged from its previous isolation: in 1885 it affiliated to the London Trades Council; in 1886 it sent representatives to a national conference of typographical unions; and in the following years it entered local politics to conduct a campaign for the placing of local body printing contracts with fair firms.

Bookbinders and Machine Rulers.[2]

As cloth binding superseded leather binding the leather workers, especially the highly skilled finishers, ceased to play a dominant role in union affairs. The great Victorian commercial expansion increased the demand for account books and ushered in a period of relative prosperity for the London Vellum Binders who specialized in making these articles. Membership of their society rose from 130 in 1850 to 843 in 1891.[3] With funds rising to over £4 per head it was for twenty years (1872–91) the wealthiest union in the industry. It was one of the first to pay out-of-work benefits and in 1890 introduced the principle of paying benefits on a sliding scale related to the state of the General Funds.

In London there were two other autonomous societies of book-binders—the old Consolidated Lodge ('The City') and the breakaway Society of Day-working Bookbinders ('The West End'). For many years relations between them were embittered by memories and distortions of the dispute which in 1849 had led to the split. Despite the able administration of T. J. Dunning, one of the leading union theorists of the times, the City Lodge made slow progress, allegedly because it had a higher proportion of the older members and in consequence had to pay more per head in benefits for sickness, unemployment, and old age. The fourth bookbinding organization in London was a branch of the Bookbinders' and Machine Rulers Consolidated Union. Although

[1] F. Willis, *The Present Position and Future Prospects of the L.S.C.*, 1881.
[2] For a detailed account, see C. J. Bundock, *op. cit.*, Book I. E. Howe and J. Child, *op. cit.*, chs. XVII–XXII.
[3] Vellum Binders' Trade Society, *76th Annual Statement*, 1899.

120 REGULATION BY UNION RULE

this union had a fairly extensive organization in the provinces, it adopted very cautious trade policies. One of the last printing unions to introduce benefits on the grand scale, its main source of weakness was the interminable rivalry of the large branches over the location of the Seat of Government. Inter-branch suspicion, and sometimes open hostility, prevented the centralization of authority which was a pre-requisite of centralized finance of insurance benefits. In 1890 however a delegate meeting decided to remodel the union, which had then a membership of 2,500, and in the following year both superannuation and out-of-work benefits were introduced.[1]

Lithographers.[2]

In the lithographic section of the industry skilled workers were divided into two groups—those who prepared the blocks (the artists) and those who worked the special printing machines. The earliest known society was that of the London Lithographic Printers (established *c.* 1833) which in 1884 had 200 members and paid most of the customary benefits. In 1888 it amalgamated with two other small societies to form the London Union of Lithographic Machine Minders. The new union prospered initially and in 1890 had 821 members.[3] About this time two other small societies were established—the London Society of Litho-graphic Music Printers, and the Lithographic Stone and Zinc Pre-parers' Society, which enrolled semi-skilled men.

In 1860 a number of small local societies of provincial lithographic printers linked up in a loose federal association with the object of giving each other information and assistance on trade problems.[4] From this association was formed, in 1879, the Amalgamated Society of Lithographic Printers which grew rapidly to a membership of 2,235 in forty branches by 1890. From its foundation it paid a number of benefits—Unemployment, Sick, Funeral, Travelling, and Emigration.[5]

THE SOCIAL PHILOSOPHY OF UNIONISM

Essential to an understanding of the printing unions of this era is a realization of their social philosophy. They propounded no revolutionary doctrine, but accepted the prevailing social and economic structure. They relied on the unaided efforts of the workmen themselves to achieve, by collective action, a satisfactory standard of life.[6] There was

[1] B.M.R.C.U. Report of Delegate Meeting, *Trade Circular*, 1890.
[2] *History and Progress of A.S.L.P.*, 1930.
[3] Board of Trade, *Fourth Report on Trade Unions*, C-6475, 1891.
[4] Central Association of Lithographic Printers, *Annual Report*, 1879.
[5] A.S.L.P., *Rules*, 1879.
[6] The best account, by a union official, is T. J. Dunning's *Trade Unions and Strikes, their Philosophy and Intention*, 1860.

CONSOLIDATION OF THE CRAFT UNIONS 121

little official encouragement of schemes for co-operative production, or for participation of workers in the control of industry. The printing journeymen accepted the general social framework of *laissez-faire* capitalism with a complacency verging at times on servility.

'We have said before that the true state of employer and employed is that of amity, and that they are the truest friends, each of the other—for each derives his revenue from the other. . . . It should be the duty of both to prevent this harmony from being interrupted. Each should consider this state their true relation, and consider its interruption the greatest of calamities.'[1]

Yet Dunning, and other leaders, were keenly aware of capitalism's particular defects, and the basic objective of their unions was the remedying of those ills which resulted from its failure to provide continuous employment at adequate rate of payment. From the start, however, there were some who preferred to place the blame for the distress upon the faults of the individuals rather than the failure of the system. The main causes of the depressed condition of a section of the workers were to be found, so they alleged, in the workers' indolence, addiction to alcohol, lack of ambition, misuse of natural endowments, or sheer selfishness.[2] Indeed the opinions of the employers regarding the vices of the working class could hardly surpass in bitterness some of the criticisms of tramps, casuals, and unemployed made by the more prosperous journeymen. The Pharisaical faction was often vocal and influential, and although staunch supporters of unionism, tended towards conservatism in policy and exclusiveness in organization.

At the other extreme were those visionaries whose belief in unionism had an almost mystical quality. They regarded it as a means of curing almost all social ills, and of transforming conditions of working life from strenuous toil, poverty and subordination to ease, comfort and dignity. Differences between the two groups were no doubt largely a reflection of personal temperament.

The majority of the members, however, tended to be highly conservative in regard to changes in the structure or function of their union, frequently rejected changes proposed by the Executive Committee or Delegate Meeting, and only after prolonged debate and fruitless tinkering with the old devices, gave their consent to any radical change.[3]

[1] T. J. Dunning, *op. cit.*, p. 73.

[2] 'Inattention, profligacy, pride and drunkenness' were given in 1842 as causes of printers' unemployment by a writer in the *Compositors' Chronicle*, (p. 168).

[3] An outstanding example of conservatism was the T.A.'s retention of Tramp Relief until 1914.

122 REGULATION BY UNION RULE

The stated objects of the printers' unions in the late nineteenth century can be divided into three groups: to raise the social status of their members, to relieve distress, and to maintain and improve conditions of employment.

In the nineteenth century, while actual physical conditions of many printing workers deteriorated, the trade was generally held in high social esteem. The unions endeavoured to remove this discrepancy by raising the economic status of their members and by encouraging a sense of professional pride, personal dignity and public service. In almost every phase of union activity the motive of moral improvement played an important part. Outstanding practical examples of this concern with 'non-economic' progress were the libraries of the London societies of compositors (1848) and bookbinders (1855). Towards the end of the century each had over 10,000 volumes. Reading rooms in the union offices provided periodicals, papers and reference books. Even the union journals, for example, the *Trade Circular* of the London Bookbinders, were concerned less with matters of local union policy or administration than with politics, economics, and social philosophy.[1]

The immediate, enduring and essential concern of the unions was, however, with the maintenance or improvement of the terms of employment of their members. How did they hope to achieve this? A detailed study of union strategy over this period shows that there were two stages. For roughly the first twenty-five years (1850–75) the unions relied mainly upon their control of the supply of labour to give them the bargaining power which would ensure 'justice' in the determination of the price of labour. T. J. Dunning put the emphasis on the need for a Society to provide a fund for strike pay and unemployment relief.

'Singly the employer can stand out longer in the bargain; and as he who can stand out longest in the bargain will be sure to command his own terms, the workmen combine to put themselves on something like an equality in the bargain for the sale of their labour. . . . This is the rationale of Trade Societies. . . .'[2]

E. Edwards, considering the long term problem of improving the unions' bargaining power, came out strongly in favour of strict limitation of apprentices.

'The only Remedy that will heal the wounds of the printing trade is Restriction of Boy Labour . . . Justice, Right and Duty thunder into

[1] See Preface to Vol. I of *Bookbinders' Trade Circular*.
[2] T. J. Dunning, *op. cit.*, p. 10. See also Dunning's evidence before the Royal Commission on Trade Unions.

CONSOLIDATION OF THE CRAFT UNIONS   123

our ears this important obligation. The *justice* of limitation is written in the absolute necessity herein proved; the *right* in the protection of our labour from its worst enemy—individual aggrandisement; and the *duty* in the requirement of citizenship.'[1]

By 1875, however, it was obvious that this could not be achieved without greatly improved organization. Furthermore, conditions of production were changing and employers were searching for new methods of organizing work to reduce the wages bill. The few simple working rules on which most unions (except the L.S.C.) relied were proving to be ambiguous and easily evaded. Furthermore, the unions had not made as much progress in organizing new areas as they had expected. Increased membership was a pre-condition of further improvement in conditions. To increase the attractiveness of membership most of the larger ones then introduced the benefits which proved the key to future success.

From the reports of the delegate meetings at which the proposed benefits were discussed it is evident that it took a long time to convince delegates (who were among the keenest and ablest of unionists) that the extra cost would be worth the added strength. But until the Central Executive had some tangible sanctions which it could apply to recalcitrant members or rebellious branches, its chances of succeeding in a vigorous and consistent trade protection policy were negligible. The attempt to do so led, as often as not, to the resignation of the disgruntled member, or the withdrawal of an entire branch. Hence the large turnover of members of the Provincial and Scottish Typographical Associations in their first two decades.

After 1875, with numbers growing and discipline assured by the sanctions made possible by the threat of loss of benefit, the unions were able to attempt stricter control of apprentice quotas, and the elaboration of more detailed, precise, and complex rules for regulating working conditions.[2]

These two broad fields of union activity—Control of Labour Supply and the elaboration of Union Rules,—are the subjects of the next chapters.

[1] E. Edwards, *The Apprentice System, the Disease and the Remedy*, London 1850. (Reprinted by T.A., 1886), p. 20.

[2] In their otherwise masterly analysis of trade union methods, in *Industrial Democracy*, 1892, S. and B. Webb made a serious misjudgement of the unions' policy in regard to 'Restriction of Numbers'. The Webbs thought that it was falling into disuse, and the example they chose—the compositors—was quite incorrect. Their description of conditions was more applicable to the decade 1860–70, *before* the unions began their successful membership campaign.

CHAPTER VIII

CONTROL OF LABOUR SUPPLY

*When an employer demands labour on terms repugnant to
our moral feelings, and which are opposed to the
common weal of society, then it is that a Trade Society
steps in and forbids the supply; and we believe that did
not Trade Societies so control the supply and demand
for labour, there would be no limit to the state of
degradation to which the bulk of the working class would
be brought . . .*

A. WAINHOUSE, *Trades Unions Justified*, 1861.

ECONOMIC THEORY

Dunning's work, *Trade Unions and Strikes, their Philosophy and
Intention*, contains the most complete theory written by a working man
of the nineteenth century on the economic function of trade unions.[1]
He maintained that the true price of labour, like that of any other
commodity, was regulated by the long-term relation of supply and
demand. But in any given market situation the actual price was determined by the immediate bargaining power of the buyer and seller. Trade
unions were necessary to protect workers from having to sell their
labour at a price below its true value because of their urgent need for
money to buy food and necessities.[2]

In this view a trade union, far from interfering with the market
mechanism, and producing a 'distortion' of prices, was a necessary
corrective to an existing tendency to distortion due to the superior
bargaining power of the employers. Furthermore, 'undue competition'
among employers acted continuously to reduce wages in a trade
depression, but there was no comparable pressure to raise wages in
busy times.

---

[1] See the tribute paid by J. S. Mill, *Principles of Political Economy*, 1862,
Vol. II, p. 542 n.
[2] *Trades Unions and Strikes* . . . p. 9. This theory is very similar to that of
Adam Smith, with his distinction between 'natural' and 'market' prices.

CONTROL OF LABOUR SUPPLY

How did the trade unions help to raise the bargaining power of the workers?

'The object intended is carried out by providing a fund for the support of members when out of employ, for a certain number of weeks in the year. This is the usual and regular way in which the labour of members of a Trade Society is protected, that the man's present necessities may not compel him to take less than the wages which the demand and supply of labour in the trade have previously adjusted.'[1]

In the process of bargaining to fix a new rate, if each side had full knowledge of the other's resources, a simple calculation would enable them both to see who could hold out longer, and the weaker party would be foolish to provoke an open conflict. Strikes and lock-outs arose chiefly because of imperfect assessment of the chances of victory, due to inadequate information. Because in real life information would often be inadequate, strikes and lock-outs were sometimes bound to occur. Dunning was emphatic that 'while strikes are always to be deprecated ... there is no proper alternative, in certain cases'.[2]

The essence of union strategy, then, lay in its control over the short-term supply of labour, and more especially, over the unemployed. The two union devices designed to control the unemployed, in order to prevent them from accepting work on terms below the union standard, were the Strike Allowance and the Out-of-work Relief.

STRIKE ALLOWANCE

By this time all trade unions were agreed that the Strike Allowance was the basis of effective collective control over working conditions. In earlier times it had taken various forms—sometimes a lump sum or 'bonus', sometimes a 'backed' or 'double' tramp card, sometimes a weekly allowance. In time, the last-named came to be the dominant form.

The strike allowance had to be adequate to meet two contingencies: to induce members to quit their situations when called upon to do so by the society, and to prevent them from drifting back into 'unfair' offices when the excitement of the original dispute had abated. By the second half of the nineteenth century strike pay was usually intermediate in value between the out-of-work relief, and the local standard wage. In the regional unions the local branches supplemented the central strike allowance from their own funds, so that strikers received almost full stab wages.

[1] T. J. Dunning, *op. cit.*, p. 11.   [2] *Ibid.*, p. 28.

126 REGULATION BY UNION RULE

The following table shows the maximum amount payable according to rule to members on strike:

Union	Date	Weekly Amount	Duration
S.T.A.	1873	20s	10 weeks
T.A.	1877	20s	15–20 weeks
A.A.P.	1893	30s	13 weeks
L.S.C.	1892	30s	10 weeks

Source: Union Rule Books

What of the man who was 'victimized'—dismissed by his employer for failure to work contrary to rule or for trade union activities? In many such cases it was obviously impossible for the Executive to obtain certain proof of the cause of dismissal, yet it was clear that in a genuine case of victimization the man who had suffered deserved a reward at least equal to that of a striker, and that unless such men *were* compensated by the union, it would be impossible to maintain organization or enforce standard working conditions. On the other hand no union was prepared to make an express rule to this effect because of the manifest danger that almost every member who was dismissed from his job would put in a claim for victimization allowance. Most of them were thus forced to leave wide discretionary powers in this matter to the Executives.

'The benefits of this rule (Strike Allowance) shall only be awarded to such members as are directed by the Committee to give up their situations; members unjustifiably discharged, or who have made a sacrifice on the part of the Society, when proved to the satisfaction of the Committee, shall be remunerated *as they may determine*.'[1]

OUT-OF-WORK RELIEF

Although different factions within each union argued vigorously over the details of the rules relating to Strike Allowance and Victimization Pay, they were almost unanimous on the broad principle on which this payment was based. On the matter of payment of an allowance to the involuntarily unemployed, however, there remained, at the time of forming the New Model unions, bitter conflict of opinion. In an industry subject to severe seasonal and cyclical variations a union was impotent unless some provision was made for relief of the unemployed. It was many years, however, before a majority of the members were convinced that the best solution lay in the provision of a weekly out-of-work allowance.

[1] L.S.C., *Rules*, 1892. T.A., *Rules*, 1877. See Musson, *op. cit.*, p. 150.

CONTROL OF LABOUR SUPPLY

Opponents raised several objections: first that such schemes would put too severe a strain upon the finances, or entail subscriptions so high that membership would inevitably decline; second, that they would be impossible to administer, and would result in a great deal of fraud and imposition; third, that they would encourage indolence and extravagance, for a man on relief would not be so keen to get another job, and those in work would not be so careful of retaining their situations.[1] Unions were eventually persuaded to give the new method a trial less by the arguments adduced in its favour than by the manifest need for some control of the unemployed, and the failure of the old methods. The administrative difficulties were overcome by the improved efficiency of union administration. In provincial areas this was largely due to speedier transport and communication which followed the extension of the railways, the telegraph, and the introduction of cheap postage.

Those unions which in 1867 had still not adopted out-of-work benefits were probably influenced by the evidence given by the Secretaries of the great Amalgamated Societies of Carpenters and Engineers—Applegath and Allan—before the Royal Commission on Organization and Rules of Trade Unions.[2]

Some provincial printing unions were highly conservative in this matter and it was not until 1872 that the P.T.A. delegate meeting voted in favour of introducing out-of-work benefit, while the S.T.A. took another ten years to be convinced of its necessity.[3]

REDUCING UNEMPLOYMENT

But as well as controlling the unemployed, the unions developed several procedures which they hoped would reduce unemployment. In the short-run these were schemes for promoting labour mobility by improving the information about vacancies, and by giving financial help to unemployed members wishing to transfer to another town.

Call Book

In the first place each local society tried to ensure that all vacancies in fair offices in the town were filled by union members or honourable tramps. This was effected by keeping at the office, or in the bar of the

[1] Correspondence in Union Journals, c. 1870–80. *Reports of T.A. Delegate Meetings*, 1856, 61.

[2] Royal Commission on Organization and Rules of Trade Unions, *First Report*, 1868.

[3] P.T.A., *Report of Delegate Meeting*, 1872. S.T.A., *Report of Delegate Meeting*, 1882. Gillespie, *op. cit.*, pp. 78–83.

128   REGULATION BY UNION RULE

society house, a Call Book in which the unemployed members signed
their names daily. An employer who wanted union men to fill a vacancy
on his staff sent a call to the same office. As men were sent to answer
calls in the order in which their names appeared in the book, the man
who had been longest out of work received the first option on the next
vacancy. Of course the employer might reject him as unsuitable, in
which case the person next on the list was sent, until one was engaged.[1]

In order to ensure that the union received notification of all fair
vacancies, each employed member was under a moral obligation—and
was often required by Rule—to notify his union of any vacancies at his
place of work. Before signing the Call Book each day a man was required to make a genuine effort to find work; the book was not opened
until 10 a.m. Any calls from employers were attended to at definite
times throughout the day unless they were specially urgent. A number
of ancillary rules developed to prevent the interception of calls, and to
ensure that discipline was maintained and available work fairly distributed.

In London the function of the Society Call Book was to some extent
usurped by the Gifts, the exclusive associations of compositors or
pressmen which had arisen about the middle of the century. Their
objects were the assistance of members in search of employment by the
operation of a Call Book, and sometimes the provision of out-of-work
relief. The oldest of these organizations among the compositors,
known as the Old London Society, claimed descent from the Trade
Society of 1816.[2] Other Gifts of compositors were The Lions (1858),
The Pioneers (1874), The West End (1870), and The Milton (1875).[3]
Membership of each was limited to one hundred; subscription was 2d
weekly. Each had its House-of-Call and its own Call Book, and attempted
to maintain a monopoly of the vacancies occurring in the district
surrounding its House-of-Call. For this reason, and because of their
exclusiveness, the Gifts became highly unpopular with a large section
of the members. They were heartily detested by provincial journeymen
also, for they made it almost impossible for tramps to get any work in
London.[4]

In 1892 a Special Committee appointed to revise the Rules advised
that in the interests of internal harmony,[5] the Gifts should be dissolved.
In future any journeyman who joined an association formed to procure

[1] Call Book rules varied slightly in detail. This account is taken mainly from
L.S.C. Rule Books.
[2] *Rules of the Old London Society of Compositors*, 1885.
[3] Rules of most of these Gifts are in the Webb Collection.
[4] *Scottish Typographical Circular*, Third Series, p. 141. According to this
source there were at least five Gifts of compositors in London in 1861.
[5] L.S.C., *Report of Special Committee*, March 2, 1892, p. 32.

CONTROL OF LABOUR SUPPLY

employment for its members, was liable to be excluded from the Society.[1]

Full data on the number of vacancies filled through the Call Book are not readily available. But an investigation by the Board of Trade showed that in the year 1892–93, when the L.S.C. had over 10,000 members, and an average of over 400 signing the Call Book each day, only ten men, on average, were found work each week.[2] Though in earlier times the Call Book was probably more important, as an employment agency, by 1892 'by far the larger number of engagements were secured through personal application made direct to overseers'. Partly to assist unemployed members to find work, most of the London unions regularly published lists of 'fair' houses.[3] By these means, then, the unions practically eliminated 'frictional' unemployment due to ignorance of vacancies.

Tramp Relief and Removal Grant

These two devices aimed to reduce unemployment by promoting mobility of labour throughout the country.

After the collapse of the N.T.A. tramping was reinstituted by the main provincial unions and continued for some decades as their main method of dealing with the unemployed. In 1862 the P.T.A. Delegate Meeting resolved to appoint a Committee to frame rules for a national scheme of tramp relief.[4] This Committee declared that the main objective of any system should be the removal of the unemployed from the large towns:

'Whilst you pay men relatively high sums on coming to large towns, you give them next to nothing to try their fortunes in the smaller ones, where many of them are no doubt deprived of getting jobs for want of the means to carry them there; hence the tendency, to some extent, of boy labour in those towns.'[5]

The S.T.A. and the provincial lithographic printers did not actively encourage tramping although most of the local branches had some provision for the relief of travellers. After 1880 tramping became of less importance as the payment of unemployment relief was adopted by the large unions. The following table shows this trend for the T.A.:

[1] L.S.C., *Report of Trade Committee*, May 1893, p. 13.
[2] Board of Trade, *Report on Agencies for Dealing with the Unemployed.*
[3] e.g. L.S.C., *Guide to the Printing Offices of London. . . .* P.M.M.T.S., *List of Fair Houses*, n.d. (St. Brides).
[4] P.T.A., *Report of Delegate Meeting*, 1862.
[5] *Report of the Committee appointed by the Delegate Meeting*, 1862.

E

130   REGULATION BY UNION RULE

AMOUNT PAID IN BENEFITS BY THE T.A. ($£$)

		1873	1878	1883	1888	1893	1898
A.	Mileage Relief	590	1243	372	634	561	608
B.	Out-of-Work Payment	145	1992	1535	2659	4569	6925
A.	as percentage of B.		407	62	24	24	12	9

Source: T.A., *Fifty Years' Record*, 1898, Appendix

Although the T.A. continued to pay tramp relief until 1913, the other unions abandoned it before the end of the century. Independent Societies, such as the London ones, often paid a lump sum to their members going 'into the country'. This was sometimes known as the tramping 'bonus'. Historically it merged into the Removal Grant, and it is often difficult to decide just when the change was made. In the L.S.C. for example the change of terminology was made in 1881, but there had been frequent modifications of rules before this.[1] The S.T.A. abolished tramp relief in favour of the Removal Grant in 1877; the amount payable was fixed at 4s per year membership, with a maximum of $£3$.[2] The London Pressmen abolished the tramping grant in 1880.

By 1890 the majority of unions had evolved a workable set of rules respecting the Removal Grant. The L.S.C. Committee, endorsing a recommendation that a fine of 10s should be imposed on any member who failed to leave London after claiming the grant, admitted that there had been numerous occasions in the past when the grant had not been used for the appropriate purpose.[3] As the L.S.C. had no country branches, it had no regular source of information regarding the state of trade in the various provincial centres; for this reason it did not (in 1890) require written evidence of a particular situation to which the applicant was allegedly going. The Machine Managers' Society, however, paid the Grant only after such evidence had been produced. As an alternative method of promoting labour mobility the Secretary could purchase a railway ticket (not exceeding $£1$ in value) for a member wishing to travel to a vacancy.[4]

The regional unions had greater scope for applying this method, for their branches acted as information agencies regarding the state of trade. On this information the Secretary could require an unemployed member to take up a vacant situation in another branch, on pain of suspension from out-of-work benefit if he refused without good reason.[5] As far back as 1877 the T.A. Executive had been permitted to pay

[1] Cf. L.S.C., *Rules*, 1848, 1871, 1881.
[2] S.T.A., *Report of Delegate Meeting*, 1877. S.T.A., *Rules*, 1877 (43).
[3] L.S.C., *Report of Trade Committee*, 1893, p. 11.
[4] P.M.M.T.S., *Rules*, 1894. (46).   [5] S.T.A., *Rules*, 1881. (49).

CONTROL OF LABOUR SUPPLY

removal expenses to a member on *strike* who wished to go to another town.[1]

Thus by the end of the Century the regional unions had developed a number of techniques for overcoming frictional unemployment within Great Britain, whether due to inadequate information, lack of resources or geographical immobility of the unemployed.

Emigration

Why not go a step further, and make a permanent reduction in unemployment, by removing some of the surplus labour to another country?

As early as 1842, a year of great distress in the London printing trade, emigration had been mooted as a means of effecting a 'permanent' reduction in the supply of labour:

'. . . the plan is simply this—In all cases where men are out of employ, and where they are thrown out of situations in consequence of *strikes*, to induce them, if possible, to emigrate, either to any of the British Colonies, or to the United States of America; and that a fund be established for the purpose of making an allowance to those who are willing to adopt the proposition, sufficient to pay their passage and something more.'[2]

An opponent of the scheme pointed out that compositors were often not physically suited to the rough life of the colonies: 'a man who for twenty years had been accustomed to wield nothing heavier than a composing stick would make but a sorry hewer of wood or buffalo hunter'.

After the collapse of the N.T.A. in 1848, emigration schemes enjoyed another spell of popularity and in 1849 a delegate meeting of the Provincial Typographical Association considered a comprehensive emigration plan preferable to the old tramping system.

'It must be obvious that if the home market be relieved of a portion only of its unoccupied labourers, those remaining are certain to be benefited by such withdrawal. . . . Abolish the present system of tramping altogether. For it, we say, substitute emigration upon as large scale as the profession can possibly afford.'[3]

A Typographical Emigration Society was established in 1852, but it lasted only one year, and sent off only fourteen emigrants.

In 1853 the L.S.C. formed an Emigration Aid Society to administer

[1] T.A., *Rules*, 1877. (22).   [2] *Compositors' Chronicle*, 1842, pp. 190, 204.
[3] *Typographical Protection Circular*, 1849, p. 23.

132   REGULATION BY UNION RULE

the allocation of grants to members wishing to leave the country, and in the next five years £800 from the funds of the Society were paid to emigrants. Although the London Bookbinders had no special Emigration Fund, in the early fifties small grants were made to members emigrating.[1] Both of these schemes lost official support after a few years, and it was not until 1871 that the L.S.C. revived its emigration fund. In the next two decades it paid out £3,625 to emigrants.[2]

By the end of the century nearly all of the larger unions had some provision for the assistance of emigrants. Rules were elaborated to prevent the misuse of the money; the L.S.C. for example gave a maximum grant of £15 but required a proportional repayment if the recipient returned to the United Kingdom within two years.[3] Trade journals and circulars frequently reprinted letters from union members who had gone to try their fortune in the new colonies. Emigrants' letters home contained details of the state of trade, the hazards of the voyage, the cost of living, and—topic of perennial interest to the British —the local weather.

The effect on the number of unemployed, however, was imperceptible.

Assistance to Leave the Trade

Rather similar to the Emigration Grant, in the effect which it was expected to produce, was the provision made by the Machine Managers' Society for the assistance of members who wished to leave the trade 'to try another business'. A maximum of £15 was payable to a member of at least ten years' standing who could show that he was unable 'from causes other than slackness of trade' to obtain employment at his usual trade.[4] As the usual reason for such inability was some form of ill-health, which disqualified a man from receiving the unemployment allowance, the object was to compensate him with a lump sum and at the same time remove him from the responsibility of the Society. Very few members made application for the grant.

LONG-TERM CONTROL OF LABOUR SUPPLY—RESTRICTION OF APPRENTICES

Emigration might be effective in reducing unemployment—if the unions could afford to encourage it on a large scale. But many journeymen did not want to emigrate, and they could hardly be forced. What other means were there of balancing the long-term supply of labour with the demand? In his fiery essay, *The Apprentice System, the*

---

[1] L.C.S.J.B., *Annual Audits*, 1849–51.   [2] L.S.C., *Annual Reports*.
[3] L.S.C., *Rules*, 1890. (40). S.J.B., *Rules*, 1889. (45).
[4] P.M.M.T.S., *Rules*, 1904. (47).

CONTROL OF LABOUR SUPPLY

Disease and the Remedy, Edwards advocated a determined policy of restriction of entry to the trade. Unions should enforce a rigid quota of apprentices to journeymen, 'fair' employers should be given every assistance, parents should be discouraged from putting their sons into printing trades, and all practicable steps should be taken to eradicate the small, inefficient master printer who tried to make up for his lack of efficiency by using the cheapest possible labour.[1]

The persistence of unemployment in the letterpress printing trades confirms the claim of the unions that apprentices were always greatly in excess of the number who could be absorbed by the industry, even when allowance was made for a reasonable rate of expansion. Edwards calculated that in 1849 there were three boys to every four journeymen, and that if the trend continued the latter would soon be outnumbered.[2]

Despite the general recognition of the seriousness of the position at first only two of the larger unions took the step of fixing a definite quota. The P.T.A. continued with the policy of the old Northern Union and placed the limitation of apprentices first among its objects.[3] The permitted quota was:

> 1 to 3 journeymen   2 apprentices.
> 4 or more journeymen   3 apprentices.

However appropriate this quota may have been when first introduced by the old Northern Union in 1834, the increasing size of printing offices rendered it more and more unrealistic. The enforcement of the rule penalized the larger offices, where apprentice training might have been most effective, and practically forced them to become non-union houses. At the same time hundreds of unindentured youths were receiving scrappy training in the 'cock robin' shops of the small jobbing printers, and growing up completely isolated from union influence. Despite the many arguments advanced against this rule—its unfairness, its weakening of the union, its encouragement of non-union houses—it remained in the Rule Book until 1911, a testimony to the conservatism of the letterpress printers. 'The apprentice rule became, in fact, the T.A. totem—quite useless but regarded with a kind of superstitious veneration. . . .'[4]

The other union which had always insisted on limitation was the London Printing Machine Managers' Trade Society which came into conflict several times with the employers on this issue. In 1858 the Committee of the Association of Master Printers reported that business

---

[1] See also Correspondence in S.T.A., *Circular*, December 1862, January 1863.
[2] E. Edwards, *The Apprentice System. The Disease and the Remedy*, p. 14.
[3] P.T.A., *Rules*, 1850, Objects.
[4] Musson, *op. cit.*, p. 182. Ch. IX of *The Typographical Association* has a detailed account of the practical problems of the T.A.'s apprentice rule.

134 REGULATION BY UNION RULE

had lately been 'obstructed' by union interference with apprentices, and resolved:

'1. That this Committee, having heard that attempts have been made in various quarters to restrict the number of apprentices at Machine, entirely repudiate such restriction.

2. That the following be the answer given to the deputation: That in the opinion of this Committee the question of the number of apprentices in each office is a question *for each individual Master to determine for himself:* and this Committee must decline any interference in the matter.'[1]

The employers clearly realized that it was essential for them to retain freedom to take unlimited apprentices if they wished to maintain their superior bargaining position. This 'privilege', indeed, was most strongly defended, forcing the unions to employ indirect tactics. The S.T.A. for example at first simply required local societies 'to use every legal means to regulate the number of apprentices introduced to the profession' and to make their own rules, to be approved by the Central Board, for carrying this into effect.[2] In 1858 while continuing to permit branches to fix the local quota it prescribed a *minimum* number—two apprentices to the firm and one to every two journeymen.[3] The reasons for this ingenious rule were, firstly, to provide specific evidence to the public that the Association was not attempting to fix a *maximum* and, secondly, to prevent a particularly enthusiastic branch from fixing a quota which, by its severity, would provoke a large number of disputes. In 1850 Edwards estimated apprentices numbered fifty-eight per cent of journeymen. By 1862 there were two apprentices for every three journeymen. It was not until 1873 that the S.T.A. took over from the Branches the fixing of a maximum quota: one apprentice to the firm and one to every three journeymen regularly employed.[4]

Four years later, after a long debate at the Delegate Meeting, the T.A. stiffened its already restrictive rule by requiring that a new firm should be allowed only one apprentice during its first twelve months of operation.[5] Similarly, the various Lithographic printers' societies which had amalgamated in 1880 attempted to reduce the ratio of boys to journeymen, and later adopted a specific rule of one apprentice to five men, with a maximum of six in any one firm.[6]

[1] A.M.P., *Annual Report*, 1858 (italics supplied).
[2] S.T.A., *Regulations*, 1852. (8).
[3] S.T.A., *Rules*, 1858. Footnote to Apprentice Rule.
[4] S.T.A., *Rules*, 1873. (11). See Gillespie, *op. cit.*, ch. 8.
[5] T.A., *Report of Delegate Meeting*, 1877.
[6] A.S.L.P., *Rules*, 1887, p. 26. See *History and Progress*, pp. 14, 17, 18.

CONTROL OF LABOUR SUPPLY

Although the other major unions had no rules expressly limiting the number which a master could take, they were not indifferent to the matter. On several occasions the London Society of Bookbinders discussed the problems of securing joint action with the other Societies to enforce limitation, for it was patently useless for any one of them to do so alone. Inter-union rivalry and the echo of past disputes prevented active co-operation.[1]

About 1890 there was a noticeable revival of union interest in the limitation of apprentices, this time accompanied by a determination to take action. In 1891 the joint Trade Committee appointed by the London Bookbinders' societies to make a full investigation of the position, reported:

'The apprentice question is the first and foremost in all questions waiting solution, and it is one on which your Committee are sharply divided. . . . Accepting the proposition that a measure of limitation is necessary or advisable, we have by a majority agreed to recommend a proportion of one apprentice to four journeymen; but indeed it would appear that a successful movement for the reduction of hours would afford scope for a more liberal proportion of apprentices.'[2]

The resolution which was actually adopted by a general meeting of the trade in April 1891, contained a rather more complicated quota rule:

'With a view to remedying the existing evils of the employment of an undue proportion of Boy workers, for the future the Trade will not recognise any shop as fair where the number of apprentices exceeds the following proportion: in shops where less than ten men are employed, one apprentice to three men; in other shops, one apprentice to four men; no shop to have more than five apprentices.'[3]

Finally the London pressmen (1893) and the provincial bookbinders and machine rulers (1892) also tightened up their rules regarding the number of apprentices permitted in fair shops.[4] These numerous examples of increasing union concern with regulating apprentices show indisputably that as far as the printing industry was concerned, the Device of Restrictions of Numbers which the Webbs claimed was falling into desuetude,[5] was in fact being introduced in a wider field, and with

---

[1] E. Howe and J. Child, *op. cit.*, p. 216.
[2] Joint Trade Committee, *Report*, February 1891.
[3] *Report of General Meeting of the Trade*, April 1891.
[4] B.M.R.C.U. *Rules*, 1892, Apprentices. A.A.P. *Rules*, 1893 Apprentices.
[5] *Industrial Democracy*, 1898, Pt. II, ch. X (a); Pt. III, ch. III (a).

136 REGULATION BY UNION RULE

greater stringency, than in any previous time since the decline of the Stationers' Company. Although their analysis of the futility of a partial application of restrictive rules was undoubtedly valid, their description of what was happening was more applicable to the sixties than to the nineties when they wrote.

Why were the Webbs led to make this serious misjudgement? Apart from errors of fact—their 'description' of actual conditions in the printing industry was largely hypothetical—they seem to have failed to grasp the difference in strategy necessary for the maintenance of the union standard in printing as compared, for instance, with cotton manufacture. It was incautious to deduce that because the cotton unions had maintained their rules by collective bargaining, without any restrictions of entry, the printing unions could do the same.

That the printers, among whose leaders were numerous men of outstanding intellectual ability, should have turned almost reluctantly to the general employment of the Device of Restriction of Numbers was *prime facie* evidence that methods which had proved successful in other industries were not considered adequate in printing. The objections, both practical and theoretical, which the Webbs raised to the limitations of apprentices were clearly recognized by the majority of unionists and had, indeed, been the subject of keen debate at meetings and in the Union journals for generations past. If, after this prolonged discussion of potential benefits and practical difficulties, with full knowledge of the public disapproval and employer opposition which it would evoke, the printers turned unanimously to the stricter regulation of the number of entrants to their trades, they presumably did so with good reason. On the other hand, the attempt to enforce an unfair and unrealistic quota, like that of the T.A., might well retard union growth.[1]

The main practical argument against limitation lay in its alleged ineffectiveness, as long as there were large areas beyond union control. But by 1880 these areas were shrinking rapidly; after a generation of consolidation the unions were expanding both in numbers and in territory. By the employment of paid full-time organizers,[2] the elimination of old rivalries, the provision of attractive benefits and other methods they were reducing the proportion of unorganized workers. Under such circumstances there was a chance that a reasonable policy of restriction of entry would prove successful.[3]

[1] Musson, *op. cit.*, p. 179.
[2] The T.A. appointed two full-time organizers in 1892.
[3] Gillespie, *op. cit.*, p. 99.

CHAPTER IX

REGULATION BY UNION RULE

*Since the dissolution of the employers' association in
1872, which circumstances, by the way, we have always
regretted, it has necessarily fallen to our lot to consider
and adjudicate upon all questions of scale and custom
that have arisen, and although representing directly the
interests of the journeymen, we have never overlooked the
fact that the interests of the employers are identical with
our own.*
L.S.C. *Annual Report of the Committee,* 1884.

RATIONALE OF REGULATION

In 1848 when the National Typographical Association broke up there
was no formal organization of printing employers with any claim to
stability or cohesion, for even the London A.M.P. had collapsed
shortly after the negotiations on the Scale. Nevertheless the terms on
which disputes had been settled, whether by tacit consent or formal
agreement, were still in operation in the large towns. Some were
reprinted in the Rule Books of the societies; others were taken for
granted as the customary basis of the regulation of working conditions.
In general, however, they were no more than simple price lists for
piecework composition, usually in newspaper offices where the need for
uninterrupted production made the provision of explicit rules more
urgent than in the more leisurely book and jobbing houses.

These price lists tended to endure despite the collapse of the parties
which had originally signed them. The most outstanding example of
this viability of piece lists was the London Scale of Prices which
survived the dissolution at different times of both the trade society and
the masters' association. Enforcement of the terms of such agreements
almost invariably devolved upon the unions, for their interest in
maintaining standard conditions was much greater than the masters',
as Edwards pointed out in 1850:

'Believe me, the preservation of the Scale rests more with ourselves

138 REGULATION BY UNION RULE

than with our employers. Whilst we are united together its conditions will continue to be respected. . . . But if the journeymen were to cease in their demands for an inviolable Scale, and permit it to be broken with impunity . . . reduction of wages would be forced upon them as a matter of necessity—and general depreciation would immediately set in.'[1]

Under the prevailing conditions, with a permanent pool of unemployed, the employers both individually and collectively were attracted by the prospect of infringement of the Scale. On the other hand, the journeymen were collectively interested in maintaining the Scale even although individuals might gain temporary advantage by infringement.

Perhaps the commonest complaint levelled by the employers against trade unions of the nineteenth century was that they were dictatorial. Certainly to the master who had hitherto fixed the wage of his workers and the terms of work without any consideration other than that of maximizing his profit, the experience of coming up against trade union rules was naturally calculated to inflame.

'Among the various conspiracies by which freedom of trade and freedom of labour have been resisted, few have been more vexatious or unreasonable than that of letterpress printers. The rate of wages, the proportion of apprentices and every minute point in the management of the business, they attempt to regulate.'[2]

To counter such charges the unions developed several arguments. In the first place, as the employers had welcomed the process by which labour was reduced to the status of a commodity, whose price was determined by the market, they could hardly complain if the sellers attempted to obtain the highest possible price. The fixing of the selling price by a wholesaler or retailer was not normally considered to be unwarranted dictation to the customer, or interference with his freedom. Why should the fixing of price by the sellers of labour be singled out for special disapproval? It did not avail him to reply that the worker was free to accept or reject his terms, for the trade unions could equally well reply that employers were free to accept or refuse *their* terms.[3]

The fact was that many employers, remembering the days before trade unionism became an effective force, were not disposed to admit that the price of labour should be settled by the market mechanism. As Dunning observed:

[1] *Typographical Protection Circular*, 1850, p. 83.
[2] *Oxford Herald*, July 6, 1843.
[3] *Bookbinders Trade Circular*, 1851. 'Wages of Labour and Trade Societies.'

REGULATION BY UNION RULE

'With them it is something which should always be at their command at their own price, resistance to which is "insubordination" and "mutiny". We should be glad to be informed wherein the ideas of such employers differ from those of serf owners in like circumstances.'[1]

Once the principle that the price of labour should be settled by some market mechanism was admitted, it was difficult to argue *on principle* against other trade union regulations, for the latter could be considered as part of the conditions of the contract of service. But the unions were not content merely to assert that they had as much right as the employers to frame rules relating to working conditions; they proceeded to show that their rules were advantageous to the employers as well as to the workers. It was obvious, for example, that in the absence of a standard wage rate, unscrupulous employers would reduce their costs by paying lower wages and thus obtain a greater share of contracts. Other firms would be forced to follow suit. The result would be all-round reductions of the prices of printing products which would bring greater profits to booksellers and other purchasers, but would certainly bring no benefits to the body of master printers. Similarly, the rule prohibiting smooting was defended on the grounds that the extra work reduced the energy and attention which the journeyman could devote to his regular job;[2] the limitation of overtime was held to encourage efficiency by its improvement in the workers' health; apprentice limitation was necessary to ensure that youths received thorough instruction.[3]

In the last resort any union rule could be defended by two pragmatic arguments. Firstly, that such rules, even if it restricted the freedom of action of the employer, provided a code which the journeymen would obey; while in the absence of such rules they would be tempted to take advantage of every opportunity to better their condition. Secondly, if rules were necessary, they should be framed by those best qualified to assess the intricacies of the technical points involved, i.e. the representatives of the journeymen.

In short, union rules were said to provide a code which reduced unfair competition among employers and facilitated the conduct of industry by giving them an expectation of a reasonable degree of stability in their cost elements. And if the employers complained about the 'dictatorship' of the unions, the remedy was in their own hands. They should agree to meet the unions on equal terms, and discuss the terms. This, however, most of the employers would not do.

[1] Dunning, *op. cit.*, p. 58.
[2] P.M.M.T.S., *List of Fair Houses* . . . (*c.* 1891), Preface.
[3] E. Edwards, *op. cit.*, pp. 6–9.

140   REGULATION BY UNION RULE

It was left then to the unions to draw up rules to 'regulate' working conditions, and to devise means of enforcing them.

THE OBJECTS OF UNION RULES

In framing the rules relating to working conditions the craft unions had three broad objects in mind: maintaining traditional rate of exchange of work effort for wages, maintaining control of a certain range of work operations for their members, and sharing this available work reasonably equitably.

The first objective is roughly expressed in the old trade union slogan of 'a fair day's work for a fair day's pay'. There were few attempts to define a fair day's work more precisely. At first most of the provincial unions simply tried to maintain the standard 'stab rate in each town. The union rule laid down a *minimum* which had to be established before a local society could be accepted for membership of the union. For example, in 1877 the T.A. rule stated: No Society to be eligible for admission that does not maintain a 'stab, or equivalent piece scale, of at least 24s per week.[1] In 1873 the minimum rate which would qualify a society for membership of the S.T.A. was raised from 20s to 24s.[2] The standard rates of the larger and more powerful local societies were well above the union minimum.

But how much work should be done for the standard wage? A simple way of measuring work effort was by time. The unions then made a rule fixing the *maximum* standard hours. In 1852 the S.T.A. rule stated that 'the regular time of labour is not to exceed 11 hours per day'. In 1873 this was altered to fifty-four hours per week. Again, many of the larger branches enjoyed slightly shorter hours. In 1877 the T.A. rule was:

'That 56 hours per week be the maximum of working time on piece or 'stab, local rules to define when a day's work begins and ends.'[3]

The unions' earliest rules, then, fixed minimum rates and standard hours. But time is only a rough measure of work effort. How hard should a man work during his employer's time? The printing unions did not explicitly fix a 'stint' or 'darg', but over the years there developed some standard of work effort which was considered 'fair'.

Hence arose the unions' opposition to speed-up, by the use of 'whips' (pace-setters) and methods of payment such as bonus, or task work which encouraged time workers to speed-up. Hence, too, the suspicion

[1] T.A., *Rules*, 1877 (73).
[2] S.T.A., *Rules*, 1873. (2).
[3] T.A., *Rules*, 1877.

REGULATION BY UNION RULE

of time dockets and recording systems would enable the employer to measure the work output of each man.[1]

The second objective, of keeping control of certain technical operations, had a long tradition, stretching back to the medieval gilds, with their rigid demarcation of trades. The craft unionists believed with almost religious faith that certain operations *should* be performed only by craftsmen. (In public debate, however, they often argued that these tasks *could* only be done by craftsmen; in other words, that non-craft labour produced inferior work.) From this assumption arose the rules which prohibited boys, women, or unskilled men from doing certain work in 'fair' offices.[2]

The third objective, of sharing the available work more equitably, prompted the rules relating to smooting (working in more than one office) and limiting overtime. As well as by placing direct limits, unions hoped to discourage it by requiring that it should be paid at higher rates.

Overtime rates were usually left to be settled by the branches. Even in 1881 the S.T.A. Delegate Meeting considered that the settlement of rates for Sunday work should be settled by the local Societies.[3] By 1880 almost all of the large provincial branches had hourly overtime rates, usually about one-quarter or one-third higher than the normal time rate.

Piecework, inevitably, was a continuous challenge to the unions, for not only did it encourage speed-up, with the danger of rate-cutting, but it tended to promote disputes among members of the union.[4] At first the actual piece-rates were regulated by local rules. The S.T.A., however, had a general proviso that the basic rate should not be less than $4\frac{1}{2}$d per 1,000 for bookwork, 5d per 1,000 for news, and $5\frac{1}{2}$d per 1,000 for jobbing. Clearly, whether or not these scales had originated in an agreement with the employers, by 1870 they had been incorporated in the body of union law.

As provincial competition grew keener employers searched for new ways of reducing the wage bill. An obvious one was to change their men from piece to 'stab according to whether the work was difficult or easy. The unions countered this with a rule requiring a fortnight's notice of such change. Some employers attempted to reduce wages by employing as many men as possible as casuals at so much per hour. Many of the local societies had an official casual rate, usually higher than the 'stab

---

[1] Musson, *op. cit.*, p. 172.

[2] E. Howe and J. Child, *op. cit.*, ch. XXI. Gillespie, *op. cit.*, ch. IX.

[3] S.T.A., *Report of Delegate Meeting*, 1881, p. 34.

[4] For a full discussion of the complexities of piecework, see Musson, *op. cit.*, pp. 169–177.

142 REGULATION BY UNION RULE

but lower than the overtime rate. Others refused to recognize such a method of payment and required that casual men should be paid standard piece rates.[1] Others again required that no journeyman should accept a position on 'stab wages for a period of less than a fortnight, and that if he continued to work in the office he should become a permanent hand, entitled to a fortnight's notice.[2]

Thus, throughout this period the craft unions attempted to formulate and enforce more and more detailed rules to regulate working conditions, in an effort to achieve their three broad objectives.

DIVISION OF AUTHORITY TO MAKE RULES

One of the most difficult problems confronting the unions in their attempt to provide a set of working rules was that of the division of legislative authority. On what basis, and with what limitations, should the power to make rules be divided between the shop organization, the branch and the supreme union authority? Historically, of course, this problem seldom became acute until some years after the formation of the union. Inevitably, however, as the central executive tightened its grip and improved the administration, it came into conflict with the powerful local branches which were reluctant to relinquish the autonomy they had enjoyed for perhaps several decades.[3]

Delegate Meeting

There were always certain rules which were laid down by the supreme body—the Delegate Meeting. These embodied the 'fundamental principles' of the union. Perhaps the most important was the one specifying the qualifications necessary for admission. Most of the craft unions required a seven years' apprenticeship to the trade,[4] although the L.S.C. was content with proof that the applicant had established a 'right to the trade' by having worked for some time in a fair office. Towards the end of the period a second fundamental rule determined the quota of apprentices. The T.A. Executive stressed the importance of clear recognition of this division of authority between the branch and the central authority:

'To accomplish this object [the limitation of labour supply] the Association has framed a Rule *to be observed by all Branches*; other

---

[1] S.T.A., *Report of Delegate Meeting*, 1881, p. 34.
[2] Glasgow Typographical Society, *Rules*, 1892.
[3] See Gillespie, *op. cit.*
[4] T.A., S.T.A., B.M.R.C.U., London Bookbinders, Pressmen, and Machine Managers.

REGULATION BY UNION RULE

objects of association, such as wages, hours, and the like, are *of local regulation*, but the apprentice rule is *uniform and general. . . .*'[1]

Branch

The branch itself had authority to fix local standard time rates and hours of work. It could not normally expect financial support from the Central executive for any forward move unless it had first obtained the latter's permission. But even if the executive advised the branch not to persevere with a 'forward' move, the branch could ignore the advice and go ahead with its campaign, relying on the adequacy of the local funds to maintain the men if they had to be withdrawn. Thus the T.A. constitution required:

'That the opinion of the executive shall be elicited before Branches initiate any movement for an advance of wages, reduction of hours, &c., and no memorial or other document bearing on these questions, or on any matter for which the Association might be held responsible, shall be issued to employers or the public without the knowledge and approval of the Executive Committee. Branches neglecting to comply with this rule will forfeit any participation in the Association funds in all those cases where unadvised action may involve the members in a dispute.'[2]

Although the Executive was required to sanction 'forward movements', in practice it seldom opposed the wishes of an important branch. For one thing a large branch was not likely to ask permission unless it had a good chance of success; secondly, during the period of consolidation the Executive hardly dared to antagonize the members of an important branch, for the threat of secession was wielded fairly freely.[3]

Chapel

The shop organization (e.g. the printers' chapel) usually enjoyed a certain amount of autonomy in agreeing on working rules relating to such matters as meal hours, distribution between piece and 'stab hands, demarcation of apprentices' and labourers' work. These varied so much from one shop to another that a general rule would not have been enforceable. In practice the degree of initiative which the chapel assumed depended upon the keenness of the members and whether the firm was a 'union house' or an 'open house'.[4] In the former case the

---

[1] T.A., 39th *Half-Yearly Report*, 1869 (italics supplied).
[2] T.A., *Rules*, 1877 (17).
[3] T.A., 16th *Half-Yearly Report*, 1857.
[4] 'Union house': only union members employed.
    'Open house': both union and non-union workers employed.

144 REGULATION BY UNION RULE

chapel obviously had more power. Generally, local organizations could not ignore the possibility that if their rules were too restrictive employers would dismiss union members and operate as a non-union shop.

The chapel seldom took the initiative in framing rules. The usual procedure was for the employer to make the rules for his establishment, and for the chapel to advise him if any of these infringed the union rules. If so, the chapel consulted the committee of the local branch and explained to the employer the amendments which would be desirable.

In the latter half of the century the old chapel customs of fines and solaces for the 'good of the chapel' still persisted in many non-union shops, but the surviving Rules of large London and Manchester chapels show that they were concerned mainly with the supervision of *union* rules and the relief of *union* rules and the relief of *union* members.[1]

ENFORCEMENT OF UNION RULES

Information

An obvious condition of the successful enforcement of any union rule was that the appropriate authority should have information regarding the matters which it wished to control. Hence from an early date the local societies framed rules requiring members to report to their committee such matters as the engagement of a non-union man, or the taking of another apprentice. The London Society of Bookbinders had made the reporting of such information one of the most serious obligations of membership as early as 1820.[2] The Trade Council of the L.S.C. laid down the following procedure:

'Any member working in an office where there is any encroachment made, or about to be made, on the authorized customs or regulations of the trade, shall give information respecting the cause of such encroachment to the Secretary, or be fined 1s.'[3]

Within a regional organization such as the T.A. it was also necessary that the branches should send full information on trade matters to the Central Executive. At first it was simply required that whenever a dispute seemed imminent the Branch Committee should send details to the Executive before taking drastic action,[4] but by 1880 most of the regional unions were not content to wait until the eleventh hour. Branch Secretaries had to forward to head office, every quarter or half year, a

---

[1] *Rules of Palmer & Howe Chapel*, Manchester, 1888 (St. Brides).
[2] London Society of Journeymen Bookbinders, *Articles*, 1820.
[3] L.S.C., *Trade Memoranda . . .*, 1864, (C.U.P., 55).
[4] T.A., *Rules*, 1877, (18).

statistical return showing local wage rates, hours of work, number of members and non-members, number of apprentices, and an assessment of the 'state of trade'.[1] For failure to make such returns individuals were sometimes fined, and occasionally a branch was suspended from membership of the union.

In enforcing observance of their rules, the unions had to deal with four different groups: non-union men, members of other unions, their own members, and the employers. Gradually they developed a range of fairly effective sanctions to apply to each.

Non-union men

Naturally the main influence which the unions exerted on non-members was directed towards drawing them into the organization. If, however, they proved resistant the unions' second objective was to ensure that at least they obeyed the important working rules. This was often possible in 'open houses', where members and non-members worked together. By daily contact with union members and minor officials the non-members were able to argue about the objects and methods of the unions, and to learn that the rules were imposed, not from an arbitrary lust for power, but in pursuance of a policy which aimed at promoting the 'good of the trade'. Furthermore, by close association with union members both at work and during leisure they made friendships and developed loyalties which made it difficult for them to contravene a union rule, even though they might think it mistaken.

A third reason for the acquiescence of the non-members lay in the prospect of a considerable degree of discomfort and possibly of monetary loss, if the branch discovered that a rule was being broken, and closed the offending office. Sometimes indeed the local societies paid strike allowance or gave a tramping donation to non-members who volunteered to leave, or keep away from, a closed office.[2] Most unions had a clause in their admission rules stating that any applicant for membership who had worked in an unfair office should pay extra fees.[3]

Union branches gave the fullest possible publicity to the actions of those workmen who infringed union rules, particularly those who accepted work in closed offices. They compiled lists of 'rats' which were collated by the executive and published in the union journal or circulated as broadsheets among the Houses-of-call.[4] Thus any journeyman who had behaved 'dishonourably' in one town had little chance of moving to another region in which a different union held control without eventually being unmasked as a 'rat', and being ostracized and

---

[1] S.T.A., *Rules*, 1880, (36); A.S.L.P., *Rules*, 1884, (9).
[2] Musson, *op. cit.*, p. 148. [3] S.T.A., *Rules*, 1885, (29).
[4] Trade Documents in St. Bride Library, and Jaffray Collection.

146 REGULATION BY UNION RULE

humiliated by the union journeymen there. On the whole, however, black-lists and 'registers of rats' were of declining importance throughout the latter part of the century, and most unions discontinued them.

Members

The problem of internal discipline was solved by the development of the auxiliary benefits which bound each member more closely to the union and gave him a direct financial inducement to retain his membership. Without such benefits the unions had to rely for punishment on fines or expulsion. The difficulty with the former was that if a fine was small the deterrent effect was also small; if on the other hand it was made large enough to compel respect, when the committee came to impose it, the member might threaten to withdraw from the union rather than pay. For reasons of sentiment and self-interest a branch committee was usually reluctant to lose a member in this way, and the system of fines became ineffectual in regard to breaches of trade rules. 'The system of fining in most instances is a failure', reported the T.A. Executive.[1]

The effects of these penalties were obvious and immediate. There was, however, another range of techniques used at all times by union authorities to deter members from infringement of the working rules. These included the methods used to develop moral and emotional attitudes which would ensure the positive, enthusiastic co-operation of members. It is impossible to read journals and reports of the unions of the late nineteenth century without concluding that this sense of an underlying moral purpose was an important factor in determining their stability and effectiveness. But such attitudes did not arise spontaneously, and it was in the careful nurture of sentiments likely to promote the 'cause of unionism' that the leaders showed their political acumen. Such phrases as 'rights and duties', 'fair' and 'unfair', the need to 'clean up the trade', abolish the 'evil of boy labour', introduce 'remedial measures', or extend 'missionary work', which were common currency, reveal the moral and emotional approach to matters which have sometimes been regarded as merely economic.

Members of Other Societies or Unions

The high proportion of casual labour and the continuation of tramp relief encouraged a high degree of labour mobility. This gave rise to a special problem in connection with the enforcement of union rule; namely, when a union member from one town was working away from

[1] *Typographical Circular*, 1877, p. 2.

REGULATION BY UNION RULE

home, whose rules did he obey, and which union was responsible for his good conduct?

Owing to the loose federal structure of the early unions, each journeyman was strictly a member of his local Society, and subject to its rules. Suppose, then, a member of the Liverpool Society obtained work in Manchester, where different working rules were in operation. It was fairly simple, as both societies were members of the Association, to provide for this case by requiring the visitor to exchange his card for a local card and thenceforth obey Manchester rules.

The problem was more complicated when the visiting journeyman was a member of a different union. Normally, of course, he obeyed the local rules, but suppose he was offered a position in an office which was 'fair' according to the rules of his own union, but 'unfair' according to the rules of the local union? If he elected not to take the situation, which union should pay his unemployed allowance? As he was not a member of the local society it could disclaim responsibility; but if it did so it ran the risk of provoking him to take work in the unfair house.

These were not merely abstract problems. On several occasions inter-union relations were severely strained by the behaviour of a group of men from one union who acted as blacklegs in a closed office because they felt no obligation to obey the local rules. For example, in 1883, some tramps from the London Society of Bookbinders took work at an office in Dublin which had been declared closed by the Executive of the Consolidated Union because women were being put on men's work.[1] When the B.M.R.C.U. protested to the London Committee the latter replied, first, that they had not received notice that the office was closed; second, that the decision was unwise and should be reconsidered. The complete failure of the London Committee to co-operate was welcomed by the employer who openly boasted that he could break any local strike by obtaining men from London.[2]

A T.A. rule expressly required that members on tramp should conform to the local rules, whether the local society was a member of the Association or independent ('non-conforming'). Local secretaries were asked to report to the executive the names of those who refused to comply, in order that disciplinary action might be taken.[3] The London Society of Bookbinders gave members travelling to the provinces Honourable Leave so that they would be free to join the local Society in any town where they obtained work.[4]

[1] B.M.R.C.U., *Trade Circular*, 1883–4, passim.
[2] L.C.S.J.B., *Special Circular*, December 1884. E. Howe and J. Child, *op. cit.*, pp. 215–20.   [3] T.A., *Rules*, 1877, (56).
[4] *Bookbinders' Trade Circular*, 1858, 'Dispute with Consolidated Union'.

148 REGULATION BY UNION RULE

Employers

The methods used by the printing unions to ensure the observance by the employers of union working rules may be divided into two groups—direct and indirect. In the first category were those sanctions which operated immediately upon the employer, such as the boycott and the withdrawal of labour. The second comprised such methods as the use of public opinion, the influencing of public authorities, and the disciplining of union members.

Boycotts had been employed with some success since early in the century. For example the L.S.C. in the course of several disputes with newspaper firms about the middle of the century attempted to persuade the public to refuse to buy the offending paper during the course of the dispute:

'Deputations were sent to the various trade organizations, inviting financial assistance; also to the principal licensed victuallers and coffee houses, who by refusing to take in the particular paper, *The Sun*, rendered the Defence most valuable assistance.'[1]

During this dispute a large number of broadsides were distributed to members of various London unions—bookbinders, carpenters, joiners, bricklayers, &c.—asking them to help to make the boycott effective.[2]

The other form of direct boycott consisted in cutting off supplies of materials to the firm in dispute. This procedure was usually embodied in the rules under the heading 'Assistance to Unfair Offices'. The S.T.A. rule, for example, read:

'No matter is to be borrowed from or lent to an unfair office under any circumstances; nor shall members knowingly assist in the composition or printing of matter which would aid an employer with whom there is a dispute in producing work professedly done on his premises.'[3]

Towards the end of the century printing unions were considering how this type of boycott could be made more effective, for example by cutting off supplies of paper or other materials. Such developments required a higher degree of inter-union co-operation than was usually possible at this time.

The normal method used in case of a serious breach of union rule was to declare the office closed and withdraw union members from it. Union leaders in the sixties and seventies impressed upon the members

[1] L.S.C., *Report of Defence Committee* (*The London Compositor*, p. 432).
[2] Trade Documents in St. Bride Library. See Musson, *op. cit.*, p. 148.
[3] S.T.A., *Rules*, 1889, (30). T.A., *Rules*, 1889, (45).

REGULATION BY UNION RULE

the need for great caution in the application of this sanction. There is obviously an important tactical difference between the closing of one office, and the simultaneous withdrawal of union labour from all shops in a town. Only the latter was called a *strike*. The occasion for such a move would normally be the concerted action of the employers in breaking a union rule. As long as the employers remained unorganized strikes were uncommon. The few which occurred in this period were invariably caused by refusal of the employers to accede to a request for a rise in wages or reduction of hours. For example, in 1872 the Edinburgh printers *struck* when the associated masters refused a memorial for a fifty-one hour week;[1] in 1865 the P.T.A. became involved in an expensive *strike* when the Liverpool Branch revised its local rules in order to reduce hours from fifty-nine to fifty-six and raise the 'stab rate to 31s.[2]

If a local branch obtained permission to conduct a 'forward movement', it composed a memorial setting out the reasons for the desired change, and presented a copy to each employer who was left to decide for himself if whether or not he would accept the new conditions. As the branch was always careful to present the memorial at the start of the busy season, the employers were usually disposed to comply. There is more than a suspicion of irony in this comment of the S.T.A.

'The employers have, in the most courteous and considerate manner, without pressure of any kind, save the moral force of the facts and arguments of the Memorial, consented to a scale which augments the price of general work at least ten per cent.'[3]

Once the busy season was past, however, they would be tempted to 'nibble at the rate' by trying some rearrangement of their staff, or by introducing a new method of working. In such cases the local branch was called on to deal with only one employer at a time. Even so it was rarely able to resist a determined effort to introduce 'unfair' conditions, for there was always a pool of non-union unemployed who were desperate to take work on almost any conditions.

For this reason the unions were extremely reluctant to order that an office should be closed, and throughout the period rules relating to the procedure to be followed in case of dispute were elaborated in order to eliminate the risk of precipitate action by local officials. The most important development of such rules was the vesting of the authority to

---

[1] S.T.A., 19th *Annual Report*, 1872.
[2] P.T.A., *Half Yearly Report*, December 1865.
[3] *Scottish Typographical Circular*, Third Series, Vol. I, p. 99.

REGULATION BY UNION RULE

close or open offices in the Central Executive. The T.A. Rule on this point was unequivocal:

'No office can be closed without the authority of the Executive; nor can any closed office be re-opened without their sanction.'[1]

Indeed this provision was more than a rule; it ranked as one of the fundamental principles of union organization. Without it the central funds would have been drained away in support of strikes started by militant branches in ignorance of the primary need to balance commitments against resources over the whole of the union's territory. On numerous occasions the central executive came in for severe criticism for failure to grant full strike pay to men who had given notice on their own initiative rather than submit to an 'unfair' rule made by their employer.[2]

When a breach of rules was reported to the Branch Committee, the usual procedure was for the Committee to require a deputation of members from the office to attend the next meeting to give full details. The Committee usually advised the chapel father or the shop steward to approach the management in a conciliatory manner. If this proved unsuccessful, the Committee reported to the Executive. If the matter was considered serious, a full-time official would attempt to obtain an interview with the management. If the latter proved determined to persist the T.A. sometimes tried to bring pressure by withdrawing all casual labour. This was done by the local Secretary with the consent of the Executive.[3] If this failed to produce a promise to conform to rule, the Executive could take the further step of requiring all union members in the office to give a fortnight's notice. At the end of the two weeks the men were withdrawn and the office declared closed.

This ultimate sanction was applied only with great reluctance on the part of the Executive, for it needed little experience of union administration to convince the officials that it was much easier to close an office than to re-open it. In this respect they were often placed in an awkward dilemma. After spending much time and energy in developing in their members an attitude of strict obedience to the union rule—an attitude frequently coloured by strong emotional or moral feelings—when a Branch reported a clear-cut instance of a serious breach, the Executive often had to advise that it was inexpedient to take strong action in the meantime. By doing this, however, they ran the risks of being considered by the members to be lacking in fighting spirit or, alternatively, of

[1] T.A., *Rules*, 1877.
[2] S.T.A., *Report of Delegate Meeting*, 1862.
[3] T.A., *Rules*, 1877, (69). This was applied for breach of the Apprentice Rules.

REGULATION BY UNION RULE

inducing a reaction of apathy and carelessness in regard to observance of union rules.

The threat of withdrawal of labour was more effective if union labour was of higher quality or efficiency than the available non-union labour. Aware of this, the unions attempted to promote a sense of pride and workmanship and indeed of citizenship. The journals and reports contain numerous references to the close association of the printing trades with such 'noble arts' as literature, painting and music, to its connection with the causes of science and universal education, and to its part in the emancipation of the working class from ignorance and political subordination.[1] Pride in the importance of printing as the 'handmaiden' of social and moral progress was closely bound up with pride in good craftmanship:

'A young man, therefore, in joining our Society, may be said to have joined a body of advanced scholars, whose greater experience enables them to be of much use to their less advanced companions. As this superior knowledge is freely communicated to all who desire it, a service is rendered not only to our fellow workmen, but also to our employers; and so long as it is the practice of this Society to thus aid its members in acquiring the highest attainable state of proficiency in their profession, its usefulness is not likely to be called in question.'[2]

Many unions did not merely encourage a high level of technical ability and responsibility, but took steps to punish members who were found guilty of wilful neglect of work. The T.A. regularly fined members for this offence, or for leaving without giving proper notice to the employer, and published the names of the offenders.[3] The London Consolidated Society of Bookbinders offered to reimburse any employer who could prove that a union member had caused him loss by spoiling work.[4] The Secretary of the London pressmen's society was authorized to repay to any employer any wages which he had paid in advance to a pressman who had subsequently failed to work.[5]

By all these specific devices then, as well as their general discouragement of drunkenness, laziness, absenteeism and poor craftsmanship, the unions attempted to gain the adherence of employers to the union rules. Not only did the unions raise the standard of efficiency of their

[1] An excellent illustration is the S.T.A. emblem. See *A Hundred Years of Progress*, Frontispiece and Notes, p. 132.

[2] P.M.M.T.S., *List of Fair Houses* (c. 1891), Preface.

[3] *Typographical Circular*, January 1877, p. 11.

[4] L.C.S.J.B., *Articles*, 1860.

[5] A.A.P., *Rules*, 1893, General Regulations.

152 Regulation by Union Rule

members; they took over, to some extent, the disciplining of them in the interests of the masters:

'Employers as a class look with very little favour upon organizations like ours, and one of the reasons why we are not subjected to greater antagonism on their part is the fact that our Association offers great facility for obtaining men, either for regular or casual employment, and gives a kind of guarantee that such men have been taught the trade, and that they will attend to the work they undertake, or be punished for their neglect.'[1]

Throughout the period the unions, beginning with a few simple rules relating to minimum conditions, gradually elaborated them to counter 'sharp practices' by the employers, or to control new methods of working. 'Regulation of working conditions' became an accepted objective.

The employers were completely excluded from the rule-making process. Militant unionists considered they had no right to be consulted.

This exclusion from participation in the framing of 'industrial' laws under which they would have to conduct their business, prompted the masters to form their own organizations to conduct collective bargaining on their behalf.

[1] *Typographical Circular*, 1877, p. 3.

PART FOUR

BILATERAL BARGAINING
1890–1920

CHAPTER X

THE TECHNICAL REVOLUTION
1890–1914

When it is remembered that throughout the United States
and in nearly every provincial town of importance in the
United Kingdom, machinery has been introduced to a
more or less general extent, it becomes a duty to
recognize that it cannot longer be treated as some
plaything to be toyed or trifled with.
L.S.C. *Report of Executive,* January 1896.

THE TECHNICAL REVOLUTION

In the quarter century before the Great War the printing industry was in a turmoil of technical and industrial development. The outcome, though obscure to contemporary observers, was obvious by the end of the War. It was nothing less than a profound and general change in both the processes of production, and the methods of organization. Whether the changes in techniques caused, or were themselves caused by, the economic changes, must remain an open question. Technical changes encouraged a larger scale of production; this in turn led to wider markets, and a search for new techniques to speed up or cheapen production still further.

Compared with the previous era, the rate of technical innovation in this period was spectacular. For almost four centuries one of the basic processes of printing—hand composition—remained practically unchanged.

Between 1850 and 1890 there were several, largely unsuccessful, attempts to invent a machine to speed up the setting of type. These all worked on the mechanism of a keyboard which would release individual letters from racks when the keys were pressed by the operator. Although the best of these machines—the Hattersley and Kastenbein models—when working efficiently under a good operator, undoubtedly were quicker than the hand compositor they were not much cheaper, for the type had to be distributed by hand and arranged in the magazines.[1] In

[1] T.A., *Report of Delegate Meeting,* 1891.

156   BILATERAL BARGAINING

the provinces this work was done by unskilled men or boys, and sometimes even by girls, and these machines were therefore used in a few
provincial news offices. In London the persistent refusal of the Society
of London Compositors to permit the distribution of type by anyone
except skilled craftsmen, practically prohibited the use of this old style
composing machine except in non-union offices such as *The Times*.[1]
The Thorne machine tried to overcome this problem of distribution by
incorporating a mechanical type distributor, but this had the handicap
of requiring specially nicked type.

Nevertheless in 1890 the Thorne was in use in two important
provincial newspaper offices, the *Manchester Guardian* and the *Bradford
Observer*, and seemed set to sweep the field. When the London *Sportsman* installed Thorne machines in 1891, and was unable to agree with
the L.S.C. on the rates to be paid to the operators, the proprietors dismissed all of their union employees, and took on non-union operators.
This dispute prompted the L.S.C. to review the whole question of
composing machinery.[2]

In the meantime, however, the Linotype machine, working on a
completely different principle, had been perfected in the United States,
where it was first used on the *New York Tribune* in 1886. In a few years
its fame had spread abroad. The Linotype, introduced into England
from the United States in 1889 was the first type-composing machine to
go into general use. It consists of a rack of matrices which are released
by a keyboard mechanism and assembled into a line. When the
operator presses a lever the line of matrices is brought into a mould into
which molten metal is then forced. The result is a 'Line o' Type', or
'slug', ready for assembling with other lines to form a galley. After the
slug has been cast the matrices are returned to their respective racks,
ready for use when needed again. A large element in the cost of hand
composition using individual letters was the cost of 'distributing' the
type after use, an operation which cost about one quarter as much as
the actual composition. The Linotype completely eliminated this
expense, for after use the slugs are simply returned to the melting pot.

First used in England in the Office of the *Newcastle Chronicle* in 1889,
the Linotype was later installed in the London office of the *Globe* and
by 1895 had established its pre-eminence for newspaper work. Apart
from the speed at which type could be set (at a conservative estimate this
was four times the rate for hand composition) the Linotype had the
additional advantage of providing type material which was not so easily
'pied', or displaced, as matter composed of separate letters. The capital

[1] For further details, see L. A. Legros and J. C. Grant, *Typographical Printing
Surfaces, the Technology and Mechanism of their Production*, Lond., 1916.
[2] *The London Compositor*, Doc. CXXI.

THE TECHNICAL REVOLUTION

cost was, of course, considerable, and to some extent this accounted for its slower application to book and job printing where production costs were a more important item than in newspaper publishing. The Linotype Company Ltd., formed in 1889 as a subsidiary of the Mergenthaler Company spent three years in equipping its works in Manchester and erecting experimental machines before production began in earnest in 1893. In two years over 400 machines were produced and the plant's output capacity extended to 500 annually. Two schools for training operators were established in London, as well as a repair depot employing over 100 mechanics.[1] By the end of 1895 the Linotype was in use in most of the large London news offices. In 1895 there were more than 250 Linotypes being operated outside of London but only thirty-three Hattersleys and fourteen Thornes. The number of case hands had dropped from 1445 to 881 since the introduction of the machines, but 60 per cent of the displaced men had found work as operators.[2]

Ten years after the introduction of the Linotype, the Lanston Corporation set up an agency in London for the sale of its machines. The Monotype had arrived. This machine consists of two parts—a keyboard which punches holes in a continuous strip of paper and a casting machine which produces individual letters. When the punched strip of paper from the keyboard was fed into the caster, compressed air forced through the holes guided a master matrix into position over the mould, and the required letter then cast and moved out into the line. The machine cast quads of the correct length to 'justify' each line. It could also be used as a simple type-caster, and, as a variety of master matrices were evolved, it eventually superseded the older type-casting equipment.

As a type-setting machine it found widest use in bookwork, though some newspapers—notably *The Times*—continued to use it. Although its output was roughly that of the Linotype it had the disadvantage of a higher labour cost than the Linotype, as it needed two people to handle it. On the other hand the fact that the paper ribbon could be stored cheaply and used an indefinite number of times made the Monotype particularly suitable for book work where later printings or editions might be required.

The revolution in presswork achieved by the introduction of high speed rotary machines was no less spectacular than that in composition. About 1900 began an importation of American machinery on a scale which provoked considerable comment in the trade journals and led to pointed criticism of British manufacturers whose machines were

[1] Linotype Coy., Ltd., *Report of Directors*, 1895.
[2] T.A., *Special Memorandum*, 1893. *The London Compositor*, pp. 498–9.

158 BILATERAL BARGAINING

alleged to be slower, less accurate, and more difficult to manage than the American. In 1901 the manager of the *Manchester Guardian* wrote:

'The course of the last ten or fifteen years in the printing trades has been one long process of education from America. An employer must reckon it part of his duties nowadays to take a trip over the Atlantic as often as possible to enquire into new processes and look up new machinery.'[1]

Progress in the operation of rotary newspaper presses was greatly accelerated after 1880 with the series of improved presses manufactured by the Hoe and Goss companies. Eight Hoe Double Supplement presses installed in London in 1887 for the production of *Lloyd's Weekly Newspaper* astonished the printing world by their capacity to print papers of from four to twelve pages at the rate of 24,000 per hour. In 1902 these were superseded by the Hoe Double Octuple presses, each of which could produce a thirty-two page paper at the rate of 55,000 per hour.

Newspaper publishers were chiefly interested in the speed, size and reliability of the machines, but the men who had to work on them were concerned with the degree of comfort and safety with which they could be operated. Other things being equal, employers tended to favour a small, compact press which would occupy less space, use less power, have less vibration. The men, however, preferred ample space between different moving parts, so that oiling and adjustment could be done with minimum danger.

'Press manufacturers were faced with application for quart sized machines to fit into pint sized rooms, and the period of press monstrosity began to dawn, and led to the "deck" type of press being placed on the market . . . men were compelled to work under ridiculous conditions, and the list of injured and maimed operatives took on alarming proportions.'[2]

Rotary presses needed a curved stereoplate to fit the cylinders, and this led to many improvements in the technique of casting stereoplates. The most important invention in this branch was the Autoplate which not only cast the plate in a curved casting box fitted to the size of the printing cylinder but trimmed off the surplus metal, bored it for fitting to the cylinder, and cooled it to room temperature—at the rate of three or four plates per minute.

[1] G. B. Diblee, 'Ca' Canny in the Printing Trades', *Economic Journal*, 1901.
[2] G. A. Isaacs, *op. cit.*, 1931, p. 79.

THE TECHNICAL REVOLUTION

In book and jobbing printing there was not the same spectacular improvement in machinery, and the flat-bed machine with a cylinder impression, such as the Wharfedale or Miehle, continued in general use. Lithographic printing was revolutionized by the discovery that offset printing, by which the print was transferred to a roller before being applied to the paper, obviated many technical difficulties and permitted the use of a wide variety of original sources—copper plates, flat stones, blocks and letterpress. Speeds were increased to an average of between 1,500 and 3,000 per hour.

ECONOMIC CHANGES IN PRINTING

General Expansion

Throughout this period the demand for printing grew steadily. Newspaper circulation rose to heights undreamed of in the Victorian era, and the reduction in the cost of books by mass production of both printing and bindings opened up the great, untouched market for those cheap editions which were the foundation of the prosperity of many large printing houses. Improvements in colour printing and photographic reproduction coincided conveniently with the rapid development of poster and display advertising, and gave renewed stimulus to the job printing trade. Thus, while the population increased at the rate of 9 per cent in each decade, the number of workers in the Paper and Printing Industry grew at roughly twice that rate.

The following table shows the gross increase in the number of workers in the paper and printing industry in this period.

EMPLOYMENT IN PRINTING TRADES
(Persons aged 10 and upwards)

	Male (000)			Per cent Increase	Female (000)			Per cent Increase
	1891	1901	1911		1891	1901	1911	
England & Wales	156	188	226	45	63	91	121	92
Scotland	22	24	31	32	14	20	25	79
Ireland	7	7	8	14	4	4	4	—
United Kingdom	186	220	264	42	81	115	150	85

Source: *Censuses of Population, 1901, 1911*

Owing to various changes in classification it is impossible to show the exact increase in each group of workers, but one outstanding feature was the rapid growth in the number of women employed. From 1891 to 1911 they had increased by 85 per cent, twice as rapidly as the men. The

160 BILATERAL BARGAINING

great part of the increase in women workers occurred in stationery and paper bag and box making trades. In both of these sections of the industry the numbers of women more than doubled in the period.

Growth of Large Firms

One of the most striking features of the economic organization of the industry was the growth of large establishments in both newspaper and general printing. The former were mostly in London or Manchester where labour costs were high, but many of the latter were situated in smaller country towns where costs were low. Owing to low wages, rates and rentals, as well as the economies of large-scale production, the competitive position of these firms was very strong, enabling them to overcome the barrier of transport costs which otherwise tended to create local monopolies.

The growth of large firms was most spectacular in the case of the London dailies. *The Times*, by no means the largest, in 1912 had a salaried staff of 300 (excluding correspondents) and a technical staff of 350 (excluding distribution).[1] On some papers the total staff, both permanent and casual, reached 2,000. Such Leviathans were not peculiar to newspaper printing. The modernized Parkside factory of Thomas Nelson & Sons in Edinburgh produced 30,000 volumes of books daily as routine work, and could double this output in an emergency. William Clowes & Sons with a large electrified factory at Beccles had over 100 printing machines in operation and employed some 1,600 workers. But such giants were not typical of the general printing trade, especially in the provinces where thousands of small jobbing firms struggled for existence, often using antiquated machinery, and sustained only by virtue of a quasi-monopoly position due to geographical situation and the sentiment or conservatism of local customers.

Location of the Industry

In this period the location of different branches of the industry changed considerably. For instance, up to the turn of the century the book trade had tended to drift from London to Edinburgh where composition costs were low owing to the fairly general employment of women compositors. After the introduction of composing machines, however, it became essential to have high quality labour in order that high output might offset increased overheads for capital charges. Edinburgh then ceased to hold a competitive advantage, and indeed, by lagging behind in the installation of the new machines, tended to lose ground. Similarly

---

[1] *The Times, Printing Number*, p. 91.

THE TECHNICAL REVOLUTION 161

in a smaller town, Warrington, the past employment of women compositors impeded the introduction of Linotypes.[1]

London, however, did not gain from the change. Partly because of high London wages, but also because of low country rentals, cheap land and non-union labour, many expanding London firms built large works at such towns as Aylesbury, Reading, Guildford, and Maidstone. The Home Counties became notorious in trade union circles as low-wage areas, and attracted the attention of the vitally interested London unions. From 1907 until 1919 the L.S.C. extended the radius of its jurisdiction from fifteen miles to forty miles from Charing Cross in order to combat the drain of book printing from the Metropolis.[2] Despite union efforts London's share of the nation's printing continued to decline, as the following shows:

WORKERS IN LONDON PRINTING TRADES
EXPRESSED AS PERCENTAGE OF THE
TOTAL FOR ENGLAND AND WALES

	1891	1901	1911
Printers	41	35	34
Lithographers	40	31	29
Bookbinders	62	52	46

Source: *Census of England and Wales*, 1901, 1911

Even outside London the industry was essentially an urban one. In rural districts only eighteen per 10,000 of the population were returned as Printers and Lithographers as compared with 116 for urban districts. In 1911 the highest density of printing employment was in such cities as Oxford (386), Reading (252), Bristol (218), and the London Metropolitan Area (211).

Competition

In this period the growth of better communications tended to widen the market for products, and also the area of competition, which in certain lines became nation-wide. There was, however, a hint of paradox in the situation when London employers refused to give wage increases because of low provincial wages, while provincial employers refused because of transport costs to the London market. Indeed, employers frequently complained that continental printing prices were so low that they attracted British customers deficient in a sense of patriotic duty.

[1] J. R. MacDonald, (ed.), *Women in the Printing Trades*, p. 46. See also P. & K.T.F., *Annual Report*, 1899.

[2] L.S.C., *Report of Committee on Extension of the Radius*. See also *Annual Report*, 1907, p. 42.

F

162 BILATERAL BARGAINING

This intensification of competition exercised a pressure on employers which produced two defensive reactions. Firstly, there was a general attempt to cut wage costs by using non-union 'unskilled' labour. Secondly, there was competitive price-cutting in the attempt to gain contracts by submitting low tenders. Larger firms which were slowly adopting improved accounting methods were precluded from taking the second course, and often had great difficulty with the first. It was no accident, therefore, that they tended to take the lead in espousing schemes for organization of employers and the introduction of standard costing procedures which would reduce 'unhealthy' competition.

TECHNICAL CHANGE AND THE WORK FORCE

All of these changes affected, either directly or indirectly, the fortunes of the workers or employers concerned. Obvious and immediate was the threat to the skilled handcraftsmen who were threatened with displacement by machinery worked by an 'unskilled' operative. Fortunately, mechanization did not result in a marked displacement of skilled labour. On the contrary, while there were pockets of 'technological unemployment' the cheapening of the product and the continuous expansion of output brought about an increase in the number of skilled workers in most departments. Nevertheless, the increase in the number of skilled men was proportionately smaller than that for all workers in the industry, partly because of the phenomenal increase in the number of women workers.

But more important was the rapid growth of a new class of men who tended the machinery but had little of the all-round training and nothing of the apprenticeship experience of the skilled journeymen. This class is called for convenience the 'semi-skilled', but the term implies only in a general way that the body of these men were less skilled than those called 'craftsmen'. In many cases the 'semi-skilled' machine operators required greater manual dexterity and occupied posts of greater responsibility than many of the 'craftsmen'. The most striking example of this anomaly occurred in newspaper printing. Some of the great rotary presses needed twenty or thirty attendants, of whom only the chief—the machine-minder or manager—qualified for entrance to the craft union. Yet he was not apprenticed to this trade, but was usually promoted through the various ranks of carrier-away, fly hand, reel hand, sup hand and brake hand.

In book and job printing works there arose a large class of workers of varying grades of skill who were occupied in the storage, handling and preparation of paper. With improvements in the technology of paper manufacture a great variety of papers especially adapted to different

THE TECHNICAL REVOLUTION

163

printing processes was produced. The job of the head warehouseman in a large firm was rightly regarded as one requiring high skill and carrying great responsibility. The numerous assistants and cutters, however, generally required little skill or training, and as they did not qualify for any of the old craft unions they became organized in the various Warehousemen's and Cutters' unions which eventually amalgamated with the union catering for workers in paper mills.

Secondly, with the increasing diversity of equipment workers tended to become more narrowly specialized. While compositors usually received a fairly general training at case work during their apprenticeship, on serving their time they settled into one of the various crafts of Linotype or Monotype operating, imposition, or hand case-work, and were rarely called upon (indeed, in some cases they were forbidden) to exercise the other skills. Printing machinemen similarly tended to become specialists in the various branches of letterpress, lithographic, copper plate or offset printing, while newspaper printing developed as a vast field with its own numerous specialities.

To some extent specialization was achieved at the cost of the all-round training which had characterized the best of the old craftsmen, but in an industry in which small firms predominated there remained a steady demand for workers with versatility and general skills. Specialization was pushed to extremes in those large newspaper firms where speed, smoothness and efficiency were demanded at all costs. Partly because of this the unions were able to impose a prohibition on apprentices in London daily news offices.

It is often stated that the introduction of machinery lightens the task of the worker and dispenses with the need for his skill. Both of these contentions were vigorously challenged by the unions. A large proportion of technical improvements consisted of devices which permitted a process to be performed either more accurately or at greater speed. In the first case the accuracy of the machine depended upon the fineness of its adjustment, which in turn reflected the skill of the operator. In the second case there was often greater nervous strain, if not greater danger, in attending the faster machines. In this particular period of technical change, in which many machines were still in the process of being made automatic and foolproof, the demands on the workers' skill and endurance were often increased rather than diminished.

TECHNICAL CHANGE AND INDUSTRIAL RELATIONS

The technical changes of this period were the immediate causes of many important changes in industrial relations. Firstly they led to the formation of the unions of semi-skilled workers, with methods and

164 BILATERAL BARGAINING

aspirations which often conflicted with those of the craft unions. The organization of these new classes of workers resulted in bitter jurisdictional and demarcation disputes. The challenge to their leadership prompted some of the craft unions to re-shape their own organizations, and to try to enrol categories of workers whom they had previously ignored.

The introduction of the revolutionary Linotype and Monotype machines prompted the formation of Users' Associations of these two machines. The long battle over the terms on which the machines should be operated resulted in the first national collective agreement in the printing industry. In most of the larger provincial towns the master printers formed their first associations to resist the steady 'encroachment' of union rule on managerial 'prerogatives'.

CHAPTER XI

COMPOSING MACHINES

If machinery is to be introduced, we claim a right to benefit by its introduction; but if it can only be made to pay at the expense of those who have served an apprenticeship to the trade, we submit that in such an event no real advantage is to be derived.

L.S.C. *Circular to the Workman of the United Kingdom,* February 1892.

MECHANICAL COMPOSITION

The displacement of the hand compositor by the composing machine is one of the classic case studies in the history of technology. The story lacks the tragic elements of other great changes such as the introduction of the power loom, and the impoverishment of the hand weavers. But it possesses several unique features which have fascinated historians. Firstly there is the swiftness of the transition: after four centuries of hand composing, in two brief decades the change, in larger offices, was complete. Secondly, the machine displaced a hand craftsman whose organization had become the archetype of the tightly knit, highly disciplined, 'aristocratic' and exclusive craft union.[1]

What happened when the forces of technological change impinged on a powerful social group committed to conserve its traditional rights and privileges? Would there be open conflict? And if so, which would win?

To understand the controversy over composing machines it is necessary to know a few technical details. The hand compositor picked his separate pieces of type from a 'case' which contained small compartments, each with one sort of letter. When he ran out of letters he had to find some set matter which was no longer needed, and 'distribute' it, placing each letter in the correct compartment in the case. This latter work *could* be done by boys or girls, but the unions insisted that it be done by compositors.

The earliest type composing machines consisted of racks of letters,

---

[1] From a practical consideration, too, this case study is very well documented.

166 BILATERAL BARGAINING

connected with a keyboard. As the operator pressed the various keys appropriate letters slid down a guide and were arranged in a line. On straightforward matter the operator could compose about three times as quickly as by hand. Distribution, however, was often *more* difficult, because of the need to arrange the letters the right way up in the racks. In order to make the machines economical to operate, owners tried to use cheap labour of boys or girls on the distribution. This was only possible in non-union houses.

Provinces

When a Hattersley (one of the most successful of these early machines) was installed in the *Bradford Times* in 1868 it was manned by four youths—one composing and three distributing. This posed the first fundamental policy problem of the P.T.A. Should it *oppose* the introduction of machines as such, or should it simply seek to *control* their operation? Opinion on the Executive Council was divided, but a majority decided to adopt the policy of control. The Council informed the proprietor that only journeymen or legal apprentices would be permitted by the union to work on the machine. When the proprietors refused to accept this ruling the P.T.A. declared the office 'closed' and withdrew its members.

During the next two decades the T.A. followed the 'control' policy in regard to the operator, but modified it in regard to distribution, allowing first non-apprenticed boys, and later girls, to do this unskilled work. The boys were permitted 'on the condition that they are not taught or engaged in the general business of letterpress printers'. Girls were indeed favoured by some, as they would be less likely to 'pick up the trade'.

During a debate on composing machines at the 1877 Delegate Meeting the Manchester delegates protested against the use of this juvenile labour, and claimed that distribution was the work of journeymen or apprentices. They argued, too, that machine operators should be paid the same 'stab or piece rates as hand compositors. They pressed the Executive to take a ballot of the members on these important policy matters. The long controversy which followed, in the pages of the *Circular*, revealed the dilemma of the membership: on the one hand the threat of displacement and unemployment, on the other public opprobium and a series of costly disputes with employers.

The Executive advised members against imposing 'unreasonable restrictions' on the working of composing machines. Their aim should be to discover how the machines 'can be most advantageously worked in the interest of the journeyman printer, without prejudice or injury to that of the employer'.

COMPOSING MACHINES

The expression of this pious ideal was probably more of an exercise in public relations than a plain statement of the Executive's real ambition. The shrewd politicians on the Council must have realized that there was not *one* journeyman's interest, for the hand compositors and the machine operators were bound to differ. And who would judge when the employers' interests were injured or prejudiced—the employer or the union?

The members' ballot gave the Executive a mandate to deal with each case on its merit, on the understanding that the T.A. would not oppose the machines provided that fair wages and working conditions were secured.[1]

During the eighties, as many more news offices installed Hattersleys, the T.A. gained further insight into the sort of problems that could arise. Case hands complained that the machine operators were kept supplied with material while hand compositors (on piecework) had to 'slate'. The first newspaper to introduce a Hattersley machine paid, for a while, the full case rate of 9d per 1,000. But as the proprietors learned more about its capabilities, the rate was cut—to 6d, to 5d, to 4d, and then to 3½d!

In 1886 the Executive invited delegates from the large Midland towns, where machines were increasing, to attend a special conference on rules for working composing machines. Copies of the agreed code were circulated to all branches. Thus by 1889 the broad principles had been established.

Firstly the union reverted to its original policy: 'Type Composing machines must be exclusively worked by Journeymen and duly recognized apprentices.'

The second policy problem was this: how and when were operators to be trained, and how were they to be paid while learning the new skills? In the provinces promising young journeymen were taught to operate the machines during normal working hours but they were not allowed to go on to piece rates until they could earn the 'stab wages for the town.

The fixing of piece rates was an extremely ticklish matter. If the rate was set too high the operator's earnings grew too high, and provoked complaints from both employers and other journeymen. But if the rate was set too low the operators would speed up, take more of the work, and leave less for the hand compositors, whose piecework earnings would be reduced. The new Rules set the piece rates at 3d per 1,000 (day) and 3½d per 1,000 (night). To protect the operator's earnings he had to be guaranteed four hours work each shift, and be paid for 'standing time'.

[1] Musson, *op. cit.*, p. 190.

168 BILATERAL BARGAINING

How was the hand compositor to be protected from the avaricious operator who would try to demand larger 'takes' of copy? The Rules tried to deal with this by forbidding operators from being given 'unduly long' takes, and by requiring that hand compositors be paid for standing time. The Rules firmly prohibited any practice which savoured of 'task work' or 'bonus work', and specifically forbade operators to mark or 'slug' their copy, or keep records of output. For the next few years these model rules guided the Executive in dealing with the introduction of scores of Hattersley machines in newspaper offices.

Thus by 1889, when the first English Linotype was installed in the *Newcastle Chronicle,* the T.A. was alerted to the nature of the problem and had worked out its basic strategy. The Linotype, indeed, simplified the problem, for it dispersed entirely with distribution. After the matter has been printed the slug is simply melted down. The question of boy or girl labour did not arise.

On the other hand, as the technique of the Linotype was radically different (type-*casting* as opposed to type-*setting*) it required a new set of detailed rules to ensure that rough justice was done to the hand compositors, who formed the great bulk of union membership.

The hand compositors were now seriously alarmed. Another machine —The Thorne—was being introduced, and the old Hattersley rules did not apply to it. Branches called urgently for a special conference to fix general rules for all machines. The conference, in February 1891, reaffirmed the principle of union control and opposition to bonus systems, but could make no headway on other aspects. When every branch of the union had its own 'stab rate, standard hours, and local customs, and the larger branches had their local piece scales, the problem of producing some uniform rules was immensely difficult. It was complicated, inevitably, by the pressure groups from the larger and stronger branches, reluctant to yield an iota of their autonomy, or to lose their traditional 'advantageous' terms.

The 1891 Delegate Meeting, the first for fourteen years, paid surprisingly little attention to the problem of machinery, and apart from resolving that hours should not exceed eight per day, or forty-eight per week, endorsed the policy of the February conference, leaving the details of working conditions to be settled by the Executive. At this stage nobody knew which, if any, of the various machines would eventually dominate the industry.

Within the next two years, however, it became clear that the Linotype was sweeping the English market, just as a few years earlier it had come to dominate in the United States. The policy of leaving the Executive to deal piece-meal with machinery resulted in a mass of anomalies which were resented by employers, journeymen and the machine manufac-

COMPOSING MACHINES

turers. In 1893 the Executive convened a meeting of machine operators to help it to frame 'a code which should be generally applicable to the working of composing machines in any branch'. There was general agreement that operators' hours should be lower than the normal. Although this was defended on the grounds of the exhausting nature of the work, a stronger motive was the hope of reducing unemployment. A standard of fifty hours (day) and forty-eight (night) was set.

How were 'stab and piece rates on machines to be fixed? The Executive decided to base them both on the 'stab rate for the branch. The 'stab rate for operators was to be not less than 5s above the case rate. Operators' piece rates varied according to the branch 'stab rate, as follows:

DAY CASE RATE

	Less than 30s	30s to 36s	More than 36s
Day Machine Piece Rate	3d	$3\frac{1}{4}$d	$3\frac{1}{2}$d
Night Machine Piece Rate	$3\frac{1}{2}$d	$3\frac{3}{4}$d	4d

The attempt to enforce these rates led to numerous disputes. But the flood of machines continued, and the hand compositors, especially the older men, were being displaced in ever increasing numbers. They called for limitations on overtime, reduction in working hours, fair sharing of copy and the elimination of piece rates.

The almost complete lack of even local masters' associations meant that the union had to rely mainly on its own power to enforce standard conditions. There was just one other possibility. The rival machine manufacturers were naturally anxious to get their products installed with the minimum of labour trouble. Could *they* be pressed or cajoled into agreeing to standard working conditions which they could enforce as part of the contract of sale, in return for a degree of union co-operation? It was one bright gleam in an otherwise gloomy prospect.

In 1893 the T.A. Executive made separate overtures to the manufacturers of the Hattersley, Thorne and Linotype, promising 'frank and honest recognition' of the machines in return for a 'beneficial influence' to be exercised by the manufacturers on their customers. Lengthy correspondence followed. Each firm accused the union of underestimating the capabilities of its product, and of encouraging operators to restrict production in order to force up piece rates. The Hattersley makers said they hoped the forthcoming Delegate Meeting would 'let well alone'; the Type-Setting Syndicate Ltd. (Thorne) said that the rate for each firm should be set independently and that the bonus system—'the most equitable and just to both employer and employee'—should be permitted.

F*

The Linotype Company was attracted by the union's offer but said regretfully, 'our influence at the present time is not, in the Councils of the newspaper owners and printers, so powerful yet as to make itself heard as authoritatively as perhaps you or we might desire'.[1]

The Company was in a dilemma. Undoubtedly it was anxious to obtain the goodwill of the unions in order to increase sales without fear of industrial strife; on the other hand it wanted as low a piece rate as possible in order to make the Linotype more attractive to potential customers.

So the gleam faded, the correspondence petered out, and the union was thrown back on its own resources. In December 1893 the T.A. called a Special Delegate Meeting at Sheffield. With winter approaching hundreds unemployed, machines still flooding into the country, the manufacturers unco-operative and the employers increasingly arrogant —the outlook was bleak. To many old hand compositors, facing at best the prospect of reduced piece earnings, at worst dismissal and either the 'road', or a few weeks on the union's meagre unemployment relief, the coming Christmas season brought little cheer.

The delegates converged on Sheffield, and assembled in the dreary conference hall: working men all—hand compositors and machine operators—elected by their fellows to deal with a problem that was growing swiftly into a crisis. Could they reconcile the differences of hand comps and operators, of pieceworkers and time-workers, of employers, unions and machine manufacturers ? Could they formulate rules to govern a technological change which had hitherto baffled the union leaders ? And could they control a process which in the past, in other trades, had brought skilled hand craftsmen down to the final degradation of the parish pauper ?

Impressed by a warning from the President that the union was faced with 'a serious development' the conference considered the adoption of a set of working rules which had been drafted by the council. On scarcely one point was there a consensus of opinion. Three main causes of disagreement were apparent. Firstly, in the absence of general rules during the past few years the branches had countenanced a variety of practices which their delegates realized could not be standardized without serious conflict; secondly, the operators were reluctant to agree to any restrictions, such as a prohibition on bonus payments or piece-work, which would reduce their high earnings; thirdly, most delegates considered it impracticable to produce a set of detailed rules which could be applied both to the large newspaper offices and to the small jobbing shops.

[1] Correspondence reprinted in T.A. *Report of Delegate Meeting*, 1893, pp. 12, 13.

COMPOSING MACHINES

The debate on piecework was particularly revealing. Thus one delegate supporting the proposal that machines be worked entirely on the 'stab system, said:

'... that when the operator was on piecework it was his entire object to earn as big a wage as possible, and by so doing, he displaced other men.'[1]

The argument that piecework promoted unemployment was opposed by those who thought that time rates robbed the operator of a 'fair' reward for his work. Said one delegate:

'By all means let it be 'stab, if you can put a limit on the production, but you cannot do that. It would not be fair to the employer, the machine, or the operator. But if this 'stab system is adopted you will find in every town in the kingdom they [the operators] will be doing piecework at 'stab pay.'[2]

The draft rules approved by the Delegate Meeting introduced no important new principle.

LINOTYPE COMPOSING MACHINE OPERATORS TERMS

	Hours	'Stab	Piece
Day	48	40s	2½d
Night	42	42s	3½d

To protect hand composition it was forbidden for machines to be operated while hand compositors were 'standing'. Copy had to be lifted 'in regular order by machine and case hands', each operator being allowed a double take.

Although the rules approved by the Conference were adopted by ballot of the membership, they were not enforced with anything approaching the rigour of other rules, but 'served as a standard to guide the E.C. and the branches in dealing with the question . . .; and modifications have continually been made as circumstances called for them'.[3] The Executive advised members that application of the rules would require 'very judicious treatment' and that local conditions would need to be taken into careful consideration. In practice the E.C. concentrated upon obtaining a reduction of working hours and on safeguarding as far as possible, the position of the case hands.

In the next few years there was a great increase in the number of Linotypes, and heavy unemployment, 'accentuated in several important

[1] T.A., *Report of Delegate Meeting*, 1893, p. 43. [2] *Ibid.*
[3] T.A., *Fifty Years' Record*, p. 113.

172 BILATERAL BARGAINING

centres through the displacement of members consequent on the introduction of composing machines'. In many branches there were strikes and other disturbances as the unemployed agitated for stronger measures to be enforced. In 1891 T.A. expenditure on out-of-work benefit was just over £2,000, the lowest for five years. In the next five years it rose to nearly £9,000, though the membership increased by less than one third.

In 1894 the Executive became seriously alarmed when it learned that the Linotype Company was advertising for youths with no experience of the printing trade to enrol as learners in classes held at the Company's school for operators.

'500 intelligent men of good character willing to learn the operation of Linotype machines and so become operators in newspaper printing offices, and be able to earn regular wages of from £2 up to £5 per week, according to efficiency, *when vacancies occur*. As fast as 500 men are trained and certified, further men will be put under training.'[1]

Such a threat to union control could obviously not be ignored, and the T.A. attempted to counter it by advertising in the leading papers and trade journals, explaining the precarious position of the hand compositors, and hoping to enlist public sympathy and trade union support. The Company had founded the school more as a move to force the unions to come to terms than as a serious attempt to provide technical training.

Throughout 1894 the T.A. did its best to enforce the observance of the draft rules. Negotiations went forward at all levels—Chapel, Branch and National executive. Where it could not gain complete acceptance the executive bargained and compromised, battling always against the militancy of some branches, the temptations offered to the operators, the desperate criticism of the hand compositors. Amazingly in this medley of conflicting interests and multi-level bargaining, not a single stoppage occurred that could be *directly* attributed to composing machines. Nevertheless the annual average strike pay for the five years 1893–97 was treble that for the period 1888–92. Surely, in this critical period, the union should have been conserving its funds to meet the main crisis? The surge of disputes may have been a reflection of the deep-seated disturbance of the membership, a rather inchoate protest against the times. But many of the disputes, especially those due to attempts to reduce hours, were indirectly related to the 'machine question', and the problem of rationing the available work more equitably.

[1] T.A., *Half-Yearly Report*, June 1894.

COMPOSING MACHINES

The relatively high piece rates required by the union were generally leading to the working of machines on 'stab. The employers disliked this because the operator had no incentive to work at maximum speed; the journeymen distrusted it lest operators should be tempted to accept bonuses. The T.A. executive considered that insistence on high rates would lead only to loss of T.A. control; in 1895 it convinced the members that the 1893 Rules should be moderated. Machine 'stab rates were reduced to ten per cent above the local case rate, and machine piece rates were based on local piece rates.

But by 1895 both union and employers were wearying of guerrilla warfare. In April 1894 an *ad hoc* meeting of Linotype users met in Manchester and resolved that piece rates should be reduced. A deputation of employers met the T.A. executive to discuss this proposal, but the latter decided that they could not agree to a rate less than the $2\frac{1}{2}$d set by the Delegate Meeting.

In 1895 a substantial body of provincial newspaper owners formed the Linotype Users' Association, with the primary object of negotiating standard conditions *throughout the whole country*. Here was a splendid chance for the executive to work for the objective of uniform conditions. Surely they would leap at the opportunity.

Not at all. On the contrary the T.A. took a very cautious line. They politely declined to attend a conference with the L.U.A., not because they were averse to meeting that body, but because they were 'not at present aware of any necessity for such a meeting'. And bearing in mind the probable reaction of some of its more vociferous branches, the Executive doubted whether the great variety of local conditions could ever be subsumed in a set of general rules.

The L.U.A., however, persisted, 'in the interests of peace and equity', and throughout 1897–98 there were numerous conferences, Council Meetings and another Delegate Meeting.

The Agreement, finally signed in December 1898, was of historic importance—the first national agreement in the industry. Even so, it contained only 'Rules for Working Composing Machines on Stab'; piece rates were too complex to generalize, and were left to local negotiation.

The Agreement confirmed that all skilled operators should be members of the T.A., and that when composing machines were installed in an office preference should be given to the hand compositors in learning to operate them. Apprentices were not allowed on machines until they had served at least three years at case. The number of apprentice operators was limited to one for each three machines. Operators wages were set at $12\frac{1}{2}$ per cent above the local case rate. Hours were forty-eight (day) and forty-four (night).

174   BILATERAL BARGAINING

This agreement, though given a hostile reception by many branches, greatly facilitated the transition to new technology.

London

During the eighties, when Hattersley machines were being installed in provincial offices, the London Society of Compositors adopted the policy which the T.A. had in 1877 rejected. It resolutely refused to allow the distribution of type by juvenile labour. In consequence hardly any composing machines were in use in London, except for a Kastenbein at *The Times*, then a non-union house. This difference in policy in fact reversed the usual sequence of technological change. Composing machines were becoming widespread in provincial news offices while London daily papers were still being set by hand!

In London the famous piecework scale, first printed in 1785, and substantially amended in 1810, remained the basis for payment of compositors. During the following eighty years, however, the number of 'trade customs' and 'house customs' multiplied. The piece scale became so complex that it was virtually unworkable, and after 1880 an increasing number of houses went over to 'stab wages. Many compositors deplored this change, mainly because earnings were reduced. In 1890–91 the L.S.C. spent much time and energy negotiating with the newly formed London Master Printers' Association on a complete revision of the hand piece scale. Having completed this major task it turned to the revision of the News Scale for hand compositors.

But even as the delegates met and argued about the revision of the scale, the world of the hand news compositor began to crumble. In 1892 the first London Linotype was installed in the office of the *Globe*. Ignoring this portent the L.S.C. pressed on with its revision of the old News Scale, and in 1893 presented a *Memorial* to the newspaper proprietors, suggesting several changes. But the London employers were prepared to do battle for the Linotype as they had not been prepared to fight for the Hattersley. They refused to negotiate on the News Scale until the L.S.C. had agreed on a scale of prices for composing machines.

Warned by reports from the United States, and more recently from the provinces, the L.S.C. reluctantly gave its attention to composing machines. It lacked the T.A.'s long experience in coping with Hattersleys; but on the other hand it had a very well disciplined union, more readily in touch with the Executive, which could be summoned to delegate or general meetings at short notice. The T.A. was an army of guerrilla bands; the L.S.C. was a panzer division.

Like the T.A., however, the L.S.C. had two main objectives: to retain a 'fair' share of work for hand compositors during the transition,

COMPOSING MACHINES

and to obtain such rates and conditions that operators would share in the benefits of technological progress, without being tempted to engage in 'speed contests'. Like the T.A., too, it settled for the policy of complete control of machines.

In February 1892, an agreement was signed with the Economic Printing and Publishing Company giving a 'stab rate to operators of 45s for forty-eight hours, as compared with 38s for fifty-four hours for hand compositors. The agreement was of only short duration, for the firm, disappointed with the low output of the operators, and incensed at the refusal of the L.S.C. to agree to a piece rate, dismissed its staff and engaged non-society labour.

As machines became more common, attitudes towards working conditions hardened. The L.S.C. was at first strongly in favour of a 'stab rate, mainly on the grounds that a piece rate would encourage high output and thus increase unemployment; the employers on the other hand wanted piece rates in order to obtain data regarding maximum capacity on different kinds of work.

When it became obvious that the Linotype had come to stay, the L.S.C. opened negotiations with the proprietors of London daily newspapers. By this time the operators were tempted by the lure of high earnings under piece rates and agitated for a change in union policy. While negotiations with the employers were at a deadlock, the union turned to the Linotype Machinery Company, hoping to exercise control of the machines through agreement with the manufacturers instead of the users. Although the parties came to an 'understanding' on a piece scale, it was never put into operation.

The first agreement with the newspaper proprietors—then the main users of the Linotype—was signed in June 1894, and was to run until the end of 1895. It contained several concessions to the union's claim to control working conditions on the machines, the most important being the stipulation that:

'All skilled operators shall be members of the L.S.C., preference being given to members on the companionship into which the machines are introduced.'

The Executive claimed that this clause—an admission of the union's exclusive right to the operation of the machine—was unique in the history of industrial relations in Great Britain. On the other hand the primary objective of protecting the hand compositor was imperfectly attained. The only provisions in this regard were that operators and case hands should commence work at the same time, and that the latter could charge for headings not composed by the operator. Nor were

176

BILATERAL BARGAINING

there any strict rules regulating transfer from machine to case, or vice versa, since in an 'emergency' an employer could make such transfer freely, although for a *permanent* transfer a fortnight's notice was required.

The following piece scales were adopted:

3¼d per 1,000 ens for daywork in Evening Paper Offices
3¾ per 1,000 ens for work in Morning Paper Offices
¼d per 1,000 ens extra on all types above brevier

As the Scale of Prices (a Hattersley scale was also included) were based on piece rates, it was necessary to include some clauses to protect earnings. Operators on morning papers were guaranteed two galleys per day of seven hours, and on evening papers twelve galleys per week of forty-two hours. Any stoppage of fifteen minutes or more for repairs was chargeable at ordinary time rate, while the usual rules regarding extra payment for bad copy, manuscript, or foreign language, etc., were to apply. Where the agreement was not specific, the provisions of the Hand Scale were to serve as a guide.

These rates were roughly one third of the hand news rates, but output on the machine was five or six times that of the hand compositors, and earnings of full time Linotype operators were approximately doubled under the new scales.[1]

'It can be asserted unhesitatingly and without fear of contradiction, that the Scale then agreed upon was from first to last most favourable to case and machine hands; and it has on more than one occasion been suggested that the employers' representatives were "caught napping" when assisting to frame it.'[2]

The Linotype Machinery Co., no less than some of the employers, was dismayed at the high earnings which operators were making, and made several attempts to induce the L.S.C. to revise the agreement. One of the most tempting offers was of a loan of £20,000 worth of equipment to be used by the union for the training of operators, in return for a modification of the terms.[3] When the union refused the Company issued a Circular in which it claimed that the L.S.C. was deliberately encouraging the restriction of output. In its counter propaganda the union while indignantly denying this charge, took the opportunity of exposing the anti-union activities of the Company.[4] In October 1895, another

[1] L.S.C., *Report of Adjourned Special Meeting*, January 1896.
[2] T.A., *Report of Delegate Meeting*, 1898.
[3] L.S.C., *Annual Report*, 1896.
[4] *Typographical Circular*, December 1894, p. 12.

COMPOSING MACHINES

mysterious circular (marked *Private and Confidential*) was distributed among London newspaper proprietors. It contained notes and suggestions for amending the Linotype scale which was due to lapse in December, and repeated the three main charges, with which the union was by this time wearily familiar, that the old rate was too high, that working rules were too restrictive, that the union's policy was subversive of technical progress.[1] Some colour was given to the last claim by the fact that a recent L.S.C. ballot had endorsed a resolution that no man should produce more than the output which his Chapel decided should constitute a fair day's work. The circular claimed that while output in America averaged 8,000 ens per hour, in London newspaper offices it was only 6,000, the difference being partly attributed to the collusion of foremen who, under the influence of union or chapel, kept back copy from the machines in order to maintain the earnings of the hand compositors.

In November 1895, the London Master Printers gave notice that they wished for a general revision of the agreement, and negotiations were renewed, though the L.S.C. Executive was not granted authority to settle the new terms. Hence the agreement reached in December was provisional only, and in accordance with union regulations, was submitted to a ballot of the members.[2] In recommending its acceptance the Executive warned members:

'that this machine question is no longer in its experimental stage, but that, on the contrary its practicability has been placed beyond all doubt. ... In voting upon this question, however, the members will do well to bear in mind that an adverse vote will probably place them—so far as public sympathy is concerned—in the undesirable position of attempting to fight machinery. Time after time charges of hostility towards the machines have been levelled against the Executive, and as often refuted. ...'[3]

Despite this warning, the members rejected the agreement. Although C. W. Bowerman pointed out that the union could not hold out against a reduction in the particularly favourable terms which had obtained under the 1894 agreement, a Special General Meeting endorsed the rejection of any compromise and agreed to pay a levy for six weeks in order to meet any 'contingencies'. A special Committee was appointed to re-cast the Scale in order to achieve a 'just balance between the interests of operators and hand compositors'.

[1] Webb Coll., B. LXXIV. 40.
[2] L.S.C., *Provisional Agreement re Machine Scale*, January 1896.
[3] L.S.C., *Report of Executive to Special Delegate Meeting*, 1896.

178 BILATERAL BARGAINING

In the meantime, while negotiations were proceeding in a somewhat desultory fashion, the Linotype Company made a successful counter-attack on the hitherto unchallenged fortress of union control.

'The last subject on my notes is the question of training schools. We have dealt with them in the Report, and I want to show you that these training schools are not entirely unproductive. The other day there was a strike at the offices of the morning newspaper, which uses Linotypes, and that newspaper appealed to us, and we furnished them with the services of 25 efficient men *and they were able to make the change from a unionist to a non-unionist office without the least disturbance to the business*. It never occasioned the loss of half an hour in bringing out the paper.'[1]

In April another dispute over the working of composing machines also resulted in the shop being closed to the union.

These defeats served to warn the workers of the risks of continuing to adopt an intransigent attitude over piece rates. In June another conference was arranged with the employers. Remembering rather bitterly the fate of the previous 'provisional agreement' the masters insisted that the union representatives should have plenary powers.[2]

The conference was successful and the new terms which, surprisingly enough, embodied only minor reductions in piece rates, came into operation in July. Several changes were made in other conditions of working, the most important being the provision that in future members of companionships into which machines were introduced were to be given facilities to learn the keyboard *in their own time*. When they had reached a certain stage of efficiency (4,000 ens per hour on test) they were to receive preference for future vacancies. The second important new rule regulated the distribution of work between case and machine hands.

'Case hands and operators to lift from separate heaps of copy, but when one heap is run out, copy is to be taken from the heap remaining.'[3]

Furthermore, not only were case and machine hands to *start* work together, but on morning papers they were also to *stop* at the same time. The employers were required to refrain from practising discrimination between case and machine in their selection of copy, and to distribute it 'in fair proportion'.

Thirdly, machines might be employed on morning papers in the

[1] Linotype Company, *Report . . . of Meeting of Shareholders*, 1 March, 1896, p. 25, (italics supplied). [2] L.S.C., *Annual Report*, 1896.
[3] Reprinted in *The London Compositor*, Doc. CXXIV.

COMPOSING MACHINES

day time 'provided that three case hands are called in to each machine, and that not more than three machines are thus employed'.[1]

Whereas the 1894 agreement had been restricted to Daily News offices, the 1896 one included Weekly News and Bookwork scales. In establishments engaged on this work, apprentices were of course employed. Youths in the last two years of their servitude could be employed on machines 'in due proportion to the number of journeymen operators—i.e., one apprentice to three journeymen operators'. Since piece or 'stab was optional in offices other than daily news, a 'stab rate of 45s for forty-eight hours was included.

The agreement worked surprisingly smoothly, but the high earnings of pieceworkers ($£4–£5$) tended to encourage employers to put them on time-work wherever possible. The union contended that this was contrary to the intention, if not to the letter, of the News Scale, and at a conference in 1898 the following equivocal 'principle' was established:

'The printer has the right to put any operator upon time work, but the representatives of the employers have agreed that such right shall be exercised with discretion, preference being given to case hands for time work.'[2]

The dry tables of union statistics tell their own tale. In the five years 1886–90 L.S.C. expenditure on unemployment relief averaged about £5,000 annually, in the next five years it leapt to an annual average of £12,000, though the membership increased from 9,000 (1891) to 10,000 (1895). Perhaps there is significance, too, in the increase in Removal Grant from an annual average of less than £100 before 1890 to nearly £400 annually in the next period. Where did these men go? Presumably to the provinces where, even if jobs were as scarce as in London, at least the cost of living was lower.

The effect on union funds was felt sharply. After rising steadily since 1881, to a peak of £30,000 in 1889, they fell over the next three years to £24,000.

But membership continued to expand, and higher contributions quickly restored the Funds. By 1900 the L.S.C. had £74,000; the crisis was over.

Monotype

The virtual settlement of conditions for Linotype operation (except for the vexed question of provincial piece-scales) by 1900 greatly facilitated the introduction of the Monotype. Unlike the Linotype, where one

[1] Most of the clauses remained unchanged. See, *Report on Collective Agreements*, 1910.   [2] M.P.A.T.A., *Circular*, 1899, p. 80.

180 BILATERAL BARGAINING

operator does both composing and casting of the type, the Monotype requires two workmen.

Were both of these men to be considered 'printers', and their operations to be controlled by the typographical unions? Or only one of them, and if so, which one?

This time the machine manufacturers took the initiative. In January 1902 the manager of the Lanston Monotype Corporation wrote to the T.A. suggesting that a rate for the operation should be fixed 'for our mutual benefit'. A few machines had already been installed, and in each case the T.A. branch was enforcing the Linotype rate. The director pointed out that physical working conditions were very different:

'In the case of the Linotype the operator has not only to attend to the ordinary composition by manipulation of the keys, but has further to supervise the casting operation, the heating of his metal, the supply thereof, the distribution of his matrices, and in general, the whole operation of composition and casting, whereas the monotype operator has an independent keyboard, practically on all fours with a type-writing machine. He is removed not only from the noise and dirt, but also from the heat which is a necessary accompaniment to the casting machine.'[1]

He suggested that it would be reasonable to fix the Monotype operators' wages and hours about midway between those for hand compositors and Linotype operators. Thus prompted, the T.A. Executive bestirred itself, inspected Monotypes at the *Manchester Guardian* jobbing office and conducted a survey to find out what practices existed in offices using Monotypes. It seems incredible that the Executive had not already been informed, but such was apparently the case.

The survey revealed the usual rich provincial mixture. Although in all 'fair' houses the operators were T.A. members, rates varied. Some were receiving the Linotype rate, some the case rate, and some were in between. Pending agreement with the Corporation, the Executive advised branches to try to obtain the Linotype terms. As the prospects of reaching agreement with the firm grew dim, the branches were left to draw up 'approved' rates and conditions, and try to get them accepted by local employers.

In 1903 the newly-formed Federation of Master Printers decided to enter directly into negotiations with the T.A. and proposed a con-ference on Monotype rates and conditions. The T.A. reacted as it had ten years earlier to the overtures of the Linotype Users' Association—with extreme caution. It was more than a year before the parties

[1] Quoted in Musson, *op. cit.*, pp. 206–7.

COMPOSING MACHINES

actually met. Although the T.A. pressed for the same conditions as Linotype operators, in order to reduce unemployment and the drain on the funds, the employers would not offer more than $12\frac{1}{2}$ per cent above case rates, and a fifty-two and a half hour week, or 10 per cent above case rates and a fifty-one hour week.

The T.A. Executive decided to accept the former alternative, and instructed its negotiating team 'to try by every means' to get the working of the Monotype *casting* machine 'into the hands of the union members'. When the conference resumed there was swift agreement on basic rates and hours. It was impossible, however, for the F.M.P., which included many non-union and open houses, to insist that all operators should be T.A. members. However, the employers agreed that in offices worked in accordance with T.A. rules, all operators should be T.A. members. This was not much of a concession, but it probably saved the T.A. from many petty disputes with individual firms. General working rules in regard to minimum earnings, payment for standing time, the sharing of 'takes', and payment for extras were much the same as in the Linotype agreement.

The employers refused to concede the right of the T.A. to control the caster. They contended that the work of minding the caster was only semi-skilled, requiring no specifically typographical training and, therefore, did not come within the jurisdiction of the T.A. This attitude was shared by a considerable number of the more conservatively minded members of the union itself.

Endorsement of the agreement was suspended for some time while the Executive attempted to force the F.M.P. to compromise on the issue of the caster attendants, but when it became clear that the union was making no headway, both Time and Piece Rules for keyboard operation were ratified in August 1905.

The T.A. paid the penalty for its negligent attitude to the introduction of Monotypes a few years earlier. Confronted with a *fait accompli*, it could only battle on rather desultorily with the organization of caster attendants. In fact, up till 1918 when the T.A. resumed the organization of caster attendants, many of them were enrolled by Natsopa and the Stereotypers' and Typefounders' societies. This issue provided a rich crop of demarcation and jurisdictional disputes for several decades.

In London the problem of jurisdiction did not arise. Having established its right to control the perforating machine, the L.S.C. disdained to enrol the non-craft caster attendants, most of whom joined the Amalgamated Typefounders' Trade Society.

In 1902 the L.S.C. appointed a Special Committee to prepare a draft scale for submission to the employers. As feeling in the union at this time was strongly in favour of piecework, where practicable, the draft

182   BILATERAL BARGAINING

which was eventually approved and submitted in 1906 included a piece rate—rather hopefully fixed at 3d per 1,000 ens for book work and 3½d for weekly news, both uncorrected. The 'stab rate was the same as that for Linotype—45s for forty-eight hours.[1] This draft scale, although adopted by the union, would not even be considered by the employers, and in 1911 a Delegate Meeting resolved that it should be withdrawn.[2]

In 1909 *The Times* changed to Monotype and installed thirty-six keyboards and casters, all operated by non-union labour, but in April 1914, following a change in ownership, the firm became a union house and over 200 employees joined the L.S.C. The question of a piece scale for operators was again brought to the fore, and a House agreement was signed some months later. It consisted of two parts—one applying to the news 'ship and one to the jobbing, with rates for uncorrected matter of 3d and 2½d per 1,000 respectively.

A general piece scale for London Monotype operators was not signed until 1923. Most machines were worked on 'stab.

CONCLUSION

By 1914 the technological revolution in composition was virtually complete. Almost all news offices throughout the country were using Linotypes, and all the main book-houses were using Monotypes.

The transition was amazingly swift and smooth. It was fortunate for the unions that the machines came on the scene during an era of great expansion in the industry. The growing demand for books and news-papers, in part a consequence of mass education, in part a consequence of new techniques of advertising, cushioned the shock to the hand craftsmen. Thousands, indeed, were displaced, but many were re-absorbed (often on worse terms) on casual work and make-up.

It was a fortunate accident, too, that the three main machines—Hattersley, Linotype and Monotype, followed each other by about a decade. This gave the unions time to adjust their attitudes and thrash out their policy. If pragmatism is a virtue then the union leaders were virtuous men. They established their 'principles', but they knew when to turn a blind eye to an irremediable breach. They modified their rules, educated their members, bargained with the employers, gave way when the opposition was too strong.

Thus the unions emerged unscathed from the process. Neither the T.A. nor the L.S.C. suffered even a temporary set-back in the growth of membership. Even the added financial burden of the extra unemployed hardly affected their funds.

[1] *London Typographical Journal*, 1906, p. 4.
[2] *Ibid.*, September 1911, p. 13.

COMPOSING MACHINES 183

On the employers' side the machines gave rise directly to the Linotype Users' Association, which developed into the Newspaper Society, and the Monotype Users' Association, which is still in existence. Indirectly, the negotiations over the Monotype scale which were in the background of the Hampton dispute, gave birth to the London Newspaper Proprietors' Association, a breakaway from the Master Printers' Association.

The urgency of the need to settle terms of employment on machines led to a revival of bilateral collective bargaining. This time, however, it was on a national, not a local level, and the T.A.—L.U.A. agreement of 1898 may fairly stand as the first national agreement. This development in turn had its influence on the internal structure of the union, tending to accelerate the trend towards centralization of authority.

CHAPTER XII

FLOOD TIDE OF
TRADE UNIONISM

*The principle expressed in this one word 'organization' is
but partially understood by the average worker. . . .
Organization is the principle of orderly combination of
any number of units which separately are absolutely
powerless to resist oppression or help themselves or others,
but which combined possess the strength of unity according
to the magnitude of the combination, the way in which it
is handled and the cohesion, loyalty and obedience to the
rules by which it is governed.*
National Society of Operative Printers' Assistants,
Annual Report, 1905, p. 7.

THE NEW UNIONS

The most spectacular change in trade union organization in this period
was the formation of unions of semi-skilled men and women. During
the nineteenth century the craft unions had succeeded in establishing
well defined spheres of influence. They fixed their limits of operation,
sometimes by a geographical boundary, sometimes by the definition of
the technical operation which they wished to control. For decades they
waged unremitting warfare against the 'encroachments' of labourers,
porters, females and boys. Their efforts were fairly successful in the
period when the others were unorganized. After 1890 they watched,
with mixed feelings, the sudden rise of Natsopa, the Warehousemen's
Union and the National Union of Paper Mill Workers. Here was a
challenge not only to the employers, but also to the craft unions' long
dynastic rule.

Natsopa—The National Society of Operative Printers and Assistants[1]
In 1889 the famous strikes of the Gasworkers and Dockers—two great
groups of unskilled and unorganized workers—sparked the flame of

---

[1] J. Moran, *Seventy-five years of the National Society of Operative Printers
and Assistants*, 1964. See also R. B. Suthers, *The Story of Natsopa*, 1930.

FLOOD TIDE OF TRADE UNIONISM

revolt among the unskilled workers in many other industries. In August 1889 the labourers in the large London printing firm of Spottis-woodes came out on strike. In a public proclamation they claimed that their wages averaged 12s–14s per week. Hours were long and irregular, overtime payment was inadequate, and working conditions were cramped, dirty, and unhealthy. As the excitement mounted, strike fever spread to other offices; by the end of the month more than forty firms were involved. A Strike Committee collected subscriptions from the public and issued an allowance. Mass meetings, with banners and bands, gathered at Clerkenwell Green in the week-ends, to hear Mrs Annie Besant and other famous orators exhorting the strikers to stand firm, and imploring other workers to support them.[1]

The main demands of the strikers were simple—a minimum wage of 20s, a standard week of fifty-four hours, and overtime of 6d per hour.

Some houses gave way, and granted these conditions. Others held out. After a few weeks, however, a committee of master printers met a deputation from the strike committee, and agreed to the minimum terms.

During the strike the Committee realized that any gains would have to be maintained by a permanent organization, and they drafted rules for a Printers' Labourers' Union. The London Society of Compositors helped the new union to find its feet. The first formal meeting of the Printers' Labourers' Union was held in February 1890. It then had over 800 members, and 'a good round sum' in the bank.

The main field of recruitment at first, however, was not the casual, unskilled labourers, but the numerous assistants who worked in the pressrooms of the large firms, especially on the rotary machines used in newspaper printing. These men were not 'labourers', and the title of the union was changed, in a few years to the Operative Printers' Assistants' Society. Later, when the Society extended beyond London, the 'National' was added. A very critical change of title was made in 1912, by the insertion of 'and' between the words 'Printers' and 'Assistants', signifying the union's claim to recruit men of craft standard.

Natsopa endured the customary growing pains of a 'mushroom' union—difficulties of administration, the development of internal factions and rivalries, occasional dishonesty of branch officials. In 1908 the union fell apart, and from the wreckage G. Isaacs began to re-build a more effective organization. By 1914 Natsopa had over 7,000 members.

Warehousemen, Cutters and Assistants.[2]

'Stirred into action by the noble example shown by the Printers' Labourers' Union and also by the dockers', Alfred Evans founded a

---

[1] See extracts from *The Star* newspaper, reprinted in *Natsopa Jubilee*, 1889–1939.　　　[2] For a detailed account, see C. J. Bundock, *op. cit.*, Book 2.

186 BILATERAL BARGAINING

union to cater for non-craft men in printers' and stationers' warehouses
—the men who unloaded, stacked, sorted, cut and folded the paper.
The first meeting was held "in an empty room with a candle on the
mantelpiece, round which we had to stand. We only mustered 33
members then, but we soon got on, and at the next meeting we had a
lamp, this time on a table, at which we sat on empty boxes. It was no
child's play then, but we all looked on it as a labour of love and spared
neither our time nor our money to perfect the organization".'[1]

The objects of the union were 'to obtain a minimum wage of 32s per
week for bookbinders' cutters, 30s per week for warehousemen and
cutters, and 24s per week for warehouse assistants, and a minimum of
time-and-a-quarter for overtime; to provide an out-of-work benefit
fund; and to endeavour to reduce the hours of labour, and regulate the
relations between workmen and employer'.[2]

There were, at this time, two London societies already catering for
warehousemen, and requiring a minimum wage of 30s and five year's
experience. They were obviously imbued with the old craft union
ideology, and looked askance at the interloper. Evans enrolled any man
over eighteen years working on paper handling. His union was quickly
engaged in disputes—with single firms—as he strove to win recognition
and the union terms. During these early disputes the older societies of
warehousemen played a somewhat equivocal role. 'Principles of
unionism' required, on the one hand, that they should support another
union; but concern for their own status suggested that they would not
be altogether displeased if the brash newcomer failed. Acrimonious
inter-union disputes led, in a few years, to the defensive amalgamation
of the two older societies. But this could not save them for long, and
in 1900 they agreed to amalgamate with the more dynamic union. By
this time Evans had extended his organization to the provinces, and
was coming into contact with Natsopa. In London the two unions had
fairly clearly defined fields of jurisdiction, but in the provinces the great
body of semi-skilled men, untouched by unionism, presented a great
attraction to both. The result was that the first union to gain support
in a firm usually won all of the non-craft workers.

The union went through several internal crises. In 1901 the Committee reported the development of an infra-union sectional organization styled the 'Jobbing Chapel', which was attempting to use pressure
group tactics to win a majority on the executive and thus promote the
interests of the jobbing (i.e. casual) hands. The Committee sternly

[1] Quoted in C. J. Bundock, *op. cit.*, p. 112.
[2] Printers' and Stationers' Warehousemen, Cutters and Assistants Union,
Rules, 1891.

FLOOD TIDE OF TRADE UNIONISM 187

called for the dissolution of this 'inner circle', and for all members to sink their petty differences in the face of a 'gigantic capitalist conspiracy to first impoverish and then crush the trade union movement'. This referred to the notorious Taff Vale Judgement of the House of Lords in 1901, under which a trade union was liable to pay civil damages for losses due to a trade dispute.

The union had to dismiss several branch officials for embezzlement of funds, or flagrant breach of union rules. These crises, however, hardly impeded its overall growth. In 1902 it began to enrol women members, taking in the London Society of Women Bookfolders which it had helped to organize ten years earlier. Later it formed women's branches in provincial towns. In 1913 the total membership was about 9,000. In 1914 the union amalgamated with the National Union of Paper Mill Workers.

National Union of Paper Mill Workers[1]

In 1890 there were three rival 'craft' unions of papermakers. The Original Society of Papermakers, founded in 1800, was a conservative and declining body clinging to the traditions of the handicraft days, and failing to adjust to the factory age. Machine-made paper workers had two unions—the United Brotherhood (1854), and the Modern Society, a breakaway union formed in 1869. These catered, however, for the men in charge of machines, and included a number of overseers and foremen. The less skilled workers had no union.

In 1890 William Ross, a man of the calibre of Evans and Isaacs in his breadth of vision and capacity for organization, formed the National Union of Paper Mill Workers, to enrol 'all male and female workers above sixteen years of age employed within the gates of a paper mill'. The preamble to the first book gave a pithy lesson in unionism:

'Of one thing you may all be assured—no amelioration of your condition as paper mill workers is possible without this Union, and combination of operatives over the entire United Kingdom. There can be no isolated and local concessions granted by employers, neither can there be successful local combinations of workers; no lessening of the number of weekly working hours; no half-holiday on Saturday; no adjustment tending to the equitable sharing of the profits of industry; and no effective support to just and humane employers can be possible without a National Union.'[2]

Because of the wide scope of its membership—it was in fact aiming at

[1] For detailed account, see C. J. Bundock, *op. cit.*, Book 4.
[2] National Union of Paper Mill workers, *Rules*, 1890.

188 BILATERAL BARGAINING

industrial unionism—with a wide variation in wages, the union had a sliding scale of contributions and benefits. From its inception it paid out-of-work allowance, as well as providing for relief of members tramping in search of work. Other benefits were paid in cases of distress, and for funeral expenses.

The Head Office of the union was in the home of the Secretary, William Ross, where for twenty years his wife acted as unpaid clerical assistant.

Conditions of working in many of the mills were shocking. Unskilled hands worked for as long as seventy-two hours per week for a wage of about 15s. Employers liked to keep the mills running continuously, for at least six days a week, with only two shifts. They enforced the rule that no man should leave until his shift mate relieved him; there were no spare hands to replace shift men delayed through accident or illness, and men sometimes had to work thirty-six or forty-eight hours continuously.[1]

Ross realized that his power to improve conditions by collective bargaining alone was severely limited by the weakness of the union (during this period it enrolled only some 5,000 of the 40,000 workers in the industry) and by foreign competition. He worked through the Labour Party, therefore, to obtain legislative restriction on imports of cheap foreign paper, and to bring the industry within the scope of the Factory and Shops Act.

But just as the formation of the Evans's Cutters' union had promoted a 'defensive' amalgamation in 1893 of the older Warehousemen's societies, so the formation of the National Union of Paper Mill Workers led, in 1894 to a closing of the ranks of the two old 'craft' societies of Papermakers, resulting in the Amalgamated Society of Papermakers. Throughout this period relations between the craft union and the industrial reunion were seldom more than civil, and the craftsmen stolidly rejected all amalgamation overtures.

Both Ross and Evans were enthusiastic apostles of industrial unionism, and as their unions expanded, they came into contact in several spheres—such as the organization of women paper folders, and cutters and warehousemen in stock rooms of paper mills. Instead of this leading to rivalry and friction, however, the leading personalities had the foresight and authority to bring their two unions swiftly into an amalgamation conference.

The meeting of delegates voted overwhelmingly in favour of the principle of amalgamation, a decision which was endorsed by a membership ballot in May 1914. With some 15,000 members the new National Union of Printing and Paper Workers was second only to the T.A. in

[1] Evidence of William Ross before Royal Commission on Labour, 1892.

numbers. The old Amalgamated Society of Papermakers clung stubbornly to its craft autonomy until 1937.

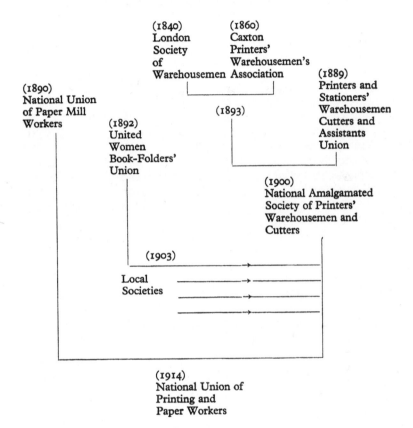

WOMEN

In the nineteenth century women were completely excluded from the craft unions. Women did not take apprenticeships to skilled trades, and therefore were not eligible for membership. Most of the union rules explicitly stated that the union was 'open to *men*' with certain qualifications. After 1900, however, some of the unions became slightly concerned lest they seem to be practising discrimination against women, and tried to maintain that they would admit women who could do the work of a man and earn a man's rate of pay. This studied piece of hypocrisy

190   BILATERAL BARGAINING

did not deceive anyone with any knowledge of the inherent conservative and exclusive outlook of the old craftsmen.[1]

In the early twentieth century the organization of women into special branches of the 'new unions' prompted the craft unions to make an agonizing reappraisal of their traditional policy. This particularly applied to bookbinders, for women continued to predominate in the 'forwarding' section of the industry. There was, on the whole, little trouble over demarcation between men's and women's work, but if the women were organized in a separate union there was a serious prospect of demarcation disputes leading to inter-union strife. The Bookbinders' Consolidated Union was, therefore, the first of the craft unions to begin to organize the women. In doing so it came into direct conflict with Evans's Cutters' Union.

Even with four unions in the field the organization of women made slow progress. In 1914 there were about 150,000 women in the industry, mainly in paper and stationery trades, but less than 10,000 in the unions.[2] Their wages were 11s or 12s per week—about a third of the standard craft rate.

CRAFT UNIONS

The growth in membership of the main craft unions over this critical period is shown in the following table:

MEMBERSHIP (000)

	1890	1900	1914
T.A.	10	16	24
L.S.C.	9	11	12
S.T.A.	3	4	5

Source: Annual Reports of Unions

In fact, despite the spectacular growth of the 'new unions', in 1914 the craft unoinists still outnumbered the non-craft, mainly because of an energetic organizing phase of the T.A. This in itself, however, was largely prompted by the provincial activities of Natsopa. After 1890 the T.A. began to organize the machine-minders which previously it had ignored and, in truth, rather despised for their lack of apprenticeship.

In evidence before the Industrial Council in 1912 the secretaries of the L.S.C., T.A. and Bookbinders' Union claimed that their organizations included 70, 80, and 90 per cent respectively of the journeymen

[1] Fair Wages Committee Enquiry, Cd 4422, p. 16.
[2] Report of the War Cabinet Committee on Women in Industry, Cd. 135, 1919, pp. 15, 56.

FLOOD TIDE OF TRADE UNIONISM

eligible for membership.[1] The Lithographic Printers' Society claimed to have enrolled 89 per cent of those working at the trade in 1908. Over the period total union membership rose from 40,000 to 90,000. The proportion of union members to all workers in the industry rose from 24 to 31 per cent. If the craft unions were as highly organized as they claimed to be—the remaining 70 per cent of workers—over 100,000— must be non-craft workers. Who was to tap this vast field of potential recruits? In 1890 the craft unions would have hotly denied that these inferior orders could be organized into disciplined unions. Evans, Ross and Isaacs had shown that it could be done.

One by one the craft unions forgot their exclusive traditions, and threw open their doors to women and male assistants.

Despite their growing membership and their high contributions, the printing unions did not build up large funds. It was not strike pay or unemployment allowance which drained away the contributions, but the burden of continually increasing payments for the superannuation benefits, inaugurated about 1880. The distribution of percentage expenditure on benefits over the period 1892–1900 is shown in the following table:

PERCENTAGE EXPENDITURE ON BENEFITS OF 7 PRINTING UNIONS — TOTAL EXPEN-DITURE

	Out-of-Work	Dispute	Sick and Accident	Funeral	Other	Super-annua-tion	Working Expenses	(£000)
1892	46	15	5	7	2	8	18	53
93	50	8	5	8	2	9	19	51
94	59	4	5	6	1	9	17	56
95	55	3	5	8	1	11	18	54
96	50	5	6	7	1	13	17	54
97	45	4	6	7	6	14	18	55
98	42	6	6	7	5	16	19	59
99	43	5	6	8	3	16	20	63
1900	48	4	5	8	3	17	16	71

Source: Board of Trade, *Report on Trade Unions*, 1901

While other benefits fluctuated slightly from year to year, the percentage spent on superannuation climbed irresistibly upward. Some part of expenditure had to be reduced to offset this. The most flexible item of expenditure was strike pay.

Unless the drain of superannuation payments could be halted, disputes would have to be kept to a minimum. But to carry this policy beyond a certain point entailed the abandoning of some of the prin-

[1] Industrial Council Enquiry . . . *Minutes of Evidence*, pp. 262, 270.

192 BILATERAL BARGAINING

ciples of unionism, or some of the hard-won standards of working conditions.

While some union leaders were keenly aware of this dilemma they were deterred from taking drastic action for several reasons: sympathy with the aged members, fear of advocating unpopular economies, and knowledge that a reduction in superannuation benefits might simply lead to the older members competing for jobs at reduced rates. In 1902 the L.S.C. Executive warned a delegate meeting to bear in mind:

'. . . that the L.S.C. is, or should be, primarily a trade union, and that although the benefits have steadily increased in number and aims, there is a distinct danger that by adding still larger and other benefits the Society will become in a sense a huge friendly benefit society, thereby in all probability weakening its force and usefulness from a purely trade union point of view.'[1]

The T.A., too, was in almost continuous difficulty over its superannuation fund. At almost every Delegate Meeting the Executive reported that the fund was in a 'very unsatisfactory condition', but despite an increase in contributions the position was no better at the next meeting. Delegates at the 1913 meeting who advocated yet another rise in subscriptions pointed out that the benefit was one of the main attractions for recruiting members.[2]

INTER-UNION DISPUTES

There are three important points to bear in mind when considering the organization of the unions and their conflicting claims to enrol certain classes of workers. First, that the provincial craft unions were developing from loose, federal 'associations' towards more highly centralized 'unions'. Second, that the New Unions of semi-skilled workers were extending outwards to the provinces after having established their nuclei in London during the burst of unionism in the turbulent nineties. Third, that the old craft unions had carefully nurtured the doctrine that each of them had the right to control a specific technical operation, such as the setting of type, or the binding of books.

Thus for a long time the Association of Correctors of the Press and the London Compositors' Society were at loggerheads over the latter's policy of enrolling readers. Many readers were, however, selected from the ranks of the compositors, and were already members of the L.S.C. Again, for a time the L.S.C. and the Typographical Association were in dispute over the right to organize the towns in the Home Counties. The L.S.C. indeed arbitrarily extended its own area of jurisdiction from a

[1] L.S.C., *Report of Committee*, 1902.   [2] See Musson, *op. cit.*, pp. 284–94.

FLOOD TIDE OF TRADE UNIONISM

radius of 15 miles to 40 miles from the General Post Office, and changed its title to the 'London and Provincial Society of Compositors'.

In the provinces there was still more trouble as the non-craft unions competed with each other and with the T.A. In 1890 the latter was primarily a union of hand compositors, with provision for the admission of machinemen but no constitutional recognition of them. By 1914 this state of affairs had radically changed. After the Special Conference in 1891, the machine-minders obtained separate representation on the Executive; steady progress was made in organization of pressrooms, and numbers of working rules were adopted. Most of the new members were minders in charge of flat-bed machines. The employers resolutely refused to recognize the right of the T.A. to enrol rotary machinemen, on the grounds that these men were ineligible under Union rules, for they had not served the prescribed apprenticeship, but had generally been promoted from the ranks of the semi-skilled. Many rotary assistants joined Natsopa when that union opened branches in the provinces. But what was to happen to an assistant who was promoted to machineminder? Should he leave Natsopa and join the 'enemy', or should he remain in the 'Assistants' union, although he was now a minder?

Many other disputes such as these racked the trade union movement in this period. The old order of craft union oligarchy was passing, but the change was resisted by those who felt that their power and prestige were threatened. Just prior to the Great War Natsopa, growing vigorously under the able leadership of George Isaacs, was in the thick of jurisdictional disputes with almost all of the craft unions. At first, when Natsopa and the Cutters' Union extended to the provinces, they clashed frequently with each other. But after they had reached a sensible *modus vivendi*, and agreed on respective spheres of influence, they both came into conflict with the craft unions. Indeed, such was the hostility of the older unions to the 'aggressive encroachments' of the new, that at one stage three of the craft unions[1] informed the Master Printers' Associations that they had formed a 'Triple Alliance for defensive purposes', and were prepared to take extreme action to prevent the craftsmen's privileges from being usurped by the semi-skilled men.

AMALGAMATION

These inter-union conflicts were obviously inimical to the success of the unions in their disputes with the employers, and there was a constant search for some remedy. The most popular panacea was amalgamation. This was the heyday of the doctrine of Industrial Unionism, and it seemed apparent to many that when all of the workers in each industry

[1] The S.T.A., P.M.M.T.S., and F.S.E.S.

194   BILATERAL BARGAINING

were united in the one union, sectional interests would be obliterated and the workers' bargaining power would be at a maximum. But although ambitious schemes for a National Typographical Union were under continuous discussion, the old letterpress craft unions were unable to yield their sovereignty or to merge their identity with a new industrial union.

The bookbinders, in contrast, made surprising progress. In 1907 a ballot of the members of four unions (three in London and one national union) gave a large majority for amalgamation. A Joint Committee was set up to wrestle with the problems of winding up the old unions, settling the *per capita* contribution to the new, transferring of members, reconciling the different benefits, and fixing a common code of working rules. In January 1911, the amalgamation was achieved and the National Union of Bookbinders and Machine Rulers was founded. For the next four years the original London Societies acted as separate branches of the N.U.B.M.R. until they were 'fused' to form the London Book-binders' Branch.

The most important amalgamation of this period was the fusion in 1914 of the National Union of Paper Mill Workers, whose membership had been comparatively constant for several years, with the more dynamic Cutters' Union to form the National Union of Printing and Paper Workers.

The main obstacle to the amalgamation of the letterpress craft unions was the disagreement between the London unions and the T.A. over the rights of branches to local autonomy in trade matters. The London societies, with a century of experience behind them, were not prepared to hand over this vital matter to an Executive which would be largely composed of provincial members. On the other hand the experience of the T.A. executive of the 'irresponsibility' of local branches set them firmly against any devolution of authority in matters vital to sound financial management.[1] Although the plan for a national amalgamation lapsed after 1909, renewed efforts were made to arrange for a single union of London letterpress workers—again without success. Alas for the hopes of an industrial union, embracing all workers in the industry working together for their common good! In 1914 Natsopa made a 'defensive alliance' with the newly formed National Union of Paper Workers, and at the outbreak of the Great War the craft unions and the 'New Unions' formed two hostile blocs.

FEDERATION

While the story of amalgamation schemes is largely one of failure, the history of the Federation in this period is one of steady, if unspectacular.

[1] T.A., *Half-Yearly Report*, December, 1911.

FLOOD TIDE OF TRADE UNIONISM

success. The idea of a federation was first mooted at the historic Typographical Conference of 1886; it took root, and in 1891 the first Printing and Kindred Trades' Federation was established. Broadly, its objects were the establishment of more uniform working conditions throughout the industry and the co-ordination of union policies, especially during conflicts with the employers. The most important rules were, therefore, those prescribing the procedure to be followed in case of dispute. The union concerned notified the Federation Secretary as soon as it was apparent that no peaceful solution could be found. Other unions were then put on the 'alert', but were not required to take active part unless non-unionists were engaged to replace the strikers. The Federation could call a conference of unions to consider what help they could give to a union in dispute, but it could not order the unions to withdraw their members. Once a dispute had been taken to the Federation Council no union was allowed to make a settlement with the employers without first obtaining the consent of all the unions involved. All unions pledged themselves not to give any assistance to an employer in dispute with a member of the Federation.[1]

The London craft unions did not join this 'National' Federation, but formed one of their own. As neither Federation had an independent income, its activity was restricted to encouraging union co-operation. The main defect, as the critics saw it, was that in the last resort each union was still only as strong as its own funds. What was needed was a scheme which would support *each* union with the funds of *all*. Such a scheme had been mentioned at the 1891 meeting, but had then gained little support.

In 1899, however, the climate of opinion changed and feeling ran in favour of a national federation with a compulsory strike fund. The new Printing and Kindred Trades Federation came into being on January 1, 1902. The chief difference between the new constitution and the old lay in the formation of a central strike fund, to which unions contributed on the scale of 1d per member on first affiliating, and 1s per member annually. Affiliated unions could draw 10s weekly for twenty weeks for every member on an 'approved' strike, or who had been dismissed for upholding the rules of his union. Each union was required to supplement this allowance with another of at least 5s per week from its own funds. These provisions put some teeth into the Federation, and by 1910 its funds had grown to over £10,000.

Early enthusiasts for federation realized that it was not sufficient to link up the unions at the national level; to complete the organization it was also essential that the workers should be united within the locality and the workshop. In the provinces energetic branches had formed

[1] P. & K.T.F., *Rules*, 1891, Objects, Dispute Rules.

196   BILATERAL BARGAINING

effective local federations of all the principal printing unions. The success of forward movements conducted by two powerful local federations at Birmingham and Sheffield gave a great boost to the movement, in which the T.A. executive was particularly active:

'Your Committee most earnestly desire that every encouragement and assistance should be rendered in establishing local federations, as in their opinion it is advisable that such bodies should be formed in every centre amongst the printing and kindred trades, and affiliated to the central body, so that when necessary the whole machinery of an extended federation can be brought into operation . . .'[1]

After the formation of the National Federation in 1901 little was heard of local federations for several years, but after 1904 there was a revival of interest in projects for completing the structure of organization. Union leaders held widely diverging views of the correct role of the Federation. Some looked towards greater centralization of authority as a means of ending internecine strife and combating the 'irresponsibility' of local union branches. Others hoped for decentralization of power and the building up of local federations as the spearhead of vigorous industrial action. A second conflict of opinion centred on the respective powers of the federation and the unions.

Gradually, however, the local federations won an official recognition in the constitution. In 1906 they were permitted to affiliate to the national body and receive copies of circulars; in 1909 they were given very limited right to send delegates to Annual Conferences. Despite fundamental differences of opinion on their function, the number of locals rose from twelve in 1904 to thirty-seven in 1914, and in the later years they played a regular part in initiating 'forward movements'.

Throughout this period almost all of the unions made provision for strengthening the organization at the workshop level. The formation of chapels or 'shop associations' was made compulsory whenever a minimum number of eligible workers was available. The new unions copied their pattern of organization from the older craft unions, making minor adaptations to suit their own conditions.

But although the Chapel was an invaluable link in the chain of union control, it was by no means wholly satisfactory. Based on the old distinctions of crafts which sometimes bore little relation to later machine production, the Chapel organization tended to split the workers, especially in London, into small groups which were sometimes uncooperative and occasionally hostile. Aware of this weakness the workers sometimes formed a House Chapel, or 'Imperial Chapel', which em-

[1] *Typographical Circular*, October 1896, p. 13.

FLOOD TIDE OF TRADE UNIONISM

braced all unionists within the establishment. By improving inter-union relations within the office they hoped to increase bargaining power. Formerly the employers had frequently encouraged inter-union hostility by playing off one against the other in such matters as recognition of rules or cards, or alterations in craft differentials.

Although the need for closer liaison at the workshop level had long been recognized, and indeed *ad hoc* co-ordinating committees had frequently been set up to help conduct disputes, it was not until 1911 that an official scheme for uniting the different workshop units was inaugurated. The P. & K.T.F. decided to give every encouragement and asistance to the formation of Federated Chapels in offices where members of more than one union was employed. Model Rules for such chapels were subsequently printed in the back of the Annual Report of the P. & K.T.F. but no information was given as to their number or influence.

For many years the most effective work of the P. & K.T.F. was its conciliation in inter-union disputes and co-ordination of efforts to increase over-all union membership. After 1908, however, the unions decided to attempt a nation-wide reduction of hours, with all acting in concert under the direction of the P. & K.T.F. In 1910 they presented to the Federation of Master Printers a demand for a forty-eight-hour working week. After a year of complicated manoeuvring, in the course of which some unions broke away from the national movement, a settlement was made on fifty-one hours. But the failure of the unions to work together did not augur well for the future of the P. & K.T.F. as a collective bargaining agency.

MASTER PRINTERS' ASSOCIATIONS

The London Master Printers' Association which had dissolved in 1870 was re-established in 1890 with the intention of eventually extending its organization to embrace the whole of the United Kingdom. Probably the employers had got wind of the intentions of the L.S.C. and the London Bookbinders to agitate for a revision of the London Scale and a reduction of the standard week. When these disputes were over the Association, then 200 strong, settled down to the task of consolidating its organization and tentatively extending its functions. It claimed that it could be of great value to the employers in representing the interests of the industry in regard to Bills in Parliament, trade tariffs and questions of copyright, as well as providing a counter to the growing strength of organized workers. The following rules are of most direct relevance to industrial relations:

'Every member and firm joining the Association thereby agrees not to conclude any modification of terms of labour with his men without first submitting the matter to the Committee and obtaining their views, which shall be communicated within one week from the receipt of notice by the Secretary.

Every member who shall receive any notice from his men requiring any alteration in the working hours, or customs, or rates of wages, shall send notice of the same to the Secretary, who shall lay it before the Committee for consideration. Should any strike occur without notice, the same action shall be taken.

It may be pointed out that freedom of action is not in any way affected, the only proviso being that proposed changes should be reported, and the advice of the Committee obtained for any point of importance.[1]

One of the first activities undertaken by the Association was an investigation of costing practice which it followed up by the issue of a Special Circular, exposing the unsoundness of many accounting procedures:

'It is notorious that, under stress and unhealthy competition, houses undertake work involving a large amount of composition at prices which allow but a slight percentage on compositors' wages, with the idea of merely covering the cost of composition, and of making a profit in other departments.'[2]

Interest in this matter was heightened by numerous reports in trade journals of the campaign being waged by the United Typothetae of America (a master printers' organization) in favour of standard costing. Selections from these reports were reprinted in the *Members' Circular*, helping to mould employer opinion in favour of reducing 'unhealthy' competition.

The formation of a permanent Master Printers' Association in London set an example for the provincial employers to follow. There, as in the capital, they were faced with important changes in technology and the growing influence and militancy of the unions. Most of them came into existence to conduct negotiations with the local trade societies, and continued for social intercourse, discussion of technical problems, and examination of the novel idea of standard costing. The objects of the Leeds association embraced a wide range—a watching brief on legislation, a benefit fund for workers, and the promotion of technical education for apprentices.[3]

---

[1] Printing and Allied Trades Association, *Rules*, 1890.
[2] *Special Circular*, November 9, 1892.
[3] M. Sessions, *The Federation of Master Printers: How it Began*, 1950, p. 188.

FLOOD TIDE OF TRADE UNIONISM 199

In June 1901 when the Federation of Master Printers was founded, local Associations existed in most of the main printing centres—Leeds, Bradford, Newcastle, Sheffield, Halifax, Derby, Birmingham, Reading, Leicester, Dublin, Edinburgh and Glasgow. In many cases, however, the formal organization was rather sketchy, and the 'solidarity' of the members was open to question.

Federation of Master Printers[1]

Confronted by the spectacle of growing national unions and a national federation of unions, the employers realized their own organization would need strengthening if they were to resist the workers' demands. In April 1901, the Federation of Master Printers came into existence, largely through the enthusiasm of Walter Hazell who became its first President. A paternalistic employer and philanthropist, Hazell did much, through his speeches and writings, to set the tone of the Federation's policy. He was no enemy of unionism, conducted in an orderly way, but believed that the time had come when organization of employers was necessary to combat the potential abuse of union power. But no less important was the need for printers to formulate a set of rules to protect themselves from the unreasonable demands of their customers.

The policy document issued in 1901 emphasized the function of the Federation as an agency for gathering and disseminating information on legal, technical and accounting problems, but also expressed the hope that later on the Federation might conduct negotiations with the trade unions. It suggested that the Federation should emulate the United Typothetae of America in the regular provision of social festivities which would help to minimize friction in business matters by improving inter-personal relations among employers.[2]

For the first few years the Federation concentrated on a campaign to raise interest in the reform of cost-accounting in order to eliminate unsound price-cutting. Even by 1904 an ex-president of the London M.P.A. thought that there had been a noticeable improvement:

'True it is that the fierce and foolish competition of previous years is modified; not, be it said, on account of a flux of business, but rather from the restraint and good sense born of the better knowledge of the liabilities of conducting a business.'[3]

In 1909 the Federation published a booklet *Printers' Costs, a System*

[1] M. Sessions, *op. cit.* See also Ellic Howe, *The British Federation of Master Printers*, 1950 .
[2] F.M.P., *Policy Document*, June 1901.
[3] F.M.P., *Members' Circular*, 1905, p. 13.

200   BILATERAL BARGAINING

of Book-keeping with Examples and Specimen Forms, which set out the principles and practice of costing.

Apart from standard costing the main activity of the F.M.P. in this period was the exercise of a vigilant watch on Parliamentary Bills likely in any way to affect the interests of master printers. With the increasing intervention of the State and local bodies in the conduct of business it became important for each industrial pressure group to exercise its influence most effectively. The Printers' unions, with their long historical association with the London Trades Council and the T.U.C. had an old tradition and not inconsiderable skill in the technique of lobbying. With the establishment of the Federation the master printers were able to make their viewpoint heard to the best advantage.

Although the main impetus to the formation of the London M.P.A. was the need to meet the growing strength of the unions, the main idea behind the formation of the Federation was to extend the principles of sound costing. H. Vane Stow, Secretary of the F.M.P. said:

'Our enemy is not the working man; our enemy is the man who will not pay enough for his work: and if we can do something to get a fair working profit for printers we shall be doing far more than [by] trying to beat down the wages of any working man.'[1]

As the Federation became firmly established it inevitably came up against the unions' efforts to alter working conditions. In 1904 it sent representatives to confer with the T.A. on compositors' and machine-minders' wages in the Home Counties, a notorious low-wage area. Two years later the Secretary took part in the negotiation of new local agreements in Manchester, and the F.M.P. became a party to the final settlement. But, in general, when the unions made a local movement the employers preferred to deal with it through the local Master Printers' Association. In 1910, however, a nationwide conflict was precipitated when the P. & K.T.F. presented a demand for an overall reduction and standardization of hours of work. In the course of the protracted negotiations the F.M.P. emerged as the national bargaining agency of the printing employers, and its signing of the Leeds Agreement in 1911 was an important development in the pattern of industrial relations.

The formation of the Federation gave renewed impetus to provincial organization, and the 'missionary work' of the Federation officials, especially on standard costing, gave a unity of purpose to the rather heterogeneous associations.

[1] Quoted in Ellic Howe, *op. cit.*, p. 6.

FLOOD TIDE OF TRADE UNIONISM

NUMBER OF PRINTING EMPLOYERS' ASSOCIATIONS

	England & Wales	Scotland	Ireland	Total
1901	30	4	2	36
1906	35	5	3	43
1913	68	9	3	80
1914	93	11	4	108

Source: Abstracts of Labour Statistics

The figures indicate the 'snowballing' rate of growth. Indeed, prior to the Great War the officials realized that the infant Federation had outgrown its swaddling clothes, and needed a new constitution. In 1911 the various Master Printers' Associations in Scotland formed an 'Alliance' to confront the unions. This had been eminently successful. An article in the *Members' Circular*[1] suggested that this example should be followed in England. Grouping the Associations would permit some decentralization, with partial autonomy on a regional basis. The Organization Committee drafted a scheme for six or eight English Alliances on the Scottish model, but owing to the outbreak of war the implementation of this reform was postponed.

The Newspaper Society

In the provinces the newspaper owners formed several rather loose regional federations to look after their general interests. The first national organization, however, was the Linotype Users' Association, formed in 1895 with the expressed purpose of negotiating with the T.A. a national agreement which would standardize working conditions throughout the provinces

Under the energetic leadership of Lascelles Carr the L.U.A. quickly established itself as the most important negotiating body in the provincial newspaper industry. As the Linotype machine was particularly suited to newspaper work, and speed of composition had long been the headache of newspaper managers, they were keen to see the machine adopted with maximum speed and minimum dislocation. The S.T.A. refused to negotiate with the L.U.A. on the ingenious grounds that it was a 'mythical body', and that the recognition of such specialized organizations to participate in settling working conditions would create a dangerous precedent.

In 1920, the L.U.A. was reconstituted as the Newspaper Society, and absorbed the other newspaper organizations. It continued to represent the interests of most newspaper and periodical houses throughout the country, with one important, and several minor, exceptions.

[1] F.M.P., *Members' Circular*, March 1914.

G*

202   BILATERAL BARGAINING

Newspaper Proprietors' Association

In May 1906 the L.S.C. reached a deadlock with the London M.P.A. in negotiations on overtime limits, night 'ships, and Monotype scale. At the same time the Printing Machine Managers' Trade Society and Natsopa became involved in a dispute with the London firm of Hamptons. At first the dispute concerned only the machine room, and the L.S.C. was not involved. The management decided to operate as a non-Society shop, and gave notice to all union members.

The L.S.C. suspected that the London Master Printers' Association was behind this decision, and that it formed part of a campaign to attack the Society in one house after another. A Special General Meeting of the L.S.C. decided to present an ultimatum to the Master Printers' Association: if L.S.C. men were not reinstated, the Society would issue a strike ballot. The Executive had the ballot printed and arranged for distribution as soon as the ultimatum expired. A 'general strike' of London compositors seemed imminent.

Alarmed at this prospect a group of daily newspaper proprietors approached the union and agreed to withdraw from the London M.P.A. and conduct separate negotiations with the Compositors, on the understanding that the Society would not involve the daily newspapers in any dispute with the masters in the general printing industry.[1]

Thus Hampton's dispute gave birth to the Newspaper Proprietors' Association, which since that date has conducted its affairs with the unions entirely separately from the general printers and the other newspaper proprietors.

[1] E. Howe and H. E. Waite, *op. cit.*, p. 317.

CHAPTER XIII

BILATERAL COLLECTIVE BARGAINING

If there is one feature which stands out in bolder relief than another it is the desire which, on all occasions and under all circumstances has been evinced by the members in favour of a signed and sealed working agreement with the employers.
Secretary of the L.S.C., *Jubilee History*, 1898, Introduction.

EXTENSION OF COLLECTIVE AGREEMENTS

In 1890 there was hardly one effective written agreement in the printing industry. By 1914 there were more than eighty, involving all of the major unions and employers' associations, and covering more than 50,000 workers.[1] This change in the regulation of terms of employment from unilateral enforcement of Union Rule to bilateral agreement was the dominant feature of the period.

Why did it occur? The impetus to the first important agreements was the technical revolution brought about by the introduction of Linotype and Monotype machines. Both sides were anxious to effect the change-over with the minimum of industrial dislocation and were prepared to compromise. There was also the urgent need for a clear statement of conditions on which the machines could be worked. Subsequently the smoothness of the transition, when considered against the magnitude of the technical change, was regarded by industrial historians as an almost classic example of how such an important change should be effected.

Indeed the agreement worked so satisfactorily that many leaders on both sides grew keen to extend this method of settling terms of employment. To employers an agreement which they had helped to draft was better than a continuous guerrilla conflict against union rules. To many unions, especially the New Unions of semi-skilled, a signed and sealed agreement with the masters' association was primarily a visible token of

[1] Board of Trade, *Report on Collective Agreements*, 1910, pp. 481–4.

BILATERAL BARGAINING

recognition of their status. It was also of course a help in their interminable battles with wage-cutting firms.

Speaking as a fraternal delegate to the conference of the S.T.A. in 1899 the Secretary of the T.A. said that his union 'rather welcomed the formation of an Association of Employers' because it made it possible to come to a workable agreement.[1] Similarly most of the employers realized that trade unions were too powerful to be ignored, and that a system of negotiation and compromise offered at least some prospect of making their point of view known.

The development of collective agreements depends upon the stability and extensiveness of organizations on both sides. In this period the rapid growth of unionism among the hitherto unorganized sections of the workers, and the building up of a nation-wide network of master printer associations, culminating in the two opposing national federations, facilitated the new method of settling terms of employment.

The transition was not always made without a struggle. On both sides were those who opposed the change. On the trade union side, although most of the London craft unions were well disposed, many of the others were deeply suspicious. In the first place there was often profound distrust of employers' associations as organizations formed primarily to break the unions. Secondly there was the pervasive conservatism of some older union officials who preferred to keep to the methods which they understood, perhaps fearful of being out-smarted at the conference table, or chary of committing their names to a document which might prove unpopular with the members. In the provinces there was the hostility of the stronger branches to being tied to a regional agreement which might slow down the pace of local 'advance'.

On the employers' side there were many who regarded the new method as cowardly capitulation to the unions. The more enlightened, however, saw that the old attitude was defeating its own purpose: far from ensuring the retention of the privileges of the employer, it led to more and more unilateral union regulation of trade customs and terms of employment. Furthermore, as many masters came to agree on the need for standard costing to prevent anarchic price-cutting, they welcomed an explicit agreement with the unions, which would fix wages at a standard throughout the industry.

But once negotiations had been successful, even on a minor issue, the process of extension tended to snowball. Contact between representatives of contending parties, with patient explanation of their respective points of view, often dispelled ignorance, suspicion and hostility, and showed that the other's position was not as unreasonable as each had supposed. Union leaders came to sympathize with the fair masters in

[1] S.T.A., *Report of Delegate Meeting*, 1899, p. 57.

BILATERAL COLLECTIVE BARGAINING

their struggle against the price-cutting employer; some of the masters appreciated that the union leaders were often more moderate in their demands than the rank and file. Officials on both sides soon realized the saving of time and trouble which resulted in conducting business with a central authority, instead of a multiplicity of dispersed individuals.

Under British law these collective agreements were 'gentlemen's agreements', and were not enforceable in the Courts. Whether or not they were observed depended on the honesty and sense of responsibility of those directly concerned, or on the sanctions which the other party could supply. Nevertheless even if particular terms or clauses were irksome, many employers came to realize that the enduring of such restrictions was not too high a price to pay for the overall stability and certainty which the agreement provided in a field where anarchy might otherwise prevail. This element of stability was particularly welcomed by the party which happened to be in the weaker bargaining position. Although they were not always treated as inviolable, agreements tended to slow down the rate of adjustment to altered economic conditions, for they provided a basis for negotiations which could be protracted almost indefinitely by the party on the defensive.

In 1912 leading officials of the printing unions and masters' organizations gave evidence before the inquiry of the Industrial Council into the working of the system of voluntary collective agreements, with the idea of considering whether it could be extended or improved. Most of the witnesses from the printing industry professed to be satisfied with the existing procedure.[1] There were suggestions that there should be monetary penalties for the deliberate breaking of an agreement, and that agreements might be given some more definite legal recognition, but on the whole the voluntary 'gentlemen's agreement' was recognized as the most adaptable to varying conditions.

Given mutual recognition the increasing amount of contact between the two authorities promoted the eventual settlement of working rules by common consent, rather than unilateral enforcement, and their expression in a written agreement in preference to the tacit or merely verbal acquiescence in union rules which had characterized the previous period. A secondary effect was the restriction of the geographical scope of such agreements to areas common to elements of the organizations on both sides. Thus the two main trends discernible in the printing industry in this period were, firstly, the great increase in the number of collective agreements, and secondly the progressive, although irregular, extension of their geographical range—from the firm to the town, the district and, finally, to the whole country. In 1898, National Agreement

[1] *Enquiry into Industrial Agreements, Minutes of Evidence*, (Cd 6953. 1913).

206 BILATERAL BARGAINING

on the introduction of type-composing machines, dealt with in the preceding chapter, was of course an outstanding exception.

AGREEMENT OF UNION RULES

An interesting transitional phase between regulation by union rule and by collective agreement is illustrated by the procedures adopted by the T.A. and S.T.A. In both cases negotiations resulting in agreements between the respective unions and the F.M.P. were conducted *on the basis of union rules*.

For several years after 1904 the F.M.P. pressed the T.A. to revise its apprentice quota. After the 1908 T.A. Delegate Meeting made alterations in the rules governing machinemen, overtime and enrolment of readers,[1] the F.M.P. agreed to attend a conference with the union, hoping to exchange recognition of the new rules in return for some relaxation of the apprentice ratio.[2]

During the preliminary manoeuvring the T.A. Executive withheld the issue of the new Rule Books, in an attempt to limit the agenda of the proposed conference to the subject of the new rules. The union was understandably reluctant to negotiate on its apprentice quota. But when the F.M.P. insisted on including apprentices, the Executive of the T.A. gave notice that the new rules would be enforced.

The situation was explosive. Galled by the intransigence of the T.A. on a matter which placed them at a competitive disadvantage in relation to London firms, many large employers were reported to be 'gravely considering whether a general lock-out would not be a lesser evil than submission to the dictates of the T.A.'.[3] More moderate counsel prevailed and the F.M.P. simply notified the T.A. that the new rules were unworkable and unacceptable. It advised all Association Secretaries to warn their members against permitting the establishment of new conditions in their shops,[4] and formed a defensive alliance with the L.U.A. and the three provincial newspaper proprietors' organizations.[5] In the same month, however, the F.M.P. also received a letter from the P. & K.T.F. demanding the establishment of a fifty-four-hour week on January 1, 1911 and a forty-eight-hour week exactly a year later. The question of the T.A. rules then became involved in the 'Hours Struggle of 1911, but both issues were solved, in the provinces, a few weeks

---

[1] T.A., *Report of Delegate Meeting*, 1908, pp. 28, 32, 54.
[2] F.M.P., *Special Circular*, June 1904, p. 111.
[3] E. Howe, *The Federation of Master Printers*, p. 24.
[4] F.M.P., *Members' Circular*, October 1910, p. 183.
[5] The Federation of Northern Newspaper Owners, The Federation of Southern Newspaper Owners and the Lancashire Newspaper Society.

BILATERAL COLLECTIVE BARGAINING 207

after the T.A. had withdrawn from the fight for the forty-eight-hour week.[1]

The 1911 'Agreement on Rules' was in many ways unsatisfactory to the Union, for several clauses were ambiguous, and were interpreted by employers to their own advantage. Nevertheless it had the important effect of opening a break in the employers' defences. Hitherto they had refused to negotiate with the T.A. on machinemen's rates, claiming with some truth, that the men were not craftsmen, and were not really eligible for membership of the T.A. During the nineteenth century the T.A. had indeed tended to ignore the machinemen. Partly this arose from the compositors' feelings of social and educational superiority over the hand pressmen—the 'pigs' and 'horses' of hoary chapel jokes. But after 1890, and especially after the 1908 Delegate Meeting, the T.A. took up seriously the task of organizing the machine rooms.[2]

By making internal union rules to negotiate their working conditions it manoeuvred the employers into making an agreement. That it was unsatisfactory was not so important; in the future it could be improved.

Perhaps inspired by the example of the T.A., in 1911 a General Delegate Meeting of the S.T.A. adopted substantial amendments to the Rules governing working conditions, notably in reducing the working week to forty-eight hours, increasing the overtime rate to time-and-a-half and restricting the overtime to nine hours weekly per man. When the Glasgow M.P.A. protested to the union executive against an attempt to enforce some of these rules without obtaining the agreement of the masters, it received a reply to the effect that the union regarded the Rules as a matter of 'internal administration', and could not admit the right of the employers to be consulted.[3] This challenge was too serious to be ignored and the gauntlet was retrieved by the newly formed Scottish Alliance. The S.T.A. was brusquely informed that any attempt at enforcement of rules in one locality would be met by a national lock-out. As the master printers showed an unprecedented solidarity, in December 1912, the Alliance gave explicit notice to the S.T.A. that unless the new Rules were withdrawn and a conference arranged, lock-out notices would be posted on the following week. At this crucial point the P. & K.T.F. intervened and was successful in effecting an agreement between the disputants on the future procedure to be adopted.[4] Negotiations were resumed, and in April 1913, the S.T.A. and the Scottish Alliance signed an agreement on working

[1] T.A. Rules Agreement, F.M.P. *Special Circular*, May 1911.
[2] Musson, *op. cit.*, pp. 223–6.
[3] F.M.P., *Members' Circular*, 1912, p. 90.
[4] P. & K.T.F., *Annual Report*, 1912, p. 90.

conditions which, significantly, began: 'We unanimously agree and recommend that the following rules, as affecting mutual interests, be adopted as National Rules.'[1]

These two cases have been treated at some length as they were both unusual and important. They were unusual in two respects: firstly, inasmuch as the employers agreed to accept and indeed enforce certain of the union rules, secondly, inasmuch as the unions had agreed to modify those rules at the request of the employers. The resulting agreements were in fact a concrete embodiment of recognition by each party of the right of the other to be consulted in matters affecting the conduct of the industry. The cases were important as they both came near to precipitating large scale work stoppages, tested the fighting organizations of both parties in each dispute, and resulted in important agreements governing working conditions. This form of agreement was not, however, adopted by the other unions.

WAGES AND HOURS

With the increasing settlement of working conditions by collective bargaining, embodying the terms in a formal agreement, a complex pattern of craft and geographical differentials was evolved.

One of the most important was the higher rate of machine operators as compared with hand compositors. The T.A. and the L.U.A. agreed that machine operators' rates should be $12\frac{1}{2}$ per cent above hand compositors' rates. The T.A. wanted a high time rate for operators to discourage employers from installing machines; it opposed the use of piece rates in order to discourage operators from producing high output. By 1913 when the position was more or less stabilized the machine rate was usually 3s–4s above the hand case rate.

London rates in all crafts were higher than in any provincial town, and in the provinces the larger towns tended to have the higher rates. Employers in high-wage areas naturally regarded neighbouring low-wage areas with indignation tinctured with envy, and if they could not move their own works into those areas they at least used them as reason for refusing to raise their own wages, and on occasions twitted the unions with failing to perform their primary function—the protection of the weak—by neglecting to fight for higher rates in those districts. Particularly troublesome to the London unions was the low-wage circle of the Home Counties. They frequently accused the provincial unions of dereliction of duty. Indeed in 1907 the L.S.C. arbitrarily extended its area of jurisdiction in order to rectify the position. On the other hand, in defending the higher London rates the

[2] Reprinted in F.M.P. *Members' Circular*, December 1913, p. 423.

BILATERAL COLLECTIVE BARGAINING

London unions were at no loss to find genuine reasons for these differentials, and quoted the higher cost of food, the greater expenditure on rent and transport, the increased strain of high speed work and the higher quality of London craftsmanship.

While employer organizations tended fairly quickly to formulate a policy of reducing geographical differentials in order to eliminate price cutting (and union policy was not antagonistic to this as long as it was done by raising the lower rates) union executives could not easily obtain authority to negotiate on national, or even regional lines, owing to the opposition of the powerful and numerically preponderant Branches which wished to retain a large degree of autonomy in the matter of wage negotiations. Only with great reluctance did T.A. Delegate Meetings give the Executive plenary power to sign national agreements, even in an emergency such as the introduction of the Linotype.

The following table shows the change in standard rates of the main London craftsmen.

LONDON CRAFT RATES

	1890	1900	1906	1906 Earnings	1913
Compositors (hand)	36s	38s	39s	40s 9d	39s
Bookbinders	32s	32s	35s	35s 3d	35s
Litho. Printers	42s	40s	40s	45s 2d	40s
Machine Managers	36s	38s	39s	—	39s

Source: *Reports on Standard Time Rates.* 1906 *Enquiry into Earnings . . . of Labour*

The pattern revealed in the above table was followed fairly consistently in the main provincial towns: machineminders received the same as compositors, while Lithographic printers tended to receive more, and bookbinders less, than compositors.

The table also indicates that a fairly steady rise occurred during this period. This conclusion is substantiated by a study of individual branch rates in provincial towns, as summarized in the following table:

PROVINCIAL CRAFTSMEN

Median Branch Rates

	1890	1895	1900	1906	1913
Hand Compositor	30s	31s	32s	32s	34s
Litho. Printer	30s	32s	33s	34s	35s
Bookbinder	28s	30s	32s	32s	32s

Source: Trade Union Reports. *Reports on Standard Time Rates*

210 BILATERAL BARGAINING

Studies of individual branch rates show that printing unions were almost uniformly successful in raising their time rates from 8 to 15 per cent. During the period, however, the Bowley cost-of-living index moved from 93 to 100. On the basis of time rates alone the craftsmen's real wages were almost constant. The semi-skilled workers were more fortunate, and especially in London and the larger provincial centres, raised their conditions from wretchedness to one of dignity and decency.

Almost all groups enjoyed an improvement in their standard of life due to reductions in the hours of work. Throughout the trade union movement there began, in the last decade of the nineteenth century, the great campaign for the eight hour day. For a while some of the printers, unions, especially those with a high proportion of pieceworkers, remained hostile, but by 1900 most of them were in support of the movement. After prolonged discussion of the best way to proceed, the unions agreed to hand over the control of the campaign to the Printing and Kindred Trades Federation. Negotiations began in 1908, and nearly two years later, after a nation-wide stoppage of work, an agreement was signed between the P. & K.T.F. and the Federation of Master Printers. This fixed the working week at fifty hours in London and fifty-one in most of the provincial centres.

INDUSTRIAL DISPUTES

All reports from the unions agreed that 1890 had been a year of prosperity for printing which had not been equalled for some time past, but in 1891 the unemployment figures rose again, and for the next five years the unions were battling against reductions in wages and attempts to break their hold by the introduction of non-unionists, in this period there were a few minor strikes over the introduction of type-setting machines, but no major stoppage. Such forward movements as were attempted were mainly confined to reduction in hours of work, such as that of the London Bookbinders, movements which had been inspired by the T.U.C. resolutions in favour of an eight-hour day, and which were to some extent supported by the prevalent view that such reduction would spread the available work more equitably.

Although the five years following 1895 were years of falling unemployment, when the unions changed gradually from defence to attack, their first efforts were uniformly unsuccessful, and in 1896 the compositors in six towns who took strike action were defeated, in each case by being replaced from the pool of unemployed. In the following year the demands for wage increases were intensified and led to several relatively large strikes. In Edinburgh and Glasgow over three hundred machineminders and lithographers, after being out for several weeks,

BILATERAL COLLECTIVE BARGAINING 211

were successful in obtaining wage increases, but a three-month strike of Glasgow bookbinders was broken by non-unionists. This was the stormiest year of the decade, as the following table shows, but even so the industry was comparatively undisturbed by stoppage.

TRADE DISPUTES

Percentage of Union Members Involved

	1894	1895	1896	1897	1898	1899	1900	*Mean*
Printing	0·1	0·1	0·1	0·3	0·1	0·1	0·2	0·1
All trades (except Agriculture, Fishing, Seamen)	3·9	3·2	2·4	2·8	3·0	2·2	2·2	2·8

Source: Board of Trade. *Reports on Strikes and Lock-outs*

Indeed of nine main industrial groupings used in these tables, printing has almost consistently the lowest percentage of members in disputes. Unfortunately this relative unimportance resulted in the figures for the industry being grouped with 'Miscellaneous' in the official Reports for the remainder of the period, so it is not possible to obtain full information.

DISPUTES IN PRINTING TRADES

	Average 1901–10	1911	1912	1913	*Average* 1910–13
	6·9	11	11	17	13
People affected	331	5649	961	3188	3266
Days lost (000)	6·0	215·9	18·6	68·6	101·0

Source: Board of Trade, *Reports on Strikes and Lock-outs*

The period 1900–13 divides naturally into two—a decade of relative tranquillity followed by three years of severe strife. The increase in average number of strikes from 6·9 to 13·0 yearly is less spectacular than the rise in average number of people directly affected from 331 to 3,266, while average days lost rose from an annual average of 6,000 to over 100,000. Within the first decade there was a burst of activity about 1907, which might at first be considered a random effect, but when the data for printing are compared with those for all industries it is seen that the two series form similar patterns.

It seems reasonable to ascribe this to a burst of activity to the outbreak of protests which had been uneasily suppressed in the period between the Taff Vale decision and the Trade Union Act of 1906. This

212 BILATERAL BARGAINING

burst subsided, 1909 and 1910 were fairly tranquil, and then the printers, like the other unions, entered upon a period of more serious conflict.

SETTLEMENT OF DISPUTES

In the nineteenth century the craft unions had elaborated a number of strict rules to prevent stoppages precipitated by impetuous branches or chapels. It was indeed a cardinal feature of the regional unions that control of the 'closing' of an office was the prerogative of the Central Executive. Typical of the rules were these of the Bookbinders' Consolidated Union:

Disputes and Grievances

1. Every means shall be adopted by the Central Executive and the Branches to prevent disputes with employers, they hereby being declared to be generally injurious to our trade; and all parties shall strive as much as possible (consistent with honour) to prevent the same, and endeavour as speedily as possible to bring matters to a good understanding between employers and employed.

2. In cases where the local Committee have any cause for suspecting that infringements are taking place, it shall be their duty to make the strictest inquiries by summoning shop constables or other men in the shop: or by any other means they may think desirable. Any communication received in this manner to be regarded as strictly confidential. Any Agreement made by any branch as to working conditions with any employer without the consent of the Central Executive shall not be recognized.'[1]

Other rules laid down, step by step, the procedure to be followed before the final decision to hand in notices was made by the Central Executive. All other unions had similar rules carefully framed to prevent irresponsible 'unofficial' (or as the Americans called them 'wildcat') strikes.

Union leaders, especially of the craft unions, constantly expressed their aversion to industrial conflict. Their attitude is epitomized in the following statement:

'We do not cultivate strikes—we abhor them—but it is better to be prepared for emergencies.'[2]

Even Natsopa, which had a very stormy history in its early years, as it

[1] B.M.R.C.U., *Rules*, 1905.
[2] T.A., *Report of Delegate Meeting*, 1898.

BILATERAL COLLECTIVE BARGAINING

fought for recognition by the masters, disclaimed any militant intention when it began to extend to the provinces:

'It must not be supposed that I go under my Committee's orders into the provinces to carry the "fiery Cross" of war in a Crusade of our union against the masters, as we all admit that there must be a master to pay the man. On the contrary I go with the white flag and olive branch of peace . . .'[1]

The Government itself, alarmed by the great stoppages of 1889–90, appointed a Royal Commission 'to inquire into the questions affecting relations between employers and employed . . . the combinations of employers and employed', and other matters. The result of the Commission's Report was the Conciliation Act of 1896, which empowered the Labour Department of the Board of Trade to appoint conciliators, or (if both sides requested it) an arbitrator, to help settle trade disputes. The printing craft unions, especially the London Society of Compositors, were strongly opposed to State-aided arbitration in industrial disputes.

The reason for this lay partly in the development of voluntary collective agreements, for the conditions which favoured them also favoured 'internal' methods of settling disputes. The craft unions, proud of their long tradition of independence, were loath to give up any shred of autonomy. It was a favourite boast that the industry had sufficient leaders with the intelligence and experience to manage its domestic affairs. State intervention carried with it the slight stigma of paternalism, of helping someone who could not help himself. This was vigorously rejected by the printers. Again, the isolation of the industry, in the sense that it had no close connections with any other broad field of labour, led to an attitude of somewhat parochial independence.

Almost all of the collective agreements of this period, therefore, contained a clause outlining the procedure to be followed in case of a dispute. Many agreements provided for the formation of a Joint Conciliation Board, or some such body, consisting of equal numbers of representatives from both sides, with perhaps an independent chairman or umpire. Referring to the establishment of such a body by the 1911 settlement, the F.M.P. commented:

'It is especially a matter for satisfaction that the agreement with the T.A. provides for reference of all disputes to a joint committee of employers and employed to hear and, if possible, determine the dispute before any action is taken.'[2]

[1] N.S.O.P.A., *Annual Report*, 1904, p. 7.
[2] F.M.P., *Members' Circular*, 1911, p. 157.

214   BILATERAL BARGAINING

Similarly the settlement of the dispute between the S.T.A. and the Scottish employers, which incorporated provision for joint discussion of grievances before action was taken by either side, was hailed as marking a new era, and as being an 'employers' charter' rather than a mere agreement.[1]

To such an extent had conciliation by these *ad hoc* Joint Boards come into favour that in 1908 the national federations of masters and unions went to considerable trouble to establish a 'permanent' National Conciliation Board for the industry. But despite the care taken in the drafting of its constitution, the National Conciliation Board never came into operation, and lapsed after a few years.

The following table shows the methods of settling disputes in this period: and clearly shows the importance of Direct Negotiation, especially in the settlement of the larger conflicts.

METHODS OF SETTLING DISPUTES IN THE PRINTING INDUSTRY (1906–13)

	Numbers of		Percentage of	
	Persons	Disputes	Persons	Disputes
Direct Negotiation	9558	48	79	56
Arbitration	94	3	1	4
Conciliation	586	7	5	8
Return to work on employers' terms	809	7	7	8
Replacement of Workers	961	21	8	24

Source: Board of Trade, *Reports on Strikes and Lock-outs*, 1906–14

Between 1911 and 1913 the printers were infected with the general industrial unrest which swept the country. Large scale stoppages involved, at some time or other, almost all of the major unions. The nationwide dispute over the reduction of hours showed that the provision of machinery for conciliation was not enough to prevent serious industrial conflict over major issues, and dispelled some of the complacency which had grown up in the preceding era of industrial peace.

UNION RULES TO RATION WORK

Thus many basic matters relating to terms of employment—wages, hours, dispute procedure, etc.—were decided by bilateral collective bargaining, and the result was incorporated in an unequivocal written agreement. But there was another range of matters which the masters still regarded as being within the domain of the 'rights of management',

[1] F.M.P., *Members' Circular*, 1913, p. 70.

and which they refused to discuss with the unions. In general these concerned the more detailed organization of the work, the assignment of jobs to employees, the amount of overtime, transfer of workers from one Department to another, and similar aspects of management.

It is impossible to understand the efforts of the unions to exercise some control over such matters, without a clear understanding of union strategy. Despite the fairly general expansion of the industry, there was a constant rate of unemployment of some 5 per cent, quite sufficient to prevent the accumulation of really substantial resources, and enough to put serious curbs on the unions' militancy in collective bargaining. Almost all of the union attempts to control terms of employment were intended to reduce the persistent core of unemployment. Despite the opposition of the employers the unions continued to make such rules, but in this period they were seldom incorporated in collective agreements.

One step generally regarded as likely to spread the available work more equitably was a reduction in the standard working week. It was not that the unions subscribed explicitly to any Work Fund doctrine, but that the facts of everyday life—the persistence of systematic overtime concomitantly with a hard core of continuous unemployment—outraged their sense of social justice.

'To live by his own industry is every man's birthright, and whoever attempts to curtail that right is a traitor to the community.'[1]

Moral sentiments were, of course, supported by consideration of union power and financial stability, for it was from the ranks of the unemployed that the masters recruited the 'rats' who broke strikes and boycotts, while the continuous drain of unemployment relief weakened the union funds. A clear statement of policy in this matter was placed in the Objects of the London P. & K.T.F.:

'To endeavour by conjoint action to deal with the unemployed question, by abolishing as far as possible overtime and piecework, and regulating the number of working hours per day until the whole of the surplus labour is absorbed.'[2]

Second only to the reduction in standard hours was limitation of the overtime which any man could work. In 1898 the T.A. Delegate Meeting resolved:

[1] *Typographical Circular*, February 1897.
[2] London P. & K.T.F., *Rules*, 1897.

216 BILATERAL BARGAINING

'That the overtime now so prevalent in many of our branches be prevented in the future, as the system is opposed to the true spirit of trade unionism, and is causing most of the want of work experienced by our members.'[1]

In 1904 the union brought in a limit of twelve hours per week. Despite strong representations from the employers, in 1908 this was reduced to eight hours. When in the settlement of the Hours and Rules Dispute in 1911 the T.A. Executive agreed to alter the limit to sixteen per fortnight, it came under heavy criticism from the members. Similarly all of the other unions, including Natsopa and the Cutters' Union, placed limitations on the amount of overtime.

A second method of discouraging overtime was by making it more costly to the employer. It was primarily to limit overtime, and not to raise wages, that the unions fought for higher overtime rates. In 1892 when the London Bookbinders won a nominal forty-eight-hour week, but without payment of overtime rates until after fifty-four hours had been worked, they found that employers simply kept their men on for fifty-four hours, thus transforming a 'reduction' of hours into an increase in wages which, though no doubt welcome to the men in employment, did not meet the union's desire for more equitable rationing of the work. Similarly in the T.A., despite the great variety of conditions obtaining in the different branches, by 1913 the body of opinion had swung in favour of standardizing the ratio of overtime rates to normal rates:

'Our experience has been . . . that the only way to get overtime stopped is to put an exorbitant charge upon it. We have had many negotiations with the employers, but this plea of emergencies or exigencies of production always comes up, and cannot be overcome.'[2]

A third device aimed at distributing work more widely was the restriction of transfer of a worker from one task to another. In particular the compositors' unions adopted rules restricting the transfer of machine operators to case work, with the object of requiring the small employer to keep a hand compositor to do the imposition and correction. In 1903 a member of the L.S.C. Executive politely reprimanded the T.A. for recently permitting an operator to transfer to case work as long as he was paid operators' wages:

'(The L.S.C.) did not recognize the dual system of transference of men from machine to case work . . . men must be engaged distinctly as Linotype or Monotype operators or as case hands . . . they had the

[1] T.A., *Report of Delegate Meeting*, 1898, p. 74.   [2] *Ibid.*, 1913, p. 34.

BILATERAL COLLECTIVE BARGAINING 217

entire London trade at their back in resisting the proposals of the employers that men should be transferred from case to machine.'[1]

In the provinces the T.A. was handicapped by the old custom of apprenticing a youth as a 'printer', and teaching him both composition and presswork, but from 1891 onwards the union attempted to have apprentices bound either to case or to machine. When the T.A. began its campaign to enrol the machinemen the latter used their influence to prevent compositors from helping in the pressroom:

'The reason we (the machinemen) cannot do as well here as in London is because compositors do a lot of machine work. In London a compositor does not think of asking for a job in the machine room, however busy they may be, but in the provinces it is quite common.'[2]

With the advent of the great number of new printing machines, the unions became concerned lest too many men should be displaced. They, therefore, made rules fixing the number of men to be employed on different makes. In this regard they were not very successful; only the London Machine Managers obtained recognition of their Society's rule that each machine above quad crown in size should have at least one machine-minder on it.

Another group of union rules intended to increase the amount of work available *to union members* were the demarcation rules based on the principle that certain technical operations should be restricted to skilled journeymen. The most persistently troublesome demarcation issue was that of the 'encroachment' of women in fields traditionally regarded as men's. This was particularly acute in the bookbinding trades where the change from leather to cloth binding reached its climax about the end of the century. In 1893 a conference of the Bookbinding section of the London Chamber of Commerce and the London bookbinding unions agreed upon a schedule of some sixteen operations which were to be regarded as the legitimate work of journeymen or apprentices. The unions, for their part, agreed to permit the engagement of women or unskilled workers on other operations.

In letterpress printing it was the encroachment of the semi-skilled men which raised the ire of the craft unions. At the 1891 Conference of Machinemen one delegate advocated the abolition of the rank of machine assistant, and the retention of *all* work to the skilled journeymen. This was rejected on the grounds that labourers were necessary to do the dirty and heavy work.

[1] T.A., *Report of Conference of Machinemen*, 1891, p. 92.   [2] *Ibid.*

218 BILATERAL BARGAINING

' "We cannot do without labourers, but we must keep them in their place," stated one delegate, with commendable frankness.'[1]

While the employers deplored such demarcation rules as an unnecessary restriction on the right of the manager to command his men to do what he thought fit, the knowledge that breach of such rules would involve a serious inter-union dispute, and perhaps a stoppage of work, acted as an incentive to careful observance. But in a period of rapid technical change and trade union expansion, conflicts were inevitable; some of the bitterest disputes were between rival unions fighting to gain a new field of work for their members.

[1] T.A., *Report of Conference*, 1891, p. 105.

CHAPTER XIV

WAR AND BOOM 1914–20

*We want some honourable bridge to be found. We cannot
break a national agreement. Whatever the consequences
may be, whether it is a strike or a lock-out, we say it has
come to that position. It is not a question of wages; it is a
pure question of honour, and if we do not maintain that
position, where is the country coming to?*
SECRETARY, Federation of Master Printers, June 1920.

IMPACT EFFECT—UNEMPLOYMENT

The Declaration of War was followed by a few weeks of commercial
chaos, as rational expectations were submerged in a sea of wild rumour.
In the 'Business as Usual' campaign to restore commercial confidence
the printers played an active part, placing special emphasis on the
importance of advertising in promoting sales. Some businesses returned
to normal with remarkable celerity: for example, the stationers and
papermakers immediately raised the prices of their stocks and defended
this action with the invulnerable argument that sentimental consideration of patriotic duty could not be expected to influence the immutable
laws of supply and demand. On the other hand some heretical employers deprecated such behaviour and made a genuine effort to co-
operate in the prevention of profiteering. The F.M.P. Costing Committee, concerned lest there should be a resurgence of price-cutting,
issued a plea for the retention of the standard costing system in all
shops.

The immediate cause of the sharp unemployment in the industry was
the drastic reduction in job printing due to the panic of manufacturers
and merchants. As confidence was restored printing orders were renewed and the industry revived. A factor which helped in revival was
hope of capturing a share of Germany's large pre-war export trade of
over two million pounds' worth of printing. Most of this was lithographic work such as picture post cards and almanacs of which almost
half a million pounds' worth was exported to Britain and an equivalent

amount to North America. A special committee appointed to deal with the capture of the German export trade worked in close alliance with the Board of Trade, which had begun a survey of markets and was collecting information and samples.[1] The impact effect of the war on newspaper printing was in general less drastic, and although it was reported in September that over fifty periodicals had suspended publication, these were mainly small journals devoted to trades and sports.

After the first numbing shock had subsided there was a frantic scramble for work, with a revival of competitive price cutting which the F.M.P. was impotent to control as it watched the patient work of two decades disintegrate on the battlefield of commercial competition. Many employers demonstrated their patriotism by urging their men to join the services but this particular form of sacrifice by the masters was more popular in the early period of labour redundancy than in the later situation of labour shortage.

What of the unions? The bookbinders were in the middle of the conference of their General Council which two fraternal delegates, Herr Kloth of the International Bookbinders' Secretariat, and Herr Bruckner of the German Bookbinders were attending. These delegates had barely time to express the friendship of the German trade unionists for their British counterparts, and the 'indignation of the German workers against the capitalists who were engineering the war' before they were recalled urgently to their homeland to take up the defence of trade union freedoms.[2] Other unions, faced with the prospect of near-bankruptcy if industrial dislocation persisted, advised the employers that they were abandoning 'forward' movements for the duration of the 'emergency', and asked for co-operation in operating an equitable system of short-time working.

Unemployment among trade union members reached a peak of 10 per cent at the beginning of 1915, but later in the year it declined steadily. By the end of the year it had stabilized at roughly 2 per cent, and the employers, faced with a continuing labour shortage, were pressing the unions to reconsider many of their rules.

DILUTION OF LABOUR

The process of substituting young people for adults, women for men, semi-skilled for skilled, was called Dilution of Labour. The aim of course was to make the fullest use of whatever type of labour was available, in order to release for military service as many fit men as

[1] *Members' Circular*, 1914, p. 339.
[2] N.U.B.M.R., *Trade Circular*, 1914, p. 98.

possible. By the end of 1915 the general labour shortage was so acute that Government officials conferred with the Council of the Federation of Master Printers. The latter pointed out that they could make no further economies in the use of labour, unless the trade unions were prepared to relax their demarcation rules.

At this stage, however, the unions, just recovered from a year of fairly high unemployment, and apprehensive of the consequences of a rumoured reduction in paper imports, were in no mood to make concessions. Nevertheless the Master Printers asked for negotiations with the P. & K.T.F., and in April 1916 the two reached a draft agreement on the general principles of dilution. This provided for the suspension of recognized trade rules and customs in cases where the unions were unable to supply skilled labour, subject to the proviso that pre-war conditions should be restored as soon after the armistice as possible. Every employee joining the Forces was to be reinstated in his previous position where this was possible provided he was capable of discharging his duties satisfactorily. Where dilution by women was introduced those women already in the trade were to be given first preference on skilled work, but if a reduction of staff became necessary the women dilutees should be the first to be dismissed. Questions of remuneration, demarcation and other details were left for settlement between each local M.P.A. and the union branches. In the event of any dispute arising under the agreement provision was made for an arbitration committee of representatives from both parties, with power to appoint an umpire in case of a deadlock.[1]

Despite considerable opposition from the rank and file, in the following three months, the agreement was ratified by all affiliated unions, except the L.S.C. and the Association of Correctors of the Press.[2] It is not possible to analyse all the individual agreements which resulted from the efforts to translate the broad principles of dilution into detailed prescriptions, but the extent to which the T.A. abandoned its restrictive rules is indicative of the general attitude. Firstly, mobility between jobs in the firm was increased—compositors, readers and machinemen could be interchanged, while apprentices were permitted to work on Monotype and Linotype machines after two years, if journeymen were not available. Secondly, mobility between firms was increased by suspension of the 'smooting' rule. Thirdly, the available labour force could be used more intensively as overtime restrictions and machine-manning quotas were relaxed. In every case the T.A. insisted on the higher wage rate being paid and some discretion was left to the chapel or branch in deciding whether in any particular firm the labour shortage warranted dilution. Finally, any dispute or difficulty was to be

[1] P. & K.T.F., *Annual Report*, 1916.   [2] *Ibid.*, 1917.

submitted to the National Officials on both sides, or failing a settlement, to a Committee of Reference.

In view of the long struggle which some of the craft unions had waged against the intrusion of women into their domain it is not surprising that the fiercest reaction was evoked against any proposal to admit women to skilled operations. By the end of 1916 the F.M.P. was soliciting the aid of the law in an attempt to prosecute several unions which had not implemented the general dilution agreement to the extent that the masters thought necessary. Even when the union executive was prepared to admit the strength of the employers' case, the rank and file often took unofficial action to vitiate a form of dilution which ran counter to their whole tradition. In this matter the craft unions, especially the Bookbinders, were reaping a harvest of trouble which they had sown in pre-war years by their selfish and short-sighted refusal to organize women workers. Later, when the Executive saw the need for such organization, in order that the work of women in binding shops might be controlled by the craftsmen, it was too late—the indoctrination of their members against women workers had been only too successful. In the interim the efforts of the Paper Workers in this field had established a claim which was to cause one of the bitterest inter-union disputes in the history of the industry.

Although the employers had originally supported a scheme for local variations of existing agreements in response to the needs of individual firms or districts, in order to provide a flexible and rapid method of dealing with each situation, by the end of 1916 the F.M.P. had come to the conclusion that it needed to keep a tight rein on the district associations. At the Council Meeting in January 1917, it decided that no local agreements should be concluded without reference to the F.M.P., in order that uniformity of concession might be secured, and the best terms possible made with each union branch.[1]

WAGE INCREASES

By the end of the first year of the war the rise in the cost of living and the decline in the number of unemployed were sufficiently pronounced to bring the unions into a general movement for wage increase. In London both Natsopa and the Warehousemen and Cutters' Society had already negotiated comprehensive agreements, incorporating wage advances, with the London M.P.A. The employers took the view that any increase in rates necessary to offset the rise in the cost of living should in equity take the form of a flat rate for the London area. Thus when the compositors and machine minders applied for increases in

[1] *Members' Circular*, January 1917.

July 1915, they were met with a gentle prevarication. In August almost all the other London unions or branches were at first also refused, but towards the end of the year most of them received a rise of 2s per week.[1]

In January 1916, the Government issued an appeal to the unions to exercise a policy of wage restraint except in so far as changes were due automatically under existing agreements, or necessary to remove local anomalies; during the next eight months the unions watched the widening gap between wage rates and the cost of living without taking any action. This passivity was partly due to the fact that most members were enjoying high overtime earnings. But as the wartime inflation gathered momentum they were forced to take defensive action. In August Natsopa took the lead again and obtained a War Bonus of 2s 6d a week; in September the London M.P.A. conceded a similar bonus of 3s to all craftsmen.

But the cost of living continued to soar. Early in 1917 when the unions pressed for further wage increases, the masters held out for more extensive relaxation of union rules. When these were conceded, a further War Bonus of 4s for men, 2s 6d for women, and 1s 6d for juveniles followed. Towards the end of the year wage rates were increased by an even larger instalment. So the process continued. Negotiations for one increase had scarcely ended before the increase in the cost of living justified the unions in pressing for another.

As the inflation continued, employers' attitudes to wage increases changed perceptibly. The first small increase was granted grudgingly, from fear of creating an awkward precedent; later, a larger increase was conceded in a spirit of compromise; later still a larger instalment was passed at a Council meeting 'without a dissentient voice'; and finally as the inflationary phase developed its full momentum wage increases were granted almost gladly in the comforting assurance that they would be more than recovered as the upward swing of prices continued. The following table shows the general movements of wages between 1914 and 1920 when the peak of the post-war boom was reached.

STANDARD TIMES RATES (LONDON)

	January 1914	*December* 1920
Bookbinders	35s	100s
Compositors	39s	100s
Machine-minders	39s	98s
Readers	44s	104s
Warehouse Porters	22s	83s
Women	17s	51s
Feeders	24s	84s 6d

[1] P. & K.T.F., *Annual Report*, 1915, pp. 50–62.

224 BILATERAL BARGAINING

The process of giving equal all-round increases had a marked effect in diminishing the proportional differentials between the rates of the craftsmen and the semi-skilled. Thus while in 1914 porters, women and feeders were paid at only 56, 44 and 61 per cent respectively of the compositors' rate, by the end of 1920 they were receiving 83, 51 and 85 per cent of the craft rate.[1]

In the provinces, too, wage adjustments were at first made very slowly, for the unions were content to enjoy the experience of full employment and a plenitude of overtime. The high level of money earnings tended to offset the rise in the cost of living and dulled the edge of the demand for increases. Applications for advances were somewhat random and unco-ordinated; in some centres the unions acted together in a local federation, in other cases groups of branches in one union attempted to establish a district rate.

Towards the end of 1917 the F.M.P. became alarmed by the new method of fixing wages which the unions were developing. Adopted with particular success by the T.A. and the N.U.B.M.R. this involved the settling of a standard rate for a fairly wide area, or Group of branches, instead of by separate towns or districts. The new approach was obviously economical in times of rapid change, but the employers gradually became aware that the end process might well be a national scale of wages which would play havoc with the existing distribution of industry based on widely varying wage rates. The action of the unions in taking the initiative in this direction without consultation with the F.M.P. was condemned 'as a step in the wrong direction', although it was admitted that there was no unanimity among master printers on the desirability of extending the scheme. Doubtless employer approval of Group standard rates was closely correlated with the relative wage level in each town. The masters had further cause for annoyance in the action of the strongly organized T.A. branches in keeping aloof from the Group system and relying on their inherent strength to obtain more favourable terms than those given to the local Group.

A special meeting of the F.M.P. Council in December 1917 resolved:

'That a conference be arranged, in conjunction with the representatives of the newspaper organizations, with the federated unions or the T.A. with a view to the settlement of the Group system; and that as the same difficulties will occur under the Group system as under the present town system, a national minimum wage should be advocated, with agreed advances for certain centres, and that any memorials for advances of wages should be on a national basis, affecting all areas, and that until

[1] *Master Printers' Annual*, 1921.

WAR AND BOOM 1914-20

such conference has been held all memorials for advance of wages should be suspended.'[1]

A joint meeting of F.M.P. and newspaper organizations resolved to approach the Unions to discuss the construction of a graduated scale of National Rates which should be recognized as the permanent basis for all future wage negotiations.

Early in 1918 the Manchester and Liverpool Branches of the T.A. applied for further substantial increases, bringing the case rate to 60s. The fears of the employers that this would lead to another round of applications from the T.A. regional groups was amply justified by subsequent events; groups covering almost the whole of the country followed the Manchester lead.[2] This was sufficient to convince the majority of the masters that more positive action should be taken to find some sort of national wage basis, for under prevailing conditions of labour shortage regional employers' associations were helpless in the teeth of a union attack. An ineffectual attempt to resist the Manchester demands collapsed when the newspaper proprietors gave way, leaving the jobbing employers with no alternative but to follow. The other groups then persisted with their demands and in June the second 'circle' was completed by the increase of 8s granted to forty-one branches in the Home Counties.[3]

By this time, however, Manchester and Liverpool were preparing to initiate the third round, and again the masters could not forbear from expressing disappointment that the unions showed so little regard for their 'principles' that they preferred to fight for sectional advances instead of uniting to raise wages in the weakest branches.[4] When the Manchester Branch applied for an advance of 15s weekly on all wages, with $12\frac{1}{2}$ per cent extra for operators, the F.M.P. decided to attempt another stand. This time the dispute was pressed to the last point. At one stage the T.A. members had handed in notices, and the masters had countered by serving notices of dismissal. But again the newspaper printers broke the ranks, and granted an increase of 10s a week. Again the general printers had no option but to follow suit.

In return the T.A. agreed to consider the formation of a National Wage Basis (although its last Delegate Meeting had rejected the idea.) In the meantime all of the other groups applied for, and obtained, the 10s increase. In many cases the various unions acted together. Sometimes the new rates incorporated local adjustments as well as the overall

[1] *Members' Circular*, December 1917.
[2] P. & K.T.F., *Annual Report*, 1918, pp. 60–67.
[3] T.A., *Half-Yearly Report*, June 1918.
[4] *Members' Circular*, January 1918, p. 16.

H

226 BILATERAL BARGAINING

increase. Thus a rough pattern of 'grades' of towns evolved. Once the grades were stabilized the granting of flat rate increases tended to make geographical differences relatively less important. For example when Town A had a rate of 30s, and Town B a rate of 36s, the difference was 20 per cent. But if their rates increased to 60s and 66s, the difference was reduced to 10 per cent. Alterations such as this caused substantial changes in the competitive position of firms in different areas.

The strong bargaining position of the trade union executives, who claimed that they were unable to control militant action by powerful local branches, quickly convinced the employers that a system of national agreements was eminently desirable. A writer in the *Members' Circular* gave expression to a point of view which was gaining wide acceptance:

'. . . it is quite apparent that, whether the reason is economic or otherwise, the epidemic of desire to increase the rates or the status of the industry has become endemic; though it is the emphatic belief of many that what is now being obtained by forceful negotiation would be more appropriately and more effectively done under the Joint Industrial Councils, or by much less aggressive methods than those at present prevailing. The most effective way of dealing with all these subjects would, of course, be by a consideration of all questions nationally . . .'[1]

NATIONAL AGREEMENTS, 1919

During 1919 a lengthy series of negotiations ended in a comprehensive set of National Agreements covering the basic terms of employment. All of the major unions were involved; on the employers' side the Monotype Users' Association and the Linotype Users' Association joined with the F.M.P. when their interests were affected. The agreements were not limited to craftsmen; women and girls in binderies, warehousemen and cutters, electrotypers and stereotypers, numerous classes of assistants and learners—all important groups were covered.

The bewildering complexity of the hundreds of different wage rates involved only two major principles. Firstly they fixed craft or skill differentials between different classes of workers in the same town. Secondly they fixed differentials between the same class of workers in different towns. Thus in future any proposed change in wage rates would involve consideration not only of its immediate local effects, but also of its impact on the whole pattern. Indeed this was a matter of almost continuous negotiation between the masters and the unions in the post-war period.

[1] *Members' Circular*, 1918, p. 243.

The following table shows the wage rates of some of the more important classes of workmen in the different grades when the first national agreements were signed:

PRINTERS' WAGE RATES, 1919
(Shillings per week)

Union	Classification	Grades					
		1	2	3	4	5	6
T.A.	Jobbing Case	75	72	69	66	63	60
T.A.	Operators (Day)	83/6	80	76/6	73	69/6	66
N.U.B.M.R.	Binders and Rulers	75	72	69	66	63	60
A.S.L.P.	Machine-minders	75	72/6	70			
	,, Rotary	85	82/6	80			
N.U.P. & P.W.	Class I	72	69	66	63	60	57

Source: National Agreements, reprinted in F.M.P., *Members' Circular*

A major reform incorporated in all of the National Agreements was the standardization of the proportionate rates to be paid for overtime work. The substance of these is shown in the following table:

OVERTIME RATES

Day	Period	Rate
Any week day	First 2 hours	Time rate $\times 1\frac{1}{4}$
	Next 3 hours	Time rate $\times 1\frac{1}{2}$
	Remainder	Time rate $\times 2$
Saturday	First 5 hours	Time rate $\times 1\frac{1}{2}$
	Remainder	Time rate $\times 2$
Sunday	All time	Time rate $\times 2$

Source: *Master Printers' Annual*, 1921

Any man who was required to start work before the usual time received time-and-a-half for such work, while a man required to work overtime which was not continuous (meal time excepted) with his ordinary day's work was entitled to an additional hour's overtime pay as 'call money'. Sometimes the strict terms of the agreement could be waived to permit the employment of men who, owing to age or infirmity, were unable to do as much as those who were physically fit.

The majority of agreements covered much the same ground and were formulated in a similar manner; indeed the sections on General Conditions were practically identical. More favourable conditions prevailing at any establishment were not to be prejudiced; on the formation of a new branch of any union the interim conditions applicable were to be those of the adjacent district; any union member

228 BILATERAL BARGAINING

required to work temporarily in a district of lower grade was to receive his old rate for the first six days.

Another important matter which was standardized was procedure for modification of the terms of the agreements. In each case a Joint Labour Committee composed of equal numbers of representatives from the Trade Union and the Federation of Master Printers, was set up. A meeting of this Committee could be called by either side, at fourteen days' notice. Strikes or Lock-outs were prohibited for a period of thirty-five days while the issue was being considered by the Committee. At the end of that time, if no decision had been reached, the parties were free to do as they wished.

An even clearer example of the trend towards national agreements and standardization of basic conditions throughout the country was the Hours and Holidays Agreement negotiated by the P. & K.T.F. This body had emerged from the war with its prestige enhanced by its successful handling of the delicate issues of dilution, apprenticeship and demobilization. The time was certainly well chosen. The general atmosphere of optimism and goodwill which followed the conclusion of the war and the more specific attitude of industrial co-operation which had shown in the scheme for 'Trade Betterment' were important factors predisposing the parties towards peaceful settlement. The relatively short series of conferences was characterized by 'reasonableness, moderation and remarkable goodwill on both sides'.[1]

The agreement laid down that the standard working week in all departments should be of forty-eight hours. The time of starting work was not to be altered, unless agreement was reached in each shop on some alternative arrangement; the same condition was to apply to any change in workshop practice. To compensate pieceworkers for the loss of earnings due to the reduction of hours, piece rates were subjected to an interim increase of 5 per cent until such time as permanent adjustments were made. At least six days in each year were to be National Holidays; if an employee was required to work on any of these he became entitled to extra rates for that day as well as a day's holiday with pay at a later date.

Each employee was entitled to one week's holiday yearly, to be taken between March 31st and September 30th, and to receive the ordinary 'stab rate for such week, or in the case of a pieceworker the average of his weekly earnings over the past six months. A minimum period of employment of twelve months was stipulated; any employee leaving a firm was entitled to a day's pay for every two months' completed service since the preceding June 30th, the base date for all calculation of holidays. Finally provision was made for the setting up of a Joint

[1] *Members' Circular*, 1919, p. 65.

Committee to adjudicate on any differences arising from interpretation or application of the agreement.

A similar agreement with representatives of provincial daily newspapers fixed a forty-five hour week for night workers.

Thus in the series of National Agreements the trade unions secured a great measure of that standardization of conditions which had long been their objective. Despite the strains to which they were later subjected, in economic depression, the General Strike and the Second World War, these agreements fixed the basic terms of employment in the industry. Though details were constantly modified to meet changing conditions, the underlying principles remained the same.

ORGANIZATION—CENTRALIZATION OF AUTHORITY

The structure of union organization after the war was not radically different from that of 1914, but the number of members had increased. Total membership of unions affiliated to the P. & K.T.F. rose from 75,000 in 1914 to 190,000 in 1920. The greatest expansion had been in the unions of semi-skilled and women workers. Natsopa, for example, grew from 6,000 to 20,000. The Bookbinders' and Paperworkers' unions had in 1920 a combined membership of over 100,000 of whom some 60,000 were women.[1] But even the old craft unions increased rapidly in comparison with pre-war growth: L.S.C. membership, almost stable at 11,000 from 1900 to 1913, rose to 15,000 in 1920.

Less apparent than the growth in numbers was the change in attitudes to union organization. The disruption of traditional workshop practices made necessary by the labour shortage in the later part of the war had shown that many old demarcation rules respecting the limitations of work of women and 'unskilled' men could not be justified on grounds of their technical incapacity. As these workers were obviously going to fight to retain the opportunities given them during the war, and had indeed been organized with great success, many of the old craft unions realized that their pre-war hegemony would not be regained. One method of resolving the clash between the separate interests was to enrol all workers in each branch of the industry in one union. Thus the Lithographic Printers amalgamated with the Stone and Plate Preparers; the Stereotypers' craft union opened its ranks to the Stereotypers' Assistants; the Bookbinders abandoned their traditional hostility to women unionists and started a Women's Section; the S.T.A. amended its constitution to provide for an Auxiliary Section of assistants and women.[2]

[1] N.U.P.B. & P.W., *First Annual Report*, 1921.
[2] P. & K.T.F., *Annual Reports*, 1918–21.

These activities aroused the suspicion of the leaders of Natsopa and the Cutters' Union, who suspected that this sudden solicitude for the assistants was due less to an access of philanthropy than to a desire to control a potentially rival faction. The immediate post-war years were thick with jurisdictional disputes which at times threatened the structure of the Federation. But despite this 'poaching' on their preserves by the craft unions, Natsopa and the Paperworkers emerged as two of the strongest unions in the industry, and under extremely capable leadership survived the successive shocks of the following period.

Owing partly to the need for some sovereign body to adjudicate on the numerous complex problems of inter-union rivalry, the Federation grew in importance. But the main factor contributing to its increased status was the urgent need for a central body to represent workers' interests to the Government and the employers on such national issues as use of manpower and post-war resumption of apprenticeship. Symbolic of the change in the effective authority of the Federation was its negotiation in 1919 of the Hours and Holidays Agreement, covering almost the whole of the industry.

On the employers' side there were similar movements; first, an increase in the number of firms which had joined the local associations; second, a centralization of authority. These tendencies were apparent in both general printing and provincial newspaper printing. In the latter a number of pre-war regional associations linked up in a national federation in 1917 and in 1920 amalgamated (with the Linotype Users' Association) to form the Newspaper Society.

The centralization of authority on both sides was the result of the need for a more efficient method of regulating wage rates than the slow pre-war process of local negotiation. The product of the new conditions was a comprehensive set of national collective agreements.

PART FIVE

———

PERIOD OF COMPROMISE
1920–45

CHAPTER XV

UNEASY TRUCE
1920–39

*Here surely we come to grips with the problem of the
future organization of industry. . . . The irresponsible
individualism of the nineteenth century, upon which our
whole industrial system was built, has had its day, and
must cease to be, if industry on its present capitalist basis
is to survive.*
SECRETARY, F.M.P. *Members' Circular*, 1933, p. 274.

INTRODUCTION

The most outstanding features of industrial relations in this period, and
certainly the ones most frequently commented on by observers, were
the comparative absence of deep-seated hostility and the infrequency
of open conflict. In many other industries the General Strike of 1926, or
the Great Depression of the early thirties led to the collapse of the
machinery for negotiation and conciliation, the liquidation of Joint
Industrial Councils, the abrogation of collective agreements, and the
intensification of industrial hostility. But in the printing industry the
constitutional machinery survived the buffetings of technical change,
economic stagnation and the upheaval of the General Strike. The
methods of regulating the relations between employers and employed,
and for settling disputes, remained basically unchanged throughout the
period.

There were, however, some critical moments: in 1921 when the T.A.
revolted against negotiated wage reductions, in 1926 when some
employers sought a punitive settlement after the General Strike, in
1932 when the F.M.P. grew very restless at the unions' delay in agreeing to wage reductions. On these and on several lesser occasions a
breakdown seemed imminent. In every case, however, it was averted
by the influence of those national leaders on both sides who, realizing
more clearly the consequences of such a step, restrained their more
impetuous colleagues.

H*

The absence of open conflict was not due to lack of important matters of disagreement. Representatives of unions and employers were in almost continuous negotiations, often on a matter regarded by one side or the other as involving a vital principle. But these issues were very seldom pressed to the point of open conflict.

Two groups of conditions, one economic, the other socio-political, contributed to this stability and continuity. Printing continued, except for a slight set-back in 1931, to be an industry with expanding employment opportunities, especially before 1930.

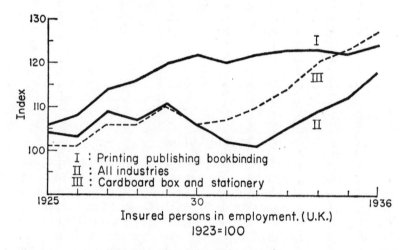

Source: *Abstract of Labour Statistics*

Secular unemployment, year by year, was approximately half as severe as the average for all industries.

Although the printers felt the impact of the Great Depression of the early thirties, unemployment did not reach catastrophic proportions. At the worst, when a quarter of all insured men in the country were unemployed, the proportion in printing was 12 per cent. Indeed unemployment in printing was roughly about *half* the average for all industries over this dismal period. In one respect printing had improved over pre-war conditions: it was much less prone to seasonal fluctuations.

Terrible though the level of unemployment seems, by modern standards, the fact that printing was comparatively prosperous and expanding helped to induce a mood of compromise, almost of complacency. Conscious of the fact that they were, if not as well off as they would like to be, at least much better off than many of their contemporaries, both sides were disposed to make concessions to preserve the prevailing harmony.

Nevertheless the substantial and persistent level of unemployment inevitably had serious effects on the funds and strategy of the weaker unions. In the thirties, too, the level of unemployment had important influence on the internal government of the unions. Organization of the men out of work to promote their own interest was no novelty in the printing trades; in the depression of 1841 and 1892 they formed pressure groups which succeeded in obtaining some modification of union policy to meet their demands for more equitable sharing of work, or the provision of relief. In the inter-war period, however, the problem assumed a new magnitude, for the prolongation of unemployment gave them more reason and more scope for better organization, and the association of the National Unemployed Workers' Movement with the Communist Party introduced a disruptive political element.

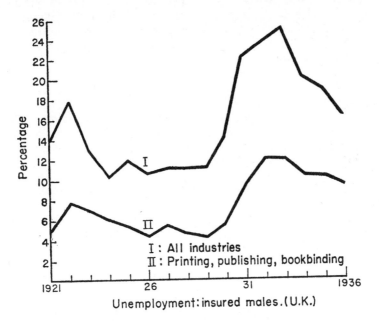

Source: *Abstracts of Labour Statistics*

Natsopa was badly shaken during the depression of 1921. The Executive's proposals for a special levy and increased contribution to meet the heavy unemployment expenditure led to a widespread

236 PERIOD OF COMPROMISE

campaign to suggest malversation of the funds. Rather than pay benefits the members balloted for suspension of benefits. Several members brought charges against the national officers, alleging that ballots were being conducted in an irregular manner. The General Secretary resigned, and his subsequent re-election was declared invalid by a High Court. According to the Union's historian, 'For nearly two years the very existence of the Society hung on a thread'.[1]

When the Paperworkers experienced their most critical internal dissension in the thirties, Natsopa was scarcely affected although a rule was adopted in 1932 requiring each official (and each future candidate) to declare that he had no connection with the 'Minority Movement'. At this time the National Unemployment Workers' Movement was building up a nation-wide organization. In many trade unions Communists gained influence and power, as the magnitude of the economic crisis led more members to approve of extreme measures for reform. Many unions were torn by internal dissension between the two factions. The communist led bloc became known as the Minority Movement, and was subjected to a steady barrage of criticism from the Labour Party and the T.U.C.

By 1932 attitudes in the Paperworkers' Union, as in the Labour Party and the Trade Union movement generally, hardened against the Minority Movement, and at the Delegate Council Meeting the N.E.C. was successful in carrying, on the casting vote of the President, a resolution debarring communists from holding official positions. On normal procedural principles this was of doubtful legality, for the President had voted to change the *status quo*. Bitterness of the unemployed was increased by the knowledge that several delegates who had been instructed to oppose the resolution had voted against the wishes of their constituents. The fact that a deputation from the Unemployed Association of the London Bookbinders' Branch, after being refused permission to wait on the Committee, entered the committee room while a meeting was in progress was magnified and distorted by the N.E.C. in an attempt to discredit the Minority Movement.

'While we have no desire to suppress the individual expression of any members' thoughts, we are determined to resist any organized attempt to disrupt the fundamental basis upon which Trade Unionism is founded.'[2]

The vigour with which the heresy hunt was conducted stood in striking contrast to the liberal sentiments which were given out for public

[1] Suthers, *op. cit.*, p. 75. See Moran, *op. cit.*, ch. 8 for a fuller account.
[2] Report of N.E.C., 1932, p. 5. See Bundock, *op. cit.*, pp. 347–8.

UNEASY TRUCE

consumption. In 1932 two active communists were expelled from the Binders' Branch after the Minority Movement published an attack on the paid officials, suggesting that they were considering the negotiation of wage reductions. As the worst of the depression passed, and the animosity faded, more tolerant attitudes were revived, and in 1936 the Delegates Council, against the advice of the N.E.C., voted to rescind the rule giving the Executive power to debar members connected with the Minority Movement from holding office.

Although the older craft unions had their troubles their existence was never threatened. Throughout the inter-war period the records of the L.S.C. are littered with copies of ballot papers:

'Are you in favour of granting –s weekly for — weeks to members who exhaust their Provident benefit, subject to a levy of –d per member for the same number of weeks ?'

Every ballot was carried. In 1932 the cost of unemployment relief was over £8 per member. Over nearly a century the London compositors had learnt the necessity of a trade union to care for its unemployed members. In the time of its greatest testing, this lesson was not forgotten.

ALTERNATIVES TO PRIVATE ENTERPRISE

The second reason for the comparative tranquillity of the printing industry was that official trade union policy did not include nationalization or socialization of the industry. In some industries this issue overshadowed all others; in printing it was hardly ever even considered. This tacit agreement on the continuation of private enterprise, even more than the forms of procedure for settling disputes, reduced the element of *class* conflict between unions and employers.

In the past, other systems of production had been advocated, but they had seldom enjoyed much support from the conservative printing unions. In the late nineteenth century, for example, there were sporadic attempts by local branches to swing their unions over to support of producer co-operatives.

'Sooner or later we shall have all trades becoming co-operative producers. There will come a day—and God speed it—when we shall do without the capitalist altogether, and we shall reap the just reward of our labour.'[1]

[1] T.A., *Report of Delegate Meeting*, 1898, p. 58.

238   PERIOD OF COMPROMISE

But in 1890 there were only four producers' co-operatives in the industry, at Manchester, Leicester, Edinburgh and London. By far the most important was the Manchester Society, established in 1869. Its workshops were models of hygiene, safety and comfort for the workers, and trade union negotiators frequently referred to them as models for other employers to emulate. The Society encouraged its members to join the appropriate union, always paid union rates, observed union conditions, and pioneered shorter hours. About 1900 it introduced the forty-eight hour week. During the long negotiations for shorter hours in the printing industry in the early twentieth century, the example of Manchester Co-operative Society was often cited approvingly by the unions.

At the end of the nineteenth century, during a decade of industrial ferment, the workers showed a short-lived burst of enthusiasm for co-operatives, and the number grew to seventeen in 1902. But in 1920 there were still only nineteen in printing, out of seventy-two for the whole of industry. The unions generally gave little encouragement to the co-operative producers' movement. They feared that the co-operative 'workers' would develop an 'employer' outlook, and lose their interest in unionism. The T.A. went so far as investing several thousand pounds in loan or share capital of some half dozen printing co-operatives, but none of the others gave even this much support.[1]

The unions' experience of a state-owned printing office did not encourage them to support nationalization of the industry. Early in the twentieth century Sir Roland Bailey, then Controller of His Majesty's Stationery Office, suggested the establishment of a large State printing works. Employers vigorously opposed the scheme which was shelved until 1914 when a Select Committee of the House reported that it was practicable to set up a small Government printing office. During the War the activities of H.M.S.O. were greatly expanded to cope with the printing of state and military documents of an urgent or secret nature.

The printing unions took little interest in this extension of State printing. Indeed many of them were hostile to the project. The management of the H.M.S.O. insisted on operating as an 'open shop', employing unionists and non-unionists on an equal footing. Even after the War, when the private master printers were constitutionally committed, through their membership of the Joint Industrial Council, to the principle of 'encouraging organization', the Stationery Office was pursuing the opposite policy. After the General Strike the Controller of the Stationery Office insisted that the representatives of the unions should explicitly recognize the open shop policy. This roused the resentment of the unions, and showed them clearly the kind of treatment

[1] T.A., *Half-Yearly Report*, December 1914.

UNEASY TRUCE

239

they could expect from a State-owned works when the government in power was hostile to trade unionism.[1]

A third threat to private enterprise came from Education Authorities, City Councils and County Councils. As early as 1920 the F.M.P. reported that it had 'in every possible way' called public attention to the fact that many such bodies were setting up their own printing works. During the next few years the Council claimed success in preventing the completion of several projects for starting municipal printing offices.

On the whole the printing trade unions showed no more enthusiasm for experiments in municipal socialism than for co-operatives or State ownership. This indifference did not stem simply from their conservatism, or from a narrow conception of the proper function of local authorities. Much of the agitation for Municipal printing works had stressed the economies that would result. The trade unionists were naturally concerned that these economies might be made at the expense of the workers. A Labour council would be unlikely to do this, but suppose a Conservative council were to take over the administration?

There was, then, no practicable alternative to the continued operation of the industry by private enterprise. Workers' co-operatives were small and few; State printing works had antagonized the unions; municipal printing plants were suspect. With this major socio-political issue eliminated the printing unions and employers were free to concentrate on the more immediate problems. In many instances unions and employers worked together to try to improve the efficiency, raise the status, and promote the expansion of their industry.

TRADE UNIONS

During the War the idea of 'industrial unionism', of one huge union for the industry, with a sectional organization catering for the needs of different sectors, such as newspapers, stationery, bookbinders, lithographic printers, gained considerable support, especially among members of Natsopa and the Paperworkers. The old craft unions, consistently refused to disband their historic associations, and merge in an organization in which their interests might be subsidiary to those of the numerically stronger semi-skilled men.

One major advantage claimed for the Industrial Union was that it would eliminate the inter-union disputes which had proliferated before the War, resulting in a considerable weakening of the trade union movement. In 1920, the leading exponent of this policy, A. Evans of the National Union of Printing and Paper Workers, arranged the amalgamation of his union with the National Union of Bookbinders. The result

[1] P. & K.T.F., *Annual Report*, 1926, pp. 31–35.

240 PERIOD OF COMPROMISE

was the National Union of Printing, Bookbinding and Paperworkers, with over 100,000 members, by far the largest union in the industry. In its ranks the Paperworkers, as it became known, enrolled skilled craftsmen, such as bookbinders, pressmen and warehousemen, semi-skilled male assistants, and women and girl working in paper mills, stationery firms and bookbinding shops.

This aroused considerable interest in trade union circles, for a controversy was then raging over the respective merits of general and sectional forms of amalgamation. Under a sectional amalgamation each group kept its identity, at least for a probationary period, and perhaps retained some degree of autonomy, so that it would not be outvoted by other groups which did not, perhaps, fully understand its problems. Sectional amalgamation had the additional practical advantage of preserving the positions of the different officials, who were not so likely therefore to oppose a scheme as they would be, naturally enough, if it threatened them with the loss of their jobs. By permitting a greater degree of autonomy in finance, payment of benefits, and such matters, too, a sectional amalgamation made it easier to work out an equitable scheme for transferring members of several unions which might vary widely in amount of funds, and in their benefit rules, to the one big union. And finally, if, after a trial of sectional amalgamation, any section wished to withdraw again, it was much easier to do so, than it would be if its members were completely and indistinguishably merged in the new union.

The Paperworkers was a sectional amalgamation, with a probationary term of five years. In fact, although its membership fell fairly steadily from the 1920 peak, this was not due to the withdrawal of any of the major sections. Indeed it engulfed several small unions during this period.

The graph shows clearly the pattern of the change in union membership, and requires little explanation. Peak membership in 1920–21 was held for only a few months before the general decline during the depression of the next two years. A recovery during 1924–25 was more than offset by the drop following the collapse of the General Strike. The sharp decline in affiliated membership of the P. & K.T.F. was almost completely accounted for by the huge losses sustained by the Paperworkers' union, while the upswing after 1933 is largely due to their recovery.

Changes in Federation membership can be almost entirely explained by the fluctuations in the Paperworkers' numbers; each of the individual craft unions maintained a stable membership, as is shown in the numbers of the L.S.C.

After recovering from an internal crisis in 1921 Natsopa practically maintained its numbers at 17,000 during the 1922 depression. After the General Strike it lost some ground, but in 1928 it began a recovery which with a slight set-back in 1931–32, brought it to 28,000 in 1939. In this year the three largest unions—Paperworkers, T.A. and Natsopa —accounted for roughly three-quarters of the total of organized workers in the printing trades.

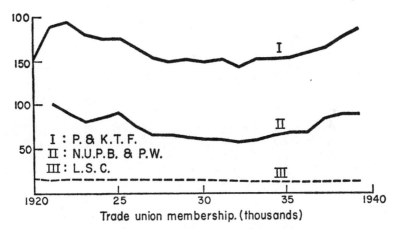

Trade union membership. (thousands)

Source: P. & K.T.F. *Annual Reports*
N.U.P.B. & P.W. *Annual Reports*
L.S.C. *Annual Reports*

ORGANIZATION OF CLERICAL WORKERS[1]

One of the most prolonged and intricate disputes of the inter-war period arose from the attempts of Natsopa to secure recognition of its right to organize and conduct collective bargaining for clerks in printing works and newspaper offices. In 1924 the union began active organization in London periodical houses, and threatened to withdraw members unless the clerks were allowed to join the union. The dispute came before the Conciliation Committee of the J.I.C. which obtained a statement from the management that no objection would be raised to the enrolment of clerks, except those in highly responsible positions with access to confidential information.[2]

Organization was interrupted by the General Strike, but the problem flared up again in 1932 when Natsopa attempted to assert its right to

[1] Moran, *op. cit.*, ch. 13.
[2] F.M.P. Council Meeting, April 1924.

242   PERIOD OF COMPROMISE

organize the clerks. When the dispute was referred to the J.I.C. there was a deadlock, representatives of both the Newspaper Society and the F.M.P. stating that their organizations were opposed to the recognition of clerical workers as members of Natsopa.[1] A special committee appointed to find some basis of agreement reported a complete failure to make progress.

In January 1936, a second Committee reported that as no agreement was possible, the matter was beyond the authority of the J.I.C. From then onwards Natsopa gradually brought pressure to bear on other newspaper houses which were most vulnerable to the threat of a withdrawal of labour. In October 1937, the F.M.P. Labour Committee reported that on three occasions members of the Newspaper Society had been asked for House Agreements covering clerical workers.[2] In the same month the J.I.C. appointed its third Special Committee on this subject!

At the P. & K.T.F. Administrative Council Meeting in May 1938 Isaacs said categorically that 'they (Natsopa) could not accept the right of the employers to dictate to any union as to whom they should organize, and whom they should not', and added that if no progress was made in the forthcoming discussions there would be trouble.[3] At the J.I.C. meeting in July he affirmed that his union was prepared to take direct action without delay.

This threat was effective and in the following month the Newspaper Society put forward proposals for negotiations. The agreement, signed in November 1938, formally admitted Natsopa's right to organize the clerks, but severe limitations were placed upon the freedom of the union to engage in collective bargaining.

PRINTING AND KINDRED TRADES FEDERATION

During the War two influences were at work gradually strengthening the influence and prestige of the Federation. Firstly, in regard to many problems arising from the War, such as dilution of labour, the services of apprentices, and the suspension of trade union rules, the Government wished to obtain some standard principles to cover the whole industry, and to obtain these with the minimum of time. As the master printers were represented at the national level by their Federation, the printers' unions also wished to speak with a united voice. The success of the P. & K.T.F. in these fields thus showed the advantages of an organization able to represent the unions of the whole industry.

[1] J.I.C., *Minutes of Quarterly Meeting*, April 1932.
[2] F.M.P., *Minutes of Council Meeting*, October 1937.
[3] P. & K.T.F., *Annual Report*, 1937, p. 40.

UNEASY TRUCE

Secondly, the highly successful working of the National Hours Agreement, which had been negotiated by the P. & K.T.F. in 1911, and substantially amended in 1918, also showed that its functions could be extended beyond the rather narrow limits envisaged by its founders, to collective bargaining.

Thus when inter-union disputes flared up after the War it was logical that the unions should consider some ways in which the Federation's power to deal with these should be made more effective. In 1919 and 1920 there were two major disputes between craft unions and unions of semi-skilled. Both of these arose from the craft unions' decision to begin enrolling non-craft workers, although the latter were already catered for by Natsopa and the Paperworkers. So serious did these disputes become that in 1924 the Paperworkers' representative on the P. & K.T.F. suggested that the Federation should undertake a searching investigation into the craft unions which were altering their rules in order to admit associated non-craft workers. The T.A., by beginning to enrol Monotype caster attendants had antagonized the Typefounders' Society, the Paperworkers and Natsopa, all of whom had certain agreed regions in which they considered they had jurisdiction over the attendants. The Society of Lithographic Printers, a craft union, altered its rules to admit the semi-skilled lithographic plate preparers, who had previously had their own small union.

The refusal of the S.T.A. to accept the Council's ruling that it should cease from enrolling certain of the assistants shocked the unions into tightening the rules. The 1928 Conference adopted a rule on Demarcation Disputes which explicitly required the unions involved to submit the dispute to an arbitration committee appointed from the Council delegates. In most cases this method of settling inter-union disputes was successful, but the controversy over the enrolment of the Monotype caster attendants kept flaring up intermittently for the next twenty years.

While the authority of the Council of the P. & K.T.F. was thus being strengthened, a peripheral movement was taking place, almost spontaneously, and certainly without much official encouragement. This was the 'Local Federation' movement, which had gained ground during the war, especially in the period preceding the National Wage Agreements. Many local union officials and members, suspicious of the centralization of power in the hands of national officials of the union or the federation, saw that one effective counter to this 'bureaucratization' or the movement was to strengthen the local industrial movement, by linking up all branches in the town into a local federation.

The actual powers of these federations, their place in the structure, and their rights and duties in relation to both the unions and the

244

PERIOD OF COMPROMISE

national federation, were for a long time very vague. Many of the national union leaders seemed to distrust them; they certainly received little encouragement, and a very scanty recognition, from the higher authorities. A succinct account of the rather submissive role which they were expected to play was given by G. Isaacs, Natsopa secretary:

'... All that was possible should be done to encourage local federations not to miss their aim of attending to local affairs. National policies were in the hands of the delegates from the unions attending as an Administrative Council, and it was for the local organizations to co-operate in order to carry out the policies that were formulated for them.'[1]

Some leaders, however, realized that the local federations would fade away unless they were given a more responsible role, with some opportunity for influencing policy, and not simply carrying out what was decided at the higher level. Some envisaged a complete network of federations at the three levels—federated chapels in each work place, local federations linking up with the branches in one town, and the national federation linking up the unions. In this way they hoped that a workable compromise would be achieved between the need for closer co-operation and the desire for autonomy.

After 1933 the national federation provided the finance for an annual Conference of delegates from the local federations. The sponsors hoped that the conference would work out a common policy in regard to problems of trade union organization at the branch level, and also help to stimulate interest in such activities as the J.I.C. Apprenticeship Selection Scheme.[2]

The first conference was reasonably successful. Stimulated by the prospect of greater participation in both the formulation and execution of policy, many local federations revived, and the number grew slowly from thirty-eight in 1933 to forty-eight in 1939. The national executive reported:

'Interest in the working of the local Federations has increased enormously since the practice of holding these annual meetings was commenced. They had been the means of indicating in what way local Federations can serve a useful purpose in our trade union organization, and local officials have not been slow to realize that their individual efforts can be supplemented to great advantage in co-operation with representatives of other organizations.'[3]

[1] P. & K.T.F., *Annual Report*, 1932, p. 25.
[2] *Printing Federation Bulletin*, November 1933, p. 1.
[3] P. & K.T.F., *Annual Report*, 1936, p. 12.

UNEASY TRUCE 245

In many cases the local officials were first to realize the advantages, and had been frustrated or discouraged by the apathy or suspicion of the national officers. It proved extremely difficult to fit the locals to play a useful part, and bring to the industrial struggle the energy, resourcefulness and initiative of branch officers, with their detailed knowledge of local conditions.

BRITISH FEDERATION OF MASTER PRINTERS

Shortly after the end of the War the master printers gave serious consideration to methods of strengthening their organization. The master printers were impressed by the almost continuous process of centralization of authority on the union side, and the growth of the P. & K.T.F. Furthermore with the signing of the National Agreements there was need for a tighter discipline, and better channels of communication if the members were to observe the strict letter of the agreements, and be kept in close touch with the executive.

The old structure, with no direct representation of the mass of the members, did not give enough real authority to the Council. The Associations were grouped therefore into twelve Alliances (including Scotland), which varied greatly in the number of associations and firms which they covered. The London Alliance comprised six associations with almost 1,000 firms; the Northwestern Alliance had four associations and only forty-two firms. In Ireland there was no Alliance, but the three master printer's associations were allowed direct representation on the Council.

As well as the full members there were a number of affiliated organizations which had limited rights to representation and voting. In 1921 these included the Master Bookbinders' Association, the Monotype Users' Association, the Master Engravers' Association, and the Federation of Wholesale Newsagents.

Under the new constitution the subscription was $\frac{1}{4}$d in the pound on wages paid, with a minimum of one guinea, and a maximum of five hundred pounds. Ultimate authority in the Federation rested with the Annual General Meeting which had full power to deal with all matters affecting the industry. In actual fact the General Meeting was much too unwieldy a body to exercise any effective control. It developed into a quasi-social function at which the formulation of policy was subsidiary to the promotion of solidarity by the extension of personal friendships and education in printing industry problems through lectures and discussions. Formal business was reduced to the adoption of the Annual Report and Balance Sheet and the endorsement of the reports of the Standing Committees.

246 PERIOD OF COMPROMISE

Effective authority lay with the Executive Council. It controlled finances, appointed the staff and fixed their terms of service, appointed the Federation representatives on the Joint Industrial Council, and generally conducted the affairs of the Federation. It met normally four times each year. As the full Council consisted of about one hundred members, it was too large for detailed executive work, and there gradually evolved a number of standing committees, on Costing, Finance, Organization, Legislation and Labour. The Quarterly Meetings of the full Council were then concerned with hearing reports from the various committees, and perhaps authorizing them to take any necessary action. Voting at all meetings was, in the first instance, on a show of hands, but a block vote by Alliances could be demanded by a one-fifth minority. In such a case each Alliance had a number of votes equal to the number of pounds contributed by it to the Federation Funds in the past financial year.

The Labour Committee was concerned with the Federation's relations with the trade unions; it was, therefore, one of the largest, busiest and most important of the Committees. It consisted of representatives of all the Alliances and affiliated organizations; in 1925 the full Labour Committee was forty-two members, a number still too large for expeditious settlement of business. The detailed work was therefore delegated to a number of sub-committees, which dealt with the following subjects: National Wage Basis, Regrading, Union Rules, Lithographers, Apprenticeship. These sub-committees in general had only advisory status; after making an investigation, or conducting negotiations, they reported back to the Labour Committee for instructions. Usually the Labour Committee met first 'to consider and define the policy' before the negotiations were begun, but sometimes, in an emergency, this was not practicable.

NEWSPAPERS

Before the Great War, there was no national organization of newspapers outside of London. In negotiations with the trade unions over the conditions of operating the Linotype machines, the provincial newspaper proprietors formed the Linotype Users' Association. Its original purpose was limited, and it did not command a great deal of authority. About the same time a few local associations of provincial newspapers were formed.

With the signing of the national wage agreements in 1919 it became necessary that there should be a single organization to represent the provincial newspaper interests. The L.U.A. was therefore reconstituted, and amalgamated with other newspaper associations, forming the

UNEASY TRUCE 247

Newspaper Society. It comprised twenty-one District Associations, with a membership which published over 120 daily and over 800 weekly newspapers. The problem then arose of the relations between this body and the Federation of Master Printers, and of its representation on the Joint Industrial Council.

In the past the F.M.P. had usually consulted the various newspaper bodies before changing any of the terms of wage agreements, and sometimes the local newspaper association had actually been given representation on the negotiation committee. But the F.M.P. complained that the various news groups were not always consistent, or in agreement, and it was therefore difficult to know just what they wanted. While the F.M.P. wanted the co-operation of the newspapers in resisting the demands of the unions, it knew from past experience that the newspapers could not be relied upon to stand firm in the face of a determined assault. News is a perishable commodity, and a strike or stoppage has much more immediate repercussions on a newspaper than on a book printer. However, in the T.A. strike against wage reductions in 1922 the newspapers exhibited an unprecedented solidarity with the other printers and won their spurs. Shortly afterwards they were granted representation of six members on the F.M.P. Labour Committee.

In London the Newspaper Proprietors' Association, an organization of the large London daily papers, continued to make its own agreements with the trade unions. It had practically no contact with the F.M.P. and very little even with the provincial Newspaper Society. The London dailies claimed that their field was so specialized and their problems so delicate that they could not afford to run the risk of a stoppage, through being associated with any other branch of the industry. Because of their extreme vulnerability to trade union action the London dailies usually granted concessions which the general trade often resisted.

One development which the unions regarded with alarm was the increasing concentration in newspaper printing, as powerful trusts absorbed less successful rivals, or several firms amalgamated to 'rationalize' distribution and reduce 'uneconomic' competition. Obviously a few papers with huge circulations, would require less production staff than a larger number of smaller papers. In 1929 the Council of the P. & K.T.F. instructed its executive 'to consider methods, legislative or otherwise, for safeguarding employees who may be displaced by amalgamations and to secure for them adequate compensation for consequential loss of employment'.[1]

Partly no doubt to placate the unions, in 1930 Lord Rothermere,

[1] P. & K.T.F., *Annual Report*, 1928, p. 30.

248   PERIOD OF COMPROMISE

after effecting a series of mergers, gave £10,000 as a personal gift to those who would lose their jobs in the changeover. But on the general principle of compensation for loss of jobs, the unions were unable to obtain any agreement from either the London Newspaper Proprietors' Association or the provincial Newspaper Society. To a considerable extent the effects of newspaper amalgamations were masked by the overall growth in this section of the industry. This itself was largely due to the great expansion of newspaper advertising. During the depression when other sectors of the printing industry actually declined, newspaper production was kept at a high level by the boom in advertising as firms tried desperately to find purchasers for their products.

THE GENERAL STRIKE

The British trade union movement emerged from the Great War greatly strengthened in numbers, with improved organization at the top level, and with confidence that its strength could be used to further the welfare of the working class. Thus in 1925 when the coal miners were threatened with wage reductions and increased hours of work, the Trades Union Congress pledged its full support to the Miners' Unions, to the extent, if necessary, of calling a sympathetic strike of other unions. The latter were put into several categories—'first line', 'second line', etc., in the best military tradition. The printing unions were put in the first line.

In 1926 the T.U.C. was called on to implement its pledge. Negotiations between the coal owners and the miners' union collapsed; the miners were locked out. At the eleventh hour, officials from the T.U.C. were in conference with the Government, hoping to avoid a major industrial conflict. At this critical stage the members of the Natsopa chapel at the *Daily Mail* office refused to handle an editorial which contained, they felt, gross misrepresentation of the issues at stake. On this pretext the Government broke off negotiations, and forced the T.U.C. either to back down or to call a sympathetic strike. Reluctantly the Council called out the first line.

The response of the workers surprised even their own leaders. Contemporary observers estimated that at least 90 per cent of the printing unionists obeyed the order. The strike lasted a week, but was called off when the miners' leaders refused to accept a compromise solution. During this great industrial upheaval the country was without regular newspapers, and the public was therefore unable to get a clear picture of events. The T.U.C. and the Government issued their respective propaganda sheets, the *British Gazette* and the *Daily Worker*, but these were naturally suspect, unashamedly prejudiced in

UNEASY TRUCE 249

their presentation, and hardly contributed to a cool appraisal of the situation by the general public.

On May 12th the T.U.C. countermanded its order calling out the second line of unions, and called off the strike, leaving the miners to struggle on alone. The 'first line' unions were left to make their own arrangements regarding the return to work.

The Federation of Master Printers immediately notified all masters that workmen should be engaged only on a day to day basis until some satisfactory scheme was worked out. It claimed that although the masters were keen to return to normal as quickly as possible the general disruption of industry prevented them from offering continuous employment. The day to day arrangements would therefore continue until industry was normal, and the unions had given some guarantee against another 'lightning' strike. The unions accepted these arrangements as a *temporary* measure.

Negotiations then began on the principle of a *permanent* settlement. In the meantime a Joint Reference Committee considered cases of friction arising as work was resumed, and was generally successful in preventing any serious stoppage. The negotiations were conducted in an atmosphere of tension, suspicion and hostility. Flushed with victory and indignant at the loss and inconvenience to which they had been subjected, some employers were thirsting for revenge. On the other side the craft unions in particular were determined not to submit to any humiliating reduction of the rights which they had patiently struggled for a century to establish. Fortunately the F.M.P. negotiators were wiser than many of the masters, and realized that any attempt to force a vindictive settlement would only sow the seeds of future hostility and conflict. Furthermore they knew enough of union politics to realize that the infliction of extremely onerous terms would only bring discredit on the moderate union leaders, and perhaps encourage extremist elements in the union to gain influence. Hence most of the punitive proposals were eventually withdrawn or modified.

The employers insisted on retaining complete liberty of action in regard to the re-employment and promotion of workers, but agreed to recommend that preference should be given to former employees. The issue which presented most difficulty was that of the position of foremen and managers in future strikes and other union activities. At first the employers pressed for a prohibition of trade union membership for this class, but later agreed to a clause which merely prohibited trade unions from calling such men out on strike. Nevertheless this clause remained highly unpopular with those craft unions which had enrolled supervisors and managers, and the Lithographic Printers delayed ratification for six weeks over this point. This delay prevented the

250

PERIOD OF COMPROMISE

return to 'normal conditions', for the F.M.P. had shrewdly insisted from the outset that the agreement would be valid only if ratified by *all* of the unions.

Other important clauses were those prohibiting 'lightning' strikes, that is, strikes in which the workers had failed to give the customary two weeks' notice, and prohibiting interference with the contents of newspapers printed by members of the F.M.P. There were also pro- hibitions on holding chapel meetings in working hours, bringing apprentices or works managers into trade disputes, and 'interference by members of the Unions with the management of businesses or with the right of the management to employ, promote or discharge members of the staff'.[1]

These terms were considered by union leaders to be much more favourable than they had at first feared. On the other hand many employers felt that the unions had got off too lightly. But in fact the transition from complete stoppage to normal conditions was effected remarkably smoothly, and as the memories of the dispute dimmed with the passage of time, most employers agreed that the settlement had been a sensible one. But there remained a core of intransigents who never forgave the unions for participation in the General Strike, and worked unceasingly to ensure that their firms did not again employ union members.

In effect then the General Strike made surprisingly little difference to the picture of industrial relations in printing. Some thought that the Joint Industrial Council would not recover from the shock, for the conciliation machinery had been flagrantly ignored, and the committee work suspended for a month or so after the Strike. Fortunately for the future of the J.I.C., when the two panels assembled for the next Quarterly Meeting, the initial tenseness was dispelled when the chair- man, an employer, made only brief and impartial reference to the Strike, and expressed a desire that the work of the Council should continue. This wish was echoed by leading union speakers, and the J.I.C. quickly settled down to its usual business.[2]

On paper the unions had been forced to make certain concessions, but these amounted in practice to little more than a token sacrifice to appease the more vindictive employers. The officials on both sides were eager to resume traditional peaceful relations. The P. & K.T.F. was pleased with the settlement:

'Taking into account the great difficulties which had to be removed before the condition of affairs assumed anything like normality the

[1] F.M.P., *Members' Circular*, May 1926, p. 184.
[2] J.I.C., *Minutes of Quarterly Meeting*, July 1926.

UNEASY TRUCE

printing trade can congratulate itself upon the speedy and peaceful way in which it settled down to work again.'[1]

The employers were equally optimistic:

'Relations between employers and employed have been subjected to a severe strain, but they have weathered the storm, and other effects of the strike have not been so great as was feared. Trade is rapidly recovering, markets are being regained, and industry as a whole has escaped the burden of extra taxation. The outlook is good.'[2]

HOUSE UNIONS

One of the most serious effects of the General Strike on printing union organization was the fillip which it gave to the formation of House Unions. Hitherto the Printing Trades Alliance had been the principal specimen of this detested genus, but after the Strike several large firms attempted to insulate themselves from general trade union conflict by binding their workers more tightly to their employers. Prominent among the new House Unions was that of the *Manchester Guardian*.

When this firm intimated that it would go ahead with the scheme, which provided benefits on an attractive scale, the P. & K.T.F. issued a circular to the employees warning them of the dangers and advising them to vote against it. But with the surprising exception of the N.U.J. members who refused to have anything to do with it, the scheme was accepted. In all departments there were a few workers who remained loyal to their old unions and refused to join the new.

The T.A. then came into conflict with the other unions over the question of whether to try to break the House Union or to try to capture control of it from the inside. The T.A. Council decided that membership of the House Union was incompatible with membership of the T.A. and expelled some 200 members who had ignored the instructions of the Executive. But the other unions had agreed with the management that membership of the House Union should not exclude a man from his old union, and in December 1926, Natsopa and N.S.E.S. secured agreements which recognized this arrangement.

Printing trade union organization in several Scottish newspapers suffered a severe setback after the General Strike. Prominent among firms which decided to operate as non-union shops were George Outram, Limited, and the Thompson–Leng combine:

[1] P. & K.T.F., *Annual Report*, 1926, p. 7.
[2] F.M.P., *Members' Circular*, 1927, p. 228.

PERIOD OF COMPROMISE

'The readiness with which the employees of these firms relinquished membership of the unions so as to return to their jobs was remarkable, except at Dundee, where a good fight is being put up to retain the right to remain trade unionists.'[1]

Here the unions' greatest obstacle to organization was the rule of the S.T.A. that union members should not work with non-unionists. In consequence unless 100 per cent organization could be achieved, it was pointless to attempt to enrol members. When the S.T.A. introduced a motion at the 1939 A.C. meeting asking the unions 'to consider what steps can be taken to organize non-union Newspaper Houses', its closed shop policy came in for general criticism from other delegates. R. Watson (S.T.A.) admitted that the executive had found it impossible to carry out the closed shop rule, and was anxious to convince the rank and file of its futility, so that at the next Delegate Meeting the rule could be deleted.[2]

The organization of workers in many offices was not simply impeded by a managerial prohibition on union membership. In many cases the welfare and pension schemes proved so successful in binding the worker to the particular firm that even when the management offered to allow employees to join a union, the offer was rejected. Older workers, with many years' contributions towards the House Scheme, stood to gain considerable benefits. On the other hand, if they joined the union they had either to pay double contributions, or lose their right to benefits of the House Union. In short, their vested interest in the latter was sufficient to outweigh any other advantages they might gain from joining the trade union. In an attempt to overcome this the S.T.A. altered its Rules to permit men over forty-five to join as Protective Members, with a low contribution which did not entitle them to welfare benefits, but this did not appeal to many workers for in all cases the firms were careful to pay trade union rates. In 1937 when the Outram Press in Glasgow withdrew its prohibition of trade union membership only a small proportion of the employees signified a desire to join their appropriate trade union. 'The position was rendered difficult by the existence of a welfare scheme inside the office.'[3]

The stationery firms of Dickinson & Company at Hemel Hempstead and Millington & Sons at Tottenham organized House Unions which required workers to relinquish membership of their former trade unions. By August 1927, it was reported that these two firms had largely succeeded in breaking the union organization in their works.[4]

[1] *Printing Federation Bulletin,* July 1926, p. 6.
[2] P. & K.T.F., *Annual Report,* 1937, p. 45.
[3] *Ibid.,* p. 16.
[4] *Printing Federation Bulletin,* September 1927, p. 3.

UNEASY TRUCE 253

The P. & K.T.F. then attempted to bring pressure on the firms by organizing a boycott of their envelopes, but at first it made little headway owing to the lack of co-operation of the Co-operative Wholesale Society.

From the beginning of the campaign a major difficulty was finding alternative sources of supply, for there were not many stationery manufacturers which observed trade union conditions. An important result was, therefore, the organization of numerous smaller firms which were induced to relax their opposition to the unions in order to qualify for the Fair List and thus share in the trade deflected from Dickinsons.[1] Within a year the Fair List grew from four to twenty-three. As the C.W.S. remained adamant in its policy of continuing to trade with Dickinsons, pressure was brought to bear upon it through some 2,000 local Co-operative Societies, many of which refused to accept the firm's products. Many football pool firms too were induced to place their large orders for stationery with firms on the Fair List.

By 1940 the Federation was victorious. All of the unions concerned had members in the firm, in some cases with 100 per cent success. Some 9,000 institutions throughout the country were supporting the campaign and as a result of intensive work over half of the firms in the Envelope Makers' Association had been put on the Fair List.

[1] P. & K.T.F., *Annual Report*, 1939, p. 24.

CHAPTER XVI

THE JOINT INDUSTRIAL
COUNCIL

*We have done much, we can do more, and by our
example we shall prove to our own satisfaction and show
to other industries that consideration, conciliation and
co-operation, instead of conflict and combat, is the wisest
way of striving to solve the economic problem with which
we have to deal.*

JOINT INDUSTRIAL COUNCIL, *Report of Annual
Convention*, 1929.

ORIGINS

On May 11, 1915, a letter in the *Newspaper Owner and the World* made
the rather startling suggestion that the trade unions should co-operate
with the employers' organizations in enforcing standard costing methods.
This would help to eliminate the suicidal price-cutting which was the
bane of both the 'fair' masters and the unions. Lengthy correspondence
followed in the pages of the influential trade journals, *Caxton Magazine*
and the *British and Colonial Printer and Stationer*. The unions in the
process engraving trade were co-operating with the masters in operating
a scheme of price control with which both parties were highly satisfied. In the course of correspondence and discussion the idea of co-
operation for wider purposes than the suppression of price-cutting
gradually gained ground, and comprehensive schemes for 'trade
betterment' were advanced by enthusiasts on both sides. In 1917 a
conference of representatives of unions and employers endorsed the
principle of greater co-operation for printing trade betterment, and all
present pledged themselves to support and encourage a scheme for
giving effect to this principle.[1]

During the subsequent discussion emphasis was placed on the need
for a more humane attitude by management. The ending of the agony
of War, and the high hopes of a new era of prosperity and social

[1] *Joint Industrial Council, Its Origin*, 1940.

THE JOINT INDUSTRIAL COUNCIL

reform, provided a climate of opinion in which such ideas received a much more favourable hearing than at any time in the past. Unions and employers vied with each other in suggesting practical ways in which the broad principles could be implemented. One of the most popular on the employers' side was some permanent organization for the settlement of incipient trade disputes. An idea which was naturally more favoured on the workers' side, was the granting to them of greater responsibility for their conditions of work, by the setting up of joint worker–management committees in each firm, rather similar to the production committee which had been very successful in the munitions industries during the War.

Another strand in the tangled skein of the Betterment Movement was concerned with the health of the workers. Printing works, because of their antiquity, tended to be cramped and uncomfortable, with the barest minimum of facilities for washing, eating meals, and resting during breaks. Only a few large modern works could compete with the best factories in more modern industries. Investigations into productivity in munitions industries during the War had revealed that improvement in such amenities resulted in greater output. Considerations of self interest thus reinforced more altruistic motives in producing a movement for improvement in physical working conditions.

In October 1916, the Government, seriously alarmed by a widespread resurgence of industrial strife, appointed a committee to consider ways of securing a permanent improvement in relations between employers and employed. The reports of the Whitley Committee, as it was called, helped to crystallize the rather nebulous ideas about the form of organization which would promote the objects of the Betterment Movement. The Whitley Committee recommended:

'The establishment for each industry of an organization representative of employers and work people, to have as its object the regular consideration of matters affecting the progress and well-being of the trade from the point of view of all those engaged in it, so far as this is consistent with the general interest of the community.'[1]

These Joint Industrial Councils should be formed by voluntary action of the existing organizations in each industry; the latter would then feel direct responsibility for their success. In the printing industry adoption of the Whitley scheme was facilitated by the high degree of organization of workers and employers, though there were a few problems regarding the representation of such independent sections as the Newspaper Society, the Bookbinders and others.

[1] *Interim Report on Joint Standing Industrial Councils*, 1918, p. 3.

256 PERIOD OF COMPROMISE

The various strands—standard costing, industrial conciliation, joint consultation, improvement in health and hygiene—were eventually incorporated in the constitution of the Joint Industrial Council, which held its first meeting in July 1919. Although the form was modelled on the recommendations of the Whitley Committee, the printers were proud of the fact that the Betterment Movement had, in principle, anticipated the ideas of the Committee.

CONSTITUTION

The Joint Industrial Council was formed as a co-operative organization of employers and trade unions. The employers had to be members of the Federation of Master Printers, and to employ at least some members of the printing trade unions. Thus non-union houses, though they could join the F.M.P., were not officially represented on the J.I.C. The trade unions had to be federated to the Printing and Kindred Trades Federation. No member of any organization 'not in harmony with the objects of both Federations' was eligible for representation on the J.I.C. The membership rule at times caused friction, for some unions contended that 'open houses', firms employing both unionists and non-unionists, should be refused admission. This contention was not generally supported, for the F.M.P. had frequently made it clear that it could not discipline its members into becoming Union Houses.[1] Among those who were definitely excluded were the House Unions which, of course, were not federated to the P. & K.T.F.

The representation of the Newspaper Society was something of a problem. At one stage it was suggested that a separate J.I.C. should be formed for the newspaper industry, but this had not been taken up, largely because of the opposition of the London Newspaper Proprietors' Association, which claimed that its interests were so distinct from those of the general printers, that it could not join with them. The position of the provincial newspaper firms was very different, for many of them also ran commercial printing departments. The unions were keen to admit the Newspaper Society, for it had in the past proved more vulnerable to union pressure than the general printers. For exactly the same reason the F.M.P. had serious reservations about admitting the Society. However, after prolonged discussion, it was allowed four representatives on the Council, and the trade union representation was increased accordingly.

The first objective of the J.I.C. was the encouragement of fuller

[1] J.I.C., *Minutes of Quarterly Meeting*, October 1924. This chapter is almost entirely based on minutes of meetings and Annual Reports of the J.I.C.

THE JOINT INDUSTRIAL COUNCIL 257

organization on both sides. The following extracts from the Objects show how the other ideas were incorporated:

'1. Standard Costing: to resist the action of those who would injure the fair standard of wages and prices by disposing of their goods or their labour at less than the standard mutually agreed upon. . . . to assist in the maintenance of such selling prices as will afford reasonable remuneration to both Employers and Employees.
2. Conciliation: to promote good relationships between employers and employed; to secure co-operation and the recognition of mutual interests; to encourage direct contact between employers and workers to devise ways and means of settling any differences that may arise.
3. Welfare: to take in hand the question of apprentice conditions; to insist upon clean, healthy workshops; to encourage full and proper ventilation, clean surroundings and decent habits; to encourage the establishment of welfare departments and the provision of meal rooms for work people.
4. Joint Consultation: to provide means for securing to work people a greater share in and responsibility for the determination of the conditions of health and comfort under which their work is carried on.'

As well as the National Council, the J.I.C. structure made provision for a network of District Committees which would send representatives to the Annual Convention, and would act as two-way channels of communication between the National Council and the firms. The Annual Convention was intended to provide an open forum for the discussion of general problems of the industry. After 1925 it functioned regularly. Experts on some selected topic, such as technical training, or costing, were invited to read papers, and these were followed by open discussion.

To complete the scheme as suggested by the Whitley Committee, Works Advisory Committees, with representatives of both management and workers, were to be set up in individual firms. In fact, very few of these were ever formed. Even the District Committees were far from flourishing. In fact, at the local level many trade union branches and employers showed apathy, if not open antagonism, to the ideas of the J.I.C., partly, no doubt, because they suspected that it would collapse at the first trade depression or major industrial dispute. Even when it was shown that the J.I.C. enjoyed a reasonably robust constitution, and survived the General Strike and the Great Depression, the problem remained: What useful work could the District Committees perform within the limitations imposed by centralization of authority on both the union and employer sides? At first some thought that the District

I

258   PERIOD OF COMPROMISE

Committees might act as 'courts of first reference' in cases of industrial disputes, in order to localize them if possible. But with the settlement of terms of employment under National Agreements, the national authorities were unwilling to allow local bodies to settle disputes, for the terms they agreed on might upset the delicate balance of wage differentials throughout the country, or be quoted as a precedent for similar settlements in other regions. The 1935 Convention was devoted to the question of how to revive and revitalize the District Committees. One employer put the position bluntly:

'You are not going to get hard-headed business men to spend their time in attending meetings with a programme that is little better than a mothers' meeting programme.'[1]

The Organization Committee battled on trying to form District Committees, but met with very limited success. However, when the Apprentice Selection Scheme of the J.I.C. was put into operation some District Committees did very useful work in forming local selection committees.

On the whole, however, the J.I.C. remained a macrocephalic monster whose head was out of all proportion to its other members. Despite the optimistic rhetoric of the Annual Conventions, the ideals of a new era in industrial relations had made little alteration to conditions at the primary level, where employers and employed met in the place of work.

THE HEALTH COMMITTEE

One of the first to be set up in 1919, the Health Committee worked steadily to improve the hygienic standard of printing offices. Although there had been a good deal of discussion of industrial disease before the War, there had been little systematic investigation, and only sporadic attempts to educate management and workers in the best methods of combating the most dangerous ones. After 1900 the increased use of fast-running machinery led to an increasing incidence of accidents. This aspect of industrial health was, however, largely under the supervision of the Factory Inspectors, and the Health Committee decided to concentrate on such diseases as lead poisoning, notorious as a hazard in the printing industry, and tuberculosis.

In 1921 it obtained the help of medical officers in compiling a short pamphlet *Precautions against Consumption*, and in designing leaflets and posters suitable for display in workshops, with simple rules to be observed in different trades. The J.I.C. also co-operated with the

[1] J.I.C. *Report of Convention*, 1935, p. 11.

THE JOINT INDUSTRIAL COUNCIL

Newspaper Proprietors' Association in organizing a thorough investigation into the health of workers in newspaper offices. The final report of the investigator showed an alarmingly high rate of tuberculosis among compositors between sixteen and nineteen years of age, and among machine-minders between thirty and fifty-nine years of age. The former was perhaps due to poor physical standard of entrants, and emphasized the need for medical examination of candidates for apprenticeship. The latter was perhaps due to higher speeds of working, the prevalence of night work, or similar conditions which would lead to deterioration in general health.[1]

In 1930 the Committee drew attention to the high incidence of dermatitis in certain branches of the industry, and supplied Dr Sybil Overton of the Home Office, who was conducting an investigation into industrial dermatitis, with case histories of printing workers who had been affected. It also went thoroughly into the problems of disinfecting factories. It used the technical skill of the Printing and Allied Trades Research Association to help in the analysis of paper, inks, dust and other materials about which there had been compaints from the workers.

The Health Committee tackled its job with enthusiasm and determination. By its patient discoveries of the relevant facts, and its constant propaganda for reform, it assisted the movement for improvement of the physical conditions of workplaces. By its thorough investigation of complaints of suspected poisonous materials it helped to allay workers' hostility to new processes. At the same time it urged employers to adopt a more responsible attitude to the health of their apprentices and employees by pointing out that in most cases good health and high productivity went together.

THE APPRENTICESHIP COMMITTEE

Before the War several of the more thoughtful leaders in the industry had been giving consideration to the reform of the apprenticeship system. The War itself focused attention on the problem by raising the special issue of what was to be done with youths whose servitude had been interrupted by service in the Armed Forces. It seemed hardly fair to force them to complete the full term of their indentures, especially at the rates of pay and under the general conditions of apprentices. On the other hand if they were granted full journeyman status, with perhaps only three or four years of training, did not that imply either that there was no real need for a seven years' training, or alternatively that semi-skilled men were being released who could not hope to master the skills in which they were supposed to be expert?

[1] Medical Research Council, *The Sickness Experience of Printers*, 1929.

PERIOD OF COMPROMISE

With the experience and insight gained in the administration of the Interrupted Apprenticeship Scheme in the years immediately following the Armistice, officers of both trade unions and employers associations revised their approach to the broad issue of trade training. Previously apprenticeship was regarded almost solely as a method of technical training, and arguments for reform had been based on allegations of inefficiency of the old system. Employers favoured any change which improved the quality of craftsmanship or led to increased labour productivity; at the same time the craft unions approved any reform which raised the status of the worker, improved his chances of obtaining employment, or offered a basis for claiming better conditions of work or higher wages. Here was a field like that of improved industrial health, where it seemed as if there was a considerable measure of common interest, and where joint action might be both practical politics and agreeably fruitful.

Another idea behind the formation of the Apprenticeship Committee was that of a national apprentice ratio which would regulate the intake in conformity with the needs of the different trades, and thus help to reduce unemployment. In fact it was from a Committee appointed to deal with the unemployment arising from the 1921 depression, that the suggestion of a national campaign to reform apprenticeship arose.[1]

Nevertheless, on both sides were some who opposed any change. The unions were suspicious lest the transfer of some of the training to technical schools might lead to the side-stepping of the unions' restrictive apprentice ratio, and lead to swamping of the labour market with a flood of trainees. Older craftsmen were haunted by the fear—by no means groundless—that the younger, more scientifically trained men, would displace them in the labour market. Others, as always, opposed from sheer conservatism—'We got along all right in the old days.'

The newly formed J.I.C. decided to tackle the problem, and appointed an Apprenticeship Committee to study the plans for reform, and make some recommendations. In 1921 officers of the Ministry of Labour, who were also making a study of the problem, reported to the J.I.C. that the position in the printing industry was chaotic: a wide variety of practices prevailed throughout the country, and even among different firms in the one locality. There was almost no attempt at systematic selection, and in many instances the training was, to say the least, inadequate. There was almost no correlation between the workshop training and the courses given in some technical schools.

But the officers did more than point to the inadequacies of the system as a method of trade training. They argued that a more liberal approach should be made to the whole problem, and that candidates for appren-

[1] J.I.C., *Fourth Report of Unemployment Committee*, January 1921.

THE JOINT INDUSTRIAL COUNCIL 261

ticeship should be considered also as young people 'training for citizen-ship', and for their future careers.[1] Reaction to the suggestion was disappointing. The masters showed strong opposition, particularly to any move which would limit their 'right' to select their own appren-tices. The smaller employers, who often gave least and gained most, under the old order, were the main objectors.

For a few years the idea was dropped. Then in 1925, largely on the initiative of J. C. Coppock, an enthusiastic advocate of apprenticeship reform, the F.M.P. formed its own Apprenticeship Committee. This drafted another scheme, aimed at meeting the objections to the first. There was no element of compulsion; a master retained the right to select his own apprentices, and the scheme was to be supervised by local Committees, preferably connected with the J.I.C. The function of the committees would be to select panels of suitable candidates for appren-ticeship, to advise employers and technical schools on trade training programmes, and generally supervise the progress of the lads under its jurisdiction. Although this scheme was commended by the J.I.C. its adoption was painfully slow. By 1930 only two District Committees, Derby and Leeds, had adopted the full scheme, but in about ten other centres local Joint Committees were exercising some measure of supervision over aspects of selection and training.

In general there was more progress in the larger centres, where organization was more thorough, and educational facilities more adequate. A disproportionately large number of apprentices, however, continued to be trained in small shops, where the equipment was often obsolete, and conditions far from the ideal. The unions proposed to eliminate this unsatisfactory training by getting the J.I.C. to agree to some scheme whereby only approved employers would be permitted to take on apprentices. On the other hand the apprentice ratios which the unions themselves enforced tended to discriminate against the large firms where conditions tended to be better.

The Depression temporarily killed interest in apprenticeship reform. At the 1933 Annual Convention of the J.I.C. a trade union leader, R. Kneale, analysed the reasons for the failure as lack of flexibility in the scheme, laziness and conservatism of both workers and masters, and the over-centralization of the power of the J.I.C. which tended to dis-courage the District Committees.[2]

In the matter of technical school training, there was substantial improvement. In 1939 over sixty schools were giving some courses in printing and allied subjects. Most of the students taking these trade courses were also given instruction in English and general subjects. In

[1] J.I.C., *Minutes of Quarterly Meeting*, January 1921.
[2] R. Kneale, 'The Apprentice', *Report of J.I.C. Convention*, 1933.

262 PERIOD OF COMPROMISE

1937 Teachers of Printing and Allied Subjects formed an Association, with the object of exchanging ideas, and co-ordinating courses to raise the standards in all schools. For this the J.I.C. could claim only a very small part of the credit. In regard to the selection of apprentices for crafts, and supervision of their workshop training a beginning, and hardly more, had been made, despite two decades of continuous propaganda by the advocates of reform. Almost nothing had been done to improve the methods of selection and training of the non-apprenticed boys and girls who elected to make their careers in the printing trades.

For the modicum of improvement that had been effected a few idealists on the J.I.C. Apprenticeship Committee deserved full credit. But against the rock wall of conservatism and entrenched interests of both masters and the older craftsmen, they battered almost in vain. Almost the only gleam of hope in a rather desolate prospect was the disposition of the new generation of masters, organized in the Young Master Printers, to tackle the problem with thoroughness and enthusiasm. Their efforts were, however, interrupted by the Second World War.

CONCILIATION COMMITTEE

Among the most important objects of the J.I.C. were the promotion of good relationships between employers and employed, the recognition of mutual interests, and the investigation of 'ways and means of settling any differences that may arise'. To further these objects a Conciliation Committee was set up very soon after the establishment of the J.I.C. The original Disputes Rule was simple and categorical:

'No Strike, Lock-out or other aggressive action shall take place in any locality until the matter in question has been placed before and considered by the District Committee, and failing a settlement being arrived at, has been remitted to the National Council, which shall meet to consider the question within six days.'[1]

In its first year the J.I.C. was called on to settle two disputes, one in the Potteries District where the combined unions had demanded a wage increase, and the other in Eastern Counties where a firm had introduced non-union labour. The successful settlement of these cases which, though not of wide importance, had both reached an 'acute' stage, was considered by contemporary observers to augur well for the success of the conciliation procedure.

In the next few years, however, there were major disturbances over the question of wage adjustments—upwards in 1920, downwards in

[1] J.I.C. Constitution, 1920, *Master Printers' Annual*, 1921, p. 38.

THE JOINT INDUSTRIAL COUNCIL 263

1921. As wage rates were settled by a network of National Agreements embodying the first approach to a wages structure for the industry, with regional, craft and sex differentials, any adjustment made by one craft, grade or region would alter a wide circle of differentials. Hence disputes, even of an apparently local character, were much too important to be settled by any but the highest authorities, and the full J.I.C. was inevitably called in to try to make a settlement. The Disputes rule was modified to require reference first to a District Committee (where one existed), then to the Conciliation Committee, and finally to the full Council.

At this stage there was by no means unanimity regarding the best form of procedure. The L.S.C. secretary stated that it should be a cardinal principle that no case should be taken up unless both parties agreed to accept the decision of the Conciliation Committee. Representatives of both the T.A. and the S.T.A. opposed this, as smacking too strongly of compulsory arbitration:

'Unions which had fought for years against arbitration could not agree to accept the decisions of a committee without consulting their Executives, or to a Conciliation Committee functioning as an Arbitration Board.'[1]

Though the Dispute Rule was subsequently amended several times, the principle of voluntary acceptance of the finding of the Committee was always maintained. Very rarely was the finding actually rejected. In fact, however, the method of resolving the disputes would perhaps be more accurately termed Voluntary Arbitration.

It was generally recognized that the settlement of trade disputes was made much easier if the parties were not permitted to take the crucial step of precipitating a stoppage. But the problem then arose, under what terms and conditions were the workmen to be engaged during the hearing of the dispute? In 1924 the Conciliation Committee adopted a rule which stipulated that both parties should conform to 'normal conditions'. This was found to be inadequate, for often the dispute hinged on just that point—what were the 'normal conditions'? Later the phrase was defined as meaning the conditions immediately prior to the dispute.

Gradually, over the years, the form of procedure adopted by the Conciliation Committee became standardized. First the terms of reference of the dispute were drafted by the Joint Secretaries, in consultation with the parties concerned. The Committee for any dispute consisted of the Chairman and Vice-President of the J.I.C., four

[1] J.I.C., *Minutes of Quarterly Meeting*, January 1922.

PERIOD OF COMPROMISE

members from each panel, selected by the parties to the dispute. Members of bodies directly concerned, such as the trade union, the firm, or the local Master Printers' Association, were not permitted to serve on the Committee.

No documents relating to the dispute were circulated to Conciliation Committee members prior to the meeting. The object of this was to prevent them from pre-judging the issue. Nor was there any attempt to imitate strict judicial procedure. Meetings had an air of informality. The primary object was to ensure that both parties felt they had been allowed a full presentation of their case, uninhibited by fear of procedural complexity. For example, if the complainant was a trade union, and the case was being presented by the national secretary, he might bring along the Secretary of the Branch concerned, the Father of the Chapel, and perhaps the worker personally involved, either to give evidence or to clarify points of detail.

After the case and the reply had been made by the respective parties the Chairman and members of the Committee would question them to make sure that the facts were clearly established. The parties then withdrew while the Committee considered points of principle involved. After some discussion it usually appeared that, in the light of some collective agreement, trade custom, or previous interpretation, one of the parties was in the wrong. Then a member of the Committee would put forward a tactfully phrased memorandum, designed to protect the rights of the injured party and at the same time save the face of the other, in order to facilitate its acceptance of the finding.

When the wording was agreed upon, the disputants were asked to come in again, and the finding was read to them. Sometimes they said there and then whether or not they accepted the verdict; usually they asked for permission to refer to higher authorities on their side. In many cases, however, the Committee itself was unable to come to any settlement of the point at issue, and the 'finding' was simply that the parties should continue to negotiate to try to find a compromise solution. If one party eventually rejected the finding, the matter was taken before the full J.I.C. where much the same procedure was followed.

At first only disputes between parties who were *both* members of the J.I.C. could be dealt with by the Committee. But in 1926, after a dispute between the London Bookbinders' Branch of the Paperworkers' Union and the Book Trade Employers' Federation had threatened the whole London binding trade with a stoppage, which would have involved many members of the J.I.C., a new clause was adopted:

'In the event of a dispute arising between an employers' organization

THE JOINT INDUSTRIAL COUNCIL 265

or a trade union which is a member of the J.I.C. and a third party which is not a member of this Council, which dispute is likely to involve working relations in the Printing and Allied Trades, as represented on this Council, then the Joint Secretaries shall at once be informed so as to enable the Council to protect the interests of its members.'[1]

Most of the disputes which came before a Conciliation Committee were over the interpretation of National Agreements. Hence, although most of them appeared to be local, arising out of trouble in one firm, the finding inevitably created a precedent which affected all other workers covered by the clause in question. In such cases the unions tended to treat the case as 'national' in scope. On the other hand, the employers were often keen to make it appear as if the issue was only a local one, and would therefore allow it to be handled by the representative of the firm. Thus any classification of disputes into 'local' or 'regional' or 'national' is very arbitrary, and often meaningless.

However, a broad distinction could be made between disputes over the terms of National Agreements, arising either from interpretation or intended alteration, and disputes arising from the application of the agreement to, say, a particular machine in a particular office. Most of the 'national' disputes were over wages or hours, and arose from trade union attempts to improve conditions for their members, though in the early thirties the major dispute was a prolonged series of manoeuvres by the employers to force the trade unions to agree to wage reductions. On major issues such as these the Conciliation Committee could not hope to find a basis for agreement, for almost all possible and acceptable compromise solutions would inevitably have been suggested in the course of the previous negotiations. This is not to say that the Conciliation Committee was useless. Several times, when negotiations had broken down, and perhaps hard words had been spoken, and the parties were refusing to meet, a tactful recommendation from the Conciliation Committee saved the day, permitted the re-opening of negotiations, and led to a settlement. In some disputes the time given for 'cooling down' while the Committee deliberated, prevented the threatened stoppage.

It is impossible to assess the effectiveness of the Conciliation Committee in settling disputes, for any assessment must be based on an estimate of the stoppages that *would* have occurred, had there been no Conciliation Committee. This would be pure conjecture. On the other hand the shrewd and able leaders on both sides seemed to be convinced

---

[1] J.I.C., *Minutes of Quarterly Meeting*, July 1926.

I*

266 PERIOD OF COMPROMISE

that the Conciliation Committee had done valuable work. Their judgement must count heavily in its favour.

SOME BLIND ALLEYS

Limited progress was made in three of the fields in which the founders had hoped that the J.I.C. would inaugurate a new era of industrial relations. It remains to record other efforts which were complete and utter failures.

Shortly after the J.I.C. was established, the printing industry felt the effects of the 1920–22 depression. The Council set up a Committee to consider ways of reducing unemployment and mitigating its hardships. This Unemployment Committee drew up several schemes of super-annuation for older workers, but the employers claimed that they could not bear the additional financial burden, and the schemes were shelved. Local schemes for retraining the unemployed, which had been partly successful in Edinburgh and Glasgow, were publicized, and details circulated to the District Committees, but had little practical effect. During the Great Depression the Unemployment Committee was revived. It made a detailed survey of the extent and cost of unemployment, but again its practical proposals were ignored.

In 1926 the Betterment Committee was set up to consider ways of raising the status and improving the economic position of the industry. On the employers' side many believed that the most urgent need was to increase the productivity of labour, and that the best ways to achieve this were to adopt payment by piece rates and relax some of the unions' restrictive rules. On the union side these methods of 'reform' naturally met with opposition; their representatives claimed that the industry would be on a sounder economic basis if management invested in more modern machinery, and tried to encourage the workers by providing better working conditions. Neither side managed to convince the other, and nothing tangible resulted from the discussions.

During the Great Depression, when there was a resurgence of price-cutting among employers, the F.M.P. turned again to the idea of enlisting the help of the unions to enforce standard costing practices. The J.I.C. appointed a Fair Prices Committee which worked out several plans for eliminating 'unfair' competition. But none of them was ever adopted, and with the return of more prosperous times, the idea was quietly dropped.

CONCLUSION

The founders of the J.I.C. hoped that it would achieve four main objects: the co-operation of employers and unions to reduce price-

THE JOINT INDUSTRIAL COUNCIL   267

cutting, the extension of joint consultation between workers and management, the improvement of health and welfare of the workers, and the elimination of stoppages by the provision of conciliation procedures.

The Health Committee did valuable educational work by giving publicity to the dangers of occupational diseases, and practical measures for combating them. The Conciliation Committee was highly successful in preventing the breakdown of negotiations on several critical occasions. Although it was generally credited with being the most successful of the J.I.C. activities, it is difficult to make an accurate assessment of its real contribution.

The Committees dealing with the major controversial issues of Trade Betterment, Unemployment and the maintenance of Fair Prices achieved practically nothing. This failure, however, served to reveal that despite the flowery rhetoric about 'common interests' of workers and employers, their objectives remained often poles apart.

In the long view, perhaps the most constructive contribution of the Council was the slow, patient work of the few enthusiastic advocates of apprenticeship reform. In the teeth of apathy and opposition from conservatives in both the unions and the employers, they propounded radical ideas of scientific selection, of thorough technical education, and of the responsibility of the industry towards those who elected to enter it to earn their livelihood.

CHAPTER XVII

TERMS OF EMPLOYMENT
1920–39

*It is probably safe to say that the printing industry today
is more regulated by collective agreement than any other,
and is correspondingly in less need of outside interference.*
SECRETARY OF F.M.P., before I.L.O. Convention, 1937.

INTRODUCTION

Throughout this period the regulation of contractual relations was
mainly effected by the 1919 series of national agreements. Apart from a
brief suspension during and after the General Strike, and occasional
disruption due to disputes, the terms of these agreements settled the
basic terms of employment of the great majority of workers in the
industry.

An important feature of the mode of adjustment of these terms to
meet altered economic or technical conditions, was the *continuity* of the
collective bargaining. Whereas before the War this had been an intermittent process, with several years of isolation between periods of
intense negotiation on important changes, from 1920 to 1939 there was
almost constant negotiation on a number of minor matters, in particular
on extra rates to be paid for skill and responsibility.

There were of course attempts to alter the *basic* conditions. In 1921–23
the employers were able to enforce wage reductions; in 1937 the
workers obtained a reduction in the standard hours of labour. Two
lengthy series of negotiations ended without effecting any alteration:
the unions' campaign to have a complete revision of the grading
pattern, the employers' attempt to effect wage reductions in the Great
Depression.

These five movements are treated in more detail in the following
sections:

TERMS OF EMPLOYMENT

TECHNICAL CHANGES AND SPECIAL RATES

Between the World Wars there were no technical developments in printing as spectacular as the introduction of machine composing and high speed rotaries in the earlier period. However, there was a continuous search for greater speeds and greater precision, and the development of such ancillary machinery as mechanical feeders, and anti-set-off devices. Newspapers changed over from the deck to the line type of printing machine, with mechanical hoists and magazine reel holders for loading the great reels of newsprint, and conveyor belts for removing the printed papers. Automatic folding and wrapping machines added to the complexity. One important new technique was the development of rotary photogravure, a process eminently suited to the production of illustrated periodicals, and the glossy women's magazines which were springing into prominence.

Probably the most important technical change in the industry was the mechanization of bookbinding. One machine performed all of the operations in making a cloth case; another did all of the 'forwarding' operations—folding, gathering and stitching in one run-through. Cutting and trimming were speeded up by the use of the continuous three-knife trimmers; blocking of the cases (printing of the title, &c.) was greatly speeded up by power-driven machines.

Partly, no doubt, this change was prompted by the unions' policy of raising wage rates, especially women's. Before the Great War many semi-skilled bookbinding tasks had been done by women or girls; but after the War the 'females' were in the unions—often to the disgust of the old craftsmen—and their rates were standardized. But at the same time other factors were operating too: the increasing demands of an educated democracy for cheap books, changes in publishers' practices, the growth of commercial circulating libraries, the need to replace equipment worn out during the War. Thus when the trade journals of the twenties carried tempting advertisements of the wonderful new machines, of American design, most of the larger bookbinding offices decided to invest in them.

These technical changes, far too numerous to be enumerated here, posed a major problem for the trade unions. Most of them were not, officially, opposed to the introduction of machinery. But at the same time they insisted, as a matter of 'principle', that the machine operator should be a member of the same union as the hand craftsman whom the machine had replaced. In general the employers were prepared to concede this. The 'control of the machine' was thus not a matter of dispute.

The second aspect of the problem, however, was more difficult.

PERIOD OF COMPROMISE

How much extra was the operator to receive, and what working rules were to apply to the machine? The unions claimed, with considerable justification, that operators should have extra pay to compensate them for the additional skill, or responsibility, or strain. Obviously the conditions of operation of no two makes of machines are exactly alike; the unions, therefore, aimed at obtaining agreement on a schedule of Extras payable for each type. When a few of these had been standardized it would be fairly easy to work out the rate for a new model, by comparing it with one of the known ones.

For example, under the National Agreement of 1918 the F.M.P. agreed with the T.A. on Extras for machine-minders in charge of five classes of machines of increasing complexity, for which the additional payments ranged from 3s to 15s. Between the Wars the T.A. was in almost continuous negotiation with the F.M.P. over the rates for new machines, or for additional gadgets such as mechanical feeders, on the old ones.

A few of these cases came before the J.I.C. Conciliation Committee, but most were settled without any serious stoppage. Bronzing attachments, feeding attachments, anti-set-off devices, machines for printing paper bags, milk bottle tops, business labels—no sooner was one point settled than another was brought forward.

Other unions took similar action. In 1923 the London Central Branch of the Paperworkers' Union, after threatening to strike, won agreement on the payment of standard Extras to operators and *assistants* on the new bookbinding machines in use in printing offices.

This did not apply to binding machines in purely bookbinding shops. The existence of two different rates for the same work performed by members of the same union (although in a different branch) was anathema to the London Bookbinders, and two years later when their demands for similar differentials were refused, they struck. The Central Branch came out in sympathy, 16,000 workers were on strike, and the dispute could easily have snowballed into a national stoppage. Indeed this was the largest strike over an industrial issue in the industry in this period, an indication of the strength of union feeling on the matter of machine rates. The settlement of the dispute involved an agreement on the procedure to be followed in future cases. First, all negotiations were to be on a national basis; second, adjustments were to be on a flat rate applicable throughout the whole country; third, men put on to learn a machine were to receive half of the Extra for the first six months; fourth, there was to be no change in the manning of machines without consultation with the unions. The Executive of the Paperworkers claimed that this Agreement gave effect to the Union's claim to share in the increased productivity of the industry. Between

TERMS OF EMPLOYMENT

1925 and 1939 some twenty additional differentials for other machines were added to the original schedules. Similarly Natsopa won a major victory in 1938 when it obtained recognition of the principle that its assistants on the more complex machines should also receive some extra payment.

WAGE REDUCTIONS, 1921–22

In the very month after a wage advance had been negotiated—November 1920—the cost of living fell seven points, initiating a trend which was to continue for the next fourteen years. As the depression deepened, the F.M.P. was threatened with internal dissension, for there was a revival of price-cutting and pervading pessimism regarding trade prospects. Master printers automatically looked towards a general wage reduction to effect a revival of the industry.[1]

In May 1921, the employers conferred with the P. & K.T.F. to try to find some means of checking the growth of unemployment and of placing the industry on a 'sounder economic footing'. This euphemism held no ambiguity for the union representatives, who had been previously consulting their colleagues in order to devise the best means of resisting the expected demands for wage reductions. The P. & K.T.F. distributed to the unions hundreds of copies of the employers' *Statement of the Present Position of the Industry*,[2] in which the author argued that the depression in printing was partly due to high costs and that an improvement could be achieved only by increasing productivity and reducing wages.

After several conferences and a special meeting of the J.I.C. the unions eventually agreed to ballot their members on an employers' revised proposal of reductions of 7s 6d and 3s for men and women respectively. Only the Paperworkers, the Lithographic Artists, the Natsopa women's section, and the Society of Women accepted the proposals.[3] The F.M.P. Wage Basis Committee then decided to instruct all members to post notices on September 1st, intimating that a reduction would come into effect on September 24th, almost a month later than the reductions applicable to the unions which had accepted the terms.

Had the unions offered united resistance they might have called the employers' bluff. But a week before the employers' notice expired the T.A. asked for separate negotiations. The ensuing conference ended in the virtual capitulation of the T.A. which agreed to recommend acceptance of the 7s 6d reduction, to take effect from January 1922. At

---

[1] F.M.P., *Minutes of Council Meeting*, January 1921
[2] *Members' Circular*, 1921, p. 169.   [3] *Ibid.*, p. 266.

272 PERIOD OF COMPROMISE

the same time, last minute negotiations were held with the P. & K.T.F. in an attempt to find some way of avoiding the threatened breakdown. The Federation representatives pressed strongly for a reduction of only 5s; alternatively they urged that the other 2s 6d reduction should be the subject of further negotiation after a few months. The employers refused to consider this, and when the others learned that the T.A. had accepted the 7s 6d reduction they realized that their own chances were negligible, and concentrated on obtaining the same terms as the T.A. In this they were successful. Shortly afterwards the L.S.C. and the Stereotypers' Society, the two strongest unions in the industry, agreed to accept reductions—*of five shillings weekly*. This destroyed the recent achievement of a uniform craft rate, and increased the London–provincial differentials.

The F.M.P. had barely time to congratulate itself on narrowly averting a crisis with the more recalcitrant unions before it was subjected to the complaints of those which had accepted the 7s 6d reduction in August (to take effect in two instalments of 5s and 2s 6d). Both the Paperworkers and the Lithographic Artists argued strongly, on grounds of equity, that the 2s 6d reduction should be postponed from September to January, to keep them in line with the other unions. The plea was rejected on the grounds that to modify an agreement would create a troublesome precedent, and (with probably unconscious irony) that 'decisions of the Federation, like every Act of Parliament, must of necessity bring hardship to someone'.[1]

Thus the employers clearly won the first round. Throughout the remainder of 1921 there were only minor disagreements which did not disturb the tranquillity of the industry. By January 1922, however, the cost of living index had fallen still further and the F.M.P. Council authorized the National Wage Basis Committee to press for further wage reductions.

Towards the end of March events moved to a climax. The Alliances unanimously rejected the T.A.'s counter proposals to discuss the re-grading of some 254 towns and empowered the Committee to take what action it thought necessary.[2] If the T.A. had hoped to stave off wage reductions by prolonged re-grading negotiations, it had overplayed its hand. A Special F.M.P. Council Meeting on March 29th decided that, as the unions seemed likely to reject a sliding scale agreement, and that notices would probably have to be served, a special J.I.C. meeting should be convened in order that any action of the Federation should be 'constitutional'. At this meeting the employers' panel agreed to postpone aggressive action until they had conferred with all of the unions concerned in about a week's time, and had discussed the situation with

[1] *Members' Circular*, 1921, p. 309.   [2] *Ibid.*, 1922, pp. 86–89.

TERMS OF EMPLOYMENT

the P. & K.T.F. at the Quarterly Meeting of the J.I.C. on April 26th.[1]

The union panel of the J.I.C. promised to try to obtain unanimity among the affiliated unions in order to simplify the negotiations, but the London craft unions and the T.A. would not join in such a move. The situation was complicated by recent amalgamations under which sections of the Paperworkers and Natsopa had autonomy for a probationary period, but in general the members of these two large unions accepted a reduction of 15s for men and 7s 6d for women to be applied in instalments between May 1922 and January 1923.

The Quarterly J.I.C. meeting was mainly occupied with finding some formula that would save the face of the union executives who would have to recommend their members to accept wage reductions. Even the T.A. spokesman stressed the need for compromise, and finally the meeting resolved that the ballots be taken on the terms already accepted by some unions, and that the results of these be made known to the employers by May 18th.[2]

On May 22nd representatives of the Newspaper Society and the Labour Committee met to consider the results of the ballots. There were no complications—all the unions, including the federated group, had rejected the 15s reduction by large majorities! Only in Scotland could the employers find cause for satisfaction; the Alliance had achieved a reduction of 15s by all unions, except the Lithographers and Stereotypers, on condition that no further reductions were made during 1923.[3]

Again the T.A. withdrew from the 'federated group', and conducted its own campaign of resistance. After further negotiation the federated group agreed to recommend that their members accept a reduction of 12s 6d for men and 6s for women, with proportionate reductions for pieceworkers and juveniles, on condition that no further reductions were made during 1923. The Litho. Printers and Artists accepted similar terms.

When negotiations with the T.A. reached a deadlock, Sir David Shackleton, from the Ministry of Labour, suggested that the dispute could be submitted to the Industrial Court for settlement if both parties gave their consent. The T.A. agreed to this procedure. Terms of reference were settled as follows:

'Should there be a reduction in the wages of the members of the T.A.?

---

[1] Report of Special Meeting of J.I.C., *Members' Circular*, 1922, p. 122.
[2] J.I.C., *Minutes of Quarterly Meeting*, April 26, 1922.
[3] *Members' Circular*, 1922, p. 176.

274 PERIOD OF COMPROMISE

If so, what amount, and how should any such reduction be divided, and at what dates ?'[1]

In the preliminary proceedings the T.A. caused a fine contretemps at the Industrial Court by pointing out that the union would not be bound by the award unless it was accepted by a ballot of the members. The masters regarded this manoeuvre as a despicable piece of chicanery but proceeded to put their case. The Award gave the reduction of 12s 6d for which the F.M.P. had applied, but the anger of the masters when the T.A. proceeded to put the issue of acceptance to the ballot knew no bounds.[2] The representatives of the other unions, many of which were already in financial difficulty, knew that if the T.A. came out on strike their own members must suffer severe unemployment. The employers promised to try to keep other union men in employment as far as was possible.

As soon as the wage reductions were enforced most of the T.A. members affected came out on strike. While many firms refused to comply with the F.M.P. order, although strenuous efforts were made to bring them into line, on the other hand some thousands of T.A. members accepted the reduction and remained at work, despite the equally vigorous efforts of the Executive and branches to bring them out.

The strike dragged on for four weeks, but the position of the T.A. was practically hopeless. It could expect little sympathy from the other unions in the P. & K.T.F. with which it had failed to co-operate, and whose members were already accepting reductions, while its refusal to accept the decision of the Industrial Court had brought public opprobrium on its head. On August 12th the T.A. Executive sent a request for resumption of negotiations and agreed to recommend its members to accept a reduction of 12s 6d in four instalments.[3] The Masters agreed to reinstate T.A. men on strike. On August 25th, the Secretary of the F.M.P. received the following laconic telegram from the T.A.: 'Majority members accepted agreement'.

Having settled the rates for the major national unions the F.M.P. then turned to the London unions—the compositors, readers, machine managers and pressmen. The suggestion of a reduction of 6s was accepted by the L.S.C. and some of the others, but not by the readers and machine managers. The London M.P.A. warned the latter that notices would be posted and threatened that those dismissed would be re-engaged only on less favourable terms.[4]

[1] Report of Meeting with T.A., *Members' Circular*, 1922, p. 219.
[2] F.M.P., *Special Circular*, July 1922.
[3] Report of Conference with T.A., *Members' Circular*, 1922, pp. 279–311.
[4] London M.P.A., *Report of Special General Meeting*, November 14, 1922.

TERMS OF EMPLOYMENT

Although the Paperworkers' union had balloted in favour of accepting the 12s 6d reduction, the large, wealthy and militant Central Branch refused to abide by this, and joined in with the London craft unions. Several hundred members were then locked out, and only accepted the reduction on condition that their minimum rates for various classifications should be increased by amounts ranging from 1s 6d to 2s 6d. Similarly Natsopa agreed to the 6s reduction only on condition that the minimum rate was raised by 2s.[1]

Only in a few cases did the local branches or chapels refuse to accept the majority verdict. The most important of these revolts was the refusal of the Irish branches of the T.A. to agree to the reductions.

Much more serious to the unions than any of these isolated instances of failure to observe the agreement, was the ill-feeling engendered between the T.A. and the others over the attempt to resist the wage reductions on its own. At the Federation Council meeting in 1923 representatives of the other unions accused the T.A. Executive of 'cynical disregard of the interests of any other body'. A long debate on the ethics of the T.A.'s withdrawal from the Federation negotiations was precipitated by the union's appeal for the payment of strike benefit. This was refused on the technical point that the T.A. had failed to seek the advice and assistance of the Federation before entering on a serious dispute.[2] 'Maintain solidarity at all costs', had for generations been the basic principle of union strategy; the T.A. for the second time had been guilty of breaking rank at a critical juncture. Furthermore, by trifling with the decision of the Industrial Court the union had given strong propaganda to those who wished to depict union leaders as powerful, irresponsible and dishonourable demagogues.

The T.A. Executive maintained stoutly that the union had a constitutional right to autonomy on wage matters, that it had kept the Federation informed of developments, and that its refusal of wage reductions was 'one of the greatest fights ever put up in the industry'.[3] While the first point was admitted, the others were contested, and the fact that the T.A. strike was soundly defeated and that other unions had suffered innocently in the process, indicated that the T.A. leaders had made a serious miscalculation of their strategic position.

REGRADING

The trade unions agreed to the last round of wage reductions on condition that they were followed by a period of 'stabilization'. Hardly

[1] *Members' Circular*, 1922, p. 443; 1923, p. 27.
[2] P. & K.T.F., *Annual Report*, 1922.
[3] *Printing Federation Bulletin*, November 1923, p. 3.

PERIOD OF COMPROMISE

had this period expired than the unions put forward extensive proposals for regrading of many country towns. Again the T.A. refused to join the federation movement, and presented its own schedule. This independence was a great boon to the employers, who were able to point to discrepancies between the two schedules, and play off one group against the other in the negotiations. Had the union's demands been moderate, they might have been considered. But by the sheer magnitude of the changes they proposed they rallied the ranks of the employers, who announced that the industry needed an extension of the stabilization period in order to complete its recovery from the depression:

'By stabilization we mean that there are to be no broad or basic changes whatever in wages, grading, and conditions. At the same time it is understood that now, as always, any genuine anomaly can be brought up by either side for consideration.'[1]

Naturally enough, there were many borderline cases, and union branches could easily show that, in many cases, they deserved higher grading; at the same time, local Master Printers' Associations could put up a good case for lower grading of many centres. Eventually two Joint Regrading Committees were set up, one for the T.A. and one for the P. & K.T.F., with representatives of the F.M.P. on both. These committees laid down the factors to be considered in assessing grading. First was the population of the town; second its proximity to a large industrial centre; third its importance as a printing centre. Other factors could be considered in special cases, but a high local cost of living was not, in itself, to be regarded as an argument for up-grading. The parties agreed that no alteration should be made until the whole list had been considered.

For almost three years, until interrupted by the General Strike, these Joint Committees worked intermittently, travelling to various centres and collecting evidence. After the Strike, the hearings were resumed, but by the time they were concluded, in 1929, and a beginning had been made in sorting out the mass of evidence, the Depression intervened. For the next few years the regrading issue was set aside as the unions negotiated desperately to stave off further wage reductions. In 1933 when trade had improved, and the Federation of Printing and Kindred Trades held its Council meeting, there was little enthusiasm for renewing the campaign for regrading.

For this there were several reasons. Firstly, under the original National Agreements, several of the non-craft unions, in particular Natsopa and the Paperworkers, had agreed to accept the same grading

[1] *Members' Circular*, 1924, p. 332.

TERMS OF EMPLOYMENT

for their branches as the T.A. grading. This meant, however, that as long as those clauses operated, their branches' rates were tied to the T.A. grading. And as the irrepressible leader of the T.A. pursued his solitary, stormy way, the others were forced to follow passively in his wake. They bitterly criticized the T.A. for trying to pursue an 'independent' line on the matter:

'The attempt to negotiate regrading by any one society acting separately can only lead to delay and confusion, and is a negation of the right of other societies to be given equality of treatment and to voice the desires of their membership . . .'[1]

One T.A. delegate, displaying a lamentable lack of appreciation of the economic consequences of the grading system, claimed that 'those unions whose activities are confined to London cannot reasonably have a voice in the grading of towns in the provinces'. Fortunately for inter-union relations, the T.A. elected as its new secretary J. Fletcher, who made haste to try to restore unity. In negotiations with the F.M.P. he put forward a strong case for both a reduction in the number of grades, and a reduction in the differential between them. The first idea caused no little stir among the employers. Their Chairman asked, disingenuously, whether the T.A. envisaged a reduction in the higher grades, or the abolition of the lower ones. The T.A. secretary replied solemnly that the latter was intended, for the former would *increase* the disparity between London and provincial rates, and further embarrass the London masters.

Then, in 1936, before the F.M.P. had clarified its attitude to the new proposal, it received a letter from the T.A. stating that the union was abandoning its attempt to modify the wage pattern by regrading individual towns, and adding a dark hint of an impending approach on 'other constitutional lines'.

When the T.A. withdrew from the field, the other unions, acting under the P. & K.T.F., tried to renew the battle, but they made no progress, and with the outbreak of the War gratefully decided to postpone the matter 'until a more opportune time'.

Thus ended, almost in fiasco, the prolonged regrading negotiations which had consumed so much time of committees, councils and conventions, and been at times a burning issue in many union branches and Master Printers' Associations. It showed clearly the difficulty of adjusting any part of an overall wage pattern once the latter had been established for a few years. The reasons are not difficult to see. On the union side, there would almost certainly have been very strong ob-

[1] P. & K.T.F., *Annual Report*, 1932, p. 15.

278   PERIOD OF COMPROMISE

jection to any *down*-grading. Thus any practicable change would have
to be an *up*-grading. But this would be certainly opposed by the
employers in that locality. Furthermore, by making the regrading
depend upon several variables, the Committees had made it almost
certain that few cases would be clear-cut anomalies on all counts. In the
end both sides wearied of a series of negotiations which were obviously
not going to produce any change of worthwhile proportions.

'REDUCTION OF COSTS', 1931–33

At the annual conference of the P. & K.T.F. in May 1931, union
leaders discussed the steps necessary to promote a revival of trade.
Like most of their contemporaries, they were woefully ignorant of the
nature of the crisis with which they were contending, and hardly two
of the speakers offered the same remedy for the depression. One
wanted a shortening of the working week, to share available work more
equitably; one advocated a reduction in the apprentice ratio; a third
favoured abolition of overtime; another wanted international control of
wages and hours of work; a few were pessimistic and unconstructive.
Only G. Isaacs, secretary of Natsopa, appeared to realize that the
depression was related to international economic adjustments, and
required drastic fiscal and financial remedies which were beyond the
power of the trade unions.

On the employers' side there was the same confusion. The *Members'
Circular* for 1931 contained many gloomy reports of reduced turnover
and increasing unemployment. Towards the end of the year appeals
to master printers to refrain from competitive price cutting assumed a
note of urgency. Like most of the union leaders, who could suggest
nothing but the traditional remedies, the masters discussed their
favourite panacea, and early in 1932 asked for a conference with the
P. & K.T.F. to discuss ways of reducing costs and stimulating the
demand for printing.

At the first conference the P. & K.T.F. pointed out that it had no
authority to negotiate on wage reductions, but was prepared to discuss
other ways of reducing production costs. Later the Federation issued a
warning to the unions to be prepared to make a stand, and reminded
them of their fundamental function:

'A trade union is not merely a philanthropic institution; . . . Its funds
are primarily intended for other purposes which must not suffer
because of financial calls to meet an unprecedented volume of unemployment.'[1]

[1] *Printing Federation Bulletin*, January 1931, p. 1.

TERMS OF EMPLOYMENT

At a subsequent conference with the unions, the Federation Executive was again asked to continue discussions with the Master Printers—presumably to gain as much time as possible—but not to consider wage reductions in any form. In the meantime the Federation of Master Printers had sent out a circular to all affiliated bodies asking them to submit reports on union rules or clauses of agreements which they found either anomalous or restrictive. The reports were collated by the Negotiations Committee, and the following 'list of subjects requiring revision' was forwarded to the unions:

Rates for Machines	Piece Work	Women's Rates
Manning of Machines	Short Time	Composing Machines
Semi-skilled Workers	Balancing of Time	Call Money

In most of these cases the employers wanted either some relaxation of rules, or some reduction in the rate of pay. Perhaps the employers, knowing how attached the unions were to these rules, thought that a feint attack in this sector might leave the wages front only lightly defended, for at the next conference they gave a strong hint that if the unions would agree to a 15 per cent wage reduction, they would withdraw the list of 'restrictive anomalies'. The unions refused to be drawn. Finally, after several more abortive conferences, the Federation of Master Printers advised each of the unions separately that it wished to negotiate an alteration in the terms of the National Agreement.

By this time the unions were better informed of the causes of the depression. At its recent Delegate Meeting the Paperworkers' Union, after discussion of wages reductions, had resolved:

'That this conference, having reviewed the proposals of the Master Printers' Federation to reduce wages and working conditions, does hereby declare its firm conviction that the depressed condition of the Printing Industry is due solely to the collapse of the world's money markets controlled by the capitalist classes, and not from any cause within the control of the industry, and as a consequence prosperity of the industry cannot be revived by the methods suggested.'[1]

The New Year, 1933, opened in an atmosphere tense with the probability of open conflict. In the provinces union branches were busily passing resolutions of support for the policy of No Reductions; in some centres mass meetings had resolved to resist any alteration of wages or working rules. But by this time the masters, in contrast, showed a disinclination to enter the lists. In his New Year message the President

[1] N.U.P.B. & P.W., *Supplement*, July 1932, p. 6.

280   PERIOD OF COMPROMISE

of the F.M.P. made no mention of wage reductions, but stressed the need for more team spirit among master printers, and announced that the Federation would launch another campaign against price cutting. During the summer trade picked up slightly, and by the end of the year unemployment had declined. Although desultory negotiations continued, the unions grew increasingly confident both of the correctness of their stand, and of their ability to resist overt action by the employers. Many employers agreed with the general contention that a deficiency of purchasing power could hardly be remedied by a further reduction in wages, and gradually their claims for reductions in costs were abandoned.

The crisis had passed, and in the following year unemployment fell substantially, union funds and membership began a slow recovery, and the unions regained the initiative.

HOURS OF WORK

The basic hours of work for most of the printing trades were governed by the 1919 National Hours Agreement negotiated between the two Federations. Alteration of the terms was not a matter for individual union action. Therefore, although the stronger unions continually pressed the P. & K.T.F. to ask for negotiations for shorter hours, the Federation officers, knowing the precarious financial position of some of the other unions, refused to take any steps which might lead to a serious dispute.

However, in 1934, when the worst of the Depression had passed, and the masters' proposals for wage reductions had been successfully staved off, the unions returned to the offensive. A special committee recommended that the Federation should press for a forty-hour week. Again the weaker unions showed a natural reluctance to be embroiled in a movement which might endanger their solvency, and perhaps their very existence. For the next few years there was no direct approach to the employers; the International Labour Office was expected to recommend that a forty-hour week should be introduced in selected pilot industries, and the British printing unionists hoped that their industry would be selected. When this hope was disappointed, they took a ballot of their members on the question of a 'forward movement'. The result showed 86 per cent in favour of an attempt at reduction of hours.

At the conference arranged with the employers, in 1936, the P. & K.T.F. spokesmen claimed that the industry could afford the shorter week, and that the workers had a right to share in the increased productivity resulting from mechanical, technical and scientific progress. The employers did not reject the proposal outright, but held out for

TERMS OF EMPLOYMENT

some concession on the union side, particularly in relaxation of apprentice ratios and overtime limits.

The P. & K.T.F. refused to discuss such matters, which were strictly not within its jurisdiction, but were governed by rules of the individual unions. They also stated firmly that when they had exhausted the conciliation procedures, they would send out a ballot to all members asking whether or not they were in favour of strike action. The employers' representatives, after some delay, offered a reduction of three hours, from forty-eight to forty-five, in the standard working week. This offer was put to a ballot of union members and accepted by an overwhelming majority.

The F.M.P., however, had the unenviable task of convincing the Alliances and other affiliated organizations that it had obtained the best terms possible. Gradually and reluctantly these other bodies gave their assent to the reduction, and the new hours came into operation in October 1937. One important condition in the new agreement was a Stabilization clause, precluding either side from asking for a major alteration in the National Agreements for a period of three years. This was resented by the Scottish Typographical Association whose members had gained rather less than the others owing to the prevalence of shorter hours in Scotland. The Lithographic Artists also were annoyed, because the Hours Movement had interrupted their negotiations for a wage increase, and this had now to be postponed for another three years. But apart from these two, the unions were pleased with the result. A few militant leaders were restrained in their praise, and urged their members to prepare to fight for another reduction at the earliest opportunity.

A survey made after a year's working of the new agreement showed that the employers were not dissatisfied either. The Costing Committee of the F.M.P. had worked out that the change would raise costs about $5\frac{1}{2}$ per cent and had urged members to try to obtain revised prices for their running contracts. On the whole the master printers had no difficulty in passing on the small cost increase to their customers.

CONCLUSION

In the inter-war period terms of employment of printing workers were determined by a large number of national collective agreements. There were three alterations of these terms. Firstly in 1921–22 the employers were able to enforce wage reductions which though substantial, left the real value of the rates considerably higher than the 1920 real value. Secondly throughout the period all of the unions enjoyed considerable success in obtaining extra payments for men doing work requiring special skill, or entailing extra responsibility or discomfort. Thirdly in 1937 the Federation negotiated a reduction in hours from forty-eight to forty-five weekly in the general trade, with smaller reductions for night workers.

There were two other attempts at a major alteration in the basic terms of employment. The unions' attempt to obtain a complete revision of the grading of provincial towns ended in failure, due in no small part to the determination of the T.A. to act alone. The attempt of the employers to enforce wage reductions during the Great Depression was foiled by the unions' negotiators who managed to prolong the discussions until the worst had passed and industry showed signs of recovery.

The following diagram shows the relation of wage rates of London compositors and bookbinders to the cost of living and to an index of wage rates in all Industries.

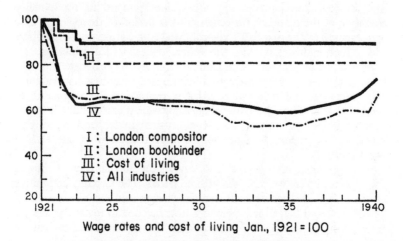

Wage rates and cost of living Jan., 1921 = 100

Source: I. Cost of Living Index, Min. of Labour
II. Index of Wage Rates, Min. of Labour
III. Weekly Wage Rate—London Compositors (case rate)
IV. Weekly Wage Rate—London Bookbinders

Thus the complex basic pattern of wage rates throughout the industry came to be made up of three strands. First were the differences in craft, sex and skill, often with a long history. Second was the somewhat erratic and arbitrary (but partly rationalized) distribution of Grade rates for different towns, based largely on historical accidents and confused by the partial application of conflicting principles. Third was the increasingly complex set of Extras for skill, responsibility or strain.

The following graph shows that printers' earnings during this period were very favourable in comparison with those of all Industries:

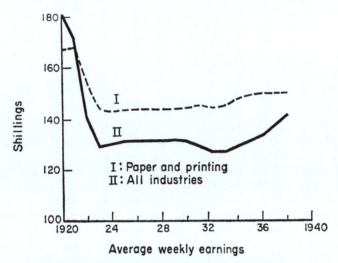

Source: A. L. Chapman & R. Knight,
Wages & Salaries in the United Kingdom, 1920–1938

A fairly common criticism of trade unions is that, by enforcing standard rates of wages, they try to bring all workers down to the same level. This charge could certainly not be sustained against the printers' unions in the twentieth century! On the contrary the complexity of these different rates was to prove a continuing source of conflict.

CHAPTER XVIII

THE SECOND WORLD WAR
1939–46

EMERGENCY MEASURES

In August 1939 the German armed forced attacked Poland. The British Government issued its ultimatum; Hitler gave no reply. On September 3, 1939, Britain was again at war with Germany.

During the hectic last few days of peace in August 1939, anticipating the outbreak of War, representatives of the P. & K.T.F. conferred with the Joint Labour Committee of the F.M.P. and Newspaper Society. Constitutionally, neither side had authority to commit its members to any agreement, but both felt that the emergency warranted extraordinary measures. The aim was to work out general rules to cover the period of dislocation immediately after the declaration of War. The printing industry would be badly hit by paper shortages and other restrictions; was there to be chaos on the labour side, with massive dismissals and re-engagement on a casual basis, or would something better be worked out?

In this first Emergency Agreement, the main feature was that employers were permitted to operate short-time working with proportionate reduction in wages.[1] Though this ran contrary to the accepted principles of many unions, the P. & K.T.F. felt it was preferable to large-scale dismissals, or changing to casual employment.[2] Other clauses permitted the alteration of working hours, to make full use of daylight and avoid 'blacking-out'. Workers transferred to other offices were to receive their old 'merit money' and 'maintenance allowance' related to their domestic circumstances. Time lost during air raids was to be paid at full rates.

Actual agreements in regard to alteration in working hours, or short time, were to be arranged at the works level by chapel and management.

Early in September a similar agreement was made with the News-

---

[1] Agreement on Emergency Conditions, August 31, 1939, *Members' Circular*, 1939, p. 306.
[2] P. & K.T.F., *Annual Report*, 1940, p. 8.

THE SECOND WORLD WAR

paper Proprietors' Association. Both agreements established a Joint Committee to consider questions of application and interpretation. These agreements were strongly criticized by several unions, who considered that the P. & K.T.F. had acted with unnecessary speed, and had conceded to the employers more than was necessary. This typified the failure, in many quarters, in the first years, to realize the requirements of 'total war'. At the next meeting of the War Emergency Committee the P. & K.T.F. conveyed the unions' strong dissatisfaction. They wanted payment to piece-workers for lost time, and for short-time arrangements to be entirely a matter between each management and Chapel.

On their part the employers strongly objected to the action of some affiliated unions which had issued to their branches a unilateral interpretation of an ambiguous clause in the agreement. The Alliances were complaining that the payment of full wages for time lost during air raids was too generous, and they wanted to reduce it to half pay.

The outbreak of the War quickly resulted in heavy unemployment in printing. The percentage of unemployed jumped from $5 \cdot 4$ in August 1939 to $8 \cdot 6$ in mid-August, and $12 \cdot 6$ in mid-October, despite the widespread introduction of short-time working.[1] Faced with lower wages, a rising cost-of-living, and growing unemployment, the unions fought strenuously to protect their members' standard of living. They tried to squeeze every pound they could from the employers, for example, by claiming that when short-time was being worked, extra hours should be paid for at overtime rates, even though still within the normal working week.[2]

In May 1940, unemployment, though falling slightly from the peak of 11 per cent in January, was still nearly double the pre-war rate. On June 5th members of the F.M.P. were settling down to a fairly dull Annual General Meeting. The meeting was interrupted by a telephone call: the Government wished to arrange an urgent transfer of printing workers to munitions. Within six hours representatives of the F.M.P., Newspaper Society and the P. & K.T.F. were in conference at the Ministry of Labour, and practical plans were under discussion.

The adopted scheme was a voluntary one, first put before the J.I.C. by Colonel Fletcher and George Isaacs, in 1940. The J.I.C. approved the idea and later obtained the endorsement of the Minister of Labour and National Service. The J.I.C. then sent out its Appeal to workers to co-operate in the scheme. The crux of it was that local committees of employers and trade unions would co-operate with employment exchanges in transferring printing workers, especially the unemployed,

[1] *Ministry of Labour Gazette*, 1939.
[2] P. & K.T.F., *Annual Report*, 1940, p. 9.

286

PERIOD OF COMPROMISE

to essential industries in which their technical skills could be readily used.[1]

From this time on the labour situation changed rapidly, and by the end of the year there was a labour shortage. In June 1940 the first War Emergency Agreement, over which there had been so much argument, was allowed to lapse.

A great defect of the Emergency Agreement was that it had no procedural provision for settling disputes. Thus after another conference on January 3rd, when disagreement continued, the F.M.P. simply issued its own recommendation regarding the interpretation of the agreement.

An interim agreement on payment for time lost through air raids during working hours reduced the employer's obligation to full pay for the first hour, and half pay thereafter. Employees would be given an opportunity to make up lost time.[2] In regard to short-time working, conditions reverted to pre-war.

A new War Agreement (No. 2) was signed on September 24, 1940. This provided that work should continue after the air raid warning, until the 'imminent danger' signal was sounded. The Government devised a scheme by which 'roof spotters' would give the second warning. This scheme could be adopted by mutual agreement—the desire of the management and a majority vote of the workers. Where this scheme was adopted, with consequent reduction of lost time, employers paid full wages for time lost. Where work had to be suspended due to enemy action, employees received half pay for the period of suspension.[3]

Another matter of serious disagreement was the procedure in regard to replacement of apprentices who joined the Armed Forces. Here there were three possible courses: to replace apprentices to maintain the normal quota in relation to the journeymen, to replace apprentices on the termination of their period of indenture, or not to replace them at all until agreement was made with the unions. In the meantime the F.M.P. wisely recommended the last course 'in the interests of good relations in the industry'.

On the matter of apprentices the War Emergency Joint Committee agreed that there should be a standstill on engagement of apprentices until April 1st, and that the underlying principle should be that every effort should be made to reinstate apprentices in their original firms. During the month the parties agreed that apprentices could be replaced when their term of indenture expired, and that the permitted number of apprentices should be the pre-war quota. A formula was devised for

[1] 'J.I.C. Appeal', *Members' Circular*, 1940, p. 112.
[2] *Members' Circular*, 1940, p. 105.
[3] War Agreement No. 2, *Members' Circular*, 1940, p. 173.

THE SECOND WORLD WAR

calculating the number of journeymen which would form the basis for the apprentice quota.

LABOUR SHORTAGE AND DILUTION

During 1941, as more and more men and women of military age were called into the Forces, and others were transferred to Essential Industries and munitions, the supply of labour eventually fell short of the demand, and for the remainder of the War the employers had the novel, and to many unpalatable, experience of coping with a labour shortage, in addition to the shortages of paper and other raw materials. The change in the labour market is dramatically shown in union expenditure on Out-of-Work benefits.

	Average				
Union Expenditure £000	1935–8	1939	1940	1941	1942
T.A.	38	58	74	8	3
L.S.C.	54	81	108	11	2
S.T.A.	9	12	20	2	–

Source: *The Typographical Association,*   Appendix
           The London Society of Compositors,   ,,
           A Hundred Years of Progress,   ,,

Both unions and employers had anticipated that there would be a need, eventually, for the replacement of craftsmen by semi-skilled, and of men by women. 'Dilution of labour', one of the main evils of industry, according to the craft union ethic, had to be admitted. In February 1941, the P. & K.T.F., Newspaper Society and the F.M.P. reached agreement on the general principles which would govern dilution schemes.

The first principle established was that any agreement on relaxation of union rules, trade customs or collective agreements was to be negotiated by the individual unions. This matter was considered too important for the unions to yield their autonomy.

Secondly, any variations agreed to should apply only for such time as the unions were unable to supply the required labour. At the end of hostilities, pre-war conditions would be resumed.

Where women were introduced to take the place of men, 'reasonable preference' had to be given to women already in the trade.

Finally, if a firm found it necessary to reduce staff, the 'substituted labour' had to be dismissed first.

A Joint Committee of the employers' organizations and the P. &

288   PERIOD OF COMPROMISE

K.T.F. had authority to arbitrate on disputes arising from the agreement.[1]

Following on this settlement of general principles, the employers began negotiations with the separate unions. By the end of 1941 a dozen dilution agreements had been signed. The T.A. Agreement, one of the first, was typical. In effect it provided that dilution agreements should be made at the local level, between the T.A. branch and the local employers' organizations. Managements and Chapels, however, were permitted to discuss 'House variations' and submit them to the local committee for approval. But in the last resort, *all local agreements* were subject to approval by the Head Offices of the T.A. and the employers' organizations. With three levels considering the problem, progress in implementing specific dilution schemes was very slow.

The T.A. agreement listed a number of matters which might be considered:

'A. Relaxation of rules relating to
   (1) manning of machines;
   (2) work upon which apprentices could be employed;
   (3) changing staff from one machine to another, e.g. from Linotype to Monotype;
   (4) "lending" men from one office to another by the day, or part of the day;
   (5) employment of superannuated union members;
   (6) limitations on overtime.
B. Substitution of men from other printing trade unions on "T.A." work.
C. Substitution of men from outside the printing industry.'[2]

The agreement covered the principles to be observed in training the new men, and the wages to be paid them during and after training.

At this stage the T.A. would not agree to admit women to craftsmen's work, but in August 1941 even this rampart was breached, and a supplementary agreement provided for the training of women as Monotype and Linotype operators, readers, machine-minders, and on 'any other T.A. operation'. Training periods varying from nine to eighteen months were stipulated; at the end of this if a woman had reached journeyman's standard, she had to be paid journeyman's wages.

[1] 'War Agreement No. 3—Variation of Trade Agreements', *Master Printers Annual*, 1946, p. 232.
[2] 'War Agreement No. 3A', *Master Printers Annual*, 1946, p. 234.

THE SECOND WORLD WAR

CHANGES IN ORGANIZATION[1]

There was no important formal changes in the main organizations in the industry. The F.M.P., the Newspaper Proprietors' Association, the Newspaper Society, the P. & K.T.F. and the individual trade unions emerged from the War with little alteration to their membership, and little change to their constitution. This in itself was in marked contrast to the First World War, which ended with phenomenal changes in union membership and funds, a new structure of collective agreements, the J.I.C. and a host of internal modifications.

True, during the 1939–45 War the P. & K.T.F. took a much greater part in negotiations on wages, but the effect of this was in general, through the flat-rate increases, to preserve the pre-war wage pattern. The unions had yielded autonomy grudgingly, because of the emergency, but were keen to regain it as quickly as possible.

In 1939 there were sixteen unions, with 217,000 members, affiliated to the P. & K.T.F. By 1945 the membership had fallen to 205,000, almost entirely due to a substantial drop in the Paperworkers' numbers in the first year of the War. Of the total 'members', however, less than one half were actually working in the industry.

In 1941 the P. & K.T.F. established its own Organization Department with one full-time organizer. During the War several large non-union firms were persuaded to open their doors to union members, but in many cases the existence of House Unions, with substantial 'fringe benefits', presented a difficult problem.

On the employers' side the most important change was the formation of a London Newspapers Provincial Association to negotiate conditions of work on London papers which were producing special editions in provincial cities—mainly, of course, Manchester.

During the first two years most of the normal work of the J.I.C. was suspended, and general meetings cancelled. A Joint Emergency Committee, however, was given powers to make representations to the Government on matters affecting the industry. This Committee was frequently in touch with Government departments, especially the Ministry of Labour, giving technical and economic advice on manpower, training, switch to munitions and so forth. During the War there was almost continuous co-operation between the officers of the P. & K.T.F. and the F.M.P. on matters of joint interest.

In October 1943, the J.I.C. held another full Council meeting, after a lapse of eighteen months. The War Emergency Standing Committee presented a long report of its stewardship, particularly in regard to

[1] For a lively and lucid account of the work of the P. & K.T.F. during the War, see *Team Work* by J. Fletcher, published by P. & K.T.F. (1945).

K

290

PERIOD OF COMPROMISE

manpower problems, and schemes for rehabilitation of disabled workers. The meeting accepted the Report on the Recruitment and Training of Apprentices, which initiated the post-war campaign to reform the system.

WAGE RATES

During the War there were three general flat-rate increases in men's wage rates, in 1940, 1941 and 1943, followed by two years of stabilization. At approximately the same time smaller increases were made in the rates for women and juveniles. In 1942 provincial grades were reduced from six to four. In 1943, for the first time, a National Agreement on apprentices' wages fixed them as percentages of the journeyman's rate. The history of these five developments is sketched below.

Towards the end of 1939 the P. & K.T.F. took the initiative and called a meeting of affiliated unions to consider the best way to conduct wage negotiations during the War. Hitherto, of course, wage negotiations had been the function of each separate union, and the basic rates were still those in the National Agreements made after the First World War, with the reductions forced on the unions in the depression of 1921–22.

The Conference of Union Executives decided to authorize the P. & K.T.F. to put forward a claim for flat rate increases of 10s for men (and women receiving men's rates), 7s 6d for other women, and 4s for juveniles. The claim was based on the increase in the official cost of living index, since the outbreak of War, from 155 to 173 (December 1, 1939), a rise of nearly 12 per cent. G. A. Isaacs (Natsopa) who presented the case, stressed that the unions' aim was not to obtain real increases, but to maintain the standard of living of their members.[1]

The employers' spokesman, Colonel Fletcher, relied on the prevalence of short-time working (admitted by the unions) as evidence that the industry could not *afford* to grant increases. He also pointed out that the cost-of-living was still *lower* than in 1922, when present wage rates had been fixed. A questionnaire sent out recently to the Alliances had revealed that the fall in volume of production was greater than the fall in wages. Considerate employers were retaining men for whom they could not find full-time work. Any increase in labour costs would only make the position worse, and lead to more dismissals. Finally he called for equality of sacrifice from employers and employed.[2]

The F.M.P. circulated the Unions' application to the Alliances, and received a unanimous rejection. A conference of union executives expressed 'serious disappointment', and called for a full meeting of the

[1] 'Application for War Bonus, P. & K.T.F. Statement', *Members' Circular*, 1940, p. 12.   [2] 'Employers' Reply', *Members' Circular*, 1940, p. 14.

THE SECOND WORLD WAR 291

J.I.C. 'in view of a probable dispute in the industry'. The employers felt that this action was hardly necessary, but made no formal objection.

After two J.I.C. conferences had proved quite ineffective, the P. & K.T.F. proposed that the dispute be referred to the newly constituted National Arbitration Tribunal. It is surely one of the minor ironies of industrial history that the printers, who had traditionally opposed 'outside' arbitration, should have been the first to obtain a hearing by the compulsory State arbitration authority.

The Tribunal consisted of the Chairman (the Hon. Mr Justice Simonds), two 'appointed members', and one member from each of the employers' and union panels.

The case was heard on August 13, 1940. The proceedings were conducted with a minimum of formality, and the atmosphere differed little from that of a Conciliation Committee of the J.I.C. The chairman, carefully trying to preserve the traditional amity of the disputing parties, congratulated them on the good relations existing in the industry. Referring to the problem of adjusting piece rates, he said, 'You are on such good terms that you might work it out for yourselves'.[1]

The Award announced a week later:

	Demand	Award
Men	10s	5s
Women	7s 6d	2s 6d
Juveniles	5s	1s 6d

The N.A.T. gave no explanation of its decision and it is perhaps sheer coincidence that the most important part (the men's rate) could be calculated by the time-honoured process of 'splitting the difference'.[2]

The employers were pleased with the verdict; union members were dismayed. At the time of the hearing the cost-of-living index was 185, 18 per cent above September 1939. The Award represented an increase of about 6 per cent to London craftsmen.

WAGE INCREASE, 1941

Throughout the winter and spring of 1940–41 the cost-of-living continued to rise. When the P. & K.T.F. held its Council meeting in May 1941, the Index stood at 200. In July a conference of affiliated Unions authorized the P. & K.T.F. to press for another increase.

This time, instead of applying for a flat rate increase, the P. & K.T.F. put up a case for graded increases varying inversely to the base rate. In

---

[1] Members' Circular, 1940, p. 148.
[2] N.A.T. Award No. 1. Printing and Kindred Trades.

292 PERIOD OF COMPROMISE

other words, workers (men, women and juveniles) on low rates should receive greater increases than those on high rates.

	Under 60s	60s– 69s 6d	70s– 79s 6d	80s– 89s 6d	Over 90s
Basic Rate	60s	69s 6d	79s 6d	89s 6d	90s
Increase Asked	14s	12s	10s	8s	6s

The application for increases for women and juvenile rates were three-quarters and one-half of the men's.

At the subsequent conference with employers, the P. & K.T.F. spokesman again relied heavily on the cost-of-living argument as the broad basis for the application, but pointed out that the unions had sunk their individual interests to the extent of asking most for those who were hardest hit.

Implementation of these increases would have had considerable impact on the effective rates payable in many lower grade provincial towns, and would have substantially reduced the regional and sex differentials. If they were later consolidated with base rates, the effect would be a radical change in the grading pattern. The employers, therefore, recommended to the Alliances that a graded increase should be rejected, and the Labour Committee authorized to negotiate a flat-rate increase.

In October the employers offered a flat-rate increase of 5s (men), 3s 6d (women), 2s (juveniles), on condition that any merit money could, at the option of the employer, be absorbed in the increase, and that employers should have the option of requiring not more than five hours of regular overtime per week.

The T.A. and S.T.A. were highly critical of the terms of settlement, but failed to gain a majority for reconsideration.[1] The unions insisted, however, that they could not *compel* their members to work overtime. The employers agreed to consider their employees' responsibilities and commitments in regard to Civil Defence, Home Guard, and their families, as well as transport difficulties and other hazards of wartime.[2]

1942 REGRADING

The national unions, whose members stood to gain most from the original graded proposals, were disappointed with the flat-rate increases. The T.A. was particularly strong in its disapproval. This was what came of associating with London! The Secretary expressed the Manchester view, 'Regrading is primarily a T.A. domestic problem'.[3]

[1] *Typographical Circular*, 1941, p. 199.
[2] War Agreement No. 6, *Master Printers Annual*, 1942.
[3] *Typographical Circular*, 1942, p. 25. See also pp. 9, 57.

THE SECOND WORLD WAR

In January 1942 the union approached the F.M.P. for a separate increase of wages on a graded basis, intimating 'that in future it would not be linked with the P. & K.T.F. wage movements'. In the following month the Paperworkers and Natsopa wrote, too, in much the same vein. If there was collusion behind this coincidence, it did not appear in the unions' proposals, which differed widely from one another. The T.A. proposals had the simple and clear effect of maintaining the existing six grades of towns, but of reducing the differential between each grade from 3s to 1s.

Grade	1942 Rate	Proposed Rate
1	87s 6d	92s 6d
2	84s 6d	91s 6d
3	81s 6d	90s 6d
4	78s 6d	98s 6d
5	75s 6d	88s 6d
6	72s 6d	87s 6d

The T.A. justified this reduction on the reduced variation in the cost-of-living, due to price controls and rationing.

The F.M.P. Joint Labour Committee replied that such far-reaching proposals deserved very full and free consideration by all Alliances and Associations. Indeed it sought its members' opinion on the whole framework of negotiating machinery, with four specific questions:

1. Whether to deal in future with the P. & K.T.F. or with the separate unions.

2. Whether to retain the structure of national agreements or revert to regional or local negotiations (as was done prior to 1919).

3. Whether the request for a *graded* increase should again be countered by an offer of a flat-rate increase.

4. Whether the whole grading system should be reviewed, with an eye to reducing the number of grades, or reducing the inter-grade differential.

After collating the replies from the Alliances the Joint Labour Committee decided that it could negotiate on some revision of the grading system, and asked for a conference with the P. & K.T.F. Thus the provincial unions' hopes for separate negotiations were stymied.

The employers' first offer was to reduce the number of grades from six to four, by up-grading the lowest three grades, and leaving wages in the top three grades unchanged. They argued that there was no case, at least on cost-of-living grounds, for a general wage increase. They

294

PERIOD OF COMPROMISE

insisted that the settlement must be accepted by all of the unions concerned.

The unions, however, pressed for a wider spread of the increases, pointing out that this would make the proposals more attractive to more people, and thus more likely to be approved by the inevitable membership ballot. Eventually another conference, at which the officers of the J.I.C. acted as informal conciliators, came to agreement on a neat compromise solution. The effect was to reduce the number of grades to four, and to halve the spread between the highest and lowest grades (from 15s to 7s 6d).

The course of the negotiations can be seen most clearly from the table opposite.

Women's grades were also reduced from six to four, with slight increases in all rates, including Grade 1.

Old Grade	Women's Rates		New Grade
	Old	New	
1	40s	41s	1
2	39s	40s	2
3	38s	39s }	3
4	37s	39s }	
5	35s 6d	38s }	4
6	34s	38s }	

The new grading applied to all non-craft workers as well as the craftsmen, and hundreds of new rates had to be calculated for the various classes of workers, as well as for male and female learners and apprentices. Nevertheless, in October, the *Members' Circular* reported that the industry had settled down quietly to the new agreement, and very few cases requiring special consideration had come before the officials. The Costing Committee of the F.M.P. calculated that the wage cost increase varied from nothing in Grade 1 to $12\frac{1}{2}$ per cent in Grade 6, over pre-war costs.

The editor of the *Typographical Circular* commented that the one threat to abrogate the National Agreement had achieved more than the previous twenty-three years of discussion, and invited members to find the moral.[1]

1943 WAGE INCREASE

In May 1941 the Cost-of-living Index ended its skyward flight and remained virtually constant until the end of the War. No basis for a

[1] *Typographical Circular*, 1942, p. 139.

T.A. AND BINDERS' RATES

Old Craft Rate	Old Grade	Employers' Proposals	P. & K.T.F. Proposals	Difference	Half the Difference	Compromise Increase	New Craft Rate	New Grade
87s 6d	1	No change Nil	No change Nil	Nil	Nil	Nil	87s 6d	1
84s 6d	2	No change Nil	Into Grade 1 + 3s	3s	1s 6d	1s 6d	86s	2
81s 6d	3	No change Nil	Into Grade 2 + 3s	3s	1s 6d	1s 6d	83s	} 3
78s 6d	4	Into Grade 3 + 3s	Into Grade 2 + 6s	3s	1s 6d	4s 6d	83s	
75s 6d	5	Into Grade 4 + 3s	Into Grade 3 + 6s	3s	1s 6d	4s 6d	80s	} 4
72s 6d	6	Into Grade 4 + 6s	Into Grade 3 + 9s	3s	1s 6d	7s 6d	80s	

296 PERIOD OF COMPROMISE

wage increase could be extracted from its monotonous hovering about the 200 mark.

The unions, fresh from a partial victory over regrading in 1942, decided to keep the tactical initiative, and press for another wage increase. This time they asked for a flat-rate increase of 20s for adults, and 15s for juveniles. J. Fletcher, presenting the P. & K.T.F. case, argued that official figures showed that wage rates for all of industry were increasing, on average, much faster than printers' wages. Printing workers were growing increasingly dissatisfied with the relative deterioration in their position. This was especially true of apprentices whose wages were very low in comparison with those of unskilled youths. The agreed wage scale for apprentices, expressed as percentages of the craft rate, was only a 'recommended' scale, and the meaner employers ignored it.

The employers rejected the claim outright, and after unsuccessful reference to the J.I.C. the dispute was submitted to the N.A.T. The parties agreed to exchange copies of their submissions *before* the actual hearing, which was set down for June 17th. The employers argued that the increase was 'inflationary', and against both the immediate national interest and the long-term interest of the industry. The unions relied heavily on the case for restoring their pre-war status.

The Award conceded most of the employers' points. No increase was given except 4s to women not doing men's work.[1]

A conference of union executives expressed 'complete dissatisfaction' with this result, and added: 'Knowing the strong feelings among the members of the Unions, the Conference is unable to reach any conclusions that will be binding on the Unions.'[2]

This was tantamount to a call for local action, and there followed a spate of wage applications from branches and chapels. Talk of an overtime ban was common, and two such cases went to Conciliation Committees of the J.I.C.

At a special meeting on August 12, 1943 the employers' negotiating committee bravely resolved that the N.A.T. award should be strictly adhered to. In the meantime, however, the flood of individual wage applications from separate unions continued to pour in to the F.M.P. office, and more chapels were threatening a ban on overtime. In some cases the ban was imposed, and the workers ignored the findings of the J.I.C. Conciliation Committee. In Scotland the S.T.A. put an official ban on overtime, and refused to appear before a Conciliation Committee of the J.I.C.

In London, especially, chapel movements for wage increases gained

[1] N.A.T. Award No. 375. Rates of Remuneration in Printing and Kindred Trades.   [2] Quoted in P. & K.T.F. *Annual Report*, 1943, p. 7.

THE SECOND WORLD WAR

momentum during August and September, and overtime bans were operating despite formal efforts by trade union officials to remove them. This continuous militant pressure at workshop level led the employers to reconsider their tactics. If they held out too stubbornly they would be faced with the enormously complicated task of negotiating with each union separately, and ran the risk of a breakdown of the complex of National Agreements.

'It seems to us unthinkable that under existing conditions we should be expected to conduct a large number of separate conferences with individual Unions, departing from the valuable war-time practice which we have hitherto followed.'[1]

In order to preserve this valuable practice they offered to resume negotiations on wage increases, on condition that all 'aggressive or coercive actions' were withdrawn. The unions agreed to the conditions, and the parties conferred on October 11, 1943. The employers' first offer was a flat-rate 5s for all men, with nothing for women or juveniles. In reply G. Isaacs said that this small offer would not allay the dis- satisfaction of the workers, and would tend to push the negotiations back to individual unions, branches and chapels. This, of course, was just what the employers were hoping to avoid. After an adjournment the employers made a more generous offer:

Men's rates:	7s 6d
Women's rates:	2s 6d
Male Juveniles:	3s od

(Female juveniles had been granted 3s by agreement in June 1943.)

In contrast to the preceding increase, which was on basic rates, this increase was added to actual wages. It was recognized, however, that the employer retained the right, wholly, or in part, after giving the appropriate notice, to reduce any merit money payments. On the other side the employee had the right to treat any such reduction as notice of discharge. Under the prevailing conditions of acute labour shortage, few such reductions were made.[2]

The most important part of the agreement, however, was the stabil- ization clause. This prohibited applications for collective increases of wages for the duration of the war and twelve months thereafter, as long as the cost-of-living remained reasonably stable. It is remarkable that the unions should have agreed to tie their own hands, as it were, for such

---

[1] Letter to P. & K.T.F. Reprinted *Members' Circular*, 1943, p. 101.
[2] War Agreement No. 8, *Master Printers Annual*, 1944.

K*

298   PERIOD OF COMPROMISE

an indefinite period. No doubt the officers were glad to get a settlement which would reduce the impetus towards decentralization of power towards branches and chapels, with its long-term implications for future union structure and policy. And at the back of their minds was the thought that if rank and file dissatisfaction grew, in future, irresistible, the stabilization clause would have to be scrapped.

The P. & K.T.F. commented that the situation immediately following the N.A.T. award was a very nasty one indeed, and that disaster had been narrowly averted by the sensible policy of reverting to 'normal negotiating methods'.[1]

APPRENTICES WAGES, 1943

In July 1943 the employers finally agreed to a definite scale of apprentices' wages. Hitherto the apprentice's pay, expressed for each year of his servitude as a percentage of the craft rate, had been only a *recommended* scale, and many employers had ignored it.

This agreement was, in fact, a major concession on a point of 'principle' by the employers. For the first time they admitted that the unions' interest in apprenticeship should be formally recognized in some respect other than the restrictive quota. The change is shown below:

B.F.M.P. Recommended Scale	New Scale	Period of Apprenticeship		
		7 years	6 years	5 years
15	20	1		
20	25	2	1	
25	30	3	2	1
30	35	4	3	2
35	40	5	4	3
40	50	6	5	4
45	60	7	6	5

The F.M.P. recommended that employers should adjust wages of present apprentices as an *ex gratia* payment.[2]

1946 WAGE INCREASE

Following war-time practice, in August 1945 the P. & K.T.F. made an application for a general increase in wage rates. The cost-of-living index was then only five points above the 1943 level.

[1] P. & K.T.F. *Annual Report*, 1943, p. 8.
[2] Agreement—Apprentice Wages, November 3, 1943, *Master Printers Annual*, 1946, p. 277.

THE SECOND WORLD WAR 299

In October 1945 the employers made an offer of 7s 6d to men, 5s 6d to women and 3s 6d to juveniles 'in a spirit of co-operation and goodwill towards those represented by the P. & K.T.F. and particularly those returning from the armed forces'. After some bargaining this was raised to 8s 6d, 7s 6d and 4s in the three categories, and accepted by the unions. The new rates came into effect in January 1946.

One vexed question arising from this type of wage increase, was whether the increase was to be added to actual wages, or to basic minimum rates. Under prevailing conditions of labour shortage many employers were paying 'merit money' or House Rates above the minimum. If they 'absorbed' or 'consolidated' these rates in the new minimum rates, many workers would receive only a small actual increase, and would be dissatisfied. Perhaps they would vote against acceptance when the draft agreement was put to the ballot. The employers' spokesmen were in an awkward position, for they were reluctant to admit that such wage payments were at all common. In all of the post-war wage negotiations this problem of 'consolidation' and 'merit money' proved difficult to resolve.

The general increase of January 1946, however, was specifically fixed as an increase in actual wages. It recognized the right of the employer to *reduce* merit money (after giving the appropriate notice), but also provided that the employee could accept such notice of reduction as notice of dismissal.

A stabilization clause provided for a standstill on wages till June 1947, on condition that the cost-of-living remained reasonably constant. The employers admitted, however, that the P. & K.T.F. had the right to make application for revision of the 1937 Hours and Holidays Agreement.

HOURS AND HOLIDAYS, 1946

The 1937 Hours and Holidays Agreement established the forty-five-hour week, continued the one week's paid annual holiday (granted in 1919), and provided for a stabilization period of three years. When the time ran out, in 1940, the country was at war and the P. & K.T.F. postponed reopening the negotiations.

An important item in the unions' post-war programme was a further reduction in hours. In March 1946, the P. & K.T.F. sent in an application for a forty-hour week and a fortnight's paid annual holiday. In the meantime, however, the Labour Government issued an urgent appeal for increased production, and Sir Stafford Cripps and George Isaacs

300   PERIOD OF COMPROMISE

(now Minister of Labour) stressed this theme to large meetings of union officers and industrialists.[1]

At the first conference the P. & K.T.F. spokesman said that the workers felt strongly that they were entitled to more leisure and the unions believed that the employers could afford to grant it. As for its effect on output, 'no greater spur to maximum effort and production could be provided than by a whole-hearted gesture by the employers on this issue'.[2]

The theme of productivity was very much to the fore. In April 1946, the J.I.C. issued a Joint Statement on Employment and Production:

I. We believe that the future well-being of the industry, and of every individual engaged in it, must depend on the maintenance of a high and stable level of employment. The responsibilities of the printing industry to the Government, to civil administration generally, and to all the other industries, are heavy, and there is no less responsibility to the workers and employers engaged in meeting the demand for the essential service of the printing industry.

II. ... we welcome the public statements recently made by Ministers of the Crown, urging the country to increase industrial production, and to improve the efficiency of our industries.

III. We therefore ... recognize our joint responsibility to see that all steps be taken to encourage the fullest production, and undertake to examine together all possible means to that end, in a spirit of joint endeavour ...[3]

The F.M.P. circulated the union proposals to the Alliances, and collated their replies. At a second conference, on May 28, 1946, the employers rejected the claims. Their spokesman argued that the labour shortage, and the growing competition from office printing machines militated against any increase in printing costs.

As the F.M.P. made no counter-offer, a dispute existed, and the P. & K.T.F. asked for immediate reference to the J.I.C. In June a Conciliation Committee failed to break the deadlock, and in July the dispute came before a special meeting of the J.I.C. This meeting failed, too, but asked the parties to resume negotiations without reference to their original mandates.

---

[1] 'Government Appeal for Increased Production', F.M.P. *Members' Circular*, 1946, pp. 41–43.

[2] 'Application by P. & K.T.F. for 40 Hour Week', *Members' Circular*, 1946, p. 64.

[3] 'J.I.C. Joint Statement on Employment and Production', *Members' Circular*, 1946, p. 64.

THE SECOND WORLD WAR 301

Although by this time the employers were prepared to concede the two weeks' holiday, the union members were growing dissatisfied with such slow progress. In July a meeting of the printing unions decided to instruct members to operate an overtime ban as from August 12, 1946, and to take a ballot on a proposal to strike.[1]

The F.M.P. reported the dispute to the Minister of Labour. The President of the F.M.P. called on members 'to meet force with firmness, avoid recrimination, and to rely on the Federation officers taking every possible step to ensure that reason and common sense will prevail, and that open dispute will be avoided'.[2]

Meetings held at the Ministry of Labour, under the chairmanship of the Chief Industrial Commissioner, were also unavailing. Nevertheless, as the date for the operation of the overtime ban grew near, the employers made further concessions. On August 7, 1946 the Council resolved to offer the unions:

(1) Fortnight's holiday with pay from July 1, 1947.
(2) A five-day week, subject to provision for mutual House or Local agreement.
(3) A reduction of normal hours to forty-three and a half, to operate from January 1, 1947.
(4) A review of the position in June 1947.

The unions rejected this offer, and re-affirmed their intention of operating an overtime ban and issuing a strike ballot.

The P. & K.T.F. had, meanwhile, been conducting separate negotiations with the Newspaper Society. Not for the first time the newspaper employers proved to be more vulnerable than the general printers, and on August 7, 1946 the Newspaper Society agreed to a fortnight's holiday, a forty-three and a half hour week for weekly newspapers as from October 1946, and further negotiations on the *date* of operation of another hour reduction. In fact, no further reduction took place, and hours on weekly newspapers were brought into line with those in general printing.

On August 12th, according to schedule, the overtime ban came into operation in F.M.P. offices. The President sent out a rallying message:

'The unions hope and expect to force a settlement under duress. . . . Dictation backed by threats and aggressive action, is a policy which must reap its own reward. To stand against such a policy, whatever in-

[1] For an account of the movement, see P. & K.T.F., *Annual Report*, 1946, pp. 10–14.
[2] 'Message from the President', *Members' Circular*, 1946, p. 135.

302 PERIOD OF COMPROMISE

convenience, difficulty and expense may be involved, is the only course open to us all.'[1]

On August 14th representatives of the F.M.P. and P. & K.T.F. met the Minister of Labour who told them he would appoint a Court of Inquiry. This was a procedure, authorized under the Industrial Courts Act, 1919, intended as a means of informing Parliament and the public of the facts and causes of a dispute. The Court of Inquiry was not primarily an arbitral or conciliatory body,[2] though it was expected that its findings would help to lead to a settlement.

The Court of Inquiry heard evidence from unions and employers for ten days between August 22nd and September 9, 1946, concluding with two lengthy submissions by the respective counsels. During this hearing the unions conducted the strike ballot. Returns showed an overwhelming vote (5:1) in favour of strike.

The Court published its Report on September 24, 1946.[3] Its first conclusion was:

'That in the General Printing Section of the Industry the demands on production are at present very large, and so far as we can foresee, are likely to continue to be very large for some appreciable time to come.'

To overcome the labour shortage there would have to be additional recruitment, especially of women and girls.

Regarding the main points in dispute, the Court concluded that the fortnight's holiday was practicable, that a reduction of hours to forty was not feasible, but that some reduction 'would be beneficial to the productive capacity of the individual worker'.

Negotiations were then renewed, but soon reached another deadlock. Having received a strong vote for direct action the unions could hardly accept the employers' original offer. A stoppage seemed imminent. Then the Ministry of Labour intervened dramatically. Representatives of unions and employers were summoned urgently to the Ministry. There officials told them that the Cabinet was considering taking drastic action, such as issuing Defence Regulations compelling employers to work on electoral registers and lists of voters, and compelling workers to work overtime if required. The emergency arose from the need to complete the papers for the municipal elections due in November.

This changed the course of the dispute. After receiving a conciliatory letter from the F.M.P., the P. & K.T.F. recommended its affiliated

---

[1] 'Message from President', *Members' Circular*, 1946, p. 137.
[2] *v.* I. G. Sharp, *Industrial Conciliation and Arbitration in Great Britain.* p. 360.
[3] 1946, Cmd. 6912, H.M.S.O.

THE SECOND WORLD WAR   303

unions to withdraw the ban on overtime. At the next conference the employers produced a trump card. While not making any further concessions on hours or holidays they offered to waive the stabilization clause of the Wage Agreement, and give wage increases of 10s for men, 7s 6d for women and proportionate amounts for apprentices. Their spokesman emphasized that the employers did not want to flood the labour market:

'I will give you this assurance right away—we as employers have no wish whatever to see a return to the days when the Unions invariably had a pool of unemployed on their books in many areas.'[1]

The new terms were accepted by 3:1 majority of the union members. Standard hours were reduced to forty-three and a half but both parties 'accepted the principle' of the forty-two and a half hour week, and would work towards achieving it when the problem of recruitment to the industry had been dealt with. The annual paid holiday was increased from one to two weeks.

To many printing workers it seemed as if the new post-war world was indeed one fit for heroes. A reduction in hours, doubling of paid holidays, and increase in wages—all at once! More important to many was the general assumption that full employment would extend into the future for an indefinite time. Older men remembered the bright hopes after the First World War—and the subsequent long depression. But to the young, who had never known unemployment, this was ancient history. The power of the workers, expressed politically through the ballot, and industrially through their unions, would prove irresistible.

The employers took comfort in the reflection that union pressure had been successfully resisted, and 'the principle of free negotiation, unhampered by action of an aggressive or coercive nature', had been maintained.[2]

As an outcome of the settlement the Employment and Production Committee of the J.I.C. set up three sub-committees to study the reduction of the term of apprenticeship, the introduction of shift-systems, and the use of incentive payments. These three topics provided material for much debate and bargaining over the following years.[3]

SUMMARY

Between 1939 and 1946 the affiliated membership of unions in the P. & K.T.F. remained almost constant. It was 217,000 in 1939, dropped

[1] 'Hours, Holidays and Wages', *Members' Circular*, 1946, p. 185.
[2] F.M.P., *Annual Report*, 1947.
[3] P. & K.T.F., *Annual Report*, 1947, pp. 14–15, 1948, p. 10.

304   PERIOD OF COMPROMISE

slightly during the War, and was 219,000 at the end of 1946. Even more striking was the stability of membership of each individual union. Nor were there any marked changes in other institutions—the Federations of employers and unions, and the J.I.C. came through the War virtually unchanged.

In general the increase in wage rates for craftsmen was approximately the same as the increase in the official Cost-of-Living Index, that is, about one-third. Because of the flat-rate general increases, lower paid non-craft men, and workers in low grade towns received slightly higher percentage increases.

Wage rates, however, are not a good index of 'real wages', as they take no account of overtime, short-time, or of extras such as House Rates and Merit Money. As there are no published figures on printers' earnings for this period it is impossible to estimate changes in 'real earnings'. The flat-rate nature of the increases resulted in a slight closing of the percentage differential between craft and non-craft rates for men, but as women received smaller increases, the sex differential remained almost constant.

The bulk of National Agreements survived the War with their main terms substantially unchanged. The P. & K.T.F. experienced some difficulty in Scotland, where the S.T.A. had established its own tradition of negotiating with the Scottish Alliance, and was extremely loath to cede its autonomy to the P. & K.T.F. The other unions with Scottish members, Natsopa and the Paperworkers were, on the other hand, content to let the P. & K.T.F. negotiate with the F.M.P. on the understanding that any agreement covered the Scottish Alliance as well as the others. After some display of nationalist intransigence by the S.T.A. the P. & K.T.F. set up a special Scottish Advisory Committee to help deal with conditions north of the border.[1]

The 1943 Administrative Council of the P. & K.T.F. discussed a number of problems relating to post-war policy, including inter-union relations, the function of the Federation, recruitment, organization, the powers of the J.I.C. The Executive then co-opted a number of prominent union officers and set up a number of Committees to deal with various aspects of Post-War Reconstruction. The reports of the committees were debated at the 1944 Administrative Council.

There was a wide variety of opinion on almost every topic. The one which excited most unfavourable comment was a proposal to strengthen the J.I.C. to give it powers to enforce 'fair prices', by Trade Unions agreeing to withdraw members from price-cutting firms. This scheme was narrowly rejected by a conference of union executives in the following year.

[1] P. & K.T.F., *Annual Report*, 1942, p. 10.

THE SECOND WORLD WAR 305

During 1914–20 adjustment to conditions of inflation and labour shortage resulted in fundamental changes in the system of industrial relations. The growth of union membership was spectacular and the balance of power shifted away from the craft unions; local agreements were replaced by National Agreements; both Federations of employers and unions emerged much more powerful; the J.I.C. was established in high hopes of 'trade betterment'; the wages pattern changed substantially.

The most surprising feature of the Second World War is, in contrast, the complete absence of change of any importance in either the institutions or the system of rules and rewards.

The period 1914–20 stands out as a watershed between the turbulent and changeful period which preceded it, and the rather stable and uneventful period which followed. The Second World War, however, belongs to this latter phase.

PART SIX

THE NEW WORLD—
FULL EMPLOYMENT

CHAPTER XIX

THE SEARCH FOR A
WAGES STRUCTURE
1947–51

WAGE NEGOTIATIONS, 1947

In the course of the wage reductions during the 1922 depression, many weaker unions had to submit to greater cuts than the stronger unions. The Stereotypers' Society and L.S.C. were able to hold out for a small cut, when the T.A., Natsopa and Paperworkers had to take a larger one. The result was a change in the pattern of wage rates established under the 1919 set of National Agreements. One of the 'principles' of these was 'craft parity', the notion that all craftsmen—lithographers, bookbinders, compositors and machinemen—should have the same basic rate in the same town. The result of the enforced wage reductions was to scrap this principle; in the provinces the stereotypers received more than the other craftsmen; in London some of the bookbinders received less than the compositors. Furthermore the London craft unions held out for smaller reductions than the national unions. This led to a widening of the gap between London and the Grade 1 compositors' rates, from 2s 6d to 11s 6d. A Manchester compositor was reluctant to admit he was worth so much less than a London man; and all other provincial craftsmen were offended that their craft rate was below the stereotypers'.

In 1947, when the T.A. received a circular letter from the P. & K.T.F. asking for its views on methods of wage payment, the union expressed the view that this twenty-five year old 'injustice did much to retard full-out productive efforts by T.A. members'.[1] The T.A. added 'the quickest and surest method of ensuring increased production in the industry is the removal of this resentment, rather than considering schemes which leave basic injustices untouched'. At a later conference with the employers the T.A. secretary stressed the importance of the issue:

'For twenty-five years we have suffered under this unfair and unjust

[1] Letter from T.A. Sec. Reprinted, *Members' Circular*, 1947, p. 149.

310   THE NEW WORLD—FULL EMPLOYMENT

discrimination. It has been a running sore in the industry as far as my members are concerned; a constant source of bitter recrimination at branch and group meetings, and an injustice that successive Executive Councils throughout those twenty-five years have promised our membership would be rectified when opportunity offered. . . . We make the claim that the service, the skill, and the general ability required by T.A. members is second to no other class of craftsman in our industry; and we shall accept second place, so far as our financial status is concerned, to no other section.'[1]

While union members of the J.I.C. were judiciously considering the alleged advantages of shift-work, the P. & K.T.F. took steps to ensure that if double day-shifts were introduced the productivity gains should be shared with the workers. In May 1947 the P. & K.T.F. put in its claim—a $37\frac{1}{2}$ hour week for shift workers, worked on five days, with payment of one-third above ordinary rates. It disclaimed any intention of negotiating actual rates, which was the prerogative of the unions, but wished to establish general principles which could then be applied to the separate National Agreements.[2]

At approximately the same time the three provincial unions with women members—T.A., Natsopa and Paperworkers—put in claims for increased rates for women workers. The recent Court of Inquiry had stressed the unsatisfactory state of female recruitment. To the unions the solution was obvious—raise their wages. In 1947 the P. & K.T.F. resolved to try to bring the adult women's rate up to 75 per cent of the men's.[3]

At the first conference on this claim, on June 16, 1947, the unions referred to the heavy drift of young women away from printing into more highly paid jobs, and pointed out that under the Trade Board agreements in the Paper Box Trade, women's rates were 75 per cent of men's. The employers, very reasonably, replied that both men and women in the paper box trade received much lower rates than those in printing, and the unions would not want their members to work under conditions obtaining in the paper box trade.

At this point there were three separate sets of negotiations in progress, namely:

[1] 'Application by T.A., Statement by Mr Riding', *Members' Circular*, 1947, p. 149. Musson, however, regarded these statements as extravagant. See, *The Typographical Association*, p. 435.

[2] P. & K.T.F., *Annual Report*, 1947, pp. 14–15. *Members' Circular*, 1947, pp. 151–2.

[3] P. & K.T.F., *Annual Report*, 1946, pp. 66–68. *Members' Circular*, 1947, p. 151.

SEARCH FOR A WAGES STRUCTURE

1. the T.A.'s nine shilling 'status differential',
2. the P. & K.T.F. conditions for shift-work,
3. the rates for women.

To the F.M.P. Labour Committee this was quite enough. But in the next month the position became chaotic as one union after another jumped on the bandwaggon and submitted wage claims.

The T.A. might declare that it was not prepared to accept less than London. But London men were equally strongly convinced that they *needed* more than provincial workers, to compensate for the increased cost of living, not to mention the fact, well known to London unions, that London craft standards were the highest in the country. And if it was 'just' for the T.A. craftsmen to draw level with the Stereotypers, was it not equally 'just' for the S.T.A., Paperworkers and Natsopa craftsmen to keep level with the T.A.?

By the end of October 1947, thirteen unco-ordinated union claims had been presented to the employers. Some were addressed to the F.M.P., some to the Newspaper Society, some to both, and others to the London M.P.A. or the Scottish Alliance! The granting of even a fraction of any one claim would have altered the craft, regional or sex differentials and precipitated an avalanche of discontent.

The employers took some consolation in the fact that the unions were divided, and their claims inconsistent and contradictory. On the other hand, the tactic of playing off one against the other was fraught with danger, even if the sheer volume of negotiations could have been dealt with. Here was the employers' dilemma.

In the end, after separate meetings of the Councils of the F.M.P. and the Newspaper Society, they agreed on a joint statement which they sent to the claimant unions and the P. & K.T.F.:

'It would be against the best interests of the industry, and against the national interest, to endeavour to deal separately with a long list of varying claims from individual unions, involving lengthy negotiations and the possibility of sectional disputes which might disrupt the industry and interfere with the primary target which has been put before every industry by the Government—namely to increase production without increase in costs.'[1]

On balance, then, the employers had decided that drawing the unions together again, in negotiations conducted by the P. & K.T.F., was the better tactic. They invited the P. & K.T.F. 'representing all the printing

[1] 'Statement of B.F.M.P. and Newspaper Society', *Members' Circular*, 1947, p. 213.

THE NEW WORLD—FULL EMPLOYMENT

trades concerned' to meet them without delay to discuss the whole situation. But would the unions, enjoying the novelty of bargaining from positions of strength, and firm in their adherence to the principle of autonomy in wage negotiations, be prepared to sink some of their differences and make a common front?

At this time the economy was in the midst of one of its frequent post-war balance of payments crises. In September 1947 the Government issued the Control of Engagement Order, in an attempt to influence the flow of labour into essential industries, without actual compulsory direction. But if voluntary persuasion was not effective the Minister had limited powers to direct labour. Printing and Bookbinding was placed in Schedule A—'very important industries and services in which the undertakings are generally undermanned'. To make matters worse there was a probability that another winter fuel shortage would lead to power failures and stoppages. To help with the problem of shedding the peak load on the Electricity Grid, the P. & K.T.F. and employers had, in the previous autumn, negotiated an agreement for staggering work hours over the winter months.[1]

It provided for the introduction of Saturday work, extension of night-shifts, payment of extra fares, and general relaxation of the limitations of the Hours and Holidays Agreements. Payment for time lost during stoppages was governed by principles laid down during the fuel crisis of 1946.[2]

Early in November 1947 the P. & K.T.F. agreed to an 'exploratory' conference, to hear the employers' views, entirely without prejudice to any of the P. & K.T.F. or union claims. The employers' spokesman stressed the difficulty and delay inevitable if the claims were pressed separately, and threw back to the unions the responsibility for resolving their differences. He emphasized the important part that printing played in promoting exports and helping the economy to survive the crisis. Finally he said categorically:

'that the procedure of separate negotiations on the major question of wages in an industry such as ours is archaic and outmoded.'[3]

The employers' first offer was:

1. to bring the craft rate in the provinces up to parity with the stereo-typers, by increase of 9s;

---

[1] 'Agreement for Staggering of Hours', *M.P.A.*, 1949, p. 294.
[2] *Ibid.*, 1948, p. 304. 'Stoppages in Production ... Arrangements to Cover Emergencies', *M.P.A.*, 1949, p. 297.
[3] 'Wages Applications', *Members' Circular*, 1947, p. 243.

SEARCH FOR A WAGES STRUCTURE

2. to add 9s to London craft rates, thus maintaining the London differential.

Later, after further meetings of the unions, the P. & K.T.F. reported that they could not agree to joint negotiations, but would proceed with their claims individually. From this point onward the story becomes very complicated.

Briefly the T.A. agreed to accept the offer of 9s, coupled with a shortened apprenticeship period and a 'productivity' clause.[1] The S.T.A. and L.S.C. imposed overtime bans and were gently reprimanded by J.I.C. conciliation Committees.

The L.S.C. dispute was then referred to the National Arbitration Tribunal.

The N.A.T. paid particular regard to the fact that in recent years the traditional differential between the rates paid to Compositors in London and the Provinces respectively, *as expressed in terms of a percentage* had progressively declined.[2]

The Tribunal therefore awarded an increase of 15s on the minimum London craft rate, with absorption of half of any existing merit money. By its explicit reference to percentage differentials the Trinbunal had revealed another skeleton in the union cupboard. It was difficult enough to agree about 'correct' differentials expressed in absolute terms. What if they were to be calculated in percentages?

WAGE NEGOTIATIONS, 1948–51

Early in 1948 the A.S.L.P. became deadlocked in dispute with the employers, and the case went before the Conciliation Committee and several special meetings of the J.I.C. At one of these meetings Colonel Lockwood (F.M.P.) put the alternatives to the unions:

'Lengthy negotiations with separate unions, ending possibly in N.A.T. awards which would probably be unsatisfactory, or else a wages structure arrived at by negotiations with all the unions together.'[3]

---

[1] 'T.A. National Agreement, Revision', *Members' Circular*, 1948, p. 37. All craft unions had, in 1947, accepted a J.I.C. recommendation that, following upon the raising of the school leaving age, apprenticeships should be reduced to 6 years. Later the unions agreed also that National Service could be deducted from apprenticeship, so long as a minimum of 5 years' craft training was completed.   [2] N.A.T. Award, January 14, 1948. (Author's italics.)

[3] 'Statement by Colonel Lockwood . . .' *Members' Circular*, 1948, p. 3.

314 THE NEW WORLD—FULL EMPLOYMENT

The long negotiations of the next three years were, in effect, an attempt to achieve the second objective by the first alternative. It was to prove a Herculean task.

Armed with the terms of the new T.A. agreement, and the N.A.T. London award, the employers drew up a new offer to the unions. This was a straightforward wage increase, without any reference to apprenticeship conditions or productivity. In February 1948, while negotiations were in progress, the Government issued a White Paper with a 'Statement on Personal Incomes, Costs and Prices', urging, in the strongest terms, a policy of wage restraint.

'In present conditions, and until more goods and services are available for the home market, there is no justification for any general increase of individual money incomes.'[1]

The Council of the F.M.P. endorsed the policy of the Federation of British Industries which advocated voluntary action by employers in support of the Government's policy. It also urged members to maintain prices and stabilize dividends at last year's level.

Should the unions press for wage increases against the advice of the Labour Government? They were in a dilemma. On the one hand the market situation was in their favour; on the other the success of the Government's policy depended upon their restraint. They could not make much use of the cost-of-living loophole clause, for the Index of Retail Prices moved only from 100 (June 1946) to 106 (February 1948) a rise of about the same order as the increase already offered by the employers.

In this situation what constituted responsible union policy? To press for wage increase approved by their members, or to disappoint their members and support the government.[2]

In March 1948, a number of unions took the simplest course, and accepted the employers' offer. The A.S.L.P. stood out, and went to the National Arbitration Tribunal, which made an Award in line with the other settlements—15s in London and 9s in the provinces.[3]

So far, so good. But in March 1948 the F.M.P. made an agreement with the Stereotypers' Society, increasing their rates by 8s 6d in Grade 1,

---

[1] Cmd. 7321, 1948, H.M.S.O.

[2] Musson, sharply critical of the unions' attitude, wrote that it revealed irresponsibility, and a 'nineteenth century mentality'. *Op. cit.*, p. 434. However for an analysis of the meaning of 'responsible wage policy', see A. Ross, *Trade Union Wages Policy*, ch. IV

[3] N.A.T. Award, March 10, 1948. 'Settlement on Wages, Terms of Four Agreements . . .', *Members' Circular*, 1948, p. 52.

SEARCH FOR A WAGES STRUCTURE

and by lesser amounts in the other grades. For two months the T.A. had enjoyed 'craft parity', by this agreement it had slipped away again.[1]

The T.A. lost no time in putting in another claim to raise its craft rates to parity with the men in the foundry. Other unions followed suit, and by July 1948 a 'second round' of claims had been submitted. The employers continued to advocate a policy of an agreed wages structure. But as long as the unions were making headway by the piecemeal approach they could hardly be expected to forswear it.

Vigorously pursuing its 'parity movement' the T.A. repudiated the clauses of the 1948 agreement which dealt with apprentices and incentive schemes. The dispute went before the Conciliation Committee of the J.I.C. which 'noted with regret' that the T.A. had taken unilateral action, and recommended the convening of a Special Meeting of the J.I.C. The debate on negotiating procedure throws a great deal of light on current procedures, and the internal political difficulties of the unions.[2]

While there was general agreement that the present situation was unsatisfactory, nobody seemed able to suggest a practicable alternative. The employers suggested a series of informal joint discussions, in which both sides could express their views freely without feeling committed. It was agreed that the full J.I.C. was much too large and unwieldy a body to enter into debate on the case for a Wages Structure. Each side blamed the other for sabotaging the approach to a wage structure in the previous year.

The union members argued that the main issue should be referred back to the constituents for further consideration. Though the employers thought that this was a further waste of time, the procedure was eventually adopted.

In December 1948 the F.M.P. wrote to the P. & K.T.F. emphasizing:

1. The employers' wish for an assurance that if a wage structure were negotiated, the unions would agree to abide by it for a number of years to enable it to become 'established'.

2. The urgent need to improve productivity in the industry, and for union co-operation in devising and applying incentive schemes.[3]

The unions, however, were unable to agree on basic principles, and the

[1] 'Foundry Agreement with N.S.E.S.', *Members' Circular*, 1948, p. 55.
[2] J.I.C. Minutes of Quarterly Meeting, October 13, 1948.
[3] 'Wages Structure, the Employers' Position Outlined', *Members' Circular*, 1949, p. 3.

316   THE NEW WORLD—FULL EMPLOYMENT

P. & K.T.F. informed the employers that it was unable to proceed with negotiations.[1]

Four of the provincial unions sank their differences and agreed to make a united approach. They demanded craft parity with the stereotypers and non-craft rates fixed at percentages of craft rates. This put the Wages Structure Negotiating Committee of the employers in a dilemma. Was half a wages structure better than none at all?

Eventually the employers decided that it would be unwise to make final agreements with a group of unions without an assurance that the others would accept the increase without another round of 'leap-frogging' claims. In the provinces an essential first step was to stabilize the stereotypers' rate. When this was achieved the F.M.P. approached the four unions to negotiate a 'draft' agreement on the understanding that it would have to be accepted by the 'non-group' unions before being ratified.

The T.A. was attracted by the offer, but objected strongly to the conditions. It balloted its members on proposals to annul the National Agreement, and revert to bargaining at the local and chapel level! As the T.A. withdrew its wages claim, it had, technically, no dispute with the F.M.P., and could not be brought before the N.A.T. Moreover the T.A. executive realized that under existing conditions of labour shortage local demands were, up to a point, irresistible. They had to act cautiously, pressing the claims in such a way that they did not create a dispute which could be taken to the N.A.T., for the latter was bound to be strongly influenced by the Government's policy of wage restraint. Nor did the T.A. want to become involved in a national strike on the scale of the disastrous 1922 one.

The T.A.'s strategy, therefore, was to 'withdraw co-operation and goodwill', by resigning from the J.I.C. and encouraging Chapels and Branches to take all action short of a strike. In Musson's words:

'What was proposed, in fact, was a return to pre-1919 conditions of guerilla warfare by branches and chapels.'[2]

At this stage four separate wage issues were keeping the unions divided:

1. Other crafts' parity with the stereotypers.
2. The London differential.
3. The provincial grading system.
4. The craft/non-craft differential.

[1] For the difficulties of agreeing on wage movements, and on voting within the P. & K.T.F., see the *Annual Report*, 1948, pp. 6-9.

[2] Musson, *op. cit.*, p. 448.

SEARCH FOR A WAGES STRUCTURE

At an informal meeting on August 29, 1949 the employers suggested the formation of a wages structure in two stages: first, settlement of craft rates, and later the non-craft rates. Again, however, the unions would not negotiate together.[1] The employers then reported an 'apprehended' dispute to the Minister of Labour, giving a history of post-war negotiations and concluding:

'As you will see from this report . . . the conciliation machinery of the industry itself has been exhausted, and there is a real danger of aggressive action at the local level which would lead inevitably to general dislocation of the industry and a hold-up in work of national importance.'[2]

Meanwhile the T.A. membership had voted strongly for a return of direct action at local level. On December 15, 1949 the T.A. gave notice of termination of the National Agreement and the War Agreements, and instructed Branches and Chapels to make local applications, using the threat of any sanctions short of a strike.

The employers applied for an injunction to restrain the T.A. from terminating the Agreements, but the application failed. Technically there was no national dispute, but each local application, with threat of coercion, did constitute a dispute, and the employers reported more than one hundred of these to the Minister of Labour. Each one of these could have been referred to the N.A.T. As the editor of the *Members' Circular* drily observed,

'The prospect of the N.A.T. sitting night and day on printing cases for an interminable period must have been one which no Ministry of Labour official could view with equanimity.'[3]

This 'brinkmanship' policy had brought industrial relations to the verge of chaos. The F.M.P. sent numerous circulars to its members advising them how to proceed when presented with local demands, published a letter in *The Times* informing customers of the situation, and opened a Defence Fund to help individuals under attack.[4]

The T.A.'s notice expired on September 26, 1949, but the annulment of the Agreement did not entail annulment of individual contracts of employment. Nevertheless in the next few days the Ministry of Labour made desperate efforts to achieve a renewal of negotiations at the national level. The T.A. executive reversed its attitude and sent telegrams to all branches instructing them to cease all aggressive action. A few days later the union and employers made a new national agreement.

[1] *Members' Circular*, 1949, p. 249.　　[2] *Ibid.*, p. 251.　　[3] *Ibid.*, p. 268.
[4] *Ibid.*, p. 269.

318   THE NEW WORLD—FULL EMPLOYMENT

The new wage rates are shown in the table:

	Grade			
	1	2	3	4
T.A. 1948 Agreement	122s 6d	121s	118s	115s
T.A. New Agreement (1949)	131s	125s 6d	123s 6d	122s
Stereotypers	131s	129s	125s 6d	122s

Thus T.A. members in Grades 1 and 4 were level with the stereo-typers, but those in Grades 2 and 3 were still below. Was this to be regarded as craft parity or not?

The employers achieved their long-standing objective of an agreement on productivity:

'Employers and members of the T.A. shall be encouraged by the parties to this Agreement to co-operate in taking all practicable steps which make for greater productive efficiency.

'It is agreed that systems of payment by results, including both individual and group bonus methods may be introduced, and that members of the T.A. shall co-operate in experiments to establish the suitability of such schemes in the industry.'[1]

A joint committee was established to consider principles and practical working of incentive schemes.

As part of the settlement the T.A. 'accepted' that the working of reasonable overtime was necessary to meet urgent production require-ments. It also agreed to a 'bonus' intake of 200 apprentices, and to renew the wartime dilution agreement. In fact the T.A. officials pre-ferred dilutees to extra apprentices, for in the event of unemployment the dilutees had to be dismissed first, and thus cushioned the impact on the craftsmen.[2] Nevertheless, there was great opposition, from branches and chapels, to the introduction of dilutees in peace-time. The T.A. Executive had to write a stiff note to its branches explaining the need for their co-operation:

'As we insist that members of the Employers' organizations must observe the wage rates, &c., set out in that Agreement, we cannot justify the refusal of our members to implement any portion of the Agreement which may not be quite so palatable as the wage rates.'[3]

[1] Agreement, T.A. (Letterpress), *Master Printers Annual*, 1950, p. 321.
[2] See Musson, *op. cit.*, pp. 428–9.
[3] Reprinted *Members' Circular*, 1950, p. 68.

SEARCH FOR A WAGES STRUCTURE

The T.A. secretary asked, in return, that F.M.P. members should be requested to act as tactfully as possible and avoid arousing the traditional shop-floor antipathy to dilutees.

New rules of procedure were devised to guide the parties in future alteration of the agreement. The most important clause laid down the principle that the rate of wages paid to any other Union should not form the basis of a claim for a wage adjustment. Finally, either party could terminate the agreement by giving six months' notice.

The agreement was accepted by a 2:1 majority of the T.A. members. Most opposition came from operators and machinemen who had to take a cut in their extras to 'absorb' some of the increase in basic rates. Others who gained little were those in low-paid towns which had not been up-graded. An increase of a few shillings a week, in exchange for important concessions, seemed a rather poor bargain after the grand ambitions and militant talk of a few months earlier. The cost-of-living had risen three points during the year, cancelling up to half of the value of the increase.

In the following month the employers quickly came to agreement with the other main provincial unions, Natsopa and the Paperworkers. Craft rates were raised to parity with the stereotypers, and general provisions and procedural rules were the same as in the T.A. agreement. Non-craft rates remained close to their old percentage of the craft rate:

	Grade			
Class IV	1	2	3	4
1949 wage at 21 years	103s 6d	100s 6d	99s 6d	98s 6d
Percentage of craft rate	79	80	81	81
1948 wage at 21 years	99s	98s	96s	94s
Percentage of craft rate	81	81	81	82

These two unions also signed an agreement on women's rates:

	Grade			
	1	2	3	4
Women's Rate	70s	68s	67s 6d	67s
Percentage of Men's craft rates	53	54	55	55

These fell a long way short of the 75 per cent which had been aimed at.

By the end of 1949, then, the employers had achieved half of a wage structure. The lithographic section in the provinces, and the London craft unions, remained to be dealt with. Would the terms of settlement with these unions disturb the delicate equilibrium in the provinces?[1]

---

[1] For a post-mortem on the breakdown of the P. & K.T.F. movement for an industry wages structure, see P. & K.T.F., *Annual Report*, 1949, pp. 42–6.

THE LONDON DISPUTE, 1950

In November 1949 the L.S.C. informed the London Master Printers' Association that the T.A. settlement had disturbed its differential in relation to the T.A. rate. It broke new ground, however, by having its claim calculated on a percentage, not an absolute amount.

Whether differentials are best maintained as percentages, or as constant amounts of money, or constant amounts of purchasing power, is a difficult problem. One thing, however, is certain; the calculation of percentages can lead to great complications. Indeed it is probable that the enormity of the complications posed by the introduction of this 'principle' had hitherto inhibited the craft unions (who stood to gain most from its application) from invoking it.

The L.S.C., however, claimed that the 9s 9d was necessary to maintain the percentage differential 'established' by the N.A.T. Award in 1948. In fact, however, the terms of the Award were not clear on this point. The tribunal had merely noted that the traditional London differential, expressed in terms of a percentage, had declined over the years. In awarding a 15s increase, however, it did not state explicitly that this was aimed at creating a correct percentage differential which should thereafter be maintained.[1]

Negotiations with the L.S.C. during April and May ended in deadlock. The Society would make no concessions on increases of apprentices or dilutees. On May 4, 1950 the Society withdrew its claims, gave fourteen days notice of a ban on overtime and withdrawal of co-operation from members of the London M.P.A.

The F.M.P. reported the dispute to the Minister of Labour, who referred it to the National Arbitration Tribunal.

To add injury to insult the Society announced that it would extend fullest co-operation to printing firms which were *not* members of the London M.P.A. and granted the demands. As an additional irritant the L.S.C. held a delegate meeting of one in every six members *during working hours* on May 25th, and proposed to hold a meeting of one in three after the Award was announced. Although the F.M.P. protested against these 'wilful interferences with production', the Ministry of Labour said that no official action could be taken.

The F.M.P. obtained an assurance from provincial members that, in the event of a stoppage in London, they would not undertake London work, nor engage the displaced labour. The Federation Defence Fund was made available to London members.

The case was heard by the N.A.T. on June 12, 1950 and the Award

[1] N.A.T. Award, June 20, 1950, *Members' Circular*, 1950, pp. 115–16.

SEARCH FOR A WAGES STRUCTURE

was published eight days later.[1] It granted an increase of 3s 6d on the minimum London craft rate, to come into operation when the ban on overtime was lifted. The L.S.C. interpreted this as an invitation to maintain the overtime ban, and in addition it encouraged members to apply other 'restrictive' sanctions.

In July, however, a large week-day delegate meeting authorized the L.S.C. Executive to cancel the ban after informal conversations with the employers, and 'before, during or after' formal negotiations. The F.M.P. remained adamant:

'There will be no negotiations whilst aggressive action in any form is continuing. . . . Industrial relations are poisoned by attempts to force issues on which there are differences of opinion. Negotiations under duress are not negotiations at all. . . .'[2]

Nevertheless, the editor of the *Members' Circular* made an heroic effort to be objective:

'It is no use trying to lay blame for this state of affairs on individuals, or unions, or employers' organizations. What is needed is recognition by all that in self-interest the industry must find a basis of respect and understanding between its representative organizations, so that between them they can work to meet present demands and plan for the future, instead of dissipating their energies, their goodwill and their chance of progress, in a series of internecine disputes.'[3]

In August 1950 the L.S.C. instructed its members to introduce additional restrictive practices into London M.P.A. houses.[4] A special meeting of employers decided that this was intolerable, and that if employees would not carry out normal duties in the customary way they should be given summary dismissal. At noon, on August 30, 1950 the London houses dismissed 3,700 employees who refused to give such assurances.

This stoppage lasted for two weeks. During this time the authorities made feverish efforts to find an escape from the impasse. When conciliation proved unavailing the Minister of Labour set up a Court of Inquiry. In September the officers of the P. & K.T.F. succeeded in

---

[1] N.A.T. Award, June 20, 1950.
[2] *Members' Circular*, 1950, p. 175.   [3] *Ibid.*
[4] A humorous paper-maker inserted an advertising leaflet in the *Members' Circular*, quoting from *The Taming of the Shrew*:

Look how thy servants do attend on thee,
Each in his office, ready at thy beck!

L

322 THE NEW WORLD—FULL EMPLOYMENT

finding a formula which led to a resumption of work under normal conditions, and renewal of negotiations.

The negotiations, however, were abortive, and on September 20th the L.S.C. reimposed the restrictive rules, and the Court of Inquiry, which had been suspended during the negotiations, resumed its hearings. The L.S.C. agreed to attend, but not to co-operate.

A mass meeting of London M.P.A. members agreed to summary dismissal of all employees enforcing restrictive rules. Some 4,000 employees were served with notices. The L.S.C. then withdrew its other members from M.P.A. houses.

The *Report of the Court of Inquiry*, issued on October 21, 1950, was highly critical of the L.S.C., evidently 'determined to exploit its key position without regard to the interests of other sections of the industry'.[1]

It gave its support to the principle of a national wage structure, and suggested that the London settlement should include stabilization clauses, cost-of-living adjustments, and provision for substantial recruitment to the industry. A substantial concession was made to the union claim on wage rates, and an increase to £7 15s minimum, with consolidation of some House Rates or merit money, was suggested.[2]

These suggestions were accepted by both sides. Work was resumed, and in November 1950 a new agreement was signed. Wages and general conditions were stabilized for five years, with a cost-of-living adjustment of 1s per point change in the official Index.

A novel departure was an annual review of the apprentice quota, and its adjustment in relation to the level of unemployment of L.S.C. members.

	Number of Journeymen when unemployment is			
	Up to 2%	2–3%	3–4%	4%
First Apprentice	1–5	1–7	1–9	Special
Second Apprentice	6–8	8–11	10–14	Methods to
Third and additional	Every 3	Every 4	Every 5	be
apprentices	up to 39	up to 40	up to 40	considered
	Every 7	Every 8	Every 10	
	above 39	above 40	above 40	

If the unemployment level reached 4 per cent special action, such as retirement of men over 65, or reduction of the working week, was to be considered. If unemployment reached 5 per cent the intake was to cease.[3]

---

[1] *Report of Court of Inquiry*, 1950, para. 59.   [2] *Ibid.*, paras. 73–79.
[3] Agreement, Letterpress (London). *Master Printers' Annual*, 1952, pp. 433–40.

SEARCH FOR A WAGES STRUCTURE

PROVINCIAL ADJUSTMENT

The raising of the London craft rate obviously would entail some adjustment of provincial rates. Taking the initiative the F.M.P. asked the P. & K.T.F. for a conference to bring conditions in the national agreements into line with the London settlement.

The unions asked that the vexed question of provincial grading should be settled, if necessary by arbitration, before negotiations began on the wage structure. The employers agreed, and devised a grading formula. Each town was given an index number calculated by adding to its population (*in thousands*) to the actual number of T.A. journeymen employed there.

	Population (000)	T.A. Journeymen Employed	Index
A	50,000	200	250
B	200,000	200	400
C	200,000	270	470

Once towns were graded, it would be simple to draw dividing lines to separate the grades. The scheme had two inestimable merits—it was simple and the basic data were unequivocal. As there was still disagreement as to where the lines should be drawn, how many grades there should be, and what differential should be fixed, these were referred to the N.A.T.

Its award,[1] issued on February 26, 1951, adopted the employers' formula, and established two provincial grades, with a dividing line above 450. In the above example, then, towns A and B are in Grade 2 and C is in Grade 1. The wage differential was fixed at 5s 6d.

Although the formula used only T.A. membership, the same grading applied to Natsopa and Paperworkers members. It did not, however, apply to the Lithographic unions, whose terms had not been settled.

With the regrading hurdle removed, negotiations began on basic rates, stabilization clauses, manpower and productivity. Provincial craft rates were raised by 12s 6d, with absorption of merit money at the employers' discretion. Rates for non-craft men, and adult women rose by 10s and 8s respectively. Basic rates were stabilized for five years. A cost-of-living sliding scale of 1s per point for men, and 9d for women, was to operate.

All unions agreed to allow substantial 'block entry' of apprentices and to renew wartime dilution agreements in case of persistent labour shortage.

[1] N.A.T. Award No. 1621, *Master Printers' Annual*, 1953, p. 334.

THE NEW WORLD—FULL EMPLOYMENT

A few awkward points were settled by reference to the N.A.T. One of these was the craft rate for London bookbinders in publishing houses, which had dropped below the L.S.C. rate in 1922, and had been a sore point in the London Bookbinders' Branch for thirty years.[1] The Tribunal awarded the bookbinders 'craft parity' with the L.S.C.[2]

Later in the year the Tribunal made an Award, along the same general lines as the others, to settle the Lithographic Printers' dispute.[3]

CONCLUSION

By this long and tortuous path, then, the industry arrived at a settlement of basic rates and conditions for the following five years. Did the overall settlement warrant the title of a 'wages structure'? It had certainly not been thrashed out and agreed upon by the unions, most of which were clinging stubbornly to their traditional autonomy in wage matters. But behind the 'constitutional' problems of how to settle differences of opinion, such as the method of voting, lay the deeper issues. What *was* the appropriate differential between the various classifications? What was the appropriate wage for a woman? To the Paperworkers' union this was a vital matter, affecting union policy, organization and future growth. To the L.S.C. it was not of immediate importance. The future growth of the Paperworkers, which already had almost half of the organized workers in the industry, *was* a matter of long-term concern to the others. Any method of proportional representation would soon lead to a swamping of the votes of the small craft unions. By joining in a united movement for a wage structure they might well jeopardize their future freedom of action, and be unable to achieve the best conditions for their members. On the other hand the constant inter-union wrangling on wages movements was time-consuming, harmful to inter-union relations, and contrary to the union tradition of 'solidarity' in the face of the employers.

This was no new problem to the unions; for at least fifty years they had been dealing with it empirically, and searching for a long-term solution. No wonder their leaders were wary of 'outside' intervention in their affairs; the proposals were usually unworkable or founded on ignorance. The 1950 Report of the *Court of Inquiry*, for example, suggested that the J.I.C. should establish two separate wage-negotiating committees—one for craftsmen and one for non-craftsmen. But the printers' leaders frequently claimed that the (admittedly limited)

---

[1] E. Howe and J. Child, *op. cit.*, pp. 276-8.
[2] N.A.T. Award No. 1675, May 30, 1951.
[3] Industrial Dispute Tribunal, Award, September 10, 1951.

SEARCH FOR A WAGES STRUCTURE

success of the J.I.C. was due to the fact that it had kept out of wage negotiations, and concentrated on areas where the common interests should have been stronger.

Furthermore it was not difficult for the craftsmen to settle craft rates, or for the others to settle non-craft rates. The nub of the problem was how to relate the one to the other. Would separate committees (including employers' representatives) be likely to succeed where conferences of union executives and the P. & K.T.F. had failed? This particular suggestion, had it been acted on, would have had only one result—the swift destruction of the J.I.C. Was this what the Court of Inquiry wanted?

The establishment of a wage structure in any industry is a difficult matter. When there are many strong craft unions, proud of their traditional autonomy, the problems are multiplied. However, people's judgement about what is 'right' and 'fair' is obviously conditioned by the position they occupy in the scale, and by their past experience. Given a new set of conditions, and a reasonable time to grow accustomed to them, their judgements will also change. What was at first rejected as an unjust innovation, will in time be accepted as part of the social order. It seemed a good idea, therefore, to have a five-year stabilization period which would give time for attitudes to be readjusted.

CHAPTER XX

BARGAINING ON
LABOUR SUPPLY

PRODUCTIVITY AND MANPOWER

In the wave of enthusiasm for social and industrial reform which swept the country at the end of the War, many trade unionists pressed the case for some scheme of worker participation in the management of industry. 'Workers' control' was generally regarded as impracticable, in the present framework of ownership and power, but 'joint consultation' seemed to provide a promising field for social experiment. Broadly speaking, three objectives could be achieved by this means: some greater measure of 'industrial democracy', improvements in welfare and physical conditions, and increased productivity. These were closely inter-related, and advocates of joint consultation differed in the priority of the objectives. Some regarded the idea primarily as an attempt to raise the workers' status in industry; others saw it as a tool of management in increasing efficiency. In 1946 the T.U.C. passed the following resolution and sent a circular to affiliated unions asking them to comment on its relevance to conditions in their industries:

'This Congress recognizes the importance of the part which Shop Stewards and Joint Production Committees played during the War and is convinced that this workshop machinery should be definitely established as a primary measure of post-war Reconstruction.

'It is convinced that it is essential for the General Council—after consultation with the unions concerned—to make recommendations for strengthening and expanding the functions of this machinery in harmony with the respective Unions so that it can adequately extend Trade Union organization, supervise agreements and act effectively on questions of welfare, safety and production.'

The P. & K.T.F. appointed a sub-Committee which reported in favour of the establishment of Works Committees and Joint Production Committees. There was, however, a general opposition to the idea of

BARGAINING ON LABOUR SUPPLY

using any compulsion in the establishment of such committees. The matter was then passed to the Employment and Production Committee of the J.I.C. Here the employers too expressed opposition to any form of compulsion. The trade unions insisted that where Works Committees were established, the union Chapel should act as the workers' unit for representation. With this recommendation the J.I.C. gave its blessing to the principle of Joint Consultation.[1] In fact very few firms took any action, and in the next few years the issue faded out of the limelight.

Productivity per se, however, came steadily to the forefront, as the British economy staggered from one crisis to another, with austerity, stricter rationing, wage freeze and eventually devaluation of the pound. Politicians, industrialists and leader writers continued to urge the need for greater productivity, and every 'responsible' high-level organization of employers and workers echoed the platitudes. But what was happening at the factory and shop level where people actually worked? The suspicion grew that perhaps methods of working were less efficient than in other countries. The Anglo-American Council on Productivity was formed to promote exchange of ideas on organizing production efficiently. In 1949–50 two teams of British printers—Letterpress and Lithographic—visited the United States to study production methods. Each team consisted of both workers and employers.

The teams' reports, published in 1951, formed the basis for a Productivity Conference convened by the J.I.C. in March 1952. The timing was rather unfortunate, as the economy was in a minor recession, and unemployment was rising. Trade Union leaders were worried how far the trend would continue. Older workers remembered the 1922 depression; many remained sceptical of the 'permanence' of full employment. Was this a time to increase productivity, and throw more workers out of their jobs? These views were frankly expressed by R. Willis (L.S.C.) who said that any opposition from the workers' side stemmed from fear of unemployment. The 'sack' had not lost its terror, and many workers felt that full employment was only temporary. He considered that a firm guarantee against unemployment was a primary precondition for changing basic attitudes to productivity.[2] Endorsing Willis's analysis, R. T. Williams (A.S.L.P.) pointed out that experience of insecurity for more than a century had made the unions reluctant to take any step which would endanger their present security. There were still employers of the old brigade who talked of using fear to discipline their employees.[3]

Referring to methods of dealing with unemployment A. J. Hubbard

[1] J.I.C. *Annual Report*, 1947–8. P. & K.T.F. *Annual Report*, 1948, pp. 15–16.
[2] J.I.C. *Report of the Printing Industry's Productivity Conference*, 1952, p. 8.
[3] *Ibid.*, p. 9.

328   THE NEW WORLD—FULL EMPLOYMENT

(Chairman of the employers' Joint Labour Committee) said that the unions had obtained clauses in recent agreements which made provisions for corrective action in the event of future unemployment. He said that consideration was being given to the establishment of a joint unemployment fund. It would be costly, and ways would have to be found of improving productivity to meet the cost.[1]

While general discussion of the Productivity Reports was in progress, a number of smaller groups studied the particular recommendations relating to practices in Composing, Foundry, Letterpress Machine, Lithography and Finishing. Most of the suggestions were of a technical nature and aroused no controversy.

The Letterpress Machine group raised the crucial question: how were the recommendations to be conveyed to individual employers and workers? Several speakers had stressed that ultimately the change had to be made at the workshop level, and that this would entail radical changes in attitudes of management and workers.

There was surprisingly little consideration of such institutional barriers to increased productivity as demarcation rules, prohibition of transfers, and machine manning ratios. R. W. Briginshaw (Natsopa) suggested that it was time the craft unions permitted new methods of entry into the skilled sections of industry. This in fact had been recommended by both the Letterpress and Lithographic teams.

Letterpress Printing

(b) The employment of dilutees should be encouraged, and it should be made possible for suitable dilutees to become craftsmen after serving an appropriate period of apprenticeship.

(c) Semi-skilled and unskilled workers should be allowed to assist craftsmen on skilled work, and should be eligible to become dilutees and possibly craftsmen, as recommended . . . above.[2]

Lithographic Printing

(a) The A.S.L.P. should open its ranks to selected semi-skilled adult assistants who should be permitted:

1. to give A.S.L.P. craftsmen a much greater amount of help in making ready and running offset printing machines than is permitted at present, and

2. to become responsible under the machine-minders' direction for loading and operating the feeder.

(b) After they have proved their suitability for up-grading, a number

[1] J.I.C., *Report of the Printing Industry's Productivity Conference*, 1952, p. 10.
[2] Anglo-American Productivity Council, *Letterpress Printing*, p. 56.

of these semi-skilled adult assistants should be eligible for training as machine-minders with eventually craft status.[1]

The A.S.L.P. officers at the conference stated that they accepted the recommendation, though it was contrary to present union practice, 'in the interests of productivity and social justice'. In lithographic printing the problem was simpler than in letterpress, because the lithographic assistants who were likely to be up-graded to craftsmen under this scheme, were already in the same union as the craftsmen.

In letterpress printing, however, the assistants were mainly in Natsopa, while the machine-minders were generally in one of the craft unions—S.T.A., T.A. or P.M.M.T.S. Up-grading of a Natsopa assistant could only be achieved if either:

(a) the craft unions admitted the right of Natsopa to enrol craftsmen, or

(b) Natsopa assistants, on being up-graded, left their old union and joined the appropriate craft union.

This problem had proved intractable for forty years, despite intermittent efforts to find a solution, and it had recently led to a bitter dispute between Natsopa and the S.T.A. which almost led to a shutdown of Scottish newspapers.

It was perhaps because they realized the complexity of such issues, and how deeply they were entangled in union history, that delegates refrained from discussing them in detail. But this is not the whole explanation. In an independent study of *Productivity and Trade Unions*, published in 1951, F. Zweig found that firms with enlightened management and good industrial relations did not complain about 'restrictive practices', in fact such management often sympathized with the unions' objectives. But this was the type of management which took an active part in the J.I.C. They were not the ones who needed converting to a more liberal approach. But how was the gospel to be brought to the heathen?

In its final session the Productivity Conference gave its approval to a general statement endorsing the conviction that 'increased productivity is essential to the well-being of our national life and our industry'. The conference recognized that among the specific difficulties to be overcome was the fear of trade unionists that increased productivity would mean less security. Unions were asked to give attention to the question of labour intake and promotion in order to settle their policy, so that the

---

[1] Anglo-American Productivity Council, *Lithographic Printing*, p. 19.

L*

330 THE NEW WORLD—FULL EMPLOYMENT

whole matter could be considered by the J.I.C. Finally the Conference made a plea for the more general adoption of Joint Consultation.[1]

After the conference the J.I.C. Employment and Production Committee prepared a number of booklets dealing with simple methods of improving workshop practice. These were widely distributed through the unions and to individual firms.

Productivity had been made respectable, at least at the top level of industry. In the 1951 Agreements the unions made considerable concessions on manpower, and both parties promised to encourage their members 'to co-operate in taking all practicable steps which make for greater productive efficiency'. How did this work out in practice? Before dealing with this question it is necessary to consider briefly the major developments in the industry in the five-year period of 'Stabilization', 1951–55.

'STABILIZATION', 1951–55

In the five years 1945–49 the printing unions' total expenditure on Dispute benefit averaged about £1,000 annually. In 1950 alone the expenditure under this head rose to £140,000 of which £127,000 was spent by the L.S.C.

In the 'Stabilization' period, 1951–55, the annual average was £35,000. In each year one or more of the unions was involved in a major dispute. Was this the sort of stability envisaged? The most important individual disputes, however, concerned a firm which was not a member of the B.F.M.P., and the London daily newspapers.

D. C. Thomson Dispute

The 1952 dispute, which promised at one stage to snowball into an industry stoppage, began when D. C. Thomson, a Scottish newspaper firm which had been non-union since 1926, discharged a Natsopa man who was acting as Father of the Chapel.[2]

D. C. Thomson was not merely a non-union firm; it was actively anti-union, and required applicants for jobs to sign a document promising not to join a trade union. Natsopa, however, had secretly enrolled seventy-five out of the one hundred employees in one office.

---

[1] In fact this was virtually the pronouncement of the last rites. Not that approval by the J.I.C. was *necessarily* the kiss of death, though it was beginning to seem so.

[2] For detailed history of this famous dispute, see C. J. Bundock, *op. cit.*, ch. 60. Also *Report of the Court of Inquiry*, July 7, 1952, H.M.S.O. Also James Moran, *op. cit.*, ch. 16.

BARGAINING ON LABOUR SUPPLY

331

When the Father of the Chapel was discharged the other Natsopa members came out on strike.

Nothing could have been better calculated to induce the printing unions to forego their interminable rivalries, and present a united front, than this attack on the fundamental principle of freedom to join a trade union. The P. & K.T.F. Council unanimously affirmed 'its determination to intensify the fight until the obstinate attitude of the firm is overcome and the infamous document denying the right of their workers to join Trade Unions is withdrawn'.[1]

The P. & K.T.F. decided to throw all of its fighting potential into the struggle against Thomson, including the use of the boycott against the firm's supplies and products. Members of the Paperworkers came out on strike rather than make or handle paper for Thomson.

The T.U.C. sent a delegation to interview the Prime Minister, pointing out that Thomson's 'document' was contrary to the International Labour Convention No. 98 of 1949, on the principle of the right to organize and to bargain collectively. Under pressure from the Government the board of D. C. Thomson's agreed to withdraw the document.

The firm would not, however, reinstate the men who had come out on strike, and in response to further boycott Thomson applied for injunctions restraining the union leaders from acting to cut off his supplies. Although these applications were refused in the lower courts, the firm appealed to the House of Lords. Thomson emerged the victor. Although the firm withdrew the document, they continued to require applicants for employment to fill in a questionnaire on which one of the questions was: 'Are you a member of a trade union?'

The P. & K.T.F. withdrew the ban on supplies to Thomson, but the T.U.C. distributed over one million pamphlets asking members to boycott Thomson publications. At the same time, however, printing unionists were handling and printing advertisements for D. C. Thomson's journals! To refuse to do so would have been 'interference with contents', and brought the unions into a direct conflict with the Newspaper Society.

In effect then, as one delegate expressed it, 'one man had beaten the Trade Union Movement of Great Britain'.[2]

In the early stages of the dispute, a visiting Indian printing union delegate had suggested a different approach. He told the P. & K.T.F. Administrative Council:

'My methods, I am afraid would be different from what you are going to do . . . I am anxious to meet him and appeal to the good in him.

[1] P. & K.T.F., *Annual Report*, 1951, p. 22.   [2] *Ibid.*, 1952, p. 35.

332 THE NEW WORLD—FULL EMPLOYMENT

Perhaps you will be successful by not handling his goods, but that may affect your workers and mean trouble and hardship. . . . In such cases, in India, we resort to Satyagraha, that is, to go on fast unto death, as a penance for the sin of Mr Thomson. I would not mind dying for this cause to solve this problem. The question of a fast is not one to be lightly undertaken, but I would gladly consider such a course, if I was convinced that it would help.'[1]

Mr Mitra's offer was not accepted at the time, and even later, when the boycott had failed, none of the British union leaders seemed to remember the suggestion.

T.A. & Machine Manning

Throughout 1952 and 1953 the T.A. and the F.M.P. had a number of disagreements over manning of new machines, and the rates payable. The issue came to a head in 1954, when the T.A. conducted a strike against a photogravure firm in Bristol. The T.A. ignored the conciliation procedure of the J.I.C. which required the restoration of normal working practice during the hearing. The employers argued that they could not negotiate with the P. & K.T.F. while an affiliated union was taking aggressive action, and suspended talks. The strike lasted fourteen weeks and affected the employment of hundreds of men from other unions. The J.I.C. conciliation machinery failed to find a basis for settlement, and for some months the union refused to submit to arbitration.

The employers referred the dispute to the Ministry of Labour and in April the Industrial Disputes Tribunal made an indeterminate award, which did not effect a settlement. The T.A. indeed boycotted the hearing. Eventually, about six months after the first notices had been handed in, the union agreed to the reference of the dispute to an arbitration panel of six members (three from each side of the J.I.C.) and an independent chairman. The Award,[2] published in July 1954, was a characteristic compromise—conceding some of the union claims and refusing others, the sort of award which would probably have resulted from independent arbitration *before the stoppage occurred*. What had the union gained by its 'militant' tactics ? It had antagonized other unions whose members had lost employment. It had also helped to destroy confidence in the capacity of the J.I.C. to act effectively in industrial disputes.

The Editor of the *Members' Circular* claimed that the difficulty of breaking a deadlock such as this indicated the need for a new approach,

---

[1] P. & K.T.F., *Annual Report*, 1951, p. 39.
[2] 'Photogravure Machine Award', *Members' Circular*, 1954, p. 206.

BARGAINING ON LABOUR SUPPLY 333

and suggested arbitration as the final stage in the dispute procedure. At the Quarterly Meeting of the J.I.C. in October the T.A. was severely criticized for failing to follow constitutional procedure. A member of the employers' panel said 'there was developing a widespread feeling up and down the country that ... so far as conciliation was concerned it was losing its influence'.[1]

The Daily Sketch Dispute

In London machine-minders in charge of rotary machines were members of the old-established craft union, the Printing Machine Managers' Trade Society, except in two offices, the *News of the World* and the *News Chronicle*. In the two latter Natsopa members were promoted to machine-minders. The P.M.M.T.S. tolerated this arrangement.[2]

In June 1953 the management of the *Daily Sketch* decided to transfer the printing of this paper to the *News of the World* office. This decision resulted in a complicated situation which revealed the difficulties of applying craft union principles in times of change. Natsopa would not agree that the *Daily Sketch* should be printed by P.M.M.T.S. men, in a 'Natsopa House'. The P.M.M.T.S. would not give up its jurisdiction over the minders in charge of printing the *Daily Sketch*.

Desperate efforts by the P. & K.T.F. to find a compromise solution were unavailing. The N.P.A. was informed that the dispute could lead to a stoppage on national dailies, for it had a rule that if one paper was stopped by a dispute, all of the others would cease publication. The P.M.M.T.S. had taken a strike ballot, and postponed the posting of notices several times, on request from the P. & K.T.F.

The P. & K.T.F. eventually asked the two unions to commence discussions, and in the event of failure, to submit to arbitration in accordance with the Federation constitution. The P.M.M.T.S. agreed, albeit reluctantly. Natsopa, however, refused, on the ground that the circularization of a letter from Lord Burnham, Chairman of the N.P.A., had seriously prejudiced the P. & K.T.F. against Natsopa. The N.P.A. then approached the Ministry of Labour, which set up a Court of Inquiry. In the meantime the *Daily Sketch* had two complete sets of machine-minders, working day about alternately, while the other set stood by.

The Court of Inquiry suggested that the present P.M.M.T.S. machine-minders should continue to work on the *Daily Sketch*, but that they should be replaced, as they left, by Natsopa men.[3] This solution was acceptable to Natsopa but not to the P.M.M.T.S. As the unions

---

[1] J.I.C. Minutes of Meeting, October 20, 1954.
[2] James Moran, *op. cit.*, ch. 14.
[3] *Report of Court of Inquiry*, September 1953.

334 THE NEW WORLD—FULL EMPLOYMENT

could not agree on a permanent solution, the P. & K.T.F. tried to obtain some form of arbitration by the Ministry of Labour. This approach was condemned by the P.M.M.T.S. which considered that the Federation should have forced Natsopa to submit to arbitration. But, as the Federation secretary said, this action would probably have led to Natsopa's withdrawal from the P. & K.T.F. Would this have led to a satisfactory solution, or would it have exacerbated inter-union friction ?[1]

The dispute dragged on through 1954. A working arrangement had been enforced by the N.P.A., on the lines suggested by the Court of Inquiry, but the P.M.M.T.S. was smarting from a sense of injustice. The T.U.C. Disputes Committee suggested that the two unions should accept the principle of a 'shared house', but this was hardly practicable given the existing tension. On October 12, 1954 the P.M.M.T.S. struck over the issue of replacements of their men on holiday. The N.P.A. ordered all other London dailies to cease publication, and the national papers were stopped for one day.

Again the P. & K.T.F. managed to find an arrangement for the resumption of work, and the unions eventually made an agreement on the lines of the T.U.C. suggestion of a 'shared house'.

At the next Administrative Council meeting Natsopa came forward with an amendment to the Federation's arbitration procedure, proposing that the panel should have an independent chairman 'drawn from the legal profession'. None of the other delegates supported the idea, and several pointedly remarked that what was needed was compliance with existing rules, not changes in the rules themselves. The amendment was heavily defeated.[2]

Why had Natsopa refused arbitration? The rule constituting the Arbitration Board stated that it should consist of a chairman selected by the Executive Committee and four others selected (two each) by the parties in dispute. The Executive was dominated by the craft unions, with several of which Natsopa had been in demarcation disputes.

Would they elect a chairman who might favour Natsopa? It was not likely. The mere existence of Natsopa machine-minders in the London area was anomalous, and contrary to the union 'principle' of one union for one area. But so long as the craft unions refused to admit the right of assistants to be promoted to craft rank, they could hardly expect Natsopa to forego one of the few avenues of promotion which the assistants possessed.

National Dailies Stoppage, 1955

The three-year stabilization period of agreements with the N.P.A. was due to expire in October 1954. Some months earlier the P. & K.T.F.

[1] P. & K.T.F., *Annual Report*, 1953, p. 37.   [2] *Ibid.*, 1954, pp. 36–38.

BARGAINING ON LABOUR SUPPLY

tried to arrange a collective movement by the ten unions concerned. Seven agreed from the start to work together and later two others joined them. Negotiations continued throughout the last four months of the year, without finality. In January the P. & K.T.F. made another joint approach, and received a slightly improved offer from the N.P.A. This was referred to the individual unions for consideration; at a meeting called in March 1955, to study the responses, the Federation was told:

One union had decided to refer the matter to arbitration.
One had accepted the offer and notified the N.P.A.
Three were in favour of acceptance, but had not notified the N.P.A.
One wanted another approach to the N.P.A.
One had decided to reject the offer.
Two had not yet made a decision.[1]

This was wage autonomy *par excellence*. Two unions with members working in newspaper offices, but not affiliated to the P. & K.T.F.— the Electrical Trades Union and the Amalgamated Engineering Union —were also keen to enjoy wage autonomy. In the past they had waited until the printing unions extracted an increase from the N.P.A., and they had then accepted a similar increase. But they began to resent being excluded from the preliminary negotiations, and went on an unofficial strike.

This led to a stoppage of national newspapers *for four weeks*! Again all the big guns of the T.U.C. and the Ministry of Labour were brought to bear, without avail. A Court of Inquiry investigated the causes of the dispute, and suggested that in future some way should be found of bringing these two unions into the negotiations. The P. & K.T.F. might well have replied that it had enough trouble bringing its own unions into line, without adding two outsiders. However, 'anxious to help as much as possible', the Federation stated that in future it would invite the E.T.U. and A.E.U. to join in negotiations. The discussion of this dispute at the Administrative Council meeting in May was surprisingly restrained. Over 20,000 people out of work for four weeks, and yet such cool, detached appraisal!

The explanation was simple: during the stoppage the N.P.A. continued to pay wages of printing employees forced to stand idle.

Review

When the main agreements were concluded in 1950, the employers' spokesman said, 'We feel we may well look forward to at least five years

[1] P. & K.T.F., *Annual Report*, 1954, p. 8.

336 THE NEW WORLD—FULL EMPLOYMENT

of peaceful co-operation on the many other jobs we ought to be doing for our respective members'.[1]

During the 1956 negotiations the employers' spokesman reviewed the operation of the stabilization period, and concluded that it had not been satisfactory. In the latter part of the period particularly the unions had felt increasingly frustrated. The unexpectedly steep rise in the cost-of-living had led to considerable 'distortion' of the wage structure, as all those rates which were calculated on the basic rate had remained unchanged. Five years was too long; it had resulted in an accumulation of business which would have been better settled piece by piece over the period. Union leaders were tied by the agreement, but chapels and members had become impatient and were taking independent action, thus driving a wedge between leadership and rank and file. On the employers' side many firms had given way on the wage front, undermining the standing of the national agreements. 'So-called Stabilization has not proved satisfactory for either side of the industry.'[2]

MANPOWER BARGAINING, 1956

The five-year period of stabilization of the National Agreements with the F.M.P. and Newspaper Society expired in November 1955. Over this period the cost-of-living bonus of 1s per point rise in the Index had grown to 33s.

In May 1955 most of the affiliated unions handed in six months' notice of termination. The employers, anticipating a round of hard bargaining, wrote to the P. & K.T.F. expressing the hope that *general* negotiations would be agreeable to the unions.

The hope was vain. From the beginning of the discussions to formulate a wages policy the L.S.C. and the Association of Correctors of the Press (a union of London readers) refused to join with the others. Others dropped out in the course of the early discussions. This left six 'united' unions which decided to press for the following advances:

1. Incorporation of cost-of-living bonus into basic wages.
2. A wage structure based on the following:
    London craft rate: £11 1s 6d.
    Provincial craft rate: £10 10s.
    Semi-skilled rate: $87\frac{1}{2}$ per cent of craft.
    General assistants: 85 per cent craft.
    Women: 75 per cent of male Class 3.
3. One grade only in the provinces.
4. Amendment of formula for calculating shift rates.

[1] *Members' Circular*, 1951, p. 4.   [2] *Ibid.*, 1955, p. 278.

BARGAINING ON LABOUR SUPPLY

The employers' first reply conceded 1, rejected 3 and 4 and indicated that they were prepared to make a wage increase provided that the unions were prepared to help in overcoming the 'acute and dangerous shortage of workers', and that arrangements could be made for the more efficient use of available labour.

As the manpower shortage was different for each union, the movement disbanded temporarily while the unions held separate discussions on rules and labour intake. Here lay the unions' problem. Fundamentally they were being asked to exchange relaxation of rules for a wage increase. At the same time both the employers and the unions wanted to arrive at some agreed wages structure. But in some sections of industry the labour shortage was more acute than in others, and some unions had more to 'put on the table' than others. To add to the difficulty, for example, in regard to labour intake, some craft unions were prepared to relax the apprentice quota, but not to admit dilutees, while others took the contrary view. Yet the granting of any concession by one union could be used by the employers as an argument against the others. The task of co-ordinating the union negotiating tactics was thus extremely difficult.

The employers, while standing firm on their refusal of changes in grading and shift rates, gradually raised the amount of the wage increase as they reached an understanding on the labour concessions the unions would make. In January 1956 four unions balloted for acceptance of the following rates:

	Old Rate	Consolidated Cost-of-Living	Increase	New Rate		
Craft, Grade 1	143s 6d	33s	18s 6d	£9	15	0
Craft, Grade 2	138s	33s	18s 6d	£9	9	6
Male Non-craft		33s	15s 6d			
Adult Women		24s 9d	12s			

The T.A., however, withdrew from the combined movement in December; the A.S.L.P. which stayed out at the start, came in to the united movement in November, rejected the employers' offer in January, and from then on conducted its own campaign.

Under the 'January terms' rates were stabilized for two years, with a cost-of-living sliding scale, and the unions made concessions in regard to increased intake of apprentices.

In January 1956, the T.A. which was making no headway in negotiations, imposed restrictions on production and refused to appear before a Conciliation Committee of the J.I.C. The F.M.P. Council resolved that:

338 THE NEW WORLD—FULL EMPLOYMENT

'The T.A. Executive is challenging the basic rights of management through the form of attack they have chosen, and that attack must be met by united action, even to the extent of closing down if required.'[1]

The employers reported the dispute to the Minister of Labour. At almost the same time the L.T.S. also imposed an overtime ban and work-to-rule campaign, and evaded reference to the J.I.C.[2] It refused to refer the dispute to conciliation, or arbitration, or to return to normal working. On February 15, 1956 the London Master Printers' Association summarily dismissed for breach of contract, all L.T.S. and A.C.P. members who refused to undertake to work in accordance with normal practice.

The Minister of Labour set up two Courts of Inquiry—one on the T.A. dispute and one on the L.T.S. dispute, both under the same chairman, Sir John Forster.

The L.T.S. claim, expressed rather confusedly, was that the craftsman's differential had been 'constantly devalued' as a result of 'flat increases, of scarcity payments, of all kinds of means of providing wages other than those laid down in agreements'.[3] The union asked for a craft rate of approximately £11 to keep an appropriate differential. But in addition it asked the Court to put a cash value on the concessions which it was prepared to make in regard to apprentice intake, relaxation of overtime rule, and co-operation in incentive schemes. This was an honest and frank bargaining approach.

The Court, however, rejected the claim that the union should be paid *anything* for relaxing its rules on labour supply.[4] On this point the Court was more doctrinaire than the employers, who realized that a bargain was being struck. In a statement to the 'united' unions, in November 1955 Jackson, Chairman of the F.M.P.–Newspaper Society Joint Labour Committee, said:

'We have stuck to our line that our recommendations are for all round cash increases to everyone, whatever rate he or she may be getting at the present time. At the same time I hope I have made it clear that our offers have been made *as part of a bargain*—the other part being that you will agree to measures to relieve the labour shortage and help *us keep down costs of production*.'[5]

---

[1] *Members' Circular*, 1956, p. 21.

[2] Many of the 'rules' which the members of the L.T.S. were instructed to obey had never been formally recognized. The aim of this tactic was to cause the maximum obstruction to production, on any pretext whatever.

[3] *Report of Court of Inquiry*, 1956, Cmd. 9717, p. 13.

[4] *Ibid.*, para. 54.

[5] *Members' Circular*, 1955, p. 282 (italics supplied).

BARGAINING ON LABOUR SUPPLY

Yet the Court itself, in its historical outline of the events leading up to the dispute, stated that the 1950 dispute was a bargain of wage increases for manpower and efficiency, and later said of the 1956 dispute, 'Again, the bargain was to be the basic rate against manpower'.[1] At the same time it suggested an increased London craft rate of £10 15s 6d, and 'a further effort to establish comprehensive national machinery on a two-tier basis for the negotiation of wages and conditions in the industry'.[2]

Here, of course, was an inconsistency which the Court did not appear to recognize. As the wage it fixed did not include a *quid pro quo* for the unions' labour offer, it must have been fixed solely in consideration of the appropriate differential for skill. How did the Court arrive at this difference? It gave no hint. (It could easily have calculated a percentage on the basis of existing non-craft rate.) Furthermore the Court denied that there was any 'traditional' craft differential; expressed as a percentage it had varied from 42·5 per cent in 1920 to 22 per cent in 1950. If the Court's suggestion was justifiable, it set a key rate for the rest of London. If it was justifiable why was it not justified? And if it was not justifiable, why should it be taken as a basis for settlement, or treated with any respect by anybody concerned? The Court seemed to have worked on the reasonable assumption that another 9s per week would be sufficiently attractive to lead to a settlement. It seriously misjudged R. Willis's tenacity in pursuit of what he regarded as the craftsmen's rights.

After a six weeks' stoppage the L.T.S. surprisingly ordered its members to return to work on March 27th, on the conditions obtaining *before* the dispute began! The reasons for this tactic were soon apparent. Following up the Court's suggestion of a two-tier structure, the L.T.S. joined with the T.A., A.S.L.P. and A.C.P. in a 'craft group' which advanced very high claims for London and provincial craftsmen. The employers replied that they would agree to the terms suggested by the Court, but nothing more.

The craft unions expressed a wish to establish the 'principle' that the non-craft rate should be 70 per cent of the craft rate. The employers' spokesman pointed out that this could not be settled without consulting the non-craft unions.

At the April conference two days of hard bargaining resulted in an agreement. The new basic craft rates were:

	Old Rate	Consolidated Cost-of-Living	Increase	New Rate
London	155s	33s	32s	220s
Provinces Grade 1	143s 6d	33s	29s	205s 6d
Provinces Grade 2	138s	33s	29s	200s

[1] *Report of Court of Inquiry*, 1956, para. 26. [2] *Ibid.*, p.19

340 THE NEW WORLD—FULL EMPLOYMENT

In return the unions agreed to block intakes of apprentices:

T.A.: 545 over three years.
A.S.L.P.: 100 over five years.
L.T.S.: 200 composing and 75 machine.

The A.S.L.P. also liberalized its apprentice quota, and for the first time agreed to permit the introduction of incentive schemes. The A.S.L.P. also agreed to the annual up-grading of twenty-members of the Multilith and Rotaprint section to full craft status after three years' training. The L.T.S. for the first time agreed to an intake of adult apprentices, aged twenty-one to twenty-five, who would be selected by a joint committee of the union and the London M.P.A. and undergo four years' training. A higher scale of wages running from 80 per cent to $97\frac{1}{2}$ per cent of the craft rate (depending upon age and year of service) was fixed.

The news of a substantial rise of the craft rate fell pleasantly on the ears of the other unions, who asked, through the P. & K.T.F. for an early conference. Jackson, the employers' spokesman, had made it clear to the craft unions that they could not expect to hold such a large margin.

'On the question of claims from other unions following a settlement with the four craft unions our policy will be to hear the claims, to consider the arguments put forward and to negotiate any alterations which may be just and fair, at the same time taking steps to achieve the two-tier structure recommended by the Court of Inquiry.'[1]

The unions were not, at this point, prepared to commit themselves to a two-tier structure. As the whole question of wages structure was due for consideration at the next Council meeting of the P. & K.T.F. they did not wish to prejudice policy decisions of the meeting. The major issue, naturally, was the appropriate differential between craft and other grades, and whether this be expressed in absolute, or percentage terms.

It was inevitable that the other unions should obtain 'craft parity' with the T.A., for their skilled workers; on this point there was no dispute. The crucial issue was the fixing of rates for the lowest paid classes of workers, men, women and juveniles.

The agreed rates, accepted by union ballot in September 1956 were:

[1] *Members' Circular*, 1956, p. 132.

	Grade 1	Grade 2
Adult Male Class I	205s 6d	200s
II	186s 6d	183s
III	177s 6d	174s 6d
IV	169s 6d	166s 6d
Women Workers		
On completion of training	120s	118s
After 4 years' experience	130s	128s

It was almost the end; the S.L.A.D.E. agreement was signed the following month. While the Negative Spotters' rate was fixed at the normal craft rate, £11, the bulk of the craftsmen received a minimum of £12 15s. In the ceramic section of the industry the basic rates were still higher. But the union did not give any firm undertaking on intake of extra apprentices; it merely agreed 'to consider any cases put forward where there is an established shortage of craftsmen which the Society cannot satisfy'. The agreement also provided that the parties should jointly consider any new techniques introduced into the industry, and come to suitable arrangements for their operation, in the first instance on an experimental basis.[1]

CONCLUSION

What effect had these rates on the craft differential? For men, the differential between the Craftsman and Class II was increased from 13s 6d to 19s, but expressed as a percentage of the 1955 Craft rate, the Class II man maintained his rate at 91 per cent of the craft rate. The Class IV rate rose from 79 per cent to 82 per cent of the craft rate.

Again, the effect of future cost-of-living bonuses, which were constant for all classes of worker, would be to reduce the percentage differential. Broadly, then, the effect of the completed agreements was to maintain the percentage craft/non-craft differential. The craft union movement for an increased differential had failed.

What of the sex differential? In 1955 the rate for an adult woman, on completion of training, was 78s, 54 per cent of the craft rate. Under the 1956 agreement this rose to 58 per cent on completion of training, and 63 per cent after four years' experience.

All of these agreements ran until May 1959, and provided for a cost-of-living bonus of 1s per point (men) above an Index of 155.

The new agreements embodied a differential between Grade 1 and 2 of 5s 6d, but this was to be reduced by two instalments of 1s 6d each in the next two years. The effect of the reduction was virtually to eliminate the provincial Grading system.

[1] 'Agreement—Lithographic Artists', *M.P.A.*, 1957, p. 400.

342　THE NEW WORLD—FULL EMPLOYMENT

At the Administrative Council of the P. & K.T.F. in May 1956 there was a long debate on future wage policy. W. A. Morrison (Paperworkers) moved:

'That, in the opinion of this Conference, recent events have demonstrated a serious lack of unity between the unions affiliated to our Federation. As a means towards restoring this unity this Conference instructs the General Secretary to call a meeting of two or three representatives from each union in the Federation, such meeting to endeavour to devise a basic wages structure for the industry.'[1]

R. Willis (L.T.S.) moved an amendment to the effect that the Conference accepted the idea of a two-tier wages structure, and that separate meetings of representatives of craft and non-craft workers should be held. The amendment was lost.[2]

The unions remained hopelessly divided. The divisions, however, was not simply on craft/non-craft lines, though this was perhaps the strongest divisive influence. The S.T.A. tended to keep out of the polarization, as did the S.L.A.D.E. And indeed the Paperworkers, with over 20,000 craft members, had more craftsmen than any other union except the L.T.S. Natsopa, too had a small craft component. To those who subscribed to traditional working class ideals of unity, mutual help and industrial comradeship, the frank adoption of 'capitalist ethics', by some of the craft unions was a depressing spectacle.

The employers had reason to be pleased with the outcome. The 1956 agreements clearly demonstrated that the less rigid union attitudes to labour supply, indicated in the 1950 settlement, was persisting. Long-established union rules, once regarded as the bulwark of union control, could be 'bought out', in return for immediate concessions. Could other union rules, restricting management's *use* of labour, also be the subject of a bargain?

[1] P. & K.T.F., *Annual Report*, 1955, p. 36.
[2] Representation on the Administrative Council of the P. & K.T.F. was roughly in proportion to membership of the union. There was no block vote; each delegate had one vote. Thus the Paperworkers and Natsopa together had about half the votes. On the Executive, however, each union was limited to one representative, and the smaller craft unions had a substantial majority.

CHAPTER XXI

PRODUCTIVITY BARGAINING
1959–62

HOURS AND WAGES MOVEMENT, 1959[1]

In the 1946 revision of the Hours and Holidays Agreement, which established the forty-three and a half hour week and the fortnight's paid annual holiday, the employers also agreed to the 'principle of a forty-two and a half hour week' to be introduced when the necessary adjustments for adequate recruitment into industry had been made with the unions concerned and when the labour situation had sufficiently improved to enable the industry to meet its obligations to the community.

In May 1958 the Administrative Council of the P. & K.T.F. unanimously voted for a Natsopa resolution urging the Federation to press forward with collective representation for the forty hour week in the general printing trade. Speakers who supported the resolution claimed that reduced hours were justified because of greater productivity, and the right of the workers to share in this by having more leisure.[2]

At the same time, however, separate conferences of craft and noncraft union executives were trying to hammer out a 'two-tier' wages policy to present to the employers when the 'stabilization' period expired in April 1959. On the other side the employers were also preparing their campaign well in advance, and making special preparations for keeping closely in touch with their constituents. A major aim this time was to keep London and the provinces 'in step'; by being manoeuvred into a London movement in 1956 the employers had been forced to give way. The London unions were the spearhead; if they could be kept in with the others, and given less room for manoeuvre, the employers would gain an advantage.

In the course of the unions' preliminary talks, four unions quickly withdrew. The Society of Lithographic Artists, which had been

---

[1] A detailed account of this dispute, written by G. G. Eastwood, is printed in the P. & K.T.F. *Annual Report*, 1959–60.

[2] P. & K.T.F., *Annual Report*, 1957, pp. 30–36.

344 THE NEW WORLD—FULL EMPLOYMENT

conducting a vigorous Charter Campaign by way of bargaining at the chapel level, and was hoping to establish the forty hour week by this approach, decided to withdraw. Natsopa withdrew because of an alleged insult to union officers who were asked to withdraw from a meeting called for craft unions. The N.U.J. and the small Society of Music Engravers withdrew because of their special problems.

In January 1959 the representatives of the two groups of unions presented their claim for:

1. A forty-hour week.
2. Ten per cent increase in London craft rates.
3. Reduction of London/Provinces differential, from 14s 6d to 10s.
4. Abolition of provincial Grade 2.
5. Continuation of present cost-of-living bonus.
6. Stabilization of three years.

Procedurally the claim was very complicated. The Hours item was a Federation one; the Wages items were presented by two groups of unions with the P. & K.T.F. acting as a co-ordinator.

There were, then, three group movements in hand:

1. A P. & K.T.F. movement for a forty-hour week.
2. A craft movement for increased wages and reduced London differential.
3. A non-craft movement for increased percentages of the craft rate for semi-skilled workers, general assistants, and women.

As well as these, however, each union had a number of special rates which it wished to have adjusted. The A.S.L.P. also had a claim for a 'redundancy bonus'.

At the first formal conference in January G. G. Eastwood presented the P. & K.T.F. case for a forty hour week, and W. A. Morrison (Paperworkers), then President of the P. & K.T.F., presented the cases for a craft increase and a non-craft increase. In general the arguments were based mainly on evidence for *past* increased productivity (based on official statistics, and company profits). Admitting that the unions had not been able to agree on a wages structure, Morrison said that the unions had reached agreement on the claims for non-craft differentials. In fact the unions were not seeking any great change, but rather a consolidation of the cost-of-living bonus, which because it was a flat rate for men, had reduced the percentage differential.

Women's rates, however, had not improved proportionately, because

PRODUCTIVITY BARGAINING 345

they received a smaller cost-of-living allowance. In 1959 women's rates were about 58 per cent of the male craft rate. The unions had abandoned their previous policy of aiming at 75 per cent of the male rate, and were prepared to settle for 66⅔ per cent.

R. A. Jackson, the employers' spokesman, had prepared an unusually thorough answer to the claims, with graphs showing (rather irrelevantly) that hand compositors were better off than in 1947, that weekly earnings in printing had risen more than the average, since 1949, for both men and women, and that profits had fallen sharply *since 1955*.

'We are fighting now in our own joint interests against foreign competition, against expansion of customers' own printing, against transfers to non-traditional printing, against inroads made by television into the field of printed advertisements.'[1]

Against this increased competition the printers had only one weapon—high quality printing at a lower cost. The only course open to both unions and employers was to explore ways of 'reducing costs and increasing volume'.

He concluded his long statement by flatly rejecting the unions' claims.

This complete rejection, with no hint of bargaining, was not altogether a surprise to the unions; they seemed to regard it as part of the usual ritual, and pressed for a second conference. Even the *Members' Circular* suggested in February that:

'If there is a determination to look at the good of the industry as a whole it will be possible to work out a solution which will not increase costs and which will avoid the kind of struggle which can only have a disastrous effect on volume of work and on security of employment.'[2]

In the March conferences, however, the employers placed more emphasis on measures to improve efficiency and productivity. Jackson remained adamant that under existing conditions the industry could not afford to raise costs still further. The unions, however, took the view that it was the employer's responsibility to find ways and means of meeting the increased costs, and they were not prepared to co-operate on this unless the employers made *some* offer.[3]

Why did not the employers make a gesture at this stage? Was there a misjudgement of union reaction, a failure to face the realities of bargaining, or were they planning a set battle? And if the last, what was the

[1] *Members' Circular*, 1959, p. 55.   [2] *Ibid.*, p. 27.   [3] *Ibid.*, p. 117.

346 THE NEW WORLD—FULL EMPLOYMENT

objective? Was it to shock the craft unions into recognizing the need for review of their traditional rules and practices, or was it to hold the line for the British Employers Confederation, against the general reduction in hours?[1]

The employers offered to go before an independent arbitrator, but the unions refused on the grounds that the absence of any offer from the employers meant that there was nothing to arbitrate about. Nor would they make any use of the conciliation machinery of the J.I.C., devised after the 1956 dispute. The unions believed that since a conciliation committee would consist in the main of the same people who had failed to reach agreement by negotiation, the prospects of a settlement by the J.I.C. conciliation machinery were non-existent.[2]

In May, however, the employers sent to the unions a 'tentative list' of twenty-two points dealing with Labour Supply, Demarcation Problems, Productivity Improvement Techniques, New Processes, Method Study, with the suggestion that if the two sides could work out ways of improving efficiency and reducing costs, some increases in wages and reduction of hours would be possible.

At this point the employers claimed that 'a settlement of the dispute is still possible'. The essence of the difference was that the unions wanted their claims to be met on past performance; the employers would only consider them in return for future concessions.

Nevertheless, the 'best' offer that the employers made was only a forty-two and a half-hour week and a $2\frac{1}{2}$ per cent increase in wages. The unions still held out for a forty-hour week and 10 per cent wage increase.

Unions then recommended their members to endorse a policy of a ban on overtime, no extension of shift work, no new apprentices, non-co-operation in the workshop, and withdrawal from participation in incentive schemes. The members voted 4:1 in favour of this policy. In June 1959 the unions called for an imposition of these five sanctions. The employers retaliated by issuing 'protective notices' to their employees to the effect that they wished to vary the terms of employment, to engage labour on a day-to-day basis. The unions informed the F.M.P. that they would not tolerate such a practice, and decided to treat the notices as notices of dismissal.

---

[1] Cyriax and Oakeshott, *The Bargainers*, 1960, pp. 109–10 suggested that the employers were keen to square the account with R. Willis, the architect of their defeat in 1956. The B.F.M.P. denies that the B.E.C. at any time made an attempt to influence the printing employers.

[2] Correspondence on this procedural point is reprinted in J.I.C. Minutes of Quarterly Meeting, April 15, 1959.

PRODUCTIVITY BARGAINING 347

Protective notices expired in the week ending June 20th, and by this time about 120,000 union members had ceased work. Up to this point Natsopa had been conducting separate but parallel negotiations with the employers, and making little progress. The other unions then invited Natsopa to join in the general dispute, and the offer was accepted. Two other unions, however, continued their policy of non-involvement, the National Union of Journalists and the Society of Lithographic Artists. The position of their members was extremely awkward, for many lost employment when the other workers went on strike.

The dispute involved, on the employers' side, only the Federation of Master Printers and the Newspaper Society. The Newspaper Proprietors' Association was not directly concerned. But Natsopa was in dispute with the Society of British Printing Ink Manufacturers, and there was a likelihood of the national dailies having to stop for lack of printing ink. This would have been very awkward for the London unions, which were levying their members in newspaper offices to help finance the stoppage in the other part of the industry. Natsopa alone was drawing £20,000 to £30,000 per week from such levies. R. Briginshaw, Natsopa secretary, arranged for stocks of ink to be pooled, and rationed to the papers. When this supply was on the point of exhaustion, he flew to Paris and arranged for supplies of French ink to be flown in. Then arrangements had to be made with picket lines and shop stewards to allow the ink to be taken from the airport to the newspaper offices.[1]

During this first week there were a number of clashes between police and picket lines, with arrests and prosecutions for disturbance of the peace. Convinced that in some of these incidents the police were exceeding their authority, a deputation of union leaders waited on the Home Secretary and presented written and photographic evidence in support of the pickets' complaints. Some stormy demonstrations took place outside firms which were continuing, with non-union labour, to print journals which had been closed down at union houses.

Meanwhile, at the top level, officials continued to search for a formula which would permit resumption of negotiations. The employers wanted an arrangement in which, in the event of a deadlock, an independent arbitrator could make a binding decision. The unions would have none of this.

At the end of the third full week of the stoppage the Chief Industrial Commissioner succeeded, after *eleven hours* of discussion with the parties, in drafting the terms of reference for an independent chairman who would conduct the proceedings. These comprised two main principles: first, that the chairman would have no power to arbitrate, but in the

[1] Moran, *op. cit.*, p. 139.

348   THE NEW WORLD—FULL EMPLOYMENT

event of a deadlock could make 'recommendations' which the negotiators would submit to their constituents; second, that there would be no
partial settlement—all issues had to be settled with all ten unions.

The issues were stated as being (i) hours, (ii) wages, (iii) domestic
claims (by individual unions), and (iv) manpower problems and
questions of improving efficiency.

NEGOTIATIONS ON SETTLEMENT

Lord Birkett accepted the invitation to act as Chairman and discussions began on July 14th. The employers quickly came forward
with an offer of a forty-two-hour week and a $3\frac{1}{2}$ per cent increase in
wages, in return for stabilization for three years, and union concessions on 'productivity'. But as the stoppage was in its fourth week,
the unions were not prepared to accept moderate gains. They held to
the line that they had already 'earned' substantial improvements in
conditions, and should not have to make further concessions.

They pressed the employers to an explicit statement of 'agreement in
principle' to the forty hour week, to be reached in stages over the next
two years. However, if the employers considered that the economic
position did not justify future reductions, the issue could be the subject
of a judicial inquiry.

To such fine (some might say 'finicky') hair-splitting had the negotiations developed, that the employers would not say that they agreed on
the principle of the forty-hour week, but at the same time said they were
not against it. Negotiations continued every day for a week, with breaks
while one side or the other held a separate conference, or referred to
constituents.

During the course of the week it became clear that settlement would
have to be worked out at two levels, a general agreement on wages and
hours covering all unions, and a number of individual union agreements
on special rates and relaxation of 'restrictive' rules. Lord Birkett
suggested, therefore: (a) a forty-two hour week immediately, to stand
for two years, with provision for a judicial inquiry at the end of 1961
if the parties could not agree on a further reduction, (b) a $4\frac{1}{2}$ per cent
wage increase immediately for two years, and a judicial inquiry in 1961
if the parties could not agree.

This was roughly half of what the unions had originally asked for.
In return, however, the unions were to make sufficient concessions on
'productivity' to satisfy the employers' basic requirements. The employers were, at the same time, to deal with the unions' domestic claims
for special rates.

These general terms were accepted by the employers on July 28th.

PRODUCTIVITY BARGAINING 349

Some unions, however, felt that they could not accept without a membership ballot. This would take three or four weeks. Suppose the members rejected the terms? One of the employers' conditions had been that a settlement was reached with *all* unions. But if work was not resumed until the results of the ballots were known, the stoppage would go on for another three weeks.

It proved almost as difficult to arrange for the terms on which the settlement could be ratified, as it was to settle the primary issues in dispute. But under the chairman's patient and skilful guidance clauses were drafted and amended, and phrases carefully reconsidered, until an acceptable formulation was reached. On condition that all union executives issued a joint statement recommending acceptance, and that at least *eight* unions voted for acceptance, the employers agreed to allow four weeks for balloting, and to pay increases retrospectively to the date of resumption of work. The unions also agreed to 'bend their efforts to obtain acquiescence' from any union which rejected the terms. All unions promised to refrain from 'aggressive action' at all levels for eight weeks from the date of resumption, which was fixed as August 6th.

The stoppage had then lasted six weeks.

Another difficult matter was the settlement of conditions for resumption.

The agreement on conditions for a Return to Work provided that work would be resumed on August 6th under the 'normal conditions' obtaining before the dispute. Both sides promised to refrain from 'punitive action or discrimination' against members of the other side engaged in the dispute.

But what of those 'open houses' in which there were some non-union men who continued in employment during the dispute, or those which had changed to 'open houses'? The Agreement provided that union members returning to work would not refuse to co-operate with other employees, and would take up work as they found it at the date of resumption. In those unions which had a 'closed shop' rule or policy this, of course, was not possible. The F.M.P. agreed with the unions' point of view that if a firm elected to operate as an 'open house', it could not complain if trade unionists chose, in future, not to work there. An instruction from a trade union banning members from working in such houses would not be regarded as a breach of the Return to Work Agreement.

Unions, however, were faced with the unpleasant task of taking disciplinary action against members who had disobeyed union instructions during the dispute, mainly by refusing the order to come out on strike. Two newspapers in Leicester, alleging victimization of employees who had stayed at work, refused to engage any members

350   THE NEW WORLD—FULL EMPLOYMENT

of the T.A. or Stereotypers' Society. This led to an extended stoppage in other departments of the papers.

The F.M.P. did not emerge unscathed either. A number of firms—mainly small ones—resigned from the Federation and conceded the unions' terms, thus enabling them to continue working during the stoppage. In March 1960 the membership had dropped to 3,958 from 4,349 a year earlier. This 10 per cent drop in membership represented, however, only about 5 per cent of the work force.

During the negotiations and stoppage the Federation had made strenuous efforts to keep constituents fully informed of developments. The effectiveness of this communication was reflected in the 'unity and determination' of the employers.

REVIEW

So ended the great dispute. It had been conducted in the full glare of publicity—from press, radio and television. For six weeks the printing stoppage was virtually the News. What effect did this publicity have on the length or the outcome? Did it make leaders less likely to compromise, because their compromise was a public spectacle, and might be interpreted as 'softness', or did it encourage a settlement, from fear of appearing too stubborn and intransigent? Did the chief participants enjoy their hour of glory, and dread the prospect of relative oblivion which would follow the settlement? Or did they dread more the prospect of a collapse of morale and discipline of their constituents, and the public humiliation of a débâcle?

Alas, until they write their memoirs, outsiders will never know.

One fact, above all others, however, stands out. Discipline on both sides was high—much higher than many both inside and outside the industry had expected. Surprisingly, the Newspaper Society stood by the F.M.P. whereas previously it had often yielded to union importunities. On the union side, too, the response of the members was overwhelmingly obedient. This was not surprising in the London craft unions, with their better communications, tight organization, and better financial resources. It was amazing, however, in the widely scattered, heterogeneous and less highly paid membership of Natsopa and the Paperworkers. Those who thought that the welfare state and the affluent society had sapped the industrial discipline of the trade unions were wildly wrong. Even the union leaders were often surprised at the strength of the rank and file support. Summing up, at the Administrative Council of the P. & K.T.F. in the following May, the President, W. A. Morrison, said:

'I have expressed the opinion that the employers were astounded at the

PRODUCTIVITY BARGAINING 351

solidarity displayed by our people. I think we must face the fact that they also were solid. It is true there were a number of firms that gave way, but, by and large, their ranks held.'[1]

The terms of the immediate settlement seemed to some observers to favour the employers. In fact the working conditions after ratification— forty-two hours and a wage increase of $4\frac{1}{2}$ per cent—was little better than the terms offered by the employers as early as July 21st—forty-two hours and a $3\frac{1}{2}$ per cent increase. Had it taken a further ten days national stoppage to achieve a 1 per cent wage increase?

This kind of consideration which some industrial observers are fond of making, is basically fallacious. The major premise of the fallacy is that unions and employers make a cold-blooded calculation of the probable costs and gains which follow from a strike, and decide that on balance a gain of so much per week in wages is worth the cost of so many weeks' lost wages or profits. Surprisingly, in a book which shows many keen insights into trade union behaviour, Cyriax and Oakeshott make this naïve error in *The Bargainers*.[2]

Even if all the items in the settlement could be assessed in money terms, they still do not complete the balance sheet, for there are many losses and gains which remain completely incalculable. Both sides gained knowledge and experience of how to conduct a stoppage—but did they gain equally? Both sides lost some members through defections —but did they lose equally? Both sides considered that the other had been taught a lesson, but was it the same lesson? And had it been equally well learnt? The answers to these questions are not known with anything approaching certainty by *anyone*. They may, perhaps, be deduced from the conduct of the parties in the next major dispute. But as they relate to internal politics and external strategy, they cannot be put into a monetary balance sheet.

Furthermore, since in effect the basic union claims were conceded in the next three years, the employers' assessment of the economic consequences of meeting the claims were proved to be wrong.[3] On the basis of many statistical calculations, R. Jackson, the employers' spokesman, described the union claims as 'staggering and unrealistic'. According to his figures the printing industry was in a mild recession, but its competitive position was so keen that any increase in costs

---

[1] P. & K.T.F., *Annual Report*, 1959–60, p. 55.

[2] G. Cyriax and R. Oakeshott, *The Bargainers*, 1960, p. 113.

[3] This judgement assumes that the unions were prepared to concede a substantial *quid pro quo*, if their claims were met. Naturally they did not give any indication of how far they would go in this direction, when submitting their claims to the employers.

352   THE NEW WORLD—FULL EMPLOYMENT

would have a sharp impact on demand, especially in the export trade.[1]

In fact, in the years after the 1959 settlement, the volume of printing and of printing exports continued to rise.[2]

The employers' facts may have been right, but their interpretation of them was highly pessimistic. Indeed, to read the continuous catalogue of woe which the employers presented in their post-war negotiations is to enter a world of almost unrelieved gloom. History has proved them wrong, time and again, but their attitude is unshakably cheerless. Perlman's famous postulate of the 'scarcity conscious' trade unionist, and the 'expansionist' entrepreneur would need to be reversed if it were to apply to the British printing industry in the post-war era.

Reviewing the dispute the *Annual Report* of the F.M.P. in May 1960, claimed that the struggle against the forty-hour week was successful, and noted that many other industries had since reduced their standard week to forty-two, in line with the printing industry.[3] The employers had conceded more than they wished, but given active co-operation between employers and union members the provisions for increasing productivity 'should make a substantial contribution towards counter-acting the rise in costs resulting from the wage increases and hours reductions'.[4]

Suspension of J.I.C.

At the Quarterly Meeting of the J.I.C. in April 1959 there was an exchange of sharp criticism between employers and unions. W. A. Morrison, General Secretary of the N.U.P.B. & P.W. said that the unions believed the employers were using the J.I.C. to attack the unions, by trying to force them to accept arbitration. Following on the stoppage in July and August, the two sides were unable to agree on a formula for settlement of national disputes, and the J.I.C. was practically suspended. No full Council meeting was held for the next three years, and several of the standing committees were also suspended. The Apprenticeship Authority, however, continued to function, and the Health and Safety Committee kept up its propaganda.

The seventy or more District Committees, which were mainly concerned with the local selection and training of apprentices, continued in operation.

The major difference was over the interpretation of Clause 2, in the Objects, which was 'to secure complete organization of Employers and

---

[1] *Members' Circular*, 1959, p. 55.

[2] P. & K.T.F., *Annual Report*, 1961–62, pp. 22–25.

[3] F.M.P., *Annual Report*, 1959–60, p. 9. This perhaps gives some support to the idea that the printing employers were asked to 'hold the line' on the hours issue.   [4] *Ibid.*, p. 15.

PRODUCTIVITY BARGAINING

353

Employees throughout the trade'. The unions interpreted this to imply the use of considerable pressure by both sides to extend membership, but the employers always claimed that they would not force their members to operate as 'closed shops'. The unions accepted this view. An issue which had caused a good deal of friction over the years was Natsopa's campaign to enrol the clerks in printing offices. On this particular point the employers had been markedly unco-operative, arguing that many clerical workers had such confidential information that they should not be expected to join a trade union.

Eventually the issue was side-stepped by the insertion of a note to the troublesome clause, to the effect that the J.I.C. had no powers to 'secure' organization of either side, and that responsibility for this matter lay with the respective parties.

The number of full Council meetings was reduced from four to two annually, and the number of standing committees was reduced from seven to four.

The new Constitution recognized the 'facts of life' in industrial disputes and removed claims for establishment or revision of national agreements from the ambit of the Conciliation procedures.

The first full Council meeting, after a lapse of three years, was held in October 1963. Speakers approved of the 'cutting out of dead wood', and 'streamlining' the constitution, and appealed for a revival of 'the J.I.C. spirit'.

PRODUCTIVE EFFICIENCY

In return for improvements in wages and the reduction in hours, the unions gave comprehensive undertakings to try to improve productivity. The totality of these arrangements is difficult to summarize, as some were common to all nine unions, and others were specific to particular unions. The F.M.P. sent out this part of the agreement, with explanatory notes, to all members, entitling it 'Measures to Improve Efficiency'. It pointed out that some measures were complete and definite, and could be implemented at once, while others required further discussion with the unions before they could be brought into operation. The following example is based on the text of the agreement and the employers' notes.[1]

1. Use of Craft Skill to Maximum Effect.

   (a) Machine Department.
      Machine crews shall co-operate in the various tasks involved

[1] Reprinted *Members' Circular*, 1959, pp. 343–6.

354 THE NEW WORLD—FULL EMPLOYMENT

in the operation of their machine and whenever practicable the craftsman shall be relieved of those subsidiary duties which can be properly carried out by an assistant under the direction and authority of the craftsman.

The note suggested that implementation of this would depend on the practice and custom of the house; and that where changes were desirable they should be discussed with the Chapel.

(b) Composing Department.
  Semi-skilled auxiliary workers of the craft unions may be employed as block and type storemen, and in clearing and sorting of furniture, lead and rule; but distribution is the work of craftsmen.

The note added that wage rates for semi-skilled auxiliary workers, and their admission to the Typographical Association, for example, would have to be negotiated with the union. In Scotland the S.T.A. already had an Auxiliary section, and in London the L.T.S. had an Allied Processes Section. This clause shows clearly the difficulty of maintaining the old demarcation rules and their consequential jurisdictional frontiers, in the face of an effort to make full use of labour.

(c) Stereo Department.
  It is agreed that in Houses where an apprentice vacancy will arise within a period of two years a prospective apprentice may carry out subsidiary non-craft duties under the direction and authority of the craftsman.

In view of the long tradition of opposition to non-apprenticed 'boy labour', this concession is quite remarkable. True the lad permitted is a prospective apprentice, but the new practice is symbolic of the general approach. Old rules are no longer rigid and unquestioned, but may be relaxed, modified, or jettisoned if need be.

Other matters dealt with in the general agreement on efficiency were:

2. Shift Work.
3. Work Study, Dockets, and Recording Systems.
4. New Processes and Changes in Methods of Production.
5. Apprentice Quotas.
6. Apprentice Training Period.

The 'formula' to govern the introduction of method study, which was later agreed to by each of the ten unions was:

PRODUCTIVITY BARGAINING

1. The circumstances in which the recommendations in paras. 2 to 6 apply are not those connected with normal management functions such as rearrangement of equipment or introduction of new equipment, but those connected with the special techniques of method study which call for active co-operation from operatives.

2. A firm guarantee should be given by an employer in inviting his employees to co-operate in the introduction of method study that no existing employee shall lose his or her employment as the direct result of applying method study. It is accepted that employers cannot be expected to give a guarantee of continuing employment if circumstances arise not connected with the introduction of method study, which reduce the opportunities for employment.

3. There should be consultation with workers and their representatives at all stages.

4. Every effort should be made to ensure that the health of employees does not suffer following the introduction of method study, one of the objects of which is to reduce unnecessary fatigue and to improve conditions of work.

5. Employers are recommended to recognize the principle that employees who co-operate in method study should participate in the benefit resulting therefrom, but it is recognized that such benefits will not necessarily be in the form of increased financial payments but may bring other advantages to employees, such as greater security.

6. The effect of method study on the total labour requirements of the various sections of the industry should be carefully watched and the position met by adjustment of agreements.

This 'formula' was the swansong of the otherwise unproductive Employment and Production Committee of the J.I.C., though in fact it was negotiated in much the same way as any national agreement.

A further series of Appendices dealt with matters pertaining to each individual union. For example Appendix 2—Typographical Association, contained five clauses providing for adult apprentices, training and interchange of monotype operators and caster attendants, and some extra rates payable to special machine-minders.

The A.S.L.P. Appendix provided for the extension of up-grading to full craft status of a number of stone and plate preparers and machine assistants. The L.T.S. Appendix provided for the transfer of apprentice 'vacancies' to other firms, with the agreement of the union, in order that the full quota might be taken up.

The S.T.A. abandoned its long-established opposition to systems of payment-by-results on a group basis, and agreed to co-operate in experiments designed to test their suitability. The S.T.A. special

M*

356 THE NEW WORLD—FULL EMPLOYMENT

agreement recommended the setting up of joint committees in firms establishing productivity schemes in order to promote full and regular consultation between Management and Chapel. The S.T.A. also agreed to co-operate in method study projects.

SETTLEMENTS, 1961 AND 1962

The 1959 settlement provided that the agreement should run for three years, but that in 1961 there should be a re-consideration of the unions' claim. The negotiations began early in 1961. The unions stood strongly for the 'balance' of their 1959 claim, namely a further two hours reduction in the working week, and an additional $5\frac{1}{2}$ per cent wage increase.

Although the employers made ritual demurring noises, there was little fire and thunder, and in June the new agreement was signed.

Hours were reduced to forty-one in September 1961.

They would be reduced to forty in September 1962.

Wages were increased by $5\frac{1}{2}$ per cent as from September 1961.

As in 1959, permitted overtime limits were extended to compensate for the reduction in hours. All of the craft unions agreed to increased quotas of apprentices, or an additional block intake. Commenting on the speed with which the new agreement had been made, the Editor of the *Members' Circular* referred to the form of settlement which is 'the most satisfactory of all, namely, a voluntary settlement by negotiation'.[1]

The national agreements, as amended by the 1959 settlement, were due to run out in August 1962. Early in the year the unions began to consider their tactics. All of the ten unions involved in the original settlement favoured a collective approach, co-ordinated through the P. & K.T.F. This time the Society of Lithographic Artists (S.L.A.D.E.) decided to join. It was no simple matter to co-ordinate the various wage claims of such an assorted bunch of unions. It was also time-consuming, as the representatives had to report back to full executives or other bodies as their own claims were modified to fit the general plan.[2]

The claim presented to the employers in April was substantial—a third week's annual holiday, 25s increase in craft rates, abolition of provincial Grade 2, increased rates for apprentices, semi-skilled workers and shift workers, as well as a number of minor items.

The employers pressed for greater flexibility in the use of the labour force, including such measures as up-grading of capable non-craft workers, greater transferability between departments, and re-training of craftsmen to new skills.

[1] *Members' Circular*, 1961, p. 222.
[2] P. & K.T.F., *Annual Report*, 1961–62, p. 30.

PRODUCTIVITY BARGAINING

The negotiations followed the classical pattern; at no time was there serious consideration of another showdown; and in August 1962 the bargain was struck.

WAGES INCREASE IN BASIC RATES

1st Pay in January	Men			Women
	Craftsmen, Class 1	Class 2	Classes 3 and 4	
1963	6s	5s 6d	5s	4s 6d
1964	6s	5s 6d	5s	4s 6d
1965	3s	2s 9d	2s 6d	2s 3d

There was a staged consolidation over the three years of 21s for men (15s 9d for women) of the cost-of-living bonus, which then stood at 29s.

As a means of simplying future calculations, all wage changes, including cost-of-living consolidation, were to take place at the beginning of the year.

The cost-of-living sliding scale was, in future, to be adjusted annually, in January, using the new Index of Retail Prices (January 1962 = 100), by 1s 10d a point for men and 1s 5d per point for women.

In regard to the claim for increased annual holidays the employers agreed that the P. & K.T.F. could present a case during the three years' stabilization, and the employers would make 'an objective assessment of the position' with them.

For their part the unions agreed to review the labour supply position from time to time, and to try to find means of dealing with the situation, including adjustments in labour intake and overtime limits.

Again there were a number of separate union agreements on the more efficient use of labour. The T.A., for example, relaxed its prohibition on 'twicing'; in small firms compositors were allowed to help run machines, and machinemen to help with make-up and imposition. Compositors could henceforth be re-trained as minders, and vice versa.

SECURITY AND COMPENSATION

The 1959–62 settlements represent a major turning-point in industrial relations in the industry. Fundamentally the history of craft unions had been a long struggle to control the supply of labour and to regulate working conditions, including the *use* of labour, by union rules. In these last negotiations the unions expressed their recognition that this policy was no longer viable. Union rules, instead of increasing the economic security of their members were endangering it. The pace of

358   THE NEW WORLD—FULL EMPLOYMENT

technical and industrial change rendered some rules unworkable; others were a prolific source of inter-union friction, and all were proving a growing burden to union officials.

These disadvantages, by no means all new, had been tolerated when there seemed some substantial compensating advantage in terms of work for union members. In a period of full employment, indeed of labour shortage, the reason for the rules had gone. The problem facing the unions was expressed by H. G. Bellingham, Secretary of the Society of Lithographic Artists, in these terms:

'In our search for security we have tended hitherto to confine our thoughts and activities to the internal domestic scene relying solely upon the control of intake of labour—apprentice ratios, &c.—as the main bastion of our defences. As a result of [new technical developments] we will be forced to realize that much more must be done if the foundations of lasting security and social well-being are to be laid for us and future generations.'[1]

The old methods were no longer adequate. But what was to replace them? Would co-operation with employers in improving efficiency *always* lead to greater job security? Or should the unions adopt the principle established in some other countries, and press for adequate compensation if workers were dismissed because of closures or amalgamations?

In the newspaper industry, in recent years, the problem of worker security had become particularly acute, as a number of amalgamations resulted in the closing down of scores of provincial newspapers, and a number of London dailies. After studying the position the P. & K.T.F. decided to press for redundancy compensation, on a scale of one month's pay for each year of service. The N.P.A., however, was not prepared to agree to this, and several Court cases threw doubt on the legality of compensation payments which were not explicit in the terms of contract.

Failing to obtain satisfaction on compensation, the P. & K.T.F. pressed for recognition of the unions' right to early notification when a newspaper was in difficulties, and proposed the following procedures:

If a newspaper is facing difficulties which might lead to closure, the management should ask to meet the union general secretaries to talk over the situation fully and frankly before any decision is taken.

Even when a decision has been taken by a management to close a newspaper, there should be consultation with the general secretaries of

[1] S.L.A.D.E., *Annual Report*, 1963, p. 6.

PRODUCTIVITY BARGAINING

the unions before the closure takes place and before any public announcement is made.[1]

The Chairman of the N.P.A. said that the Association would recommend to its members that there should be consultation with the unions at two stages: first when the paper began to decline, and second when a firm decision to close down had been made. For the unions W. A. Morrison said that was as far as they could expect the employers to go; the success of the recommendation would depend on the spirit in which it was interpreted.

Early in 1963 the P. & K.T.F., following up suggestions made by the Royal Commission, arranged to meet the N.P.A. to discuss Negotiating Machinery, Redundancy and Compensation, and Pensions.

On the first point the unions did not wish to make any variation in existing practice; each union would retain autonomy. While the unions were formulating detailed proposals on the other topics the N.P.A. had also been busy, and published a memorandum 'Efficiency of Production', in which it argued that existing staffing arrangements needed careful scrutiny, perhaps by a firm of professional consultants. Broadly the objective would be 'realistic' staffing, with reduction in casual labour and a simplified wage structure. In return, schemes for redundancy pay, pensions and sick benefits could be worked out.

The P. & K.T.F. circulated copies of the N.P.A. Memorandum to the unions for their comment. The need for some policy in regard to pension plans was made evident by two incidents reported by the unions. The management of *The Scotsman* had decided that membership of the firm's pension fund should be a condition of employment; the *Daily Mirror* group was introducing a pension scheme with a condition of compulsory retirement at sixty-five. The P. & K.T.F. decided to ask for union views on firms insisting:

(1) on membership of a pension scheme being a condition of employment;

(2) on a medical examination for applicants for employment;

(3) on compulsory retirement at sixty-five.

The union replies showed a wide variety of practices in newspaper offices. In general the unions opposed medical examinations, compulsory retirement, and compulsory membership of House pensions schemes.

The unions agreed that the P. & K.T.F. should approach the N.P.A. to try to arrange an industrial pension scheme with transferable rights.

[1] P. & K.T.F., *Annual Report*, 1960–61, p. 12.

360   THE NEW WORLD—FULL EMPLOYMENT

Realists, they recognized that they would have to give something in return by way of increases in productivity. Here, however, was a procedural difficulty. The agreements on wages and staffing were basically union agreements, but in nearly all cases there were also special Chapel agreements which gave much more favourable terms to the workers. How could these be standardized, or modified in a uniform way, if each union conducted separate negotiations? And how would the Chapels react?

On almost every concrete issue the unions were divided. Early in October 1963 the N.P.A., in reply to a notification by the P. & K.T.F. that an independent inquiry under the aegis of the P. & K.T.F. would not be possible (because of some unions' opposition to the use of industrial consultants) said that it had decided to issue a press statement regretting that after eight months, the unions had made so little progress. Further efforts to bring the unions to agreement failed.

At the Administrative Council of the P. & K.T.F. in May 1964, the President, J. M. Bonfield, asked bluntly:

'Are we taking the necessary steps to adapt our thinking, our attitudes, and our policies to entirely new problems? For there can be no doubt that the situation we are facing is a revolutionary one.

'I don't know what answers you would give to these questions. But my impression is that we have hardly begun to think about them in any constructive or positive way. . . . As for the employers, they may well feel frustrated sometimes by our lack of policy and direction, but they must take great comfort from the thought of its long-term consequences.'[1]

[1] P. & K.T.F., *Annual Report*, 1963–64, p. 50.

CHAPTER XXII

EPILOGUE

*Fundamentally, I suggest, we all whether we are
conscious of it or not, ask for three things from our
labours: a decent livelihood (of one standard or another);
some kind of security for our dependents if anything
befalls us; and security for our old age. Given these three
things most of us will do our job for its own sake. It is not
greed but fear that is the cause of man's inhumanity to
man.*

F. BISSET, Secretary of F.M.P., *Members' Circular,*
1933, p. 275.

THE PAST

In a fundamental sense there is no conclusion to be drawn from the
study of history, for history is never concluded, and the pattern of
future development can never be predicted with much certainty.
Nevertheless the 'inexorable exigencies of historical antithesis' (to use
Tawney's memorable phrase) should not be allowed to permit the unchallenged acceptance of the attractive paradox that the only thing to be
learnt from history is that men learn nothing from history. For this
study has revealed —at least to me—that some men *do* learn from history
not perhaps as quickly as a strong believer in the rationality of *homo
sapiens* might wish, but slowly, uncertainly, and with many a false
deduction from the mass of cloudy premises with which they are
confronted.

In regard to the search for security it is tempting to say briefly, 'Plus
ça change, plus c'est la même chose'. From the earliest times there is
the recurrent theme of insufficient jobs. The heartfelt plea of the 'poore
prynters' in 1577, 'That they maie have worke', has echoed down the
centuries, its underlying poignancy muffled at times by the confusion
and circumlocution with which it was expressed. But the workman
who composed that phrase would surely have endorsed the sentiments
of his successor three hundred years later who wrote:

362 THE NEW WORLD—FULL EMPLOYMENT

'To live by his own industry is every man's birthright, and whoever attempts to curtail that right is a traitor to the community.'

Thus from the earliest records we find that the obligation to help a comrade to find work, or to give him relief when he was unemployed, was generally recognized. The early craft gilds and the Stationers' Company both had such provisions written into their constitutions. The obligation extended, at least in theory, to both master and man, particularly in that period when the social cleavage between them was not acute, and the small scale of production resulted in close personal contact. But in the late eighteenth century, when the masters emancipated themselves from this responsibility, the workmen began that long series of experiments in autonomous organizations which aimed at reducing unemployment and relieving the unemployed. The first trade societies were often uncertain as to which of these should be their primary aim, and many plumped strongly for the charitable function. Indeed some were driven almost against their own inclination to engage in collective bargaining, particularly during the rise of the cost-of-living during the Napoleonic Wars.

In the nineteenth century they recognized that the relief of the unemployed was a strategic necessity, in their struggles with employers, if the union rules were not to be continually sabotaged by unemployed men desperate to obtain work, under almost any conditions, to provide for their families.

It is only against this background of the continuous struggle with the problem of unemployment that the efforts of the journeymen to regulate terms of employment begin to make sense. This point needs to be emphasized, for a generation has grown up since the Second World War, under conditions of almost continuous full employment, and they will find it, naturally enough, difficult to understand much of the tradition of trade unionism unless they realize the conditions under which union rules or collective agreements were determined in pre-War years.

Broadly the trade unions attempted to improve the standards of their members by imposing a set of rules to be observed by masters and men. Critics of trade unions, particularly those obsessed with the elegant and unrealistic theory of perfect competition, invariably tend to regard most, if not all, such 'restrictive' rules as detrimental to the optimum distribution of resources.

This was not the view usually taken by a large section of the employers. Indeed many employers, and usually the largest and most efficient, were only too pleased to co-operate in any plan which brought some degree of certainty and stability into the industry. Although the

EPILOGUE 363

master printers opposed the introduction of each new rule which extended the field of union control, once adjustment to the new conditions had been made, many masters stood to lose from a return to the anarchy prevailing before its introduction. Indeed few masters, at least by the end of the nineteenth century, believed in 'free competition'. They were, however, staunch upholders of 'fair competition'. By this they meant competition on the basis of overall efficiency, with all competitors paying equal wage rates and observing similar conditions in regard to hours of work, manning of machines, and other matters affecting costs.

Now in regard to 'fair competition' the masters were greatly assisted by the general union policy of standardizing an increasing range of labour cost elements, for this helped to reduce the element of 'unfair' competition from firms which continually tried to cut prices by such means as whittling down the rates, operating machines at dangerous speeds, 'economizing' on safety devices and workers' amenities. And while such methods might not pay in the long run, for the best workers would drift away from such firms to those where conditions were better, in the short run they might be very profitable indeed, especially in an industry where most contracts were obtained by tender. And in the long run, as Keynes observed, we are all dead.

Other critics, while admitting that some trade union rules, especially those regulating wage rates or hours or work, are justified, make a distinction between such rules, and others which are categorically condemned as 'restrictive'. It seems, however, almost impossible to state the criteria by which these 'restrictive' rules are to be separated from the others.[1] All rules are in some sense restrictive to somebody. During the twentieth century the master printers, by collective bargaining with the unions, came to agree to observe an ever-increasing range of rules. The interesting feature of this process is that, once they had come to the point of recognizing the existence of the unions, and of their right (and power) to enforce these rules, the masters were often very keen to see them extended.

The unions defended the rules by arguments based on the need to protect the health, comfort, or efficiency of the worker; in many cases they obtained the impartial support of experts in the field of industrial medicine and hygiene. But it was the experience of the munitions factories during the Great War which showed incontrovertibly that increased productivity could be obtained by shortening the work periods and providing reasonable amenities. Indeed if a decrease in

[1] For instance, in 1936, when Hilton and others published their study of 'restrictive' rules, *Are Trade Unions Obstructive?* they excluded high wages, but did not say why.

M**

364 THE NEW WORLD—FULL EMPLOYMENT

productivity is the main criterion for selection of 'restrictive' rules, very few rules would qualify, *if the workers' health and efficiency in the long run is to be taken into account,* and not merely his output over a short period.

The loss of productivity in the long run through the premature exhaustion of the workers by severe strain on high-speed machines, by the increase of accidents due to fatigue, by the decline in general health from working in ill-ventilated offices, and eating and drinking in un-sanitary workrooms, can never be estimated. But until such costs are known it is patently absurd to condemn out of hand any rule which leads to an immediate reduction of productivity. Nevertheless many of the printers' rules were 'restrictive' in particular situations. This is inevitable from the nature of a general rule; it will have application to a number of situations, on the margin or periphery, where it may be in-convenient to the employer, and indeed an embarrassment to the union. The printers, with their extremely democratic union structure, always debated such matters at length before making a decision, and one factor which they took into account was the probable impact of the new rule on public opinion, and on the 'friendly' employers. Often there was a vocal minority in the union which opposed the rule. Yet, once it had been passed, what was the union to do in the cases where its application would bring hardship? If it made a few exceptions it would be deluged with applications from other masters claiming exemption too. The union had to decide, in the light of experience, by weighing the advantages obtained in some shops against the disadvantages accruing in others, whether on balance the rule was good or bad. The ethical standards of the workers and the unions were no doubt, in many cases very different from those of the employers. The important point to make clear is that the judgements were often ethical, and not merely economic, in the narrow sense of the term. And it would be a bold man who would maintain today that in the matter of the ethical bases of their behaviour, the trade unions were inferior to the employers of the past.

THE FUTURE

The 1959–62 settlements accomplished the third major development in the industry since the end of the Second World War. The sequence of these developments seems in retrospect to have a certain logic, but there is little published documentary evidence to support the hypothesis of a planned campaign by either side. Yet if in 1945 someone had set down, for the employers, the objectives they should try to achieve in the next two decades, and had listed them as a Wage Structure, Revision of

EPILOGUE

Union Rules on Labour Intake, and Revision of Union Rules on Labour Utilization, many would have dismissed the idea as Utopian.

These rules, as this study has shown, were basically concerned with the security of the craftsman. Some rules enhanced craft security at the expense of the employer, and perhaps ultimately at the expense of the consumer, others protected the craftsman by denying work or promotion to non-craftsmen and women. Once the latter were effectively organized their efforts to increase their own security and improve their status brought them increasingly into conflict with the older unions. This conflict began before the Great War, but it was moderated in the inter-war period by the weakened financial position of the non-craft unions, the overall weakening of union bargaining power, and the general realization of the need for a united front.

But after the Second World War full employment, buoyant finances and steady growth of union membership brought a resurgence of independence, and a sharpening of inter-union conflict. What should union policy be in a period of prolonged labour shortage? On a strictly economic interpretation of union behaviour the correct policy was to press for wage increases to raise the price of labour and bring supply and demand into 'balance'. This was the justification of the 'militant' policy of the L.S.C. in 1950 and 1956. On the whole, however, the unions found it much more difficult than they had anticipated to take advantage of the favourable labour market. Just as in the 1930–32 Depression the employers had been unable to obtain wage reductions, so in post-war years the unions were handicapped by a variety of institutional arrangements and associations—government policy, T.U.C. policy, P. & K.T.F. constitution, membership of the J.I.C., and procedural rules in collective agreements. Furthermore, there were divisions of interest and disagreement on priorities not only from one union to another, but among various groups within each union. Thus, although in 1950 a majority of union members approved of the cost-of-living sliding scale of 1s per point, which seemed to be *of general advantage*, five years later there was considerable disagreement over it. The addition of a substantial flat rate bonus had, in effect, eroded craft and London differentials, and seriously disturbed the premium for shift and overtime working. The resolution of internal union interests, especially in a large heterogeneous union such as the Paperworkers, was a feat in itself. To resolve the different inter-union interests seemed impossible. The two-tier idea, favoured by the Courts of Inquiry, was basically unsound and, had the unions perisisted in it, might well have wrecked the P. & K.T.F. and the J.I.C.

Nevertheless, the fact that the giant Paperworkers union could operate successfully threw into sharp contrast the niggling attitude of

366 THE NEW WORLD—FULL EMPLOYMENT

the craft unions. And, whereas in times of slow technical and economic change they could work out their respective spheres of influence in comparative leisure, a period of swifter change threw them into confusion. The introduction of the smaller lithographic machines blurred the distinction between the plate maker and the printer; the development of web-offset and photo-composing blurred the clear division between letterpress and lithography. Demarcation agreements were made but they were often arbitrary, difficult to enforce, and sometimes as much of a nuisance to the unions as they were an irritant to employers.

'Trade Agreement and negotiating commitments with Employers' Federations and kindred unions on matters relating to demarcation issues and the daily application of Society rules and usages are beginning to really test to the limit the Society's administrative structure which, whilst adequate to meet the demands of former years, is beginning to creak at the present moment.'[1]

After a decade of full employment, however, some at least of the union leaders began to question the major premise on which traditional security policy was based, namely, a chronic and persistent shortage of work. R. Willis, secretary of the L.S.C. was the first to accept the change, and to work out the consequences. If his union's apprentice quota was no longer needed (at least in its present form) why not try to cash it in? Furthermore, it might well prove to be a wasting asset, for if the labour shortage continued, printing would be forced away from London.

The Courts of Inquiry, in 1950 and 1956, were most reluctant to face this proposition openly, and their recommendations were hopelessly confused. The employers, however, were more realistic, and the 1950 and 1956 settlements were in essence a wage increase in exchange for all round increase in labour supply, either by block intake or relaxation of quotas.

By 1959, after nearly two decades of full employment, more of the unions were aware that their traditional rules on use of labour were also of less immediate value, and in the long run, by raising costs and lowering productivity, might be endangering the security of British workers. The employers wanted them removed—well, what would they offer? It seems that this conception of the nature of the 1959 bargaining strategy gradually became clear as the unions realized that they would not be granted anything on the basis of past achievement.

The fact that relaxation of apprentice rules in 1950 and 1956 had not proved harmful to union interests was conducive to a favourable

[1] S.L.A.D.E., *Annual Report*, 1960, p. 6.

EPILOGUE 367

consideration being given to relaxation of other rules. In one decade then the unions developed, almost unwittingly, a completely new attitude to their traditional rules. No longer sacrosanct and inviolable 'principles', they became objects of commerce, to be put on the bargaining table and assessed in terms of cash.

Were the unions squandering their inheritance? Or were they making an intelligent assessment of present, as against future values, and deciding to sell out before the market collapsed? The concept of a 'sale' is really inappropriate. The unions have not lost title to these rules, and if economic conditions changed, the old rules (or others) would be swiftly imposed. In point of fact, for most of their history, few unions had been able to enforce their rules absolutely; the policy of the Executive had usually to be tempered to the wind of economic conditions. Prolonged full employment, and increased union bargaining power, had simply changed the basic conditions. Instead of the unions having to expend money to uphold the rules, employers were prepared to expend money to have them relaxed.

The long-term consequences of this development on union strategy, structure and function must be of fundamental importance.[1]

The breakdown of 'horizontal' demarcation frontiers will facilitate the amalgamation of craft unions hitherto entrenched behind these frontiers. Here it is significant that in 1955 the London craft unions of compositors and machine-minders amalgamated to form the London Typographical Society, and that in 1964 the new L.T.S. amalgamated with the T.A. to form the National Graphical Association—just over one century after the first National Typographical Association collapsed. In 1962 the Monotype Casters' and Typefounders' Trade Society was amalgamated with the Paperworkers' Union. During 1964 the Stereotypers discussed amalgamation with Natsopa, and the Lithographic printers considered joining in with the new N.G.A.

What effect will the new changes in techniques and organization have on the 'vertical' demarcation between craft and non-craft? This distinction has already grown increasingly artificial; it will crumble more quickly as arrangements for up-grading of semi-skilled men, shortening of apprenticeship, and intake of adult apprentices continue to operate. Again the 'aristocratic' Society of Lithographic Artists provides an apt example. In 1954 the Society formed an Auxiliary Section to permit it to enrol the operators of small Lithographic printing machines, and thus 'control this development, but at the same time avoid diluting the established Litho. trade'. Eight years later, however, the National Organizer reported that the policy had not succeeded,

[1] For a discussion of this in another context, see Allan Flanders, *The Fawley Productivity Agreements*, 1964, especially chs. V and VI.

368 THE NEW WORLD—FULL EMPLOYMENT

and that the majority of Auxiliary members were engaged on full Litho. work.

'It may be asked how it was that Auxiliaries were allowed to progress on to full Litho. work, but by establishing them on a basis of *no up-grading* to *full craft status*, we had perhaps introduced a Trojan horse into our policy. All workers naturally seek to improve their ability and status, and perhaps we were imposing an unnatural burden upon them.'[1]

On this analysis, the 'logic of events' of productivity bargaining must lead to a decline in 'craft consciousness' and will eventually sound the death knell of craft unionism.

What of apprenticeship—for centuries considered the essential corollary of craftsmanship? In many other industries the formal apprenticeship, with its fixed term and strict indentures, has disappeared. In printing it has been maintained more by the unions' wish to use it as a limitation on entry than by the employers' concern with it as a system of training. Since the formation of the J.I.C., however, enlightened and liberal men have battled to improve the system to ensure better selection of apprentices, better practical training in the workshops, and continued theoretical training in technical schools. Against the solid phalanx of backwoods employers, to whom apprentices were primarily a source of cheap labour, the reformers made little progress. Since the Second World War, however, more has been achieved. The persistent efforts of men like Charles Batey (Printer to the University of Oxford) have resulted in the gradual extension of areas where the J.I.C. schemes are wholly or partly in operation.

Progress, however, has been painfully slow. Will the same snail's pace of adaptation be adequate in the future? It seems unlikely. If employers will not agree voluntarily to necessary changes, should compulsion be used? Compulsory general education is now accepted as a part of the social system; future exigencies may well require that continuing technical education must also be subject to greater control. This may well mean putting more emphasis on the selection of suitable employers. Certainly compulsory day-time release must come. But technical education alone will produce only an efficient operator; what will replace pride of craftsmanship when the crafts are gone? Yet if work is to be satisfying and meaningful, its social purpose as well as its techniques must be understood. Herein lies the case for a broadening of the concept of apprenticeship to include some modern equivalent of the medieval notion of training for citizenship.

To regard apprenticeship only as a means to attaining technical

[1] S.L.A.D.E. *Annual Report*, 1962, p. 18. (Italics supplied.)

EPILOGUE

efficiency is to neglect one of the great challenges of industrial civilization. Can man find an equal measure of meaning and satisfaction from the operation of machines as, under the best conditions, he obtained from his skill in the days of handiwork?[1] The old-time printers, bookbinders and papermakers were proud of the association of their trades with education, art and science. Can education, art and science now combine to develop, in the tradesmen of the future, an interest and pride in good workmanship?

The end result, however, will depend not only on changes within industry, but on changes in education, social services, and the pattern of the social structure. The short-term product may be a form of industrial union, but depending on the environment in which it operates this union may have different functions from the present day. Collective bargaining, over the past century-and-a-half has tended to grow more centralized. Given a continuance of full employment and rapid technological change, centralized collective bargaining becomes increasingly unnecessary (from the viewpoint of workers' security), and indeed an impediment to rapid adaptation. The future trend will be towards decentralization. Indeed this is already happening in sections of the industry, with the proliferation of House and Chapel agreements, but it has not generally been formally recognized.[2] Changes in the pattern of bargaining will require appropriate adjustments to union structure, and the re-allocation of levels of authority.

At the same time, however, there will be greater need for officials at the top level to have time and facilities for keeping abreast of technical, economic, educational, social and political changes, not only in this country, but also abroad, especially in countries which may be markets or competitors. The F.M.P. has shown an awareness of this, and in recent years sent teams of observers to many continental countries to study techniques, organization and industrial relations. Trade unions, generally, lag behind in this respect. The officials are overburdened with administration and the research staff are virtually non-existent. But successful adaptation to change is surely facilitated by fore-knowledge, and by knowledge of the methods tried in other countries.

Obviously a great deal depends upon the general social provisions for security. The more generous the arrangements for unemployment

---

[1] See, for example, George Bourne, *The Wheelwright's Shop*, and *Change in the Village*; and W. Kiddier, *The Old Trade Unions*, 1930.

[2] Except by the Society of Lithographic Artists, which, for a period in 1960–61, deliberately gave up bargaining at the national level in favour of Chapel bargaining. It later reverted to national bargaining. *Annual Report*, 1960, p. 9; 1961, p. 22.

370 THE NEW WORLD—FULL EMPLOYMENT

benefit, and old age pensions, the better the arrangements for re-housing and re-training workers made redundant by technical change, the less opposition there will be to schemes for more effective use of labour. In the nineteenth century the craft unions built up their own extensive social services to members; in the twentieth century many of these have become of declining importance, and several unions have terminated their superannuation schemes. So far, however, the State has made slow progress in making adequate provision for unemployed or retired workers, and the rise in the cost-of-living has constantly eroded the real value of social service payments. The employers' organizations have shown marked reluctance to make a determined effort to provide a greater measure of security. For thirty years, on and off, they have been talking about an industry Pension Plan, to no avail. The idea is fraught with difficulties, one of which is the growing number of House pension schemes instituted by individual firms. These, of course, do not carry transferable rights, and tend to bind the workers to the firm. An extension of House pension plans, or other non-wage benefits,[1] will inevitably affect the relative hold of the trade union and the firm on the loyalty of the workers. It is not that these employers deliberately set out on a long-term policy of subverting the union. On the contrary, it is usually the firms with the friendliest relations with the unions which go in for fringe benefits. Management wants security, too, and in times of labour shortage, generous welfare schemes may help to reduce turnover, so long as the firm keeps one step ahead of the Jones's.

Taking a very long term view, the major question perhaps is: will there be a need for trade unions at all? For the foreseeable future the answer is surely in the affirmative. But it is no less certain that in response to changes in technology and social organization the unions will have to adapt themselves—their structure and strategy—more swiftly than they have in the past, if they are to play an effective part in protecting the workers' security and raising their status.

One general factor which was influential in determining the history of industrial relations was the tradition of 'independence' manifested by both sides. Partly this was due to the sheltered nature of the industry, which resulted in a measure of continued (relative) prosperity; partly it derived from an unfortunate experience of outside arbitration; to some extent it was a reflection of the printers' proud boast that their ranks contained enough men of talent and ability to allow them to solve their own problems. To attempt any sort of quantitative evaluation of this factor would be foolish; on the other hand to ignore it would be to deny what leaders on both sides have continually reiterated. On both

[1] The term 'fringe benefits' is already in some instances a mis-nomer, for the non-wage benefits approach in value the wage itself.

EPILOGUE 371

sides there developed a pride in the discipline, moderation, lack of violence and ability to compromise—characteristics which are, in fact as well as in myth, part of the British tradition of political and industrial development.

Whether those characteristics will continue to carry the printing industry—or the British nation—forward to meet the urgent social and international problems of the future it is not for the historians to say.

GLOSSARY

Chapel (since seventeenth century): Organization of journeymen and apprentices in a printing house. Later incorporated in structure of trade unions.

Clicker: head of a companionship, *q.v.*

Closed House: one in which union members were forbidden to work.

Companionship ('ship): a group of men (usually compositors) working together, paid by the piece, and organized by a clicker.

Establishment: see 'stab'.

Fat: straightforward matter on which a man on piece-work could earn good wages.

Father of Chapel: head man of chapel; later, a shop steward. (Also Mother of Chapel.)

Lean: difficult work on which a man on piece rates could not earn high wages.

Mixed House (or Office):
    (1) Paying both by time and piece,
    (2) Employing both union and non-union men,
    (3) Combined news and jobbing office.

Open House: both union and non-union men employed.

Slating: waiting for copy to set. Originally each man wrote his name on a slate when he ran out of copy; new copy was given out in order of the names on the slate.

Smooting: practice of taking part-time job in another office.

Society House (=union house): one in which only society or union men were employed.

Stab (to be on stab): to be paid time rates, usually weekly.

Standing Time: time spent by piece hands waiting for copy.

SELECT BIBLIOGRAPHY

STATIONERS' COMPANY

1. E. Arber, *Transcript of the Registers of the Company of Stationers.*
2. Greg and Boswell, *Records of the Court of the Stationers' Company, 1576–1602,* 1930.
3. *A Sketch of the History and Privilege of the Company,* 1871.
4. C. R. Rivington, *A Short Account of the Worshipful Company of Stationers,* 1903.

TRADE UNION HISTORIES

1. E. Howe and H. E. Waite, *The London Society of Compositors, a Centenary History,* 1948.
2. E. Howe and J. Child, *The Society of London Bookbinders,* 1951.
3. A. E. Musson, *The Typographical Association,* 1954.
4. S. C. Gillespie, *A Hundred Years of Progress, The Records of the Scottish Typographical Association,* 1953.
5. C. J. Bundock, *The National Union of Printing, Bookbinding and Paper Workers,* 1959.
6. R. B. Suthers, *The Story of Natsopa,* 1930.
7. James Moran, *Seventy-five Years of the National Society of Operative Printers and Assistants,* 1964.
8. *The History and Progress of the Amalgamated Society of Lithographic Printers, 1880–1930,* 1930.
9. Monotype Casters' and Typefounders' Society, Diamond Jubilee, 1889–1949. *Sixtieth Annual Report,* 1949.
10. S.T.A., *A Fifty Years' Record, 1853–1903,* 1903.
11. L.S.C., *A Brief Record of Events . . .,* 1899.
12. Leeds Typographical Society, *Centenary Souvenir, 1810–1910,* Leeds, 1910.
13. Cork Typographical Society, *Centenary, 1806–1906.*
14. Manchester Typographical Society, *Centenary, 1797–1897.*

PRINTING AND KINDRED TRADES FEDERATION

1. J. F[letcher], *Our Fifty A.C's.* n.d.
2. *Sixty Years of Service 1901–61,* 1961.

THE BRITISH FEDERATION OF MASTER PRINTERS

1. M. Sessions, *The Federation of Master Printers, How it Began,* 1950.
2. E. Howe, *The British Federation of Master Printers, 1900–1950,* 1950.

374 BIBLIOGRAPHY

UNION JOURNALS

1. *Compositors' Chronicle*, 1840–43.
2. *The Printer*, 1843–45.
3. *Typographical Gazette*, 1846–47.
4. *Typographical Protection Circular*, 1849–53.
5. *Typographical Circular*, 1852——.
6. *London Press Journal*, 1858–59.
7. *Bookbinders' Trade Circular*, 1850–77.
8. *Scottish Typographical Journal*, 1861–1908.
9. *Scottish Typographical Circular*, 1908——.
10. *London Typographical Journal*, 1906——.
11. *Natsopa Journal*, 1917——.
12. *Paperworker*, 1940——.
13. *Printing Federation Bulletin*, 1923–58.

See also the numerous Reports of Executives, Delegate Meetings, and of Special Committees set up to study particular problems.

EMPLOYERS' JOURNALS

1. *Master Printers' Circular*, 1897–1902.
2. *Members Circular*, 1902——.
3. *Linotype Users' Association, Monthly Circular*, 1897–1904.
4. *Linotype Notes*, 1898–1908.
5. *Master Printers Annual*, 1921——.

MISCELLANEOUS

1. J. Hilton (ed.), *Are Trade Unions Obstructive*, 1935.
2. P.E.P., *The British Press*, 1938.
3. F. Zweig, *Productivity and Trade Unions*, 1951.
4. V. M. Cornfield, *The Effect of the Industrial Revolution on Workers in the Printing Trades.*
5. National Association for the Promotion of Social Science, *Report of the Committee on Trade Societies*, 1860.
6. T. J. Dunning, *Trades' Unions and Strikes, their Philosophy and Intention*, 1860.
7. E. Edwards, *The Apprentice System, the Disease and the Remedy*, 1851.
8. A. Wainhouse, *Trades' Unions Justified . . . with Hints to Operative Printers*, 1861.
9. E. Howe, *The London Compositor*, 1947.
10. J. R. MacDonald (ed.), *Women in the Printing Trades*, 1904.

BIBLIOGRAPHY

JOINT INDUSTRIAL COUNCIL

1. Minutes of Quarterly Meetings. These are reprinted in B.F.M.P. *Members Circular.*
2. *Reports* on Recruitment and Training for the Industry 1945, Workshop Training of Apprentices 1957, Scheme for Selection and Training of Apprentices, 1957.
3. C. Batey, *Craftsmanship in the Printing Industry*, 1960.
4. *Report on Productivity Conference*, 1952.

HISTORY OF PRINTING

The following histories contain some information regarding management, customs, wages, chapel rules and such matters.
1. E. G. Duff, *The Printers, Stationers and Bookbinders of London and Westminster from 1476 to 1535*, 1906.
2. G. H. Putnam, *Books and Their Makers*, 1897.
3. J. Moxon, *Mechanick Exercises*, Vol. II, 1682.
4. P. Luckome, *Concise History of the Origin and Progress of Printing*, 1770.
5. C. Stower, *The Printer's Grammar*, 1808.
6. J. Johnson, *Typographia*, 1824.
7. W. Savage, *Dictionary of the Art of Printing*, 1841.
8. C. Knight, *The Old Printer and the Modern Press*, 1834.
9. J. Southward, *Practical Printing*, 1882.
10. G. Isaacs, *The History of the Newspaper Printing Press*, 1931.

OFFICIAL PUBLICATIONS

1. Select Committee on Artisans and Machinery, *Second Report*, 1824.
2. Select Committee on Combinations of Workmen, *Second Report*, 1838.
3. Royal Commission on Rules and Organization of Trade Unions, 1867, *Reports.*
4. Royal Commission on Labour, 1893, *Reports.*
5. Board of Trade, *Report on Profit-Sharing*, 1894, *Gain Sharing*, 1895.
6. Board of Trade, *Reports on Changes in Wages and Hours of Labour*, 1894——.
7. Board of Trade, *Reports on Trade Unions*, 1887——.
8. Board of Trade, *Reports* on Standard Time Rates and Standard Piece Rates.
9. *Report on Collective Agreements*, 1910.
10. Industrial Council, *Report on the Enforcement of Industrial Agreements*, 1913.
11. Royal Commission on the Press, *Report*, 1949.
12. Royal Commission on the Press, *Report*, 1962.

See also the *Reports* of the various Courts of Inquiry into printing industry disputes.

INDEX

A.A.P. (Amalgamated Association of Pressmen), 126
Accident compensation, 74, 191
A.C.P. (Association of Correctors of the Press), 338, 339
Advertisement duty, 32, 107
Advertising, 248
Agreements, National, *see* National Agreements
Alien workmen, 17, 21, 49
Allan, Mr, 127
Amalgamated Engineering Union, 335
Amalgamated Society of Carpenters, 127
Amalgamated Society of Lithographic Printers, 120, 134, 209, 227, 243, 249–50, 273, 313, 314, 319, 323, 324, 327–9, 337, 339, 340, 344, 355
Amalgamated Society of Papermakers, 188–9
Amalgamated Typefounders' Trade Society, 181
Amalgamation: of newspapers, 247–8, 358–9; of unions, 193–4, 229–30, 239–40, 246–8, 273, 367
Anglo-American Council on Productivity, 327
Apprentice System, the Disease and the Remedy, The, 132–3
Appeal to Parents and Guardians, 68
Applegath, Mr, 127
Apprentices, 17, 21, 22, 27–31, 34–5, 36, 39–42, 48, 51, 64–70, 77, 79, 163, 173, 179, 217, 242, 244, 260, 286–7, 313, 318, 346, 354, 367, 368; quota, 79, 80, 83–91, 95, 96–8, 114–15, 122–3, 132–6, 139, 142–3, 206, 278, 281, 298, 322, 323, 337–9, 354, 356, 366; and dilution of labour, 221, 320; wages, 290–1, 296, 298–9, 303, 356. *See also* under J.I.C.
Apprentices, Statute of (1563), 54, 64, 66–8
A.S.L.P., *see* Amalgamated Society of Lithographic Printers

Assistance, to leave trade, 132
Assistants, 185, 186, 191, 193, 226, 270, 271, 328–9, 336, 344
Autoplate, invention of, 158

Backhouse, John, 79
Bailey, Sir Roland, 238
Barbers, 18
Barker, Christopher, 20, 23
Batey, Charles, 368
Bellingham, H. G., 358
Benefits: dispute, 330 *et passim;* funeral, 117, 118, 120, 188, 191; fringe, 370; out-of-work, 74–5, 82, 103, 117, 125–7, 172, 188, 191, 287; sick, 26–7, 117, 120, 191, 359; sliding scale, 119; travelling, 120; *see also* various
'Benefit societies', 50, 76
Besant, Annie, 185
Bible, production of, 83, 94, 109–10
Bills in Parliament, 197, 200
Briginshaw, R. W., 328, 347
Birmingham, 115, 196, 199
Birkett, Lord, 348–9
'Blacklegs', 147
Black lists, 146
B.M.R.C.U., *see* Bookbinders and Machine Rulers' Consolidated Union
Board of Trade, 213, 220
Bonfield, J. M., 360
Bonus systems, 140, 168, 169, 170, 173, 318
Bookbinders' and Machine Rulers' Consolidated Union, 119–20, 147
Bookbinders and Machine Rulers, National Union of (N.U.B.M.R.), *see* National Union of Bookbinders and Machine Rulers
Bookbinders' Branch, London, *see* London Bookbinders' Branch
Bookbinders' Consolidated Relief Fund, 84, 99
Bookbinders' Consolidated Union, 85, 97–8, 114, 135, 190, 212
Bookbinders, early, 44, 72–3

INDEX

377

Bookbinders', London Consolidated Society of, *see* London Consolidated Society of Bookbinders

Bookbinders, Master, 48–9, 54, 62–3, 65, 71–3, 83, 84, 97, 112

Bookbinders', National Union of, *see* National Union of Bookbinders

Bookbinders' Societies, London, *see under* London

Bookbinders, women, 62, 65, 109–10, 190, 217, 222, 226, 269

Bookbinding, craft of, 16, 20, 21, 47, 71; expansion in, 72, 119; numbers employed in, 107; demarcation problem, 217

Booksellers, 18, 22, 47, 49, 55, 68–9

Booksellers of London and Westminster, To The, 69

Book Trade Employers' Federation, 264

Bookwork Scale, 179

Bowerman, C. W., 177

Bowley cost-of-living index, 210. *See also* Cost-of-living index

Box making trade, 160

Boycotts, 148, 331–2

Bradford, 199

Bradford Observer, The, 156

Bradford Times, The, 166

Brake hand, 111, 162

Branch, the 143–6, 150 *et passim*

Bristol, 161, 332

British and Colonial Printer and Stationer, 254

British Employers' Confederation, 346

British Federation of Master Printers, 245, 298, 330; formation, 180, 199; negotiations on Monotype, 180–1; and hours of work, 197, 206–7, 210, 280–2, 301–3; and wages, 200, 219–22, 225, 226, 233, 247, 270–2, 274, 275–7, 290, 293–6, 298, 301–3; organization, 201, 228, 247, 289–90, 304–5; and apprentices, 206, 261; and negotiations, 213; and costing, 219, 281, 294; and municipal printing schemes, 239; and clerical workers, 242; and General Strike, 249–50; and J.I.C., 256; and Depression, 279–80; and wages structure, 311, 313–17, 319–21, 323;

and machine manning, 332–3; and manpower bargaining, 336–8; and productivity, 300, 346, 347, 349, 350–1; and method study, 353–56, 369

British Gazette, 248–9

British Industries, Federation of, 314

British Printing Ink Manufacturers, Society of, *see under* Society

Broadsides, 21

Burnham, Lord, 333

Call Book, the 127–9

Call money, 227

Carpenters, Societies of, 127

Carr, Lascelles, 201

Carrier-away, 111, 162

Casual labour, 141–2, 146, 150, 186, 284, 359

Caxton Magazine, 254

Caxton, William, 20

'Certification', 82

Chapel, the 26, 35–9, 55, 58, 89–91, 143–4, 150, 196–7

'Character notes', 49

Chartism, 88–9

Chief Industrial Commissioner, 301, 347–8

City, the 18, 25

'City Brothers, The', Lodge, 53

City Council, 17–18, 28

'City, The', 119

Clerical workers, 241–2, 353

Clicker, 42

Closing of offices, 145, 148–50, 212

Cloth binding, 109, 111, 119

Clowes, William and Sons, 160

'Cock-robin' shops, 48, 133

Combination Acts, 50, 53, 59, 63, 64, 69, 74, 76, 96

Combinations, 49–50

Commonwealth, 24, 29

Communist Party, 235–7

Companionship (of compositors), 42–

Composing machines, *see* various

Composition, craft of, 20, 25, 37, 109, 110, 165

Compositors' Chronicle, 76, 89, 90, 95, 101, 102

Compositors, hand, 20, 47, 167, 173, 208; wages, 25, 42–44, 48, 70–3; hours, 44, 166–8, 208–9; Chapel,

378 INDEX

37; companionship, 42–4. *See also* Compositors' Unions

Compositors, news, Societies of, 51, 55, 73, 74–6, 118, 174–7, 179

Compositors' Scale of Prices, 43, 51, 63, 70. *See also* London Scale

Compositors' Trade Society, 51, 55, 57–8, 63–4; Apprentices, 66–70; wages, 72–3; hours, 73; other societies, 74–5, 193

Compositors, women, 95, 110–11, 117, 161, 224

Conciliation Act, 213

Consolidated Lodge, the, 119

Continent, printing prices on, 161

Control of Engagement Order (1947), 312

Cooperative bindery, idea of, 62, 95

Cooperative societies for women, 110

Cooperative Wholesale Society, 253

Cooperative workshops, 95

Copperplate, 44, 159, 163

Coppock, J.C., 261

Copyright questions, 197

Correctors of the Press, Association of, 192, 221, 336

Cost accounting reform, 199–200

Costing, standard, 254, 256, 257, 266

Cost-of-living: in First World War, 222–4; in Second World War, 285, 290, 291, 292, 293, 299; after 1945, 311, 314, 319, 362, 370; adjustments for, 322, 323; bonus, 336–7, 341 344, 357; sliding scale for, 337, 357, 365

Cost-of-living index, 210, 290, 291, 294–6, 298, 304, 336, 341

Court of Assistants, 22–7, 34–5, 41, 42

Craft Gilds, 16–18, 23, 26–7

'Craft parity', idea of, 309, 315, 316, 318, 319, 340

Cripps, Sir Stafford, 299–300

'Crown, The', public house, 50–1

Cutters, 163

Cutters' Union, 163, 186, 188, 190, 193, 194, 216, 222, 226, 230

'Cuz', 36

Daily Courant, 32

Daily Mail, 248

Daily Mirror, 359

Daily News Compositors, Society of, 118

Daily Sketch dispute, 333–4

Daily Worker, 248–9

Dayworking Bookbinders' Society (The West End), 88, 119

Deacon, 36

Dean of Westminster, 24

'Deckle', the 85–6

Demarcation rules, 143, 217–18, 229, 243, 328, 346, 354, 366, 367

Depression, the, 233, 234–6, 257, 261, 266, 271, 276, 282, 309, 365

Derby, 80, 81, 199, 261

Device of Restriction of Numbers, 135–6

Dickinson and Co., 252–3

Dilutees, 318–19, 320, 328, 337. *See also* London, dilution of

Disputes, methods of settling (Table), 214

Dockers' Strike, 184, 185

Drummond, C. J., 119

Dublin, 85, 91, 94, 199

Dumfries, 116

Dunning, T. J., 84, 89, 94, 119, 121, 122, 124–5, 138–9

Dundee, 252

Dunton, John, 40–1

Eastwood, G. G., 344

Economic Printing and Publishing Co., 175

Edinburgh, 82, 91, 98, 110, 112, 116–17, 149, 160–1, 210–11, 266; Cooperative Society, 238; Master Printers' Assoc., 199; Press and Machinemen's Society, 117

Edwards, E., 122–3, 132–3, 137–8

Electrical Trades Union, 335

Electrotypers, 226

Emigration Aid Society, 131–2

Emigration Grants, 117, 118, 120, 131–2

Engineers, 111, 127

Engravers, 245

Envelope manufacture, 111, 253

Equitable Society, 83

Evans, Alfred, 185–6, 187, 188, 191, 239–40

Factory Act, 112

Factory and Shops Act, 188

INDEX

379

Factory Inspectors, 258
Fair competition, 363
Fair List, the, 253
Faithfull, Emily, 110
Fares, payment of extra, 312
Faulkner, Mr, 49, 62
Feeders, 223–4
Finishing, 20, 44, 56, 71, 119
Fletcher, Colonel J., 277, 285, 290, 295
Fly hand, 111, 162
F.M.P., *see* Federation of Master Printers
Foremen, 108, 249
Forster, Sir John, 338
Forwarding, 20, 56, 190, 269
Franklin, Benjamin, 36
'Friendly Societies', 50–1

Gasworkers' Strike, 184
General Strike, 233, 238, 240, 241, 248–51, 257, 268, 276
General Typographical Association of Scotland, 80, 101–2
Gent, Thomas, 36
Germany, 219–21
Gifts, 58, 128
Gilboy, E. W., 44
Glasgow, 91, 116, 199, 207, 210–11, 266
Globe, The, 156, 174
Gorgon, The, 64
Goss Company, 158
Grand National Consolidated Trade Union, 76
Great Fire, The, 32, 39
Green Man, The, public house, 53
Guildford, 161
Guildhall, 18, 19, 27, 31

Halifax, 199
Hamptons dispute, 183, 202
Handbeaters, 94
Hattersley composing machine, 109, 155, 157, 166–9, 174, 182
Hazell, Walter, 199
H.M.S.O., 238–9
Hoe Company, 158
Hoe Double Octuple press, 158
Hole in the Wall, The, public house, 51
Holidays, 228, 230, 299–303, 343, 356–7. *See also* Hours

Home Counties, 161, 200, 208–9, 225
Home office, 259
Hours Agreement, National (1911), 243, 280
Hours and Holiday Agreements, 228, 230, 299, 312
Hours and Rules Dispute (1911), 216
Hours and Wages Movement (1959), 281, 343–6
Hours of work, 73, 91, 112–13, 140–1, 143, 145, 168– , 173, 175, 200, 210, 214, 238, 278, 280–1, 282, 284, 299–303, 310, 312, 343–6, 348, 356
Hours Struggle, 206–7
Householders, 24
House-of-call, 86– , 98, 128, 145
House Unions, 251–3, 256, 281
Hubbard, A. J., 327–8

Illuminators, 15
Imposition, 163, 216
Incentive schemes, 318, 338, 340
Incentive payments, 303
Index of Retail Prices, 314, 357
Industrial Council, 190, 205
Industrial Court, 273–5
Industrial dermatitis, 259
Industrial Disputes Tribunal, 332
Industrial unionism, doctrine of, 193, 239–
Ink, printing, 109, 347
Inquiry, Courts of, 302, 310, 321–2, 324–5, 333–5, 338–40, 358, 365–6
International Bookbinders' Secretariat, 220
International Labour Convention, 331
International Labour Office, 280
Interrupted Apprenticeship Scheme, 260
Ireland, Typographical Association of, 275
Irish Typographical Union, 80–1, 101–2
Isaacs, G., 185, 187, 191, 193, 242, 244, 278, 285, 290, 297, 299–302

Jackson, R. A., 338, 340, 345, 352
Jaffray, Mr., 89
J.I.C., *see* Joint Industrial Council
J.I.C. Apprenticeship Committee., 244, 259–62, 267, 352, 368

380 INDEX

J.I.C. Betterment Committee, 266–7, 305

J.I.C. Concilation Committees, 257, 262–, 267, 270, 296, 300, 313, 315, 332–3, 337, 338, 346

J.I.C. Disputes Rule, 262–6

J.I.C. Employment and Production Committee, 303, 327, 330, 354–5

J.I.C. Fair Prices Committee, 266–7, 304

J.I.C. Health Committee, 258–9, 267, 352

J.I.C. Productivity Conference, 327–30

J.I.C. Unemployment Committee, 266–7

Jobbing Chapel, the 186–7

Joint consultation principle of, 257, 326–7, 330

Joint Industrial Council, 233, 241–2, 244, 247, 250, 255–67, 365; and wage reductions, 271–3; and Second World War, 285, 289, 291, 294, 300, 303, 304; and wage structure, 310, 313, 316, 324–5; and productivity bargaining, 352–3,

Joint stock firm, the, 108

Journeymen Bookbinders' Friendly Society, 50, 54, 55; disputes, 62–3, 83–4 and apprentices, 67–8; and piecework, 72–3, 83; reorganization, 83

Journeymen Bookbinders' Lodges, 53–6, 62, 83, 84, 85, 87, 94

Journeymen's Foundry, 96

Juvenile labour, 95, 112, 156, 165–6, 184, 290–2, 296–7, 299, 302, 354

Kastenbein composing machine, 109, 155, 174

Kent papermakers' strike, 52

Kilmarnock, 116

Kneale, R., 261

Labour and National Service, Ministry of, 285, 289, 302

Labour, dilution of, 220–2, 242, 287–8, 318, 323. *See also* Dilutees

Labour government, the, 299, 314, 316

Labour, Ministry of, 260, 273, 317, 320, 332, 333–4, 335, 338

Labourers, 143, 184, 185, 217–18

Lanston Monotype Corporation, 157, 180

'Learners', 109

Leeds, 198–9, 200, 261

Leicester, 199, 238, 349–50

L'Estrange, Roger, 33–4

Libraries, 122, 269

Licensing Act (1662), 32

Lieutenant of the Tower, 24

Lightning strikes, 250

Limners, 15, 18, 19

Linotype machine, 156–, 161, 163, 164, 168, 169, 170–1, 174, 177, 182–3, 201, 203, 209

Linotype Machinery Company Ltd, 157, 169, 170, 172, 175, 176, 178

Linotype User's Association, 164, 173, 183, 201, 206, 226, 230, 246

Lions, The, 128

Lithographic Artists, Society of, *see under* Society

Lithographic Plate Preparers' Society, 243

Lithographic Printers, Amalgamated Society of, *see under* Amalgamated

Lithographic printing, 107, 159, 163; in provinces, 210–11, 319

Lithographic Stone and Zinc Preparers' Society, 120

Liverpool, 115, 225

Liverymen, 22–3, 29

Lloyd's Weekly Newspaper, 158

'Local Federation' Movement, 243–5

Lockwood, Colonel, 313

Lodges, *see* Journeymen Bookbinders

London and Provincial Society of Compositors, 193

London Bookbinders' Branch, 194, 197, 216, 236–7, 264, 270, 324

London Chamber of Commerce, 217

London Consolidated Society of Journeymen Bookbinders, 84, 87–8; and benefits, 84, 132; and apprentices, 97, 135; and tramping system, 84, 98–9, 147; and work standards, 151;

London Cooperative Society, 238

London Dispute (1950), 320–2

London General Trade Society of Compositors, 74

London Lithographic Printers, 120

INDEX

381

London Machine Managers' Society, 217

London Master Printers' Association, *see under* Master Printers

London Newspaper Proprietors' Association, 174, 183, 248, 256, 333–5, 347, 358–60

London Newspapers' Provincial Association, 289

London Pension Corporation, 108

London Printing Machine Managers' Trade Society, 133

London Scale of Prices, 71, 74–5, 89, 91, 113, 118, 137–8, 174, 176, 197

London Society of Compositors (L.S.C.), 114; formation of, 117–19; rules, 123, 144; benefits schemes, 126, 129, 130–2, 179, 192, 287; 330; disputes concerning, 112–14, 148, 156, 192, 202, 213, 263, 313, 320–2; membership of, 142, 161, 190–1, 193, 208, 229, 240–1; policy concerning machinery, 156, 174–83, 216–17; and New Unions, 185; and dilution of labour, 221; and unemployment, 237; wage policy, 272, 274, 282–3, 309, 324; and productivity, 327; and manpower bargaining, 336; policy, 365

London Society of Lithographic Music Printers, 120

London Trade Society of Compositors, 74

London Trades Council, 119, 200

London Typographical Society, 338–40, 342, 354, 355, 367

London Union of Compositors, 75–6, 81, 82, 87, 95, 98, 128

London Union of Lithographic Machine Minders, 120

London Vellum Binders, 119

Lovejoy, John, 62

Lovett, William, 89

L.S.C. J.B., *see* London Consolidated Society of Bookbinders

L.T.S., *see* London Typographical Society

L.U.A., *see* Linotype Users' Association

L.U.C., *see* London Union of Compositors

Machine managers, 108, 112–13, 162 209, 249, 274; societies, 130, 132, 133, 202, 217, 329, 333–4

Machine minders, 111, 117, 162, 190, 193, 200, 206, 207, 210, 221–3, 270, 328

Machine operators, 166– , 208–9, 217, 221, 319

Machine rulers, 135, 194

Magnet Coffee House, 88

Maidstone, 161

Maintenance allowance, 284

Manchester, 81, 160, 225, 238, 289

Manchester Guardian, The, 156, 158, 180, 251

Manpower bargaining (1956), 336–42

'Martyrdom' (1786), of bookbinders, 57, 62

Master Engravers' Association, 245

Master Printers' Association, 183, 193, 201

Master Printers' Association (London) 112–14, 133–4, 137, 174, 177, 197–8, 199, 200, 202, 222–3, 274, 311, 320–2, 338, 340

Masters of Craft Gilds, 18

Master Printers, Federation of, *see* British Federation of Master Printers

Mayor of London, 17, 18

Meal hours 143

Meckanick Exercises, 35–6

Medieval manuscripts, 15–

Membership, of unions, 146–7, 190, 229, 240–1, 289, 303–5, 365

Mercers' Company, 19

Mergenthaler Company, 157

Mergers, 248

Merit money, 284, 299, 304, 322, 323

Method study, 346, 353–6, 359

Miehle, the, 159

Mileage relief, 99, 115–16

Mileage Relief Association, 115–16

Mill companies, 58–9

Millington and Sons, 252

Mills, working conditions in, 188

Milton, The, 128

Miners' Unions, 248–9

Minority Movement, the 236–7

Modern Society, the, 187

Monasteries, 16

Monotype Casters' and Typefounders. Trade Society, 367

382 INDEX

Monotype machine, 157, 163, 164, 178–83, 202, 203
Monotype Users' Association, 164, 183, 226, 245
Morning Post, 118
Morrison, W. A., 342, 344, 351, 352, 359
Moxon, Joseph, 26, 35–9 43
M.P.A.(London), *see* Master Printers' Association
Municipal elections (1946), 302
Municipal printing works, 239
Music Engravers, Society of, *see under* Society

Napoleonic Wars, 51, 59, 71, 93, 362
National Agreements, 205–6, 226–9, 258, 263, 265, 268, 270, 276, 279, 281, 290, 297, 304–5, 309, 310, 316, 317–18, 336
National Arbitration Tribunal (N.A.T.), 291, 296, 298, 313, 314, 316, 317, 320–1, 323–4
National Association for Promoting the Social and Political Improvement of the People, 89
National Conciliation Board, 214
National Graphical Association, 367
National Holidays, *see under* Holidays
National Society of Operative Printers and Assistants, *see* Natsopa
National Typographical Association, 79, 81–3, 96, 98, 103–4, 114, 117, 129, 131, 137, 367
National Typographical Union, 194
National Unemployed Workers' Movement, 235–6
National Union of Bookbinders, 239, 255
National Union of Bookbinders and Machine Rulers (N.U.B.M.R.), 194, 209, 217, 220, 223, 224, 227, 229
National Union of Journalists, 251, 344, 347
National Union of Paper Mill Workers, 184, 187–8, 194
National Union of Printing and Paperworkers, 188–9, 194, 222, 227, 229, 230, 236, 239
Natsopa: membership, 181, 184–5, 193, 229, 240–1, 243; in provinces, 190, 212–13; and alliance Paper-

workers, 194, 230; and Hamptons dispute, 202; and overtime, 216; and wage negotiations, 222–3, 271, 273, 275–7, 293, 304; and Depression, 235–6; policy, 239; and clerical workers, 241–2, 353; and General Strike, 248; and House Unions, 251; and wage structure, 309–11, 319, 323; and productivity, 328–9, 347, 351; and Thomson dispute, 330–1; and *Daily Sketch* dispute, 333–4; and manpower bargaining, 342; and hours of work, 343–4; amalgamations, 367
Negative Spotters, 341
Nelson, Thomas and Sons, 160
Netherlands, 21
Newcastle, 199
Newcastle Chronicle, The, 156, 168
News Chronicle, 333
News of the World, 333
Newspaper firms, 64; and apprentices, 68; and wages, 73, 137, 118; disputes with L.S.C., 148
Newspaper Owner and the World, 254
Newspaper printing, 32–3, 107, 163; stamp duty, 107; machinery 111–12 *et passim*
Newspaper Proprietors' Association, 202, 225, 247, 259, 284–5, 289
Newspaper Society, 183, 201–2, 230, 242, 255, 256, 273, 284, 285, 287, 289, 301, 311, 331, 336, 338, 347, 350
Newspapers, 32–3, 107, 159, 220; provincial, 156, 174, 206, 224, 229, 230, 246, 247, 248, 256, 259
News sheets, 25
New Unions, the 184–90, 192, 194, 203 *et passim*
New York Tribune, The, 156
Non-union men, 145, 149, 151 *et passim. See also* Blacklegs, Rats
Northern Typographical Union, 77–9, 101–2, 133
Note of the State of the Company of Printers, 20, 23
N.S.E.S., 251
N.T.A., *see* National Typographical Association
N.T.U., *see* Northern Typographical Union

INDEX

383

N.U.B.M.R., *see* National Union of Bookbinders and Machine Rulers
N.U.P.B. and P.W., *see* Printing, Bookbinding and Paperworkers, National Union of
N.U.J., *see* National Union of Journalists
Nurseries, 77

Offset printing, 159, 163
Oiler, 111
Old London Society, 128
One Tun, The, public house, 53
'Open houses', 143, 145
'Open shop', 238
Operative Printers' Assistants' Society, 185
Original Society of Papermakers, 85, 86, 187
Orwin, Thomas, 24
Outram, George Ltd, 251-2
Overtime, 91, 113, 139, 141, 142, 202, 206, 207, 215-16, 221, 223, 227, 279, 281, 285, 292, 318, 338, 356-7, 365; bans on, 296, 297, 301-3, 313, 320-1, 338, 346
Overton, Dr Sybil, 259
Owen, Robert, 89
Owenite Builders' Federation, 76
Owenite Unions, 52
Oxford, 161
Oxford Compositors' Trade Society, 77

Paisley, 116
Pamphlets, 21, 25, 32
P. & K.T.F., *see* Printing and Kindred Trades' Federation
Paper, 32, 51, 107, 108, 109, 111, 162-3
Paper bag trade, 160
Paper box trade, 310
Paperfolding, 188
Papermakers, Amalgamated Society of, 188-9
Papermakers, Original Society of, *see under* Original
Papermakers' Societies, 44, 51-3, 56, 58-9, 85-6, 187
Paper Mill Workers, National Union of, *see* National Union of Paper Mill Workers

Paper Mill Workers, National Union of, National Union of Paper Mill Workers
Paperworkers' Union, *see* Printing, Bookbinding and Paperworkers, National Union of
Parliamentary Scale, 118
Pendred's list, 33
Pensions, 359, 370
Periodicals, 32-3, 68, 301
Petition, the, 58
Pioneers, The, 128
Place, Francis, 49-50, 89
Plague, the, 32
'Plan of Union for the Whole Trade in Great Britain and Ireland', 84
P.M.M.T.S., *see* Printing Machine Managers' Trade Society
Porter Labour, 95, 111, 184, 224
Prayer Book, the, 109
Pressmen, 20, 25, 37, 47, 48, 94; and apprentices, 42, 135; wages, 43-4, 71, 73
Pressmen's Friendly Society, 50-1, 58, 64, 73, 112-13, 151
Price-cutting, 49, 91, 162, 199, 220, 254, 267, 271, 304, 363
Printer, The, 81, 89
Printers' and Stationers', Warehousemen, Cutters' and Assistants' Union 186
Printers' Costs, a System of Bookkeeping, 200
Printers' Grammar, The, 43
Printers' Labourers' Union, 185
Printers, master, 20-4, 31, 33, 34-5, 48, 55, 93, 108, 112; and apprentices, 66-7, 69, 80; and Edinburgh disputes, 82, 91
Printing and Kindred Trades' Federation, 95-97, 200, 206, 207, 210, 215, 221, 228, 229, 230, 240-1, 242-5, 247, 250-1, 253, 365; and J.I.C., 256; and wages, 271-4, 276-7, 310-13, 315-16, 321, 323, 325; and reduction of costs, 278; and hours of work, 280-1, 343-4; and Second World War, 284-5, 287-93, 295-6, 298-305; and productivity, 326, 336, 340, 342, 351, 356, 357, 358-60; and D. C. Thomson Dispute, 331; and machine-manning, 332; and *Daily Sketch* dispute, 333-4;

384 INDEX

and National Daily stoppage, 334–5

Printing and Allied Trades Research Association, 259

Printing and Paper Workers, National Union of, *see under* National

Printing, Bookbinding and Paper-workers National Union of (known as Paperworkers), 240–1, 243, 365, 367; and wages, 269–73, 275, 276–7, 309–11, 319, 323, 324; and reduction of costs, 279; and Second World War, 289, 293, 304; and D. C. Thomson dispute, 331; and productivity, 342, 351

Printing Machine Managers' Trade Society (London), 202, 329, 333–4

Printing presses, 20, 22, 23, 24, 29, 34, 47, 108–9, 111, 159, 193; rotary machines, 109, 111, 155– . *See also* Various

Printing Trades Alliance, 251

Producer cooperatives, 237–8

Productivity, 300, 310, 311, 313, 315, 318, 323, 326–30, 343–60, 363–4, 36–8

Provincial Newspaper Society, 247, 248

Provincial Typographical Association, 114–16, 123, 127, 131, 133, 149, 166

Publishers' editions, 72

Pykard, Henry, 18

'Rats', 100, 102, 115, 117, 145–6, 215

Readers, 192, 206, 221, 223, 274

Reading, 161, 199

Red Lion, The, public house, 87

Redundancy bonus, 344, 358–59

Reel hand, 111, 162

Regulation, rationale of, 15', 40

Removal grants, 117, 118, 130, 179

Reply of the Journeymen Bookbinders, 94

Restrictive practices, 329, 337–38, 346, 363–4

Retail Prices, Index of, 314, 357

Retirement, 359, 370

Review, Defoe's, 32

Rolling machine, 94 *et passim*

Ross, William, 187, 188, 191

Rotary machine-minders, 111, 117 *et passim*

Rotary photogravure, 269

Rothermere, Lord, 247–8

Royal Commissions, 127, 213, 359

Saturday, working on, 187, 227, 312 *See also* Overtime

Scale of Prices, London, *see under* London

Scribes, 15

Scriveners, 15, 17, 19

Scotland, General Typographical Association of, 80, 101–2

Scotland, lithography in, 273; newspapers in, 251–2

Scotsman, The, 116, 359

Scottish Alliance, 207–8, 273, 304, 311

Scottish Typographical Association, 116–17, 123, 126, 127, 129, 134, 140–1, 148, 149, 190, 201, 206–0, 214, 229, 243, 252, 263, 281, 287, 292, 296, 304, 311, 313, 329, 342, 354, 355–6

Seditious literature, 21–2, 29, 33, 39

Self, Henry, 119

Semi-skilled labour, 109, 111, 162, 181, 210, 217, 220, 224, 336; New Unions of, 163–4, 184, 192, 203, 229

'Set-off', 109

Shackleton, Sir David, 273

Sheffield, 114, 196, 199

Shift work, 310, 311, 312, 336–7, 346, 354, 356, 365

Shop stewards, 90, 150, 196

Short-time working, 220, 294–5, 286, 290

Simonds, Hon. Mr Justice, 291

S.L.A.D.E., *see* Society of Lithographic Artists

'Slating', 167

Smith, Adam, 71, 91

'Smooting', 139, 141, 221

Society for Promoting Christian Knowledge, 83

Society of British Printing Ink Manufacturers, 347

Society of Brothers' Lodge, The, 53

Society of Lithographic Artists, 271–3, 281, 341–4, 347, 356, 367–8

Society of London Daily News Compositors, 118

INDEX

Society of Music Engravers, 344
Society of Women Employed in Bookbinding, 110
Southward, J., 108
S.P.C.K., *see* Society for Promoting Christian Knowledge
Spectator, Addison's, 32
Sportsman, The, 156
Spottiswoode's, 185
S.T.A., *see* Scottish Typographical Association
Stabilization, 275–6, 290, 299, 303, 314, 322, 325, 330, 336, 337, 343, 344, 348, 357; clauses, 281, 297–8, 299, 322, 323
Standing forms, 26–7
Standing time, 167, 171
Star Chamber, 23, 24, 29
Star, The, 85–6
State decree, (1403), 18
Stationers (booksellers), 18, 20, 21–3
Stationers' Company, 19–25, 29–31, 33–5, 40, 54, 59, 64, 136
Stationers' Gild, 19
Stationers' Hall, 30
Stationery manufacture, 111, 160, 190, 219
Steamdriven printing machinery, 94
Stirling, 80
Stereotypers' Society, 181, 226, 229, 272, 273, 309, 311–12, 314–16, 318–19, 350, 367
Stone and Plate Preparers' Union, 229
Strike card, 100
Strike pay, 79, 118, 122, 125–6, 172, 191
Strikes, 63, 64, 69, 80, 82, 86, 116, 347–52; causes of 125; definition of, 149; over machinery, 172, 332; in provinces, 210–11; rules concerning, 212; during Second World War, 301–2; London (1950), 321–2; D. C. Thomson, 331; *Daily Sketch* dispute, 333–4; National Dailies, 334–5
Struggle, The, 84, 91, 96, 97
Sun, The, 118, 148
Sunday, working on, 227, *See also* Overtime
Superannuation, 117, 118, 191–2, 266
Supervisors, 249
'Sup hand', 111, 162

T.A., *see* Typographical Association
Taff Vale Judgment, 187, 211
Task work, 140, 168
Tatler, The, Steele's, 32
Taxes on knowledge, 107
Teachers of Printing and Allied Subjects Association, 262
Tea Half Hour Strike, 62–3
Technical education, 260, 261–2, 267, 368
Textwriters, 15–21
Thomson-Leng combine, 251
Thompson, Robert, 87, 89, 90
Thomson, D.C., dispute, 330–2
Thorne composing machine, 109, 156, 157, 168, 169
Three Jolly Butchers, public house, 53
Times, The, 47, 51, 66, 75, 156, 157, 160, 174, 182, 317
Timperley, C. H., 32
Trade Betterment, 228, 254–6
'Trade Societies', 48, 50, 61– , 64– , 128
Trade tariffs, 197
Trade Union Act (1906), 211
Trades Unions and Strikes, 124–5
Trades Unions Congress, 200, 210, 236, 248–9, 326, 331, 334, 335, 365
Tramping Document, 99–101
Tramping Strike Card, 100
Tramping system, 92, 98–104, 115–16, 129–31
Tramp relief, 77, 79, 80, 82, 84, 85, 99–104, 117, 129–31, 145, 146, 188
Treadle platen, 109
T.U.C., *see* Trades Unions Congress
'Turnovers', 29, 34–5, 39–40
Twicing, 357
Typefounders, 49, 96; societies, 181, 243
Type-Setting Syndicate Ltd., 169
Typographical Association, 116, 367; and benefits, 126, 130–1, 147, 172, 192, 287; and apprentices, 133, 134, 136; policy concerning machinery 166– , 173, 180–1, 182, 183, 216–17, 332–3; and wages, 140–1, 167– , 224–5, 227, 270, 271–5, 276–7, 282, 292–3, 295, 309; membership, 190–1, 241; policy, 142–4, 150, 151, 166, 172; disputes concerning, 192–3, 194, 243, 247,

386 INDEX

263, 292–3; and cooperatives, 238; and House Unions, 251; and dilution of labour, 221, 288; and overtime, 215–16; and collective agreement, 206– ; and wages structure, 309–11, 313, 314, 315, 316, 317–20, 323, 329; and man-power bargaining, 337, 338, 340; and productivity, 350, 354–5, 357

Typographical Association of Scotland, General, see General Typographical Association

Typographical Association, National, see under National

Typographical Emigration Society, 131

Typographical societies, 76ff.

Typographical Union, National, 194

Typographical Unions, National Conference of (1886), 119, 195

Unemployed Workers' Movement, National, 235–6

Unemployment, 126– , 171– , 210– , 215, 219–20, 222, 234–7, 280; and J.I.C., 266–7, 285, 318, 322, 327

Unemployment Relief, 103–4, 118, 120, 122, 129, 179, 191, 237, 362, 369–70

'Unfair offices', 75, 79, 82, 99–100, 102, 115, 125, 145, 147, 149–50

Union Executives, Conference of (1939), 290

Union Rules, Agreement on (1911), 207

Union Society, 51, 58

Unionism, 120–3

United Brotherhood, the, 187

United Friends' Lodge, The, 53

United Typographical Association, 81

United Typothetae of America, 198, 199

Unskilled labour, 156, 162, 217, 229. See also Various

Vane Stow, H., 200

Vellum Binders, 56, 119

Victimization Pay, 126

Voluntary Arbitration, 263

Wages– early disputes, 25–6, 43–4; rates, 72–3, 83, 112–13, 125, 143, 210, 223, 282–3; standard rates, 113,

125, 139, 140–2, 145; machine rates, 166–71, 173, 208–9, 270; increase in First World War, 222–226; national rates, 224–6; national agreements concerning, 226– , 243, 245, 263; and J.I.C., 262– ; special rates, Extras, 270–1, 281–3; reductions, 271–6, 281, 282, 309; regrading, 275–8; in Second World War, 284–6, 290–9, 303–5; House Rates, 299, 304, 322; consolidation of, 299; and manpower bargaining, 336–42; craft rates, 337, 339, 356–7; and productivity bargaining, 343– , 348–51, 356–7;

Wages, differentials in, 309–11, 313, 316–17, 319–20, 338–41, 344

Wages, grading in, 226–7, 263, 268, 271, 272, 275–8, 282–3, 292–5, 304, 309–14, 318–19

Wages, London, 209, 309, 311, 313, 316, 321, 336, 339, 344

Wages, piecework, 25, 43–4, 48, 63, 70– , 118; rates, 72–3, 83, 113, 140; price lists for, 91, 137; union rates for, 141–2; machine rates, 166–71, 173– , 208; national agreements concerning, 228; in Second World War, 285

Wages, provincial, 209, 309–13, 319, 323–4, 344, 336, 339, 344; grades, 275–8, 290, 292, 293, 316, 319, 323–4, 336–7, 341, 344, 356

Wages structure, 309–25, 336–7, 344, 359, 364; two-tier, 339–40, 342, 343, 365

Wales, unionism in, 79

Walter, John, 67

War Bonus, 223

Wardens, 18, 19

Warehouse porters, 223

Warehousemen, 163, 184, 186, 188, 222, 226

Warrington, 161

Watkins' Bible Shop, 110

Watson, James, 44

Watson, R., 252

Wealth of Nations, The, 71

Webb, S. and B., 52, 59, 135–6

Weekly newspapers, 301

Welfare, and J.I.C., 257

West End, The, 128

INDEX

Westminster Abbey, 19
Wharfedale, the, 159
'Whips', 140
Whitchurche, Edward, 24–5
Whitley Committee, 255, 247
Wholesale Newsagents, Federation of, 245
Williams, R. T., 327
Willis, R., 327, 339, 342, 366
Women: numbers employed, 159–60; in paper mills, 187; and unions, 184, 187, 188, 189–90, 191, 222, 229, 269; and demarcation, 217; and dilution of labour, 220–2, 287; rates of pay, 223–4, 226, 271, 290, 291, 292, 294, 296, 297, 299, 303, 304, 310–11, 319, 323; and T.A., 288; and Second World War, 302; and manpower bargaining, 336–7, 341; and productivity, 344–5
Women Bookfolders, London Society of, 187

Women Employed in Bookbinding, Society of, 110
Women, Society of, 271
Working week, the, 197, 206–7, 210, 215–16, 228, 238 278–9, 280–2, 299–303, 310, 343–6, 350–1, 356
Works advisory committees, 255, 257
World War, First, 218– , 365
World War, Second, 284, 285, 287–8, 289–90, 300, 302, 317, 364–5. *See* Chapter 18
Writers of Court Letter and Text Letter, 18

Yeomen, of Stationers' Company, 22, 29
Young-Delcambre composing machine, 95
Young Master Printers, 262

Zweig, F., 329